LIBRARY OF NEW TESTAMENT STUDIES

411

formerly the Journal for the Study of the New Testament Supplement series

Editor
Mark Goodacre

PAUL AND THE GOSPELS

Christologies, Conflicts and Convergences

EDITED BY
MICHAEL F. BIRD
JOEL WILLITTS

B L O O M S B U R Y
LONDON • NEW DELHI • NEW YORK • SYDNEY

Bloomsbury T&T Clark
An imprint of Bloomsbury Publishing Plc

50 Bedford Square
London
WC1B 3DP
UK

175 Fifth Avenue
New York
NY 10010
USA

www.bloomsbury.com

First published by T&T Clark International 2011
Paperback edition first published 2013

British Library Cataloguing-in-Publication Data
A catalogue record for this book is available from the British Library.

ISBN: HB: 978-0-567-61742-2
PB: 978-0-567-45812-4

Library of Congress Cataloging-in-Publication Data
A catalog record for this book is available from the Library of Congress

Typeset by Pindar NZ, Auckland, New Zealand

Contents

ABBREVIATIONS

AASF	Annales Academiæ Scientiarum Fennicæ
AB	Anchor Bible
ANRW	*Aufstieg und Niedergang der römischen Welt: Geschichte und Kultur Roms im Spiegel der neueren Forschung.* Edited by H. Temporini and W. Haase. Berlin, 1972–
ANTC	Abingdon New Testament Commentaries
ATR	*Australian Theological Review*
BBR	*Bulletin for Biblical Research*
BDAG	*Greek-English Lexicon of the New Testament and Other Early Christian Literature*. W. Bauer, F. W. Danker, W. F. Arndt and F. W. Gingrich. 3rd edn. Chicago, 1999
BECNT	Baker Exegetical Commentary on the New Testament
BHT	Beiträge zur historischen Theologie
BJRL	*Bulletin of the John Rylands University Library of Manchester*
BRev	*Bible Review*
BZ	*Biblische Zeitschrift*
BZNW	Biblische zur Zeitschrift für die neutestamentliche Wissenschaft, Supplement
CBQ	*Catholic Biblical Quarterly*
CBR	*Currents in Biblical Research*
CITM	Christianity in the Making
ConBNTS	Coniectanea biblical New Testament Series
CQ	*Church Quarterly*
DJB	*Dictionary of Jesus and the Gospels*
DNTB	*Dictionary of New Testament Background*
EDNT	*Exegetical Dictionary of the New Testament*
EQ	*Evangelical Quarterly*
ER	*The Encyclopedia of Religion*. Edited by M. Eliade. 16 vols. New York, 1987
ESV	English Standard Version
ET	English translation
ExpT	*Expository Times*
FFF	*Foundation and Facets Forum*
FG	Fourth Gospel

FRLANT	Forschungen zur Religion und Literatur des Alten und Neuen Testaments
HDR	Harvard Dissertations in Religion
HR	*History of Religions*
HTKNT	Herders theologischer Kommentar zum Neuen Testament
HTR	*Harvard Theological Review*
HTS	*Harvard Theological Studies*
ICC	International Critical Commentary
JBL	*Journal of Biblical Literature*
JETS	*Journal of Evangelical Theological Studies*
JGRChJ	*Journal of Greco-Roman Christianity and Judaism*
JRH	*Journal of Religious History*
JSHJ	*Journal for the Study of the Historical Jesus*
JSNT	*Journal for the Study of the New Testament*
JSNTSup	Journal for the Study of the New Testament, Supplement Series
JSOT	*Journal for the Study of the Old Testament*
JTI	*Journal of Theological Interpretation*
JTS	*Journal of Theological Studies*
LAB	Ps.-Philo, *Liber Antiquitatum Biblicarum*
LHJS	Library of Historical Jesus Studies
LNTS	Library of New Testament Studies
LXX	Septuagint
MT	Masoretic Text
NCB	New Century Bible
NHMS	Nag Hammadi and Manichaean Studies
NIB	*New Interpreter's Bible*
NICNT	New International Commentary on the New Testament
NIDNTT	*New International Dictionary of New Testament Theology*
NIGTC	New International Greek Testament Commentary
NJB	New Jerusalem Bible
NovT	*Novum Testamentum*
NovTSup	Novum Testamentum, Supplement Series
NRSV	New Revised Standard Version
NT	New Testament
NTL	New Testament Library
NTM	New Tribes Mission
NTR	New Testament Review
NTS	*New Testament Studies*
OT	Old Testament

PBM	Paternoster Biblical Monographs
PTMS	Pittsburgh Theological Monograph Series
RTR	*Reformed Theological Review*
SBLDS	Society for Biblical Literature Dissertations Series
SBLMS	Society of Biblical Literature Monograph Series
SD	Studies and Documents
SecCen	*Second Century*
SJT	*Scottish Journal of Theology*
SNTSMS	Society for New Testament Studies Monograph Series
SNTW	The Studies of the New Testament and its World
SP	Sacra Pagina
SPCK	Society for Promoting Christian Knowledge
SSEJC	Studies in Scripture in Early Judaism and Christianity
TDNT	*Theological Dictionary of the New Testament*
TrinJ	*Trinity Journal*
TRu	*Theologische Rundschau*
TS	*Theological Studies*
TynB	*Tyndale Bulletin*
TZTh	*Tübinger Zeitschrift für Theologie*
UBSGNT	United Bible Societies' Greek New Testament
VC	*Vigiliae christianae*
VCSup	Vigiliae christianae, Supplement
VoxRef	*Vox Reformata*
WBC	World Biblical Commentary
WUNT	Wissenschaftliche Untersuchungen zum Neuen Testament
ZNW	*Zeitschrift für die neutestamentliche Wissenschaft und die Kunde der älteren Kirche*
ZTK	Zeitschrift für Theologie und Kirche

Contributors

Michael F. Bird is a Lecturer in Theology at Crossway College and honorary research associate at the University of Queensland, Australia. He holds a Ph.D. from the University of Queensland.

James G. Crossley is Reader in New Testament Studies in the Department of Biblical Studies at the University of Sheffield, England. He holds a Ph.D. from the University of Nottingham, England.

Paul Foster is Senior Lecturer in New Testament Language, Literature and Theology at the School of Divinity, University of Edinburgh, Scotland. He holds a Ph.D. from Oxford University, England.

Mark Harding is the Dean and Chief Executive Officer of the Australian College of Theology, Sydney. He holds a Ph.D. in New Testament from Princeton Theological Seminary, USA.

Joshua W. Jipp is a Ph.D. candidate at Emory in the Graduate Division of Religion, Atlanta, USA. He is currently working on his dissertation on the book of Acts.

Colin G. Kruse is Lecturer in New Testament at the Melbourne School of Theology. He holds a Ph.D. from Fuller Theological Seminary, Pasadena, USA.

David Morlan is a Pastor at Fellowship Denver Church, USA. He holds a Ph.D. from Durham University, England.

Stanley E. Porter is President and Dean as well as Professor of New Testament at McMaster Divinity College, Ontario, Canada. He holds a Ph.D. from the University of Sheffield, England.

Christopher W. Skinner is an Assistant Professor of Religion at Mount Olive College, North Carolina, USA. He holds a Ph.D. from The Catholic University of America, Washington, DC.

Joel Willitts is an Associate Professor in Biblical and Theological Studies at North Park University, Chicago, USA. He holds a Ph.D. from Cambridge University, England.

Preface

Michael Bird and I have known each other for nearly a decade and it is with pleasure we present this project to readers. The subjects of Paul and the Gospels are ones that both Mike and I are extremely interested in and so it was quite natural for us to work together on this book project. The book's subjects represent the topics of conversation Mike and I have been having over the past decade. We've both contributed essays in areas where we are at home and we invited experts, some senior and some junior, to also contribute essays.

We wish to thank our contributors, James Crossley, Paul Foster, Stan Porter, David Morlan, Mark Harding, Colin Kruse, Chris Skinner and Joshua Jipp. Their scholarly effort will ensure that this volume will make a contribution to the study of Early Christianity. We also wish to thank my research assistant, Joshua Wooden, who was responsible for formatting the essays and creating the indices. Without his assistance the manuscript would not have seen the light of day, at least not in the time frame required.

Finally, Mike and I want to dedicate this book to our graduate professors. For me these are the teachers such as the late Harold Hoehner, Darrell Bock and Daniel Wallace of Dallas Theological Seminary, as well as Scott Hafemann of Gordon-Conwell Theological Seminary. For Mike they are Jim Gibson, Jeff Pugh, Les Ball and Stan Nickerson of Malyon College.

These teachers were the ones who laid the foundation of our thinking about the Apostle Paul and the Gospels. While they may now recognize very little of what they first taught us, their influence remains significant. To these teachers we say a great big thank you.

Joel Willitts

Introduction

Michael F. Bird

Marcion adopted only 'one gospel' comprising of a truncated version of Luke. Marcion's justification for this single Gospel was based on Rom. 2.16, where Paul referred to 'my gospel' with the singular 'gospel' (εὐαγγελιον) as opposed to the plural 'gospels' (εὐαγγελια).[1] In this sense, in his quest for one authentically Pauline gospel, Marcion was among the first to try to relate the Apostle Paul to the four Gospels that were eventually canonized by the early church. This led to competition between the Marcionites and the proto-orthodox in the second century as to which Gospels were in accord with the Pauline gospel. Tertullian summed up the debate: 'I say that my Gospel is the true one; Marcion, that his is. I affirm that Marcion's Gospel is adulterated; Marcion, that mine is' (*Marc.* 4.4).

There are a myriad of issues that arise if we attempt to investigate the relationship between Paul (the man, letters, tradition) and the 'Jesus Books' that came to be known as 'Gospels'. The relationship between Paul and the canonical Gospels can be framed in terms of his influence on their formative traditions. That is to say that the canonical Gospels may have been shaped at the oral and redactional level by persons who had either consciously embraced or deliberately rejected elements of Paul's teaching. The influence of Paul upon 'heretical' groups in the early church was more than obvious to several of the Heresiologists.[2] As such, it would be of no surprise then to discover that several 'other' Gospels had also been influenced by Paul.

The influence of Paul upon the Gospel texts and traditions is too vast to explore in one place. The scope of the current volume is more limited and is concerned with two primary questions: (1) what is the relationship between

1. Helmut Koester, *Ancient Christian Gospels: Their History and Development* (Harrisburg, PA: Trinity Press International, 1990), pp. 35–6.

2. Cf. e.g. Irenaeus, *Adv. Haer.* 4.41.4; Tertullian, *Marc.* 1.15, 20; 2.14; 4.2, 3.

Paul and the earliest Christian Gospels in terms of their origins, setting and theological character and (2) in what ways are the earliest Gospels a reaction to Paul and his legacy, such as appropriation, development or polemic? That is the task given to the contributing authors.

The possibility that the Gospel of Mark is influenced by Paul has been a long-standing position undergirded primarily by acceptance of the tradition that 'Mark' was none other than 'John Mark' a one-time travelling companion of Paul (Acts 12.25; 13.13; Phlm. 1.24; Col. 4.10; 2 Tim. 4.11) and later an attendant of Peter (1 Pet. 5.13). The fortunes of that theory have swayed with a powerful criticism of the traditional view levelled by Martin Werner nearly a hundred years ago. Werner regarded the agreements between Paul and Mark as deriving from general Christian teaching and not due to Pauline influence on Mark.[3] However, ten years ago Joel Marcus noted a resurgence in the view that Mark was flexibly a 'Paulinist'.[4] Amid this debate two studies about Mark and Paul are included by James G. Crossley and Michael F. Bird, who take diverging views on this subject.

The first study on Mark and Paul, by Crossley, pursues a line analogous to Werner. While not ruling out more direct influence in specific instances, Crossley proposes that the Mark and Paul overlaps are often part of general Christian instruction. Furthermore, he even raises the possibility that the influence might have been reversed and Paul was an interpreter of Mark or Markan tradition. Crossley examines several proposed examples of Mark's advocacy of Pauline thought (election in Mk 4.1-20; Last Supper in Mk 14.22-25; unclean food in Mk 7.19) that he denies are uniquely Pauline when Mark is properly understood. Crossley also notes that Paul and Mark would have, unsurprisingly, faced similar issues, such as constructing an atonement theology, dealing with the issue of the inclusion of Gentiles into Christian communities and developing a distinctive messianism. Crossley concludes, with due caution, that determining precise influence is a very difficult question. However, he maintains that Mark and Paul may owe their shared interests and perspectives to the 'swirling mix of ideas' in the early Christian movement.

The second study on Mark and Paul is by Michael F. Bird, who regards the Gospel of Mark as containing a synthesis of Petrine tradition and Pauline theological perspective. Bird accepts the Papian testimony that John Mark was the author of the second canonical Gospel. Yet, regardless of whether it was John Mark or not, Bird attempts to show the presence of Petrine features in the text and distinctive Pauline perspectives as well (distinctive in the sense of

3. Martin Werner, *Der Einfluss paulinischer Theologie im Markusevangelium: eine Studie zur neutestamentlichen Theologie* (Giessen: Töpelmann, 1923).

4. Joel Marcus, 'Mark – Interpreter of Paul', *NTS* 46 (2000), pp. 473–87.

either unique to or characteristic of Paul). In the end, he concludes that there are cogent reasons for seeing Mark as influenced by Paul, though admittedly some points of agreement are more probable than other proposed agreements. Bird suggests that Mk 7.19; 10.45 and 13.10 are the most likely indications of Pauline influence on Mark. Yet Bird also acknowledges that Mark remains in many ways a very independent thinker and he is neither slavishly bound to Paul's theological framework nor hypnotically attached to Paul as his only theological teacher. Mark is more than willing to incorporate other traditions into his narrative even when they grate, potentially or actually, against Paul's own perspective. In many ways, the position of Mark vis-à-vis Paul is perhaps more analogous to that ordinarily attributed to Luke. Mark writes a Gospel to tell the story of Jesus for believers and interested persons. In the process, Mark provides a synthesis of the Pauline gospel and the Petrine testimony about Jesus.

The legacy that F.C. Baur and Walter Baur bequeathed to subsequent generations was a scholarly tradition that identified an essential division within early Christianity into its Gentile and Jewish species. These species are normally labelled respectively as Pauline and Petrine and the theological trajectories of the primitive church are often traced to the divisions and attempts at reconciliation between these two parties.[5] Indeed, Matthew has been viewed as the quintessential anti-Paulinist by many.[6] Martin Hengel was even bold enough to assert that if Matthew had been the last word on Christian theology then Paul would be a heretic.[7] That assumption is, however, put to the test by two authors.

Joel Willitts engages the subject of Matthew and Paul by utilizing a descriptive approach combined with a post-New Perspective on Paul framework. For Willitts, too many comparative studies between Paul and Matthew have a skewed view of Paul as *contra* Judaism, and this has resultantly led to a naturally antagonistic analysis of the Jewish Matthew with the anti-Jewish Paul. Willitts opts for a more nuanced perspective of Paul as Torah-compliant and he sees Paul and Matthew sharing the same ideological space of 'apostolic Judaism'. Broadly speaking, then, Paul and Matthew belong to the same web of Graeco-Roman associations operating under the umbrella of Diaspora synagogues. That context includes the co-existence of ethnically mixed members of Jews and Gentiles and is ideologically bound within the common Judaism

5. Cf. e.g. Michael Goulder, *A Tale of Two Missions* (London: SCM, 1994); idem, *Paul and the Competing Mission in Corinth* (Peabody, MA: Hendrickson, 2001). For a response, see Michael F. Bird, 'The Early Christians, the Historical Jesus, and the Salvation of the Gentiles', in *Jesus from Judaism to Christianity* (ed. Tom Holmén; Tübingen: Mohr/Siebeck, 2010).

6. Cf. e.g. David C. Sim, 'Matthew 7.21–23: Further Evidence of its Anti-Pauline Perspective', *NTS* 53 (2007), pp. 325–43; idem, 'Matthew's Anti-Paulinism: A Neglected Feature of Matthean Studies', *HTS* 58 (2002), pp. 767–83.

7. Martin Hengel, 'Zur matthäischen Bergpredigt und ihrem jüdischen Hintergrund', *TRu* 52 (1987), p. 362.

of the Second Temple period. Willitts notes that, while Paul and Matthew share this socio-religious context, nonetheless, they deal with different topics, for different reasons and to achieve different ends. But Willitts does note two key points of similarity between Paul and Matthew, viz. Davidic messianism and eschatological recompense according to deeds. In the end, Willitts rejects the idea of Matthew as anti-Pauline. Instead, he contends that Matthew can be understood as pro-Pauline if by that one means having a shared theological outlook with Paul, or Matthew can be judged to be unPauline if by that one means that Matthew does not share Paul's rhetorical concerns and is essentially disinterested in Paul.

Paul Foster begins by noting the anachronism of juxtaposing Paul and Matthew within early Christianity, because there was no concept of 'Christianity' in the first century and there is a non sequitur because Paul's letters and Matthew's Gospel have a temporal distance between them. That aside, Foster thinks that it is possible to compare and to contrast their respective outlooks in relation to several themes that indicate either conflict or confluence. These themes include use of the Hebrew Scriptures, attitude towards the Torah, Christological beliefs, perspective on the Gentile mission and reflection on community structures. On the Hebrew Scriptures, Foster proposes that Paul and Matthew both apply Scripture to support their Christological and salvation-historical purposes. As for the Torah, Paul's and Matthew's attitudes towards it are notoriously complex and disputed, yet Foster questions whether the received wisdom of Paul viewing the Torah as abrogated and Matthew regarding the Torah as changelessly enduring is accurate. Paul assigns a limited place for the Torah among Gentiles and Matthew believes that Jesus brings a new Torah to his people. According to Foster, Paul and Matthew both exhibit a strong internal struggle concerning the relationship of the Torah to God's purposes. On Christology, there is a Christological overlap between Matthew and Paul in affirming Jesus as 'Lord' and 'Christ' and the deficiency of a purely Davidic Christology. Foster recognizes that their Christological affirmations do not always coincide and they are simply different in their portrait of Christ. Concerning the Gentile mission, Foster is wisely reserved in that Matthew clearly affirms a place for Gentiles in the church, but the questions of whether Matthew thought that Gentiles should obey the Torah or whether Matthew's own community was involved in the Gentile mission are moot. Foster also contends that Paul's ecclesiastical structures are somewhat inconsistent and the details of structure in Matthew's community are largely unknown. In sum, Foster recognizes that the Gospel of Matthew does not appear to be Pauline or unPauline; it is simply non-Pauline, though points of intersection do emerge with some shared core commitments, beliefs and affirmations as part of the wider Jesus movement. Foster surmises that Paul has not left a discernible imprint upon the Gospel of Matthew.

The Lukan and Pauline corpora have been natural companions in New Testament interpretation. This is especially true of interpreters who have accepted the traditional ascription of the authorship of the Third Gospel to Luke the physician, who have regarded the 'we' sections of Acts beginning at Troas (Acts 16.11) as indicating Luke's companionship with Paul on his travels, and have regarded the entire Pauline letter collection as authentic, whereby Luke's presence with Paul in his ministry is accepted (Col. 4.14; 2 Tim. 4.11; Phlm. 1.24). Yet, even if there is a historical link between the figures of Paul and Luke, one cannot help but notice a certain paradox in Luke-Acts. Paul is one of Luke's heroes in his history of the early church and yet Luke's theology at points is distinctly unPauline. Luke has nothing on justification by faith, he accentuates resurrection/exaltation over the cross, and he appears to soften down Paul's apocalyptic worldview. As Martin Hengel wrote: '[Luke] respects Paul to the very highest degree as a divinely-gifted missionary, charismatic, and church-planter, even though he partially distances himself from him theologically, under the influence of the Jerusalem tradition . . . and its Jesus tradition, which provided him with the impulse for his gospel.'[8] My own contention is that the distance that some commentators place between Paul and Luke is needlessly exaggerated.[9] Luke is clearly committed to the Pauline paradigm for the inclusion of the Gentiles, but he is deliberately eclectic in drawing upon other streams of early tradition as well. In light of that, the nexus between Paul and Luke is explored in essays by Stanley E. Porter and David Morlan.

Stanley E. Porter notes the divide in scholarship between those who regard Luke's theology as harmonious with Paul's theology and those who regard Luke as radically dissimilar to and even incompatible with Paul. Porter notes several convergences between Luke and Paul. First, both Luke and Paul utilize the Old Testament in a manner that shows they share a common interpretative practice to establish a major theme or concept by means of quotations. Second, Luke's Christology is not anywhere as near as low as often thought. Luke and Paul possibly share a consonant perspective of Jesus as 'Lord', even if their conception of 'Lord' did vary somewhat in emphasis. Third, while Luke certainly does not stress the atoning nature of Jesus' death as Paul does, nonetheless, Porter suggests that Luke is probably influenced by Paul's Eucharistic tradition in 1 Cor. 11.23-25 and he shares Paul's view of Jesus' death as covenantal and expiatory. The primary difference according to Porter is that Luke places Jesus' death in a larger narrative of Jesus' life, death, resurrection and ascension. Fourth, Porter

8. Martin Hengel, 'The Stance of the Apostle Paul Toward the Law in the Unknown Years', in *Justification and Variegated Nomism: Volume 2 – the Paradoxes of Paul* (eds D.A. Carson, P.T. O'Brien, M.A. Seifrid; Grand Rapids, MI: Baker, 2004), p. 76.

9. Cf. Thomas R. Schreiner (*New Testament Theology: Magnifying God in Christ* [Nottingham: Apollos, 2008], pp. 299–304), who shows the parity of Paul and Luke on Jesus' atoning death.

believes that Luke and Paul are more compatible on the *parousia* than often assumed. Paul appears to have anticipated a staged return of Christ rather than an imminent return and Luke is far less grounded in the Church age than often supposed. Both Paul and Luke illustrate the tension between the teaching of Jesus and expectations of his immediate return. In sum, Porter does not think that Luke was a disciple or conceptual servant of Paul, but such an observation does not shut down the capacity for a historical or theological rapprochement between their respective writings.

David Morlan gives a specific case study that explores the theology of repentance in Luke and Paul especially as it relates to their understandings of conversion and human/divine agency. According to Morlan, for Luke and Paul conversion played an important role in the early Christian experience. He provides an extended comparison of Luke 15 and Romans 2 where he shows the precise theological profile of Luke and Paul on repentance. These profiles show some sharp contrasts between them; most notably, that Luke viewed traditional notions of repentance to be useful in his theological conception of conversion while, for Paul, repentance, as it was traditionally understood, was itself rendered ineffective by the power of sin. While showing a complex relationship between human and divine agency in conversion, both Luke and Paul understand *successful* conversion to be impossible without the intervention of an agency outside of the pre-convert.

The overall consensus of scholarship is that there is no apparent relationship between Paul and the Gospel of John in terms of dependence and influence upon each other. As Robin Scroggs put it, 'what is important to Paul, John ignores; and what is important to John was not learned from Paul'.[10] Still, if Paul and John both had periods of ministry in Ephesus, though not necessarily in the same period, then one could envisage some sort of relationship between the two traditions emerging in that locality, even if the interaction between those two streams has not left any discernible imprint in our extant sources. One might even dare to imagine what a discussion between the disciples of Paul and the disciples of John in Ephesus in the late first century would have been like. Another matter for reflection here is the parity of their spheres of thought within the discourse of a New Testament theology. C.H. Dodd was quite optimistic about the kerygmatic unity of Paul and John, but not everyone shared his optimism.[11] Any attempts at theological unity still have to face the facts that Paul and John speak a very different language, they use a dissimilar repertoire of images for Jesus and they are probably addressing completely

10. Robin Scroggs, *Christology in Paul and John: The Reality and Revelation of God* (ed. G. Krodel; Eugene, OR: Wipf & Stock, 1997), p. 105.

11. C.H. Dodd, *The Apostolic Preaching and Its Developments* (London: Hodder & Stoughton, 1936), p. 73.

different issues in their respective literary works. That is not to say that they have nothing in common: a Christology of sonship, the importance of faith and a critique of unbelieving Israel are areas that immediately leap to mind as points of contact between them. My own suspicion is that a synthesis of their theological frameworks is not simply possible; it definitely took place in the early church.[12] As for the respective theological and social positions of Paul and John, Colin G. Kruse and Mark Harding both contribute essays dealing with the relationship between the Fourth Gospel and the Apostle Paul.

Kruse traces what Paul and John both have to say about a number of particular themes. These themes include God the Father, Jesus Christ the Son, Holy Spirit, Scriptures, Mosaic Law, humanity and its need, the work of Christ, union with Christ, the church and its ministers, mission and Israel/the Jews. In each case he points to the similarities and differences between the two authors. Granted the obvious uniqueness of materials between the two corpora and given that the Fourth Gospel probably did not make use of Paul's letters, Kruse maintains that 'Paul and John drew upon the same wellspring of primitive Christian tradition' as part of their response to the revelation of God in Jesus Christ.

Harding takes a slightly different approach by assessing the possibility that Paul influenced the traditions in the Fourth Gospel concerning the Law, the 'Jews', Christology and eschatology. He proposes that a prima facie case for Paul's influence on the Johannine tradition is possible given that both Paul and John had residences in Ephesus for extended periods. In the end, Harding believes that the similarities between the letters of Paul and the Fourth Gospel are most probably not due to direct literary influence, but derive from the likelihood that Paul and the Fourth Gospel owed much of their theological perspectives to Christian Hellenists who cast the message of Jesus into the Greek idiom and took the message of Jesus to Gentiles of the eastern Mediterranean. He advocates that view in direct contrast to W. Bousset and others who asserted that Paul and John both drew on pagan influences. Harding also believes that the closest point of contact between the Pauline letters and the Fourth Gospel is in the realized eschatology, the language of resurrection as a present experience and the developed Wisdom Christology of the post-Pauline letters of Ephesians and Colossians. While direct influence is not likely here, he leaves open the possibility that the Fourth Gospel and Ephesians/Colossians share a similar theological trajectory.

The relationship between Paul and the *Gospel of Thomas* has not occupied

12. Cf. D. Moody Smith, 'The Love Command: John and Paul?', in *Theology and Ethics in Paul and His Interpreters* (eds E.H. Lovering and J.L. Sumney; FS V.P. Furnish; Nashville: Abingdon, 1996), pp. 207–17.

many minds.[13] If Paul and John are as different as apples and oranges, then Paul and Thomas are as different as apples and astronauts. In my view, the *Gospel of Thomas* represents a reinterpretation of Synoptic and independent Jesus traditions that are filtered through an esoteric and proto-Gnostic grid. But just as Paul was important for proto-orthodox forms of Christianity he was also significant for 'other' forms of Christianity. Marcion arguably attempted to ride Paul through an über-Hellenistic roller coaster with a massaged version of Luke, while the Ebionites are purported to have rejected Paul's apostolic authority and arguably found Matthew conductive to that end. Irenaeus points to the preference of certain 'heretical' groups for specific Gospels: Marcion with Luke, Ebionites with Matthew, Docetists with Mark and the Valentinians with John (Irenaeus, *Adv. Haer*. 3.11.7; 3.15.1). But what of Paul? Paul could certainly be appealed to as the precedent for certain doctrinal innovations about cosmology and salvation by several dissident groups (e.g. Irenaeus, *Adv. Haer*. 1.3.1, 5; 1.8.2). How, then, did the framers of the *Gospel of Thomas* relate to Paul in terms of the tradition history of their Gospel and with respect to their own ideological perspective? That question is tackled by Christopher W. Skinner and Joshua W. Jipp.

Skinner offers a literary and theological comparison between Paul and the *Gospel of Thomas* on certain key nodes. First, he compares several sets of texts (*Gos. Thom*. 3/Rom. 10.5-8; *Gos. Thom*. 17/1 Cor. 2.9; *Gos. Thom*. 53/Rom. 2.25-29); and other passages that contain a spirit versus flesh polarity (*Gos. Thom*. 29/2 Cor. 4.7 and *Gos. Thom*. 87/Rom. 7.13-25). He believes that these texts are all dependent upon Paul and deliberately modify Paul's original point in favour of an altogether different perspective. Second, Skinner examines theological ideas in Paul and the *Gospel of Thomas* and concludes that rejection of Paul's theological perspective 'is part of the warp and woof of Thomasine Christianity'. In Skinner's mind, the authors of the *Gospel of Thomas* were familiar with Pauline ideas, but ultimately rejected them as having any cogency for explaining the ongoing significance of Jesus.

The study by Joshua W. Jipp begins by noting how several scholars have alleged a commonality between Paul and the *Gospel of Thomas* on the 'image of God' and a shared tradition of reading Genesis 1–3 in light of Hellenistic philosophy. Since most of these parallels are found in 1 Corinthians, Jipp proceeds to contrast the perspective of Paul in 1 Corinthians with the framers of the *Gospel of Thomas* in relation to several loci including death and the human predicament, salvation as transformation and bodily practices. Jipp concludes

13. The exception here is Simon Gathercole, 'The Influence of Paul on the *Gospel of Thomas* (53.3 and 17)', in *Das Thomasevangelium: Entstehung – Rezeption – Theologie* (eds J. Frey, E.E. Popkes and J. Schröter [BZNW 157]; Berlin: Walter de Gruyter, 2008), pp. 72–94.

that, although Paul and the *Gospel of Thomas* share common words and motifs in their construction of salvation, *Thomas* imagines a protological return to an androgynous state towards the first Adam, while Paul holds an eschatological conception of conformity to the pattern of Jesus as the second Adam. Both construct their idea of salvation in dialogue with Genesis 1–3. Whereas *Thomas* sees humanity tragically alienated from its own image that is apprehended by seeking knowledge of one's true origins, for Paul transformation occurs by incorporation into the redemptive work of the Messiah. Paul can also apply bodily images for salvation in direct contrast to *Thomas* that denigrates worldly and physical existence. In the end, Jipp proposes that the *Gospel of Thomas* represents an esoteric and ascetic tradition that seeks to refashion the self through an alternative conception of the self, the discovery of the self and through the transformation of the self. *Thomas* thus rejects more 'mainstream' influences like Paul that are still attached to their Jewish religious heritage. As such, *Thomas* shares some features with Paul yet disagrees markedly with many aspects of his theology. On the whole, *Thomas* displays the 'remarkable richness and diversity that comprised the formation of early Christianity [rather] than a direct reaction to Paul'.

That is the shape of the studies as they stand and it is our hope that they will contribute to the study of the reception of the Apostle Paul in the early church.[14]

14. Cf. Albert E. Barnett, *Paul Becomes a Literary Influence* (Chicago: University of Chicago Press, 1941); Andreas Lindemann, *Paulus im ältesten Christentum: Das Bild des Apostels und die Rezeption der paulinischen Theologie in der frühchristlischen Literatur bis Marcion* (BHT 15; Tübingen: Mohr/Siebeck, 1979); William S. Babcock (ed.), *Paul and the Legacies of Paul* (Dallas: Southern Methodist University, 1990); Wayne A. Meeks and John T. Fitzgerald (eds), *The Writings of St. Paul: Annotated Texts, Reception and Criticism* (Norton Critical Editions in the History of Ideas; 2nd edn; New York: Norton, 2007); Daniel Marguerat, 'Paul après Paul: une histoire de reception', *NTS* 54 (2008), pp. 317–37; Michael F. Bird and Joseph A. Dodson (eds), *Paul in the Second Century: The Legacy of Paul's Life, Letters, and Teaching* (LNTS 412; London: T&T Clark, 2011).

1

Mark, Paul and the Question of Influences

James G. Crossley

I. *Introduction*

That Paul influenced Mark's Gospel in some way is now a major view in the history of scholarship. Notable scholars over the past hundred years have pushed this view, including Benjamin Bacon, J. C. Fenton, David Seeley, Michael Goulder, William Telford and Joel Marcus.[1] Nearly a century ago, Martin Werner's arguments that Paul did not really influence Mark – and where they did agree was on matters generally found in Christianity – were once deemed 'influential' in some scholarly literature. However, it does seem, as Joel Marcus noted a decade ago, that the tide has now started to turn.[2] This essay will challenge and qualify this influential scholarly tradition. First, we need to establish what kinds of things we might mean by 'influence'.

In terms of how we might understand Pauline influence on Mark, this can be as straightforward as a direct interpretation of a Pauline verse or saying or related kinds of influence: Mark could have been in some sense allegorizing Pauline theology, adapting ideas floating around the Pauline churches, or, as David Seeley suggested in light of what he saw as similarities and differences between Mark and Paul in the case of Mk 10.41-45, 'indirectly acknowledging a theologian he could not completely ignore, but whose theology he did not

1. See e.g. B. W. Bacon, *The Gospel of Mark: Its Composition and Date* (London and New Haven: Oxford University Press and Yale University Press, 1925); J. C. Fenton, 'Paul and Mark', in D. E. Nineham (ed.), *Studies in the Gospels: Essays in Memory of R. H. Lightfoot* (Oxford: Blackwell, 1955), pp. 89–112; M. D. Goulder, 'Those Outside (Mk 4:10-12)', *NovT* 33 (1991), pp. 289–302; D. Seeley, 'Rulership and Service in Mark 10:41-45', *NovT* 35 (1993), pp. 234–250; W. Telford, *The Theology of the Gospel of Mark* (Cambridge: Cambridge University Press, 1999), pp. 164–169; J. Marcus, 'Mark – Interpreter of Paul', *NTS* 46 (2000), pp. 473–487; M. D. Goulder, 'Jesus' Resurrection and Christian Origins: A Response to N.T. Wright', *JSHJ* 3 (2005), pp. 187–195.

2. M. Werner, *Der Einfluss paulinischer Theologie im Markusevangelium: eine Studie zur neutestamentlichen Theologie* (Giessen: Töpelmann, 1923); Marcus, 'Mark – Interpreter of Paul', p. 474.

fully approve of.'[3] Such ideas can and have been applied to themes in general, such as a theology of the cross, and to specific sayings, such as Mk 7.19: 'Thus he declared all foods clean' (lit. 'cleansing all foods'; cf. Mk 7.15) apparently picking up on 'I know and am persuaded in the Lord Jesus that nothing is unclean in itself; but it is unclean for anyone who thinks it unclean' (Rom. 14.14). We will return to these examples shortly.

There is another kind of influence, one to some extent associated with Werner and one that I will not entirely abandon in this essay: the general cultural context of earliest 'Christianity' (or whatever we wish to call its manifestation in its first decades). Mark and Paul were both part of the same general movement we call Christianity and Paul clearly felt that this movement would best suit his views after his conversion, so we simply cannot rule out the possibility of general Christian influence on both Mark and Paul. As we will see, this argument is stronger if the supposedly more precise links are shown to be problematic in terms of influence. It is clear that, while Paul and others had a distinctive influence, they were also part of the same movement with interweaving and overlapping trends. With these thoughts in mind, would it be such a surprise if we find overlapping themes in the Pauline corpus and Mark if it could be definitively shown that there was no direct influence? Presumably not. Again, we will return to these issues in due course.

There is, of course, another option: Mark or Markan tradition influenced Paul. If we take Mark (as opposed to simply Markan tradition) influencing Paul, this would require an early date for Mark (e.g. c.40 CE), as advocated more recently by myself and by Maurice Casey in his recent book on the historical Jesus.[4] If the earlier dating is correct, it might mean that we have to reverse the influence and think of Paul as interpreter of Mark, particularly in the case of

3. Seeley, 'Rulership and Service', p. 249.

4. J. G. Crossley, *The Date of Mark's Gospel: Insights from the Law in Earliest Christianity* (London and New York: T&T Clark/Continuum, 2004); M. Casey, *Jesus of Nazareth: An Independent Historian's Account of his Life and Teachings* (London and New York: T&T Clark/Continuum, 2010). See also M. Casey, *Aramaic Sources of Mark's Gospel* (Cambridge: Cambridge University Press, 1998). For other attempts at dating Mark earlier than the standard 65–75 CE view, see e.g. A. Harnack, *Date of the Acts and the Synoptic Gospels* (London and New York: Williams and Norgate/G. P. Putnam's Sons, 1911); W. C. Allen, *The Gospel according to Saint Mark with Introduction and Notes* (London: Rivington, 1915); C. C. Torrey, *Documents of the Primitive Church* (London & New York: Harper & Brothers, 1941), pp. 1–40; J. A. T. Robinson, *Redating the New Testament* (London: SCM, 1976), pp. 106–117; G. Zuntz, 'Wann wurde das Evangelium Marci geschrieben?', in H. Canick (ed.), *Markus-Philologie* (Tübingen: Mohr Siebeck, 1984), pp. 47–71; J. W. Wenham, *Redating Matthew, Mark and Luke* (London, Sydney, Auckland, Toronto: Hodder & Stoughton, 1991), pp. 136–182, 238; E. E. Ellis, 'The Date and Provenance of Mark's Gospel', in F. Van Segroeck (ed.), *The Four Gospels 1992* (Leuven: Leuven University Press/ Peeters, 1992), pp. 801–815; M. Mosse, *The Three Gospels: New Testament History Introduced by the Synoptic Problem* (Milton Keynes: Paternoster, 2007). Cf. J. Moffatt, *An Introduction to the Literature of the New Testament* (3rd edn; Edinburgh: T&T Clark, 1918), p. 213; R. Wegner (ed.), *Die Datierung der Evangelien* (Paderborn: Deutsches Insitut für Bildung und Wissen, 1983).

the more precise parallels between Mark and Paul. However, we do not have to reverse the interpretative flow, even if we were to date Mark as early as c.40 CE. Paul was, of course, active at that point and was, presumably, developing at least some of the ideas that would forever become associated with him. The early dating of Mark does not affect the idea of similarities being due to generally similar Christian and Jewish influence on both Mark and Paul. I will raise issues of dating where it may affect the argument of this essay.

II. *Mark interpreting and/or advocating Paul or Pauline thought? Some precise examples*

One of Benjamin Bacon's key arguments concerning Pauline influence on Mark was focused on the hiding and elect group understanding of a mystery in Mk 4.1-20, combined with the use of Isa. 6.9. For Bacon, this was clearly related to Paul's ideas in Romans 9–11. Bacon was clear on what he saw as some kind of Pauline influence on Mark:

> So singular a combination of Old Testament [Isa. 6.9] quotation with current logia in the interest of a particular form of anti-Jewish polemic apologetic is difficult to account for unless we suppose the evangelist to have been familiar with the parallel argument of Paul, which employs the same quotations in the same interest.[5]

As ever, the point is worth making that Bacon works with the assumption that Mark used Paul, arguing as he was for a later date for Mark. It could be the case that, for all we know, Paul used Markan tradition, found it very useful and adapted it for his present needs. But in the case of the odd shared scriptural passage we could simply be dealing with coincidence. Indeed, it is worth stressing that Romans 9–11 is somewhat different from Mk 4.1-20. Mark does not have all the key Pauline ideas concerning the salvation of all Israel, the inclusion of the Gentiles to provoke Israel to jealousy, a branch grafted onto an olive tree, and the hardening of Israel's heart. If Mark was using Paul in any direct sense, would we not expect some of these major issues to come through? Would they not have been crucial to Mark too? Alternatively, if we think of an elect group understanding the truth, alongside a very early concern about persecution in the Gospels, Acts and Paul, then we already have a general Jewish and Christian context for the Markan passage. While we cannot rule out a direct influence one way or the other on the use of Isa. 6.9, the evidence simply does not demand the conclusion that Mark used Paul and the general context is, at the very least, just as plausible an explanation.

5. Bacon, *Gospel*, p. 263.

Bacon also believed, as others have, that the 'last supper' tradition in Mk 14.22-25 is evidence of 'direct use' (though not direct *literary* use) of 1 Cor. 11.23-25: 'such expressions as "the new covenant in my blood" are of Paul's own coinage. Paul is original. Mark is dependent.'[6] But, against Bacon, it is important to stress that here we have an example of Paul using an earlier tradition and so clear evidence of how the waters can be muddied (or should that be swirled?) in terms of influence. Moreover, it is significant that a variant reading of Mk 14.24 actually has to *add* καινης, which is effectively a 'Pauline' addition (1 Cor. 11.25). Furthermore, the contexts in Mark and Paul are quite different and this could be significant. Casey has argued persuasively for Mk 14.12-26 as a translation of an early source depicting Jesus' last Passover while the Pauline version is a 'comprehensive rewriting' in light of the problematic meals at Corinth and removed from its Passover setting.[7] But whatever we make of this argument, the point stands that we have two very different uses of the 'last supper' tradition and evidence of Paul using an earlier tradition which, presumably, could have been available to Mark. It is extremely difficult, to say the least, to make the case that Mark used Paul in any direct sense, and, given the Passover setting of Mark and the textual variant at Mk 14.24, there is certainly not any serious evidence to suggest, as Bacon did, that Mark used stereotyped 'words of institution' from Pauline churches.[8]

Supposedly one of the clearest examples of Paul influencing Mark (also developed by Bacon) is the apparent parallel passages already noted here, Rom. 14.14 and Mk 7.19. Marcus, for instance, believes that for Mark, like Paul, 'the Law was passé for Christians'. Mark, according to Marcus, even expressed this point 'in terms that are remarkably similar to those of Paul in Rom. 14' and then compares Mk 7.19 with Rom. 14.20.[9] There are, however, a number of problems with this view. We will return to the notable differences between Mark 7 and Romans 14 but, for a start, the linguistic parallels are not precise. If we assume for one moment that Mark (and indeed Paul) is doing away with the food laws, then why must the influence be necessarily Pauline? We have at least one memory of clean and unclean in relation to food laws being associated with *Peter* (Acts 10–11.18) so it is clearly possible that such sentiments, unsurprisingly, were more widely spread than being found just in Rom. 14.14 and Paul's thought. Perhaps, then, Paul was taking up an independent tradition. Perhaps, Paul was developing something like a more free-floating saying. After all, the related saying in Mk 7.15 appeared to have been something taken up

6. Bacon, *Gospel*, p. 269.
7. Casey, *Aramaic Sources*, pp. 219–249 (248).
8. Bacon, *Gospel*, p. 269. For further discussion of Bacon, see Crossley, *Date of Mark's Gospel*, ch. 3.
9. Marcus, 'Mark – Interpreter of Paul', p. 485.

independently elsewhere (*Gos. Thom.* 14), with hints of a different exegesis of an alternative form of the saying in Mark 7 itself (Mk 7.18-23).[10] In terms of the idea of Mark using Paul, is there not an underlying assumption that Mark and Paul are saying more or less the same thing? Can we not entertain the idea that Paul and Mark developed the saying independently (and one which may very well go back to the historical Jesus in some form) and differently (and the grammatical problems with Mk 7.18-19 means we should be very careful when trying to establish precise meaning)? If we switch the influence around (Mark/Markan tradition influencing Paul) then Paul could have been creatively developing a tradition to suit his own needs. All these options make it very difficult to establish flow of influence and they also bring us to alternative readings of the situation.

I have elsewhere suggested an alternative reading of Mk 7.19,[11] a reading taken up in different ways by Richard Bauckham, Markus Bockmuehl and Steve Moyise, for instance.[12] I argued that Mk 7.19 is better understood as 'all foods permitted in the Law are clean'. In other words, Matthew understood Mark correctly in his Mk 7.19 parallel when he said, 'but to eat with unwashed hands does not defile' (Mt. 15.20). This is based on the transmission of impurity in hand-washing law, where impurity is transmitted from hands to food to eater (via a liquid) and thus making the insides impure (cf. Mk 7.15). According to this reading, Mark's Jesus rejects this transmission of impurity and argues that all food permitted in the Torah is clean, irrespective of whether hands are clean or unclean. This is also consistent with the detailed and accurate discussion of table purity in Mark's editorial additions (Mk 7.3-4), the heavy emphasis on 'tradition' versus the commandments in Mark 7, and the broader portrayal of Jesus as Law-observant in Mark and the Synoptic Gospels.

In a recent detailed reading of Mark's Gospel in imperial contexts, Adam Winn, however, claims that this reading of Mk 7.19 is problematic because Mark's audience is 'almost certainly Gentile' and it seems unlikely that they would be able to undertake such a 'complicated reading without assistance

10. B. Lindars, '"All Foods Clean": Thoughts on Jesus and the Law', in B. Lindars (ed.), *Law and Religion: Essays on the Place of the Law in Israel and Early Christianity* (Cambridge: James Clark, 1988), pp. 61–71 (62–63, 65–66, 68–69).

11. Crossley, *Date of Mark's Gospel*, ch. 7; J. G. Crossley, 'Mark 7.1-23: Revisiting the Question of "All Foods Clean"', in M. Tait and P. Oakes (eds), *Torah in the New Testament* (London and New York: T&T Clark/Continuum, 2009), pp. 8–20.

12. M. Bockmuehl, 'God's Life as a Jew: Remembering the Son of God as Son of David', in B. R. Gaventa and R. B. Hays (eds), *Seeking the Identity of Jesus: A Pilgrimage* (Grand Rapids/Cambridge: Eerdmans, 2008), pp. 60–78 (69–70, n. 19); S. Moyise, *Evoking Scripture: Seeing the Old Testament in the New* (London & New York: T&T Clark/Continuum, 2008), p. 27; R. Bauckham, 'In Response to My Respondents: *Jesus and the Eyewitnesses* in Review', *JSHJ* 6 (2008), pp. 225–253 (233–235). See also D. A. J. Cohen, 'The Gentiles of Mark's Gospel: A Jewish Reading' (Ph.D. thesis, Australian National University, 2006), pp. 150–171; D. I. Brewer, 'Review of J. G. Crossley, *The Date of Mark's Gospel*', *JTS* 57 (2006), pp. 647–650 (649–650).

from the author'. Winn then adds that 'Crossley himself must spend *seven pages* to explain the complex halakic debate' as key for understanding impurity and that Mark's readers 'certainly' did not have this knowledge and that it is 'virtually as certain' Mark did not intend this too.[13] These are not particularly strong criticisms. On the issue of audience, Winn is too confident about their ethnic make-up, particularly as we actually have no direct evidence whatsoever about the ethnic make-up of the audience, other than there presumably being at least some Gentiles (cf. Mk 7.3-4), which, for all we know, could be anything between one Gentile and a complete audience of Gentiles. Given Mark's detailed knowledge of Jewish legal practices (Mk 7.1-5), it is a fair assumption that Mark could have been ethnically Jewish, or at least had strong familiarity with halakic practices. If so, then was Mark, a Jew or someone learned in halakic practices, writing for an entire audience of Gentiles who had no such interests? How can we be so certain about Mark intending his readers not to know about halakic knowledge when he actually writes about immersing beds, pots and individuals? And this, of course, followed closely by a story where Jesus talks of Gentile dogs and Jews being served first and a general narrative context framed by two feeding miracles, one for Jews and one for Gentiles (more on this shortly).

To complicate the matter further, even Paul, the one Jewish person we do associate with a Gentile audience, gave some incredibly complex arguments that have puzzled people throughout the ages and which no doubt owe much to his detailed training in Jewish contexts, including, presumably, Pharisaism. Did all the Gentiles in the audience really know how to interpret Paul's letters? The answer is 'presumably not' because Paul's letters were interpretatively problematic early on (2 Peter 15–16). Perhaps some people were more aware of the intricacies of Paul's arguments than others and perhaps some church leaders would interpret on behalf of others, perhaps converts from synagogues (cf. Acts 18.8). Winn appears to have resorted to a monolithic reconstruction of Mark's audience in relation to Mark 7, about which we actually know very little historically. As for the language that Winn's counterarguments are 'certain' and 'virtually certain', I think it is fair to say that this language is a little too cut and dried, not only because we do not know very much at all about the audience but also because not everyone agrees with Winn! As for taking *seven pages*, this was also because not enough New Testament scholars have looked into issues surrounding hand washing and it is a complex area. Indeed, many of us would need at least seven pages to understand the complex Jewish background to Paul's thinking; E. P. Sanders famously devoted hundreds of pages to the

13. A. Winn, *The Purpose of Mark's Gospel: An Early Christian Response to Roman Imperial Propaganda* (Tübingen: Mohr Siebeck, 2008), p. 55.

background to covenantal nominism in *Paul and Palestinian Judaism*! I have to say I am puzzled by the relevance of this particular counterargument made by Winn; despite hand-washing and related purity laws being mentioned, should we simply provide minimal treatment because they are seemingly unusual practices?

III. *Paul and Mark (unsurprisingly) faced similar issues: Jesus' death and suffering*

In 1 Cor. 1.23, Paul famously commented that 'we proclaim Christ crucified, a stumbling block to Jews and foolishness to Gentiles'. Presumably this was not a problem for Paul alone. As has long been pointed out, crucifixion was a shameful punishment and a highly problematic issue across the ancient world,[14] while the Pauline interpretation of the curse in Deut. 21.23 as crucifixion (Gal. 3.13) has a well-known parallel in the Dead Sea Scrolls (4Q169 frags 3-4, col. 1.6-9; cf. 11QT 64.6-13). Add to this the issues surrounding a *messianic* figure crucified and clearly this was the sort of problem the earliest Christians would almost inevitably encounter. Like Paul, Mark has to deal with the problem of Christ crucified and this comes through in Mark 8–10 where there is a clear development of 'son of man' sayings emphasizing suffering, Peter's criticism of the idea of Jesus suffering corrected and the justification of Jesus' mission by the highest of authorities (God, Moses and Elijah) at the Transfiguration in contrast, again, to the actions of Peter. Like Paul, Mark goes out of his way to defend the significance of Jesus' suffering but they have their own distinctive twists on the story and this can only be said to be a parallel in the general sense of both unsurprisingly facing a similar problem. *Could* one have directly influenced the other? Certainly! Can this be shown in any reasonably definitive way from Mark 8–10 and its big emphasis on Jesus' suffering? No, it cannot.

More precisely, though, some scholars have seen an engagement with a Pauline view of atonement in Mk 10.45 (cf. Rom. 3.23-5; 5.8-9, 18-19; Gal. 3.13; 1 Cor. 7.23; and Lk. 22.24-27): 'For the Son of Man came not to be served but to serve, and to give his life as a ransom (λύτρον) for many.'[15] But, again, there are too many notable differences, most obviously Paul using neither λύτρον nor ὁ υἱος τοῦ ἀνθρώπου. It could be argued with Seeley that here 'Mark is indirectly acknowledging a theologian he could not completely ignore, but whose theology he did not fully approve of.'[16] However, even if

14. M. Hengel, *Crucifixion in the Ancient World and the Folly of the Message of the Cross* (London: SCM, 1977).

15. For discussion see Crossley, *Date of Mark's Gospel*, ch. 3.

16. Seeley, 'Mark 10:41-45', p. 249.

Seeley is right, it is far from certain which came first and when ideas were developed. As ever, we should note that it is possible that Paul could have formulated such views anytime after his call/conversion and this influenced Mark or that atonement ideas were generally 'in the air' around earliest Christianity.

It is also quite possible that such views were developed by Jesus himself and, notably, some of the major proponents of the idiomatic Aramaic use of the 'son of man' sayings have pointed out how such an idiom could be used in contexts of humiliation, danger, death and modesty.[17] And Jesus, after all, must have known that he was going to die after what happened to John the Baptist, his conflict with opponents over the Torah and the healing mission, and his action in the Temple. A crucial background to all of this, and one which would have been known to Jesus and the earliest Christians, is that of the Maccabaean martyrs and their suffering for the benefits of others (e.g. 2 Macc. 7.32-38; *4 Macc.* 17.20-22; cf. Dan. 11.35), which would probably have been remembered yearly at Hanukkah.[18] The tradition of the Maccabaean martyrs also suggests that redemptive suffering could have been present from Jesus onwards and does not require Paul to have first developed such ideas in Christianity. Furthermore, in Paul there is clearly a universalizing view whereby Jesus' death would benefit Jews and Gentiles; there is no explicit indication in Mark and, for all we know, the Markan tradition could be retaining a view whereby Jews were the major beneficiaries of Jesus' death (compare the use of 'the many' at Qumran).

Clearly, then, there are similarities between Mark and Paul – an emphasis on the suffering of Christ and problems this emphasis entailed – but they are obviously at a general level, which makes it very difficult to posit direct dependence or influence. Interestingly, Joel Marcus noted the problems of preaching a theology of cross in Corinth[19] and while the location of Mark's Gospel is difficult to ascertain (Marcus goes for Syria), Corinth is not an obvious choice. What this already shows is that anyone who upheld something like a theology of the cross would have encountered problems across the empire. However, Marcus did make the theology of the cross the centrepiece of his analysis of Mark as

17. See e.g. G. Vermes, 'The Use of בר נשא/בר נש in Jewish Aramaic', appendix E in M. Black, *An Aramaic Approach to the Gospels and Acts* (3rd edn; Oxford: Oxford University Press, 1967), pp. 310–328; M. Casey, 'General, Generic and Indefinite: The Use of the Term "Son of Man" in Aramaic Sources and in the Teaching of Jesus', *JSNT* 29 (1987), pp. 21–56.

18. See e.g. M. D. Hooker, *Jesus and the Servant: The Influence of the Servant Concept of Deutero-Isaiah in the New Testament* (London: SPCK, 1959); C. K. Barrett, 'The Background of Mark 10.45', in A. J. B. Higgins (ed.), *New Testament Essays: Studies in Memory of T. W. Manson* (Manchester: Manchester University Press, 1959), pp. 1–18; C. K. Barrett, 'Mark 10.45: A Ransom For Many', in *New Testament Essays* (London: SPCK, 1972), pp. 20–26; J. Downing, 'Jesus and Martyrdom', *JTS* New Series 14 (1963), pp. 279–293; M. de Jonge, *Jewish Eschatology, Early Christian Christology, and the Testaments of the Twelve Patriarchs: Collected Essays of Marinus de Jonge* (Leiden: Brill, 1991); Casey, *Aramaic Sources*, pp. 193–218.

19. Marcus, 'Mark – Interpreter of Paul', pp. 481–482.

interpreter of Paul. Marcus argues that Mark focuses on the cross more single-mindedly than the other Gospels, that Mark stresses a paradoxical apocalyptic demonstration of divine power amid human weakness and death and that this is only really paralleled at the time in Paul, at least before 70 CE. Let us assume this is a fair reading. Does it still mean Mark has to be an interpreter of Paul? Here we are back to the issue consistently being raised here: it could be that Mark and Paul moved in similar circles and shared similar ideas; it could be that there were a significant enough number of Christians sharing such a view pre-70 CE but we simply do not have sufficient material to be sure one way or another (Marcus does note that there are difficulties dating any material apart from Paul and, to a lesser extent, Mark, in this period and that traditions about Jesus' death may have had an influence[20]). And, if we date Mark earlier, should we then be thinking 'Paul – interpreter of Mark'? Many options remain open. Marcus may well have the connection right but it is another thing to push too hard in terms of Mark as interpreter of Paul, plausible though the argument may be.

IV. *Paul and Mark (unsurprisingly) faced similar issues: Gentiles*

On almost any dating of Paul's letters and Mark's Gospel, both were active when Gentiles were present in earliest Christianity and this was an issue almost impossible to ignore. However, in a recent Ph.D. thesis, Daniel Cohen provided a 'Jewish reading' of Mark's Gospel that claimed Mark's Gospel is a Jewish text with little, if any, interest in a Gentile mission.[21] This startling and impressive thesis makes some powerful points, particularly in pointing out that the story of the Gerasene demoniac does not necessarily have anything to do with a 'proto-gentile mission' or anything of the sort. My reservation concerns texts such as Mk 13.10 and 14.9 that in the abstract do not have to be read in light of Gentiles attracted to the Christian movement, but when contextualized it seems difficult to think that no one would have transmitted such sentiments without being aware of their resonance in the context of the movement that was attracting non-Jews. If this is the case, we remain on the radar of a major legacy of Pauline thought: justifying the inclusion of Gentiles.

Certainly there are similarities in the idea of 'Jew first' (Rom. 1.16) in Mark. For instance, in the story of the Syro-Phoenician woman, the Markan Jesus notoriously says, 'Let the children be fed first, for it is not fair to take the children's food and throw it to the dogs' (Mk 7.27) while the Syro-Phoenician woman replies to Jesus (and gains a positive response), 'Sir, even the dogs under the table eat the children's crumbs' (Mk 7.28). The two feeding miracles at the

20. Marcus, 'Mark – Interpreter of Paul', pp. 481, 484–485.
21. D. Cohen, 'The Gentiles of Mark's Gospel'.

beginning and the end of Mk 6.30–8.21 look very much as if they are structured to have a major feeding miracle for 5,000 Jews first (Mk 6.31-44), paralleled by a not-quite-as-major feeding miracle for 4,000 Gentiles (Mk 8.1-9).[22] But are these examples evidence of Pauline influence on Mark? Marcus suggests that 'only Mark among the NT writers gives to one of his stories, that of the Syro-Phoenician woman, an interpretation that echoes Paul's formula "to the Jew first, but also to the Gentiles"'. If parallels such as this are coincidences, Marcus suggests, then 'they are amazing coincidences'; if not, as Marcus believes, then 'they provide further evidence of Pauline influence on Mark'.[23] However, while of course not wanting to rule out connections between Markan and Pauline ideas, this sort of thinking was hardly news in early Judaism and earliest Christianity, as is often noted. Aspects of early Judaism, naturally enough, had a tendency to privilege Jews, with, in certain cases, Gentiles coming on board in some (usually lesser) way (cf. e.g. Isa. 25.6; 45.22; 56.6-8; Zech. 2.11; 8.20-23; Tob. 14.6-7; *1 En* 90.30-33; *Sib. Or.* 3.616, 716-718, 752-753; *t. Sanh.* 13.2; *b. BQ* 38a). It may even be that this sentiment was taken up by the historical Jesus and so providing influence from another angle.[24]

Similarly, it seems clear enough from Paul that others were advocating something like a 'Jew first' schema. There seems, at least, to be some degree of agreement between Paul and the Jerusalem leaders on the issue of the inclusion of Gentiles in Galatians 1–2 and it is noticeable that Paul speaks to Peter with the following shared assumption that obviously implies Jewish superiority: 'We ourselves are Jews by birth and not Gentile sinners' (Gal. 2.15). And, of course, 'Jew first' is part of the narrative scheme of Acts, though the case could also be made for 'Luke – interpreter of Paul'.[25] With these backgrounds in mind, we cannot assume Mark is being directly influenced by Paul (or vice versa) and doubly so when it is clear that Mark does not use the distinctive language used by Paul. Indeed, the Markan language is, if anything, more damning than Paul and the interaction with a Gentile is exceptional: there is nothing like the concern for Gentiles in Mark as there is in Paul. In the instance of Gentiles and earliest Christianity, the context for the Markan language is simply too

22. J. Marcus, *Mark 1-8: A New Translation with Introduction and Commentary* (New York: Doubleday, 2000), pp. 404–515; J. G. Crossley, *Why Christianity Happened: A Sociohistorical Account of Christian Origins* (Louisville: Westminster John Knox, 2006), ch. 4.

23. Marcus, 'Mark – Interpreter of Paul', p. 487.

24. See further, J. Jeremias, *Jesus' Promise to the Nations* (rev. English edn; London: SCM, 1967); E. P. Sanders, *Jesus and Judaism* (London: SCM, 1985), pp. 212–221; M. F. Bird, 'Jesus and the Gentiles after Jeremias: Patterns and Prospects', *CBR* 4 (2005), pp. 83–108; M. F. Bird, *Jesus and the Origins of the Gentile Mission* (London and New York: T&T Clark/Continuum, 2006).

25. Cf. P. Vielhauer, 'On the "Paulinism" of Acts', in L. E. Keck and J. L. Martyn (eds), *Studies in Luke–Acts* (Philadelphia: Fortress, 1980), pp. 33–50.

broad to posit any direct influence from anywhere in particular, at least with any degree of certainty.

Some scholars have also suggested more precise influence on missional issues – more specifically, the use of the word εὐαγγέλιον. It is easy to get the impression that εὐαγγέλιον was introduced into the NT by Paul and so, if someone were to push this impression further, Mark might be said to have been a development of this. K. Kertelge, for example, argued that Mark 'takes up the keyword "gospel" from early Christian missionary language', and this early Christian missionary language is largely due to Paul.[26] However, Kertelge's view needs to be qualified. In fear of overkill, one option might be to stress, once more, that Paul could have influenced Mark very early on if Paul took up this language just after his call/conversion. Yet, for all we know, it is possible that such language could have been acquired independently from any number of places associated with Christian circles and some of this language may have originated from Jesus (and note the preaching of the gospel/good news of the kingdom of God in Mk 1.15), who was in turn influenced by the Hebrew Bible/Septuagint, especially Isaiah (e.g. Isa. 40.9; 41.27; 52.7; 60.6; 61.1). Like Matthew and Luke picking up and running with earlier words found in Mark, Paul may truly have liked εὐαγγέλιον and so we often associate such language with him.

In this light we should not forget that there are significant Pauline words *not* used in Mark and significant Markan words *not* used in Paul. Indeed, would not the argument for direct use of Pauline letters be much stronger if favourite Pauline words were recurrent throughout Mark? This should be a warning, which Werner-influenced scholarship is right to heed, that we should be very careful in positing the more direct Pauline influence on Mark in terms of linguistic analysis. As Howard Clark Kee also warned, 'none of the characteristic theological language of Paul appears in Mark, or if roughly similar terms occur, they are used in a significantly different conceptual framework'.[27] To sum up the old argument: the possibilities are multiple and no particular argument has a strong case to be definitive.

V. *Paul and Mark faced different problems: The Torah*

For all the uncertainties in reconstructing Christian origins, we can probably say with some certainty that Paul faced controversy over whether at least some

26. K. Kertelge, 'The Epiphany of Jesus in the Gospel (Mark)', in W. R. Telford (ed.), *The Interpretation of Mark* (London: SPCK, 1985), pp. 78–94 (79). Cf. W. Marxsen, *Mark the Evangelist* (Nashville: Abingdon, 1969), pp. 117–150.

27. H. C. Kee, *Community of the New Age: Studies in Mark's Gospel* (Macon: Mercer University Press, 1977), p. 6.

Christians should be observing the Law. According to Marcus, we recall, for both Mark and Paul, 'the Law was passé for Christians'.[28] While a clear case can be made for Paul thinking things such as circumcision, Sabbath observance and food laws, if not the entire Law, were no longer required for salvation or justification, this sort of view is not found in Mark. On the issue of the Sabbath, for instance, Mark does not deal with the situation of whether the Sabbath should be observed or not; instead, he deals with the issue of how Jesus *interpreted* the details of Sabbath observance in ways that were similar to other halakic debates in early Judaism. In Mk 2.23-28, Jesus disputes with Pharisees over whether plucking grain is acceptable on the Sabbath. Plucking grain is not banned in the Torah but interpretations of the Sabbath commandment could push in this direction (cf. *Life of Moses* 2.22; CD 10.22-23) and there were disputes among Jews over related issues, such as whether or not it was acceptable to pick fruit from the ground on the Sabbath (*m. Pesah.* 4.8). Similarly, the healing controversy in Mk 3.1-6 does not break any biblical commandment as such and Jesus defends himself with reference to the well-known justification of saving life on the Sabbath.[29] In light of the earlier discussion of food laws in Mark, we have a further, similar argument on this issue too. This is different to the sorts of situations we find in Paul where circumcision is not required of Gentiles, along with, perhaps, observance of the commandments in general. Moreover, on issues relating to (presumably) the Sabbath and food, Paul sees those who observe such things as weaker in faith but accepts such practices if done in honour of the Lord (Rom. 14.1-8). But this means, of course, that such practices are no longer required and that there are now a significant enough number of people not observing them.

It is, therefore, extremely difficult to see how Pauline thought is influencing Mark on the issue of Law, or, indeed, if Mark even knew of the specific Pauline views on the Law we have come to associate with the letters of Galatians and Romans. Given the absence of controversy over the observance of the Law itself (rather than controversy over correct interpretation of the Law), and given the interpretation of Mk 7.19 as stated earlier, it may be the case that Mark still assumes that observance of the Law is still practised by his audience. Even if Mark was aware of non-observance, he shows no serious indication of such a phenomenon and no indication of a Pauline view that the Law is a thing of the past or a Pauline view that the Law has no role in salvation and justification. If this reading is right, what it again shows is that Mark and Paul were facing

28. Marcus, 'Mark – Interpreter of Paul', p. 485.

29. For a full examination of the Law in Mark's Gospel, see Crossley, *Date of Mark's Gospel*, especially chs 4, 6 and 7. See also Casey, *Aramaic Sources*, pp. 182–184 and L. Doering, *Schabbat: Schabbathalacha und-praxis im antiken Judentum und Urchristentum* (Tübingen: Mohr Siebeck, 1999), pp. 450–454, for further discussion of Sabbath and the Gospel tradition, including the issue of extending the idea of saving life on the Sabbath to include Jesus' healings.

different circumstances. Would Mark (or indeed Jesus) have agreed with Paul's solution to the problem of Gentiles and Torah observance? Maybe, maybe not: we simply do not know how others would have reacted in Paul's situation and so we should take seriously the option that we are dealing with different figures in different contexts in this instance.

VI. *Christology and conflict*

One of the most frequent readings of Markan Christology in a sense deemed to have some kind of Pauline influence is that involving 'corrective Christology'. Simply, crudely and perhaps obviously put, Mark is said to correct that which was deemed a false Christology with that deemed a true understanding of Jesus. More specifically for our purposes, this approach is frequently employed to show that Mark, like Paul (cf. Galatians 2; Romans 14–15), is in dispute with a form of Jewish Christianity, associated variously with Peter, the Twelve and Jesus' family in Mark, and which insisted on the observance of the Law.[30]

Before we turn to the relationship (or not) between Mark and Paul more precisely on this issue, it is worth looking at the role of corrective Christology in Markan scholarship in a little more detail as it provides crucial scholarly background information. One of the most influential arguments on the role of misunderstanding in the Christology of Mark is that of Joseph Tyson, who argued that the Markan Jesus' messiahship is not to be confused with a conventional Jewish nationalistic royal messiahship and so Mark makes 'relatively little' of a Son of David theology. This, it is argued, is linked to the conflict between Jesus and his family and Jesus and his disciples who represent the Jerusalem church and hold 'only a mildly modified Judaism'.[31] The debate over rank in the kingdom of God (Mk 10.35-45) implies that the disciples in Mark understood Jesus in terms of royal messiahship and that for Mark this understanding is misguided.

Although Tyson is aware that the evidence for the Jerusalem church representing such a Jewish view is not strong, he does note that the Jerusalem

30. See e.g. J. B. Tyson, 'The Blindness of the Disciples in Mark', *JBL* 80 (1961), pp. 261–268; J. D. Crossan, 'Mark and the Relatives of Jesus', *NovT* 15 (1973), pp. 81–113; Goulder, 'Those Outside'. For an alternative approach which has the failed followers as examples of the difficulties of discipleship see e.g. R. C. Tannehill, 'The Disciples in Mark: The Function of a Narrative Role', in Telford (ed.), *Interpretation of Mark*, pp. 134–157; E. S. Malbon, 'Fallible Followers: Women and Men in the Gospel of Mark', *Semeia* 28 (1983), pp. 29–48; L. W. Hurtado, *Lord Jesus Christ: Devotion to Jesus in Earliest Christianity* (Grand Rapids/Cambridge: Eerdmans, 2003), pp. 310–314. For different critiques of 'corrective Christology' see e.g. J. D. Kingsbury, *The Christology of Mark's Gospel* (Philadelphia: Fortress, 1983); Tannehill, 'Disciples in Mark', pp. 141–142; Marcus, *Mark 1-8*, pp. 75–79; S. W. Henderson, *Christology and Discipleship in the Gospel of Mark* (Cambridge: Cambridge University Press, 2006), e.g. pp. 3–15.

31. Tyson, 'Blindness', p. 40.

church did form a 'kind of family dynasty' set up by James and, according to the report in Eusebius, included many of that family. This group, taking 'the form of a mildly modified Judaism', struggled with Paul, especially over issues of apostolic authority and biblical Law. Mark agreed with the latter.[32] This Christological conflict is therefore clearly constructed in terms of a categorical distance between Judaism and Markan Christianity. Moreover, according to Tyson, a key influence in the difference was Mark's (and Paul's) concern for Gentiles and so, for Mark, 'Jesus is much more than a nationalistic Messiah to the Jews. He has significance for all the world, and this significance cannot involve the strait-jacket limitation imposed by a hierarchy of relatives and friends of Jesus.'[33]

There are problems with this approach. The view that there was a Jewish Christian dynasty imposing a nationalistic Davidic Messiah is not clear. The conflicts between Paul and the Jerusalem church, as Tyson notes, concern issues of Law rather than the James group advocating a narrow nationalistic Messiah with little concern for Gentiles. In fact, a pro-nationalism downplaying concern for Gentiles would be very unlikely. After all, James, along with Peter and John, gave 'the right hand of fellowship' to Paul and Barnabas and accepted their mission to the Gentiles (Gal. 2.9; cf. Acts 15). As we have seen, there was also a well-established view in early Judaism of eschatological restoration that included Gentiles and this does not seem to have been contradicted in early Christianity. This evidence, combined with the fact that the Jerusalem church is only shown as openly *accepting* the Gentile mission, means that it is speculative at best to say that Mark is rejecting a 'Jewish view' current in Christianity. Mark no doubt would have disagreed with any Jews who focused too strongly on Jews alone but not all Jews thought like this. We might add to all this that the disputes with family and the disciples in Mark do not, in sharp contrast to Paul, directly involve the Law and its validity and Jesus even defends his disciples on the issue of plucking grain on the Sabbath, which, as we saw, is the kind of interpretative dispute known in early Judaism.[34]

It could be argued that I am being a little unfair in using Tyson as an example of this sort of Christology that downplays Judaism, given that he wrote the article before the impact of scholars like E. P. Sanders and Geza Vermes. However,

32. Tyson, 'Blindness', p. 39.

33. Tyson, 'Blindness', p. 41.

34. It might be worth adding that if we accept the popular idea that Mark polemically fires at Jesus' family, which is said to be similar to Paul's disputes with the Jerusalem church, this still does not demand Pauline influence. Conflict over issues surrounding family could well have been generated from the ministry of the historical Jesus and social upheavals in Galilee (see e.g. H. Moxnes, *Putting Jesus in His Place: A Radical Vision of Household and Kingdom* [Louisville: WJK, 2003]). We should not assume, of course, that Paul was the only person to have tensions with fellow Christians, including issues arising in/with Jerusalem, in earliest Christianity (Acts 6.1-6).

Tyson's view remains influential and this sort of thinking partly underlies the Mark-Paul connection made in scholarship.[35] William Telford, as he acknowledges, is strongly influenced by Tyson in his reading of Markan Christology:

> [T]he essential point being conveyed by the evangelist to the reader, in my view, is that the designation 'Christ' is not to be understood in its Jewish, nationalistic, political and triumphalist 'Son of David' sense, but in the sense in which it later came to be understood by Hellenistic Christianity, that is, as a divine being who is to be identified with the community's exalted 'Lord'. What I would detect in Mark therefore is a move away from a 'Son of David' Christology, one embodied, I suspect, in the characters of the Markan text (Peter, the disciples, blind Bartimaeus and the Jewish crowd who are later to crucify him). At the narrative level, this Christology may be implied in Peter's rejection of a non-triumphalist Messiahship (8.31-32) . . . as well as the desire of his disciples to occupy a privileged position at Jesus' right and left hand 'in his glory' (10.35-45). At the historical level, although here one can only speculate, Mark may be in tension with a Jewish-Christian estimate of Jesus which laid considerable emphasis on Jesus as the 'Son of David'.[36]

For Telford, this sort of thinking attributed to Mark is evidence of similarity with Paul because Paul, too, appears to reject a 'Son of David' Christology in favour of a higher 'Son of God' Christology. Paul may, according to Telford, acknowledge the priority of a Son of David Christology in Rom. 1.3-4 but from then on Paul 'disowns it by sheer neglect'.[37]

But none of the Markan passages discussed back up this (at times, admittedly speculative) argument either, or at least they do not point to any particularly significant link with Pauline theology in terms of a Son of David Christology. It seems unlikely that Mark even has any real concern with a Davidic Christology,[38] as I have discussed in more detail elsewhere.[39] In the case of blind Bartimaeus there is no explicit critique of the title and he is portrayed more as daringly faithful when he calls to Jesus as Son of David (10.48). That said, the phrase Son of David may mean nothing more than Jesus as a good Jew, like a daughter of Abraham (Lk. 13.16) or a son of God (e.g. Exod. 4.22; Deut. 32.5-6, 18-19; Sir. 4.10; *Ps. Sol.* 17.27[29]; *m. Taan.* 3.8). In fact, when the crowds mention David in Mark 11 it is precisely in this sense: they bless the coming kingdom of 'our father' David (Mk 11.10). This is hardly an attack on a Davidic Christology and we should not assume that this specific crowd was blamed by Mark for the crucifixion.

35. This comes through, for instance, in Marcus, 'Mark – Interpreter of Paul'.
36. Telford, *Theology*, p. 37.
37. Telford, *Theology*, p. 166.
38. But cf. Kingsbury, *Christology*, pp. 102–114.
39. Crossley, *Date of Mark's Gospel*, pp. 76–79.

The closest we get to a Markan rejection of a Son of David Christology is Mk 12.35-37 but this is aimed at the scribes, not Peter and the disciples. Nor is it a criticism of a broader Jewish view: the large (Jewish) crowd thought this a wonderful piece of teaching. The reason why the Davidic language might have been used here is that the narrative now locates Jesus in Jerusalem and its environs, the area of the king. As for Telford's argument that Peter rejects a non-triumphalist Messiah, Peter specifically criticizes Jesus for saying *the son of man* must suffer (Mk 8.31-33).[40] In its present literary context there clearly is a concern to emphasize the suffering of Jesus but Mark does not go so far as to say that it should be viewed over against a triumphalist Messiah. As for the question of authority in Mk 10.35-45, a text noted by Tyson, there is no mention of Son of David and no mention of Messiah. Furthermore, the text does not actually reject the possibility of James and John suffering and sitting at Jesus' side, it is just not up to Jesus to decide (Mk 10.39-40). Perhaps Mark, like Telford's Paul, rejected a Son of David Christology through 'sheer neglect' but neglect is not a strong enough category by which to assess a Pauline influence on Mark or vice versa.

'Son of God' is one Christological title deemed to have been influenced by Paul, and this was precisely the title emphasized by Mark and Paul at the expense of a Son of David Christology in Telford's reading. While it is obviously difficult to disagree with the point that the title 'Son of God' was important for Mark, there are differences over precisely what this means and from precisely where Mark got the title, particularly in comparison with Paul or the not-particularly-helpful category 'Hellenistic (church)'. Telford, for example, notes that the title 'Son of God' is 'capable of being interpreted in either a Jewish sense or a Hellenistic sense' and, following Bultmann's lead, plumps for the latter (with Paul thrown into the mix) in his interpretation of Mark.[41] As the title is admitted by a whole host of Markan characters, apparently culminating with the confession of the Roman centurion at the cross (Mk 15.39), and not recognized or confessed by Jesus' original followers, Telford suggests that Mark represents a Pauline-influenced Gentile Christianity that viewed Jesus as the divine 'Son of God' who came to suffer and die on the cross. And it is the secrecy motif that invites the reader to view him as such. Typically of Markan scholarship, this Christology is constructed as something distinctly different over against Judaism. Telford claims it 'is in tension both with Jewish estimates of Jesus (teacher, prophet and healer) as well as Jewish-Christian

40. Cf. Kingsbury, *Christology*, p. 95.

41. Telford, *Theology*, pp. 52, 166–169; R. Bultmann, *Theology of the New Testament* (vol. 1; New York: Charles Scribner's Sons, 1951), pp. 128–133. For a critical review of scholarship on a more 'Hellenistic' understanding of 'Son of God', usually associated with the so-called 'divine man', see e.g. Kingsbury, *Christology*, pp. 25–45.

ones'. Jewish-Christian estimates of Jesus were more 'in keeping with Jewish monotheism', 'not his divinity (nor his cross?)' but rather his 'triumphant status as the Jewish Messiah'.[42] Telford concludes:

> By both employing and correcting the emphases of these separate traditions, by a discriminating use of Christological titles, and, above all, by means of the secrecy motif, Mark has presented these traditions in such a way as to leave his readers in no doubt as to the significance that ought to be attached to the historical figure of Jesus, namely, that he is the supernatural 'Son of God'.[43]

Against Telford, none of the references in Mark point unambiguously to a correction of an alternative 'Jewish' understanding of 'Son of God'. In the Transfiguration scene the best evidence is that Peter mistakenly makes booths. This may well be functioning in relation to Peter's denial of Jesus as the suffering 'son of man', hence the narrative parallel in Mk 8.31-33, but this does not mean that there is a denial of Jesus as Son of God by the Jewish Peter. On the contrary, Peter and the other Jewish disciples present accept Jesus as God's beloved Son (9.9). The only problem they have is with the meaning of resurrection (9.10) and why Elijah must come first (9.11-13).

But what of the centurion who confesses in notable contrast to the first disciples? This argument is not necessarily as strong as is often thought. As noted earlier, Jewish disciples appear to accept that Jesus is God's beloved Son after the Transfiguration. In fact it is possible that, if anything, it is the centurion who may have misunderstood who Jesus was. In an important article, Earl S. Johnson makes a strong case for the lack of a definite article and the imperfect tense in Mk 15.39 ('Truly this man *was a* son of god' [ἀληθῶς οὗτος ὁ ἄνθρωπος υἱὸς θεοῦ ἦν]) representing not quite what would be expected of the Markan Christian (note Mk 1.11 and 9.7 are in the present tense), possibly something to be more associated with Roman/pagan thought.[44]

It should also be mentioned that the view of a 'Hellenistic' Son of God, as opposed to a more 'Jewish' Son of God Christology, is suspect on the grounds that the two key scenes – namely, the Baptism (Mk 1.9-11) and Transfiguration (Mk 9.2-8) – are immersed in fairly conventional imagery in early Judaism. Among other things, the voice from heaven in the Baptism is clearly in the tradition of the *bath qol*, there is an allusion to Ps. 2.7, and the tearing of the heavens echoes MT Isa. 63.19.[45] The echoes of Sinai in the Transfiguration epi-

42. Telford, *Theology*, p. 53.
43. Telford, *Theology*, p. 54.
44. E. S. Johnson, 'Is Mark 15:39 the Key to Mark's Christology?', *JSNT* 31 (1987), pp. 3–22.
45. See Kingsbury, *Christology*, pp. 61–68, for further criticisms of the 'Hellenistic' baptism of Jesus.

sode are well known, and in addition note the white clothing (9.3) that denotes the importance of purity before God (e.g. Dan. 11.35; *War* 2.123; cf. Isa. 1.18; 6.1-7),[46] an allusion to Tabernacles (9.5) and the presence of two of the most significant figures in Jewish tradition. Given all these points, and not to mention the abundant Jewish language surrounding the 'Son of God', a good case can be made that this Markan Son of God is at the very least plausibly read in the general context of early Judaism rather than simply interpreting such language in light of Paul and/or something sometimes unhelpfully called 'Hellenistic' in distinction. As Elizabeth Struthers Malbon rightly put it concerning the term 'beloved Son' used in the scenes of the baptism and Transfiguration in Mark:

> The two scenes are impressively high in drama but amazingly low in content concerning what it means for Jesus to be called God's Son. The actions of Jesus ('enacted Christology') and the words of Jesus about God ('deflected Christology') confirm that the widespread Jewish understanding of the person obedient to God as a 'son of God' is shared by the Markan Jesus.[47]

And this leads us to a big problem with Markan Christology, particularly in terms of 'divinity': it is often too vague in relation to Paul's Christology. Certainly, we can say that issues of authority and/or suffering are tied in with terms such as 'son of God' and 'son of man' and the general issue of a theology of the cross is no doubt a clear similarity between the two. We can, of course, note that the Markan Jesus will return with the clouds of heaven and sit at his father's right hand. But to say that Mark holds a dramatic Christology in the sense of a Pauline passage such as Phil. 2.6-11 is hardly clear, for the simple reason that Mark does not tell us enough in the way of content and detail. Ultimately, it is very difficult to tell how far Mark and Paul might have agreed with one another on certain Christological issues but this should warn us about the problems involved in positing Pauline influence on Mark: would Mark really have been so non-explicit about sentiments such as those found in Phil. 2.6-11 if he had known about them?

And to what extent were there any first-century Christians who were openly denying a 'divine', and supposedly non-Jewish, Pauline/Hellenistic Son of God Christology?[48] Not even Paul, not one to hold back on polemic, attacks anyone for rejecting such a Christology. We certainly do get conflict over, and

46. Against Marcus, 'Mark – Interpreter of Paul', p. 475, n. 11, who pushes in the direction of an Adam Christology partly on the grounds that it is Jesus' clothes rather than face shining.

47. E. S. Malbon, 'The Christology of Mark's Gospel: Narrative Christology and the Markan Jesus', in M. A. Powell and D. R. Bauer (eds), *Who Do You Say I Am? Essays on Christology* (FS J. D. Kingsbury; Louisville: WJK, 1999), pp. 33–48 (42).

48. As Paul was a Jew utilizing Jewish tradition, the distinction between 'Jewish' and 'Hellenistic-and-Pauline' Son of God is problematic.

a long defence of, Jesus' sonship in John 5 but this is in conflict with 'the Jews' and is simply not the kind of material found in Mark. In fact, no Christology before John's Gospel (problems with the crucified Christ aside) appears to be all that controversial within Christianity (cf. Jn 6.60-66), at least in the sense of controversy over establishing some sort of 'divinity', nor indeed is there any explicit evidence prior to John of conflict with 'the Jews'.[49] This counts strongly against key aspects of Telford's suggested reconstruction.

VII. *Concluding remarks*

So, what can we say about influence when it comes to Paul and Mark? When analysed closely, some of the key passages where Paul is often said to have influenced Mark do not necessarily support such a conclusion. Sometimes the language is too different and the themes sufficiently widespread in earliest Christianity that it is extremely difficult to pinpoint precise influence. It is perhaps worth re-stressing that with so many ideas floating around in earliest Christianity, perhaps some or many generated by the historical Jesus, and so many shared problems when facing the world (a crucified messianic figure and inclusion of Gentiles are the most obvious examples), then it is no surprise that two of the earliest, if not the earliest, documents / collection of documents overlap. Werner was certainly onto something when he pointed out the importance of early Christianity as a general context to explain similarities between Mark and Paul. Yet, Marcus may also be onto something when he notes some of the more precise similarities between the two, though with so many key differences (on Law and aspects of Christology in particular) there is no smoking gun to make us conclude with the idea of 'Mark – interpreter of Paul' (or vice versa) in the stronger sense advocated by Marcus. Of course, while scholars may have overstated Pauline influence on all things early Christianity, we can hardly forget that Paul was a major figure presumably known among many or most Christian groups across the empire. But he was also active from the 30s CE onward and he interacted with a range of different groups, no doubt

49. Against L. W. Hurtado, 'Pre-70 C.E. Jewish Opposition to Christ-Devotion', *JTS* 50 (1999), pp. 35–58. Hurtado points to passages such as Stephen's speech in Acts 7, conflicts in the early chapters of Acts (e.g. Acts 4.1-22; 5.27-42) and the blasphemy charges in Mk 2.7 and 14.65 as evidence of opposition to the cultic worship of Christ prior to John. However, these passages are more concerned with other issues, usually the *authority* of the mission of the first Christians than with Christ's being. The issues with Stephen's speech are more to do with a clash over the correct interpretation of the Law (cf. 1 Kings 8; 2 Chronicles 6–7; Ps. 132[131].12; Isa. 66.2, 5). See further Crossley, *Date of Mark's Gospel*, pp. 126–131. Cf. P. Doble, 'Something Greater than Solomon: An Approach to Stephen's Speech', in S. Moyise (ed.), *The Old Testament in the New Testament: Essays in Honour of J.L. North* (Sheffield: Sheffield Academic Press, 2000), pp. 181–207 (192–201).

influencing them, no doubt being influenced by them.[50] It seems reasonable enough to suggest that there are overlaps and shared interests that emerged from the swirling mix of ideas and it seems reasonable enough to suggest that one was at least aware of the other, perhaps one (or both) even taking a precise idea here and there from the other.

50. Cf. M. B. Thompson, 'The Holy Internet: Communication between Churches in the First Christian Generation', in R. Bauckham (ed.), *The Gospel for All Christians: Rethinking the Gospel Audiences* (Edinburgh: T&T Clark, 1998), pp. 49–70.

2

MARK: INTERPRETER OF PETER AND DISCIPLE OF PAUL

Michael F. Bird

I. *Introduction*

Although Μᾶρκος (Greek) and *Marcus* (Latin) were very popular names in the Graeco-Roman world, the second-century Christian tradition was unanimous that the Μᾶρκος ('Mark') from ΚΑΤΑ ΜΑΡΚΟΝ in the title of the second Gospel referred to 'John Mark', a relatively minor figure known from the book of Acts and the Epistles. This John Mark was a helper to Paul and Barnabas (Acts 12.25; 13.5), to Barnabas alone (Acts 15.36-41) and to Paul alone (Phlm. 1.24; Col. 4.10; 2 Tim. 4.11). A connection between Peter and John Mark is made in 1 Pet. 5.13 where Peter calls Mark his 'son', and also in Luke's account of the Palestinian church where Peter visits John Mark's home on at least one occasion (Acts 12.11-17). A summary of what the NT contributes to the knowledge of John Mark is succinctly given by Richard Bauckham:

> John Mark, a member of a Cypriot Jewish family settled in Jerusalem and member of the early Jerusalem church, was then in Antioch, accompanied his cousin Barnabas and Paul on their missionary journey as far as Pamphylia, later accompanied Barnabas to Cyprus, and is finally heard of in Rome, if Philemon is written from Rome, where 1 Peter also places him.[1]

If John Mark was a one-time missionary companion of Paul and then later, as tradition suggests,[2] the scribe of Peter in the composition of a Gospel, this would have several ramifications for the study of Early Christianity. John Mark

1. Richard Bauckham, 'For Whom Were the Gospels Written?', in *The Gospels for All Christians: Rethinking the Gospel Audiences*, ed. R. Bauckham (Grand Rapids, MI: Eerdmans, 1998), p. 35. For a further study see the comprehensive work of C. Clifton Black, *Mark: Images of an Apostolic Interpreter* (Columbia: University of South Carolina Press, 1994).

2. Cf. Papias' statement from the 'elder' recorded in Eusebius, *Hist. Eccl.* 3.39.15 (c.110–125 CE), and similar statements can be found in the anti-Marcionite prologue (c.160–180 CE), Irenaeus, *Adv. Haer.*

would stand as a personal link between Paul and Peter; thus, the Markan Gospel would represent the literary deposit of a figure who was personally involved with two of the most influential personalities of the pre-70 CE church. However, several scholars simply bypass this debate by situating the Gospel of Mark in an environment, theologically and geographically, beyond the immediate purview of either Paul or Peter.[3] Personally, I am rather optimistic about the authenticity of the Papian testimony concerning John Mark's composition of the second canonical Gospel, if only for the reason that no serious alternative ever presented itself for consideration in the early church.[4] But even if one rejects the Papian testimony, we are still left with the question of the place of the Gospel of Mark in early Christianity. Which school, community or trajectory does the Gospel of Mark fit into?

The relationship of Mark vis-à-vis Peter and Paul has always cast its shadow over Markan scholarship. Earlier generations of scholars were divided over whether the Gospel of Mark endeavoured to defend Paul against the Jerusalem church (e.g. G. Volkmar, A. Loisy), if Mark was simply the work of a Paulinist (e.g. B.W. Bacon, J. Weiss, C.G. Montefiore, J.C. Fenton), or if Mark was representative of a Hellenistic Christianity independent of Paul (M. Werner, A.E.J. Rawlinson, F.C. Grant, A.M. Hunter, W.G. Kümmel, H.C. Kee). C.H. Turner argued that Mark's point of view was identical to Peter's and also reflected Peter's teaching without Pauline influence.[5] In contrast, B.W. Bacon was able to remove Petrine influence altogether by making Mark dependent on 1 Peter, implying that the Papian testimony was the attempt to bring the Petrine churches under the aegis of the Pauline gospel.[6] F.C. Baur regarded Mark as a second-century Petrine-Pauline compromise.[7]

The problem is that it does not seem possible to put all the eggs in either the

3.1.1-2 (180 CE), Clement of Alexandria (Eusebius, *Hist. Eccl.* 2.15.1-2; 6.14.5-7) (c.180–200 CE), and implicitly in Justin (*Dial.* 106.3) (150 CE).

3. For instance, James G. Crossley (*The Date of Mark's Gospel: Insights from the Law in Earliest Christianity* [JSNTSup 266; London: T&T Clark, 2004]) rejects the authenticity of the tradition that associated John Mark with Peter (pp. 17–18), but also argues that there is no clear evidence for Pauline influence on Mark (pp. 47–55). Crossley dates the Gospel of Mark to the mid-40s CE when the Christian movement was still Law-observant (pp. 208–9).

4. See the Appendix at the end of this chapter.

5. C.H. Turner, *The Gospel According to St. Mark: Introduction and Commentary* (London: SPCK, 1931).

6. B.W. Bacon, *Is Mark a Roman Gospel?* (Cambridge: CUP, 1919); cf. J.C. Fenton ('Paul and Mark', in *Studies in the Gospels: Essays in Memory of R.H. Lightfoot*, ed. D.E. Nineham [Oxford: Blackwell, 1955], p. 111) who sees a stronger case for a Mark-Paul link than for a Mark-Peter association.

7. F.C. Baur, *Das Markusevangelium nach seinem Ursprung und Charakter* (Tübingen: Ludw. Friedr. Fues., 1851); cf. with a different chronology to Baur, a Peter-Paul synthesis in Mark: David Dungan, 'The Purpose and Provenance of the Gospel of Mark According to the "Two-Gospel" (Griesbach) Hypothesis', in *Colloquy on New Testament Studies*, ed. B. Corley (Macon, GA: Mercer University Press, 1983), pp. 145, 151–6; Black, *Mark*, p. 208.

Pauline or the Petrine baskets concerning the origin of the Gospel of Mark.[8] Also, even if 'Paulus versus Petrus' is the matrix for locating the Markan Gospel, the relationship of this Gospel to those two persons may be far more sophisticated than often envisaged. The first polarity is whether Mark is *either* a pro- or a-Pauline document. The second polarity is whether the Gospel is really the unpolished collection of Peter's reminiscences about Jesus *or* a string of community traditions made by anonymous authors. Yet both dichotomies fail to recognize that the problem may not be reducible to singular alternatives and the actual relation of Paul and/or Peter to the Gospel of Mark may be far more complex than the options stated. The subject of Pauline and Petrine relation to the Gospel of Mark has been studied and restated many times before, but very rarely are the subjects studied together. Therefore, the thesis that I wish to advance in this essay is that the Gospel of Mark points to an early synthesis of Peter and Paul: *Petrine testimony shaped into an evangelical narrative conducive to Pauline proclamation*. The way that I will attempt to demonstrate this is by, first, examining features of the Gospel indicating Petrine tradition and, second, identifying traits in the Gospel that reflect Paul's distinctive theological character.

II. *Gospel of Mark as Petrine testimony*

The difficulty of identifying a Petrine tradition in Mark is that we have very few sources that we can safely and unhesitatingly attribute to Peter. The later pseudepigraphical works attributed to Peter (*Gospel of Peter*, *Apocalypse of Peter*, *Acts of Peter*) are exactly that, pseudepigraphical. Second Peter is almost universally regarded as being pseudonymous and 1 Peter is also contested as to its actual links to the historic Peter. The speeches and narratives depicting Peter in Acts – though containing a mix of tradition, memory and testimony – are filtered through a Lukan theological grid. Paul's representation of Peter swings from warm affirmation to factual neutrality to polemical opposition, and he has only a paucity of information about Peter anyway. Peter very quickly became a revered figure in some pockets of early Christianity (e.g. Mt. 16.17-20; *1 Clem* 5.1-4), but he was also cordially displaced by authors (John 20–21) and at other times aggressively disparaged (*Gos. Thom.* 12). New Testament scholarship has been haunted by the 'Quest for the Historical Jesus' and obsessed with the 'Quest for the Historical Paul', but the 'Quest for the Historical Peter' is without doubt the more arduous task because of our dearth of information

8. Bruce Corley, 'Seminar Dialogue with David Dungan', in *Colloquy on New Testament Studies*, ed. B. Corley (Macon, GA: Mercer University Press, 1983), p. 166.

about him.[9] Thus, we have no control source against which we can compare the Gospel of Mark with in order to identify Petrine tradents. How then are we to identify and evaluate Petrine traditions in the Gospel of Mark? Our best bet is to look at features that might represent Petrine perspective in Mark and try to correlate them with the memories of Peter floating around in early Christian sources.

Several scholars object to this endeavour of trying to detect Petrine elements in Mark on the grounds that Mark is not especially Petrine.[10] Reasons adduced against a Petrine source for the Gospel of Mark include: (1) Mark was probably derived from multiple sources and traditions, not simply from a single Petrine source. (2) Mark is not the most Petrine Gospel. Peter is portrayed more positively in the Gospel of Matthew (e.g. Mt. 16.17-19) and Matthew includes additional material about Peter not found in Mark (e.g. Mt. 14.28-31; 16.17-19; 17.24-27). It could even be said that Peter is portrayed as more humanly authentic in the Gospel of Luke (e.g. Lk. 5.8; 22.61) than in the Gospel of Mark. (3) If anything there is a polemic against Peter and the disciples in the Gospel of Mark that is not conducive to the appropriation of a Petrine source. (4) If it were not for Papias we would have no reason for postulating a Petrine tradition behind Mark. I think that all of these points are contestable.

In response, first, I concur that Mark probably represents an assortment of various Jesus traditions circulating in the church that 'John Mark' picked up in his various interactions with Christian communities in Palestine, Syria and Rome. Still, I would add that leading figures like the apostles and teachers were very much the custodians and transmitters of this tradition so that we should not rule out Peter or a Petrine circle as at least one source for Mark.[11] Second, that Peter is portrayed comparatively better in Matthew than in Mark is not an argument against a constructive and sympathetic treatment of the character of Peter in Mark. It only means that Peter was revered in more than one stream of the early church. In addition, the author of Matthew, writing out of a Palestinian context, may simply have had more traditional material about Peter available to

9. Cf. Oscar Cullmann, *Peter: Disciple, Apostle, Martyr* (Philadelphia: Westminster, 1953); Pheme Perkins, *Peter: Apostle for the Whole Church* (Minneapolis: Fortress, 1994); Michael Grant, *Saint Peter: A Biography* (New York: Scribner, 1995); Eckhard J. Schnabel, *Early Christian Mission* (2 vols; Downers Grove, IL: InterVarsity Press, 2004), vol. 1, pp. 702–28; Bart D. Ehrman, *Peter, Paul, and Mary Magdalene: The Followers of Jesus in History and Legend* (Oxford: OUP, 2006), pp. 15–120; Markus Bockmuehl, 'Peter between Jesus and Paul: The "Third Quest" and the "New Perspective" on the First Disciple', in *Jesus and Paul Reconnected: Fresh Pathways into an Old Debate*, ed. T.D. Still (Grand Rapids, MI: Eerdmans, 2007), pp. 67–102; James D.G. Dunn, *Beginning from Jerusalem* (CITM 2; Grand Rapids, MI: Eerdmans, 2009), pp. 1058–76; Martin Hengel, *Saint Peter: The Underestimated Apostle* (Grand Rapids, MI: Eerdmans, 2010).

10. Cf. e.g. Joel Marcus, *Mark 1–8* (AB; New York: Doubleday, 2000), pp. 23–4.

11. On this point see Michael F. Bird, 'The Purpose and Preservation of the Jesus Tradition: Moderate Evidence for a Conserving Force in its Transmission', *BBR* 15 (2005), pp. 178–80.

him to include in his Jesus Book. We must remain agnostic about what traditions Mark knew about Peter and why he chose to omit other traditions if he knew about them. Third, the so-called polemic against Jesus' disciples in the Gospel of Mark reads too much into too little.[12] The misunderstanding and failure of the disciples are narrative devices in Mark about epistemology and discipleship – knowing and following Jesus – and attempts to freight them with internecine Christian polemics are blandly overstated. For case in point, Matthew retains the Markan Jesus' charge of ignorance against the disciples for their misunderstanding of his figurative statement about 'yeast' (Mk 8.14-21/Mt. 16.6-12) and he likewise retains Mark's pericope where Peter is publicly rebuked before the other disciples (Mk 8.33-38/Mt. 16.23-28), yet it would be odd to conceive of a Matthaean polemic against Peter and the eleven disciples. Therefore, Mark is not 'assiduously involved in a vendetta against the disciples',[13] for if he is so involved, then, he has chosen a painfully contradictory way of showing it. Fourth, as to whether or not the Papian tradition of a Peter-Mark association is the only reason for suspecting a Petrine tradition behind Mark needs to be tested by the internal evidence of Mark itself and to that task I now turn.

A first area indicating Petrine features in Mark is the device of *inclusio* as the Markan narrative is bracketed with references to Peter as the first and last disciple mentioned (Mk 1.16; 16.7). This point is forcefully argued by Richard Bauckham who notes the importance of eyewitness testimony among Graeco-Roman historians of antiquity and he proceeds to argue:

> The two references form an *inclusio* around the whole story, suggesting that Peter is the witness whose testimony includes the whole. If the device of *inclusio* is intended to indicate that Peter was the main eyewitness source behind Mark's Gospel, then it is coherent with the evidence . . . of the remarkable frequency with which his name occurs in Mark.[14]

Bauckham identifies a similar literary device of using eyewitness *inclusio* in Lucian's *Alexander* and Porphyry's *Life of Plotinus*, which indicates that Mark (and in other ways Luke and John too) has framed his narrative by using a Graeco-Roman literary device that accents the value of eyewitness accounts in historiography.[15]

12. Cf. e.g. T.J. Weeden, *Mark – Traditions in Conflict* (Philadelphia: Fortress, 1971), p. 50; T.V. Smith, *Petrine Controversies in Early Christianity* (WUNT 2.15; Tübingen: Mohr/Siebeck, 1985), pp. 187–90.

13. Weeden, *Traditions*, p. 50.

14. R. Bauckham, *Jesus and the Eyewitnesses: The Gospels as Eyewitness Testimony*, (Grand Rapids, MI: Eerdmans, 2006), p. 125. Cf. Martin Hengel (*The Four Gospels and the One Gospel of Jesus Christ* [trans. J. Bowden; Harrisburgh, PA: Trinity Press International, 2000], p. 82): 'Simon Peter is as a disciple named first and last in the Gospel to show that it is based on his tradition and therefore on his authority.'

15. Bauckham, *Eyewitnesses*, pp. 132–45.

Furthermore, the introduction to Peter in Mk 1.16 is emphatic as it said that Jesus 'saw Simon and *Simon's* brother Andrew' (εἶδεν Σίμωνα καὶ Ἀνδρέαν τὸν ἀδελφὸν). When two brothers are named in Mark, the second brother is usually related to the first brother with the genitive phrase τὸν ἀδελφον αὐτοῦ ('his brother') as the case in 1.19 with 'James the son of Zebedee and *his* brother John'. Alternatively, Mark can also repeat a proper name in place of a pronoun as is the case in 1.19 with 'Simon's brother' and also in 3.17 and 5.37 with 'James [the son of Zebedee] and John the brother of James'. While the feature is undoubtedly stylistic rather than forensic, the double reference to Simon in 1.16 makes for genuine prominence. Robert Guelich commented: 'The double reference to Simon most likely indicates his relative stature in Mark's Gospel.'[16]

Concerning Mk 16.7, in the penultimate verse of the Gospel, the angel tells the women at the tomb, 'go, tell his disciples *and to Peter* (καὶ τῷ Πέτρῳ) that he is going ahead of you to Galilee; there you will see him, just as he told you'. Peter's position is equally prominent again and likely reflects a tradition that Peter was the first individual disciple to see the risen Jesus (cf. 1 Cor. 5.5; Lk. 24.34). The words 'and to Peter' are superfluous and intrusive, which is possibly why it is omitted from Mt. 28.7.[17]

Second, it is readily apparent that the character of Peter is the most dominating personality among the disciples in Mark. Commenting on Mk 1.16, Vincent Taylor noted that, proportionately to its size, Mark mentions Peter more frequently than Matthew or Luke. Taylor inferred: 'The vividness with which the personality of the Apostle is presented in Mk is characteristic of the Gospel and is in harmony with the Papias tradition'.[18] Martin Hengel commented similarly:

> This unique accumulation of mentions of Peter in the substantially shorter Gospel calls for a meaningful historical explanation. Here the main question is not the significance of the Galilean fisherman Simon for the historical Jesus' circle of disciples . . . but first of all why the earliest Gospel puts such unique emphasis on him a bare forty years after the Passover at which Jesus died and around five years after his martyrdom.[19]

16. Robert A. Guelich, *Mark 1-8:26* (WBC; Dallas: Word, 1989), p. 50.

17. Admittedly, a double reference to a name is a very weak limb to hang a whole argument about authorship and authenticity on. Also the mention of Peter as the first eyewitness of Jesus' postmortem appearances could be derived from a common tradition known widely in the early church, or it might be part of Mark's narrative restoration of Peter among the disciples, and thus not necessarily indebted to firsthand accounts given to Mark. That said, the argument being put forward is cumulative and when the Petrine *inclusio* is set beside further evidence, including the clear prominence of Peter in Mark, the character perspective of Peter in the story, and the affinities of Mark's outline with Peter's speech in Acts 10, then the *inclusio* observation becomes more compelling as part of a larger discernible pattern in Mark's Gospel.

18. Vincent Taylor, *The Gospel According to St. Mark* (London: Macmillan & Co., 1952), p. 168.

19. Hengel, *Four Gospels*, p. 83.

Not only is Simon Peter the most frequently mentioned of Jesus' followers in Mark[20] – and with two exceptions he is the only disciple to directly converse with Jesus in Mark – but also he is the most vocal and most active at key moments. Peter is the disciple who makes the confession of Jesus' messianic identity and tries to rebuke Jesus for his melancholic remarks on martyrdom (Mk 8.29-33), Peter is the only disciple who speaks at the Transfiguration scene (Mk 9.5), Peter is the disciple who claims that Jesus' close circle of followers have left everything to follow him (Mk 10.28), Peter is the one who draws attention to the withering of the fig tree (Mk 11.21), Peter is prominent in the last supper as he swears not to desert Jesus (Mk 14.29), Peter is the one rebuked for failing to keep watch in Gethsemane (Mk 14.37) and Peter follows Jesus to the place of his trial where he later denounces Jesus. (Mk 14.54-72). Thus, Peter is there at the commencement of Jesus' ministry, he is a protagonist and antagonistic at the messianic revelation at Caesarea-Philippi, a bewildered observer at the filial revelation on the mountain, the anti-hero of the passion narrative and the first of the disciples to see the risen Jesus.

Third, the Markan Gospel operates in places from a point of view that is best described as Petrine.[21] In the Gospel, Peter is not a flat, two-dimensional character, but a complex figure complete with naiveté, enthusiasm, virtue, zeal and lament. Peter has a representative function at the narrative level as speaking and acting for the Twelve. But in a tradition-historical approach, the Petrine focalization suggests that Mark's own sources probably reflect an interior point of view from within the circle of the Twelve. Bauckham, building on the work of C.T. Turner, suggests that the third-person plural verbs in Mark could easily stand in place of a first-person perspective (i.e. eyewitness account). For instance, whereas Mk 1.29 reads, 'They left the synagogue and came into the house of Simon and Andrew with James and John' it could naturally be transformed into, 'We left the synagogue and came into our house with our fellow-disciples James and John' (see similarly Mk 1.35-37). Not to jump the gun, much of this can be attributed to Markan style and narratological construction, but the device may also have been embedded to some degree in the sources of Mark and it remains consistent with eyewitness perspective. That does not make Mark a mere source book of Peter's autobiographical anecdotes, though it is suggestive that Peter's teachings, which exhibited traits of being a spokesman for the Twelve, strongly influenced the construction of the Markan narrative.[22]

20. See the tabulation of data in Bauckham, *Eyewitnesses*, pp. 148–9. Cf. earlier Béda Rigaux, *The Testimony of St. Mark* (Chicago: Franciscan Herald, 1966), p. 49, who also noticed the prominence of Peter in Mark.

21. Bauckham, *Eyewitnesses*, pp. 155–82.

22. Bauckham, *Eyewitnesses*, p. 180.

In which case, 'Mark was not the inheritor of a completely faceless tradition, but one which already bore the impress of Peter's experience'.[23]

Fourth, it is possible to show the affinity of the Markan outline with a source that is also believed to have its origins with Petrine tradition, viz. Peter's speech in Acts 10.36-41. C.H. Dodd noted long ago the correlation between Peter's speech in Acts 10.36-41 to Cornelius and the Markan outline. The speech represents an early summary of the kerygma in the primitive church.[24]

Acts 10.36-41	*Mark's Gospel*
36 You know the message God sent to the people of Israel, telling the gospel of peace through Jesus Christ, who is Lord of all. 37 You know what has happened throughout Judea, beginning in Galilee after the baptism that John preached 38 how God anointed Jesus of Nazareth with the Holy Spirit and power, and how he went around doing good and healing all who were under the power of the devil, because God was with him. 39 We are witnesses of everything he did in the country of the Jews and in Jerusalem. They killed him by hanging him on a tree, 40 but God raised him from the dead on the third day and caused him to be seen. 41 He was not seen by all the people, but by witnesses whom God had already chosen by us who ate and drank with him after he rose from the dead.	1.1: 'The beginning of the gospel about Jesus Christ, the Son of God'. 1.14: 'And so John came, baptizing in the desert region and preaching a baptism of repentance for the forgiveness of sins.' 1.10: 'As Jesus was coming up out of the water, he saw heaven being torn open and the Spirit descending on him like a dove.' 1.16–10.52: Narratives that ascribe healings, exorcisms and miracles to Jesus. chs 11–15: Jerusalem is the final location for Jesus' ministry. 15.1-39: Focus on the crucifixion. 16.1-8: 'He is not here, he has risen!'

In Acts 10, Peter's speech is epitomized by Luke for inclusion in his apostolic narrative, yet its structure and themes are clearly in accordance with the Markan outline.[25] We could explain that by way of: (1) Luke projecting the Markan outline into his own composition put into the mouth of Peter; or (2) Luke working from a source that included accounts about Peter's preaching that correspond with the Markan outline. The marks of source material are arguably apparent in 10.36-37 where the switch from 'the word' (τὸν λόγον) in v. 36 to 'the

23. William L. Lane, *The Gospel According to Mark* (NICNT; Grand Rapids, MI: Eerdmans, 1974), p. 12.

24. C.H. Dodd, 'The Framework of the Gospel Narrative', *ExpT* 43 (1931–32), pp. 396–400; idem, *The Apostolic Preaching and Its Developments* (London: Hodder & Stoughton, 1936), pp. 46–52. But note objections in Black, *Mark*, pp. 203–4.

25. Lane, *Mark*, p. 11.

matter' (ῥῆμα) in v. 37 is needless and non-Lukan (see a similar juxtaposition of λόγος and ῥῆμα in 10.44).[26] Also, the parenthetical remark 'who is Lord of all' (οὗτός ἐστιν πάντων κύριος) in 10.36 is intrusive and again non-Lukan. In addition, the allusions to Isa. 52.7 and 61.1 may echo primitive kergymatic preaching deriving from a Palestinian source.[27]

The similarity between the Gospel of Mark and the Lukan speech attributed to Peter does not stem from Luke following Mark, but from Luke and Mark both incorporating material from a homogenous source with an identical conception of the apostolic discourse. We have intra-narratival reasons for attributing these sources, directly or indirectly, to the apostle Peter, given the attribution of the speech to Peter by Luke and the presence of Petrine perspective in Mark. If Mark's Gospel is a rendering of the apostolic preaching, the obvious question is from which apostle does Mark's narrative take its shape? If we accept the Petrine nature of the speech in Acts 10 then we have a legitimate bridge between Mark's outline and Luke's précis of Petrine preaching.

What I have argued is that the Petrine bookends in Mark correspond to the literary device of eyewitness *inclusio* that Bauckham identified in Graeco-Roman sources. There is a clear prominence of Peter at key junctures of the Markan Gospel and a Petrine perspective in the narrative is detectable as well. Added to that is the observation that the Markan outline has a close affinity with Luke's account of Peter's preaching in Acts 10.36-43. Taken together this lends credible support to the claim that the Gospel of Mark is informed by Petrine testimony. This does not establish beyond all reasonable doubt that the Gospel of Mark was written up based upon the personal reminiscences of Simon Peter, although it is certainly consistent with the theory and in the very least suggestive of a close link between the Gospel of Mark and the Petrine tradition.[28]

26. Besides the proximity of the two words in Peter's speech to Cornelius in Acts 10.36-37, 44, the nouns λόγος and ῥῆμα only appear in relative proximity again in Acts 16.36, 38.

27. Joseph A. Fitzmyer, *The Acts of the Apostles* (AB; New York: Doubleday, 1998), pp. 459–60.

28. Crossley (*Date of Mark's Gospel*, pp. 17–18) concedes the validity of the latter point that a link may still exist between the Gospel of Mark and Petrine tradition. John H. Elliott ('The Roman Provenance of 1 Peter and the Gospel of Mark: A Response to David Dungan', in *Colloquy on New Testament Studies*, ed. Bruce C. Corley [Macon, GA: Mercer University Press, 1983], pp. 181–94) also noted affinities between 1 Peter and the Gospel of Mark and their participation in a common tradition. E. Earle Ellis ('The Date and Provenance of Mark's Gospel', in *The Four Gospels 1992*, eds F. Van Segbroeck, C.M. Tuckett, G. Van Belle and J. Verheyden [4 vols; FS F. Neirynck; Leiden: Brill, 1992], vol. 2, pp. 814–15) goes beyond the evidence when he infers that Mark was composed in Palestine (i.e. Caesarea) and delivered his Gospel to the churches in Italy in the mid-60s CE. So that: 'Mark's Gospel was initially the Gospel of the Petrine mission. It had episodic antecedents that were read in Petrine congregations in Palestine in the forties. After it was utilized by Luke and (revised and) transmitted to Rome, it became the possession of important churches in Palestine and in Italy and, in time, of the church as a whole.'

III. *Gospel of Mark as Pauline proclamation*

Although there are said to be a number of themes in Mark influenced by Paul's viewpoint (e.g. election, use of Scripture, fulfillment, mystery, faith, Christology, *parousia*), I shall focus here on commonalities around the loci of a theology of the cross, salvation and the attitude to the Law as these demonstrate the clearest examples of Pauline tradents in Mark.[29]

a. *Theology of the cross*

A first area of comparison between Paul and Mark has to be the centrality that they both assign to the cross of Jesus as the definitive saving event performed by the God of Israel. All of the canonical Gospels climax in Jesus' passion and resurrection. The preaching of the cross was a feature of general Christian proclamation according to Acts (2.23-26; 4.10; 10.39; 13.28; 20.28), it was prominent in the Catholic Epistles (esp. 1 Pet. 1.2, 19; 2.21-23; 3.18; 4.1 and Heb. 9.11-28; 10.19, 29; 12.24; 13.12, 20), memorialized in Eucharistic meals (1 Cor. 11.23-26), celebrated in primitive hymnic/confessional materials (e.g. Rom. 4.25; Phil. 2.8; Col. 1.20) and Jewish and Roman polemics against the Christian movement ridiculed its message of the cross (e.g. 1 Cor. 1.18-25; Justin, *Dial.* 32; *Alexamenos Grafitto*). I for one doubt whether there were forms of Christianity pre-70 CE that did not assign a significant place of some kind to the cross of Jesus in their identity-forming narrative, ethics and theology.[30] Paul's focus on the cross is distinctive not in the sense of being entirely unique but insofar that his kerygmatic and paraenetic references to the cross possess several characteristic features. These features include nullifying the application of proselyte models of conversion to Christian Gentiles (Romans 4; Galatians 3–4), a general antithesis between Jesus' death and the Mosaic law in light of his apocalyptic worldview (Gal. 2.15-21; Rom. 7.1-6), a highly specified soteriology that employs various images for what the cross achieved

29. I seriously contemplated having a section on Mark's and Paul's Christologies. But it was my conclusion that Mark's Christology is indebted to a pre-existence/suffering/exaltation pattern that was indeed shared by Paul and perhaps indebted to him in some respects, but the pattern was simply too widespread in early Christianity to be able to show specific Pauline influences upon Mark's formulation of it. Still, I would say that it was (a) the concept of a suffering Messiah and (b) Jesus' identity as the 'Son of God' that marks out the Christological accordance between Mark and Paul.

30. The quest for a 'cross-less' Christianity has been the Holy Grail of much research in North American biblical scholarship in its aim to find a version of Christianity free from the atonement theology that it finds so repugnant. The esoteric/proto-Gnostic Christianity of the *Gospel of Thomas* is best understood as a second-century phenomenon. If there was a written collection of Jesus traditions that we call Q, the absence of references to Jesus' death in it (if there was such an absence) does not necessarily mean that the compilers and users of such a document had no knowledge or interest in the significance of Jesus' death and resurrection. On Q and Jesus' death, see Larry Hurtado, *Lord Jesus Christ: Devotion to Jesus in Earliest Christianity* (Grand Rapids, MI: Eerdmans, 2003), pp. 235–44; James D.G. Dunn, *Jesus Remembered* (Grand Rapids, MI: Eerdmans, 2003), pp. 151–2.

(e.g. justification, forgiveness, reconciliation, adoption and atonement) and an identification with the crucified Jesus establishes the grounds for a new meta-identity that includes Gentiles, Greeks and Jews within its scope (1 Cor. 7.18; 12.13; Gal. 3.28; 6.15; Col. 3.11). Paul's own account of the fulcrum of his preaching was that it was the 'word of the cross' (1 Cor. 1.18) and in his proclamation 'Jesus Christ was publicly portrayed as crucified' (Gal. 3.1).

Coming to Mark we observe an equally distinct focus on the cross; so much so that Martin Kähler could call Gospels in general, and Mark in particular, a 'passion narrative with an extended introduction'. Similarly, Jack Kingsbury labelled Mark 'the Gospel of the Cross'.[31] Mark's Gospel is dominated by the looming crucifixion of Jesus and this is the most formative element of its narrative and theological fixtures.[32] Jesus' death is intimated as early as Mk 2.20 in the parable of the bridegroom and the mounting opposition intends to put Jesus to death as early as Mk 3.6 with a joint plot by the Herodians and Pharisees. The death of John the Baptist in Mk 6.6-31 raises the question of what will happen to Jesus and his followers who, like the Baptist, are willing to announce the news of the kingdom despite powerful people moving against them. The moment when Jesus is finally acknowledged as the Messiah by Peter (Mk 8.29) is met by the first of three passion predictions (Mk 8.31; 9.31; 10.33-34). Indeed, the restoration of Israel is intimately tied up with the sufferings of the Son of Man (Mk 9.12).[33] Later the request of James and John to sit at the right and left hands of Jesus in his glory is met with invitations to share the same cup and undergo the same baptism, metaphors of the forthcoming passion (Mk 10.35-40).[34] Jesus' death is also explicitly said to be a means of redemption (Mk 10.45).[35] The parable of the tenants, in which the son is killed and thrown out of the vineyard, further inflames the authorities in seeking to arrest Jesus (Mk 12.12).[36] The foreshadowing of the cross comes to an abrupt end in Mark 14, which accelerates towards the crucifixion. It is narrated that the chief priests and scribes 'were seeking how to arrest him by stealth and kill

31. Martin Kähler, *The So-Called Historical Jesus and the Historic Biblical Christ* (Philadelphia: Fortress, 1964 [1892]), p. 80, n. 11; J.D. Kingsbury, 'The Significance of the Cross within Mark's Story', in *Gospel Interpretation: Narrative Critical and Social-Scientific Approaches* (ed. J.D. Kingsbury; Harrisburg: Trinity Press International, 1997), p. 95. See further Peter G. Bolt, *The Cross from a Distance: Atonement in Mark's Gospel* (Downers Grove, IL: Apollos, 2004).

32. Cf. Michael F. Bird, 'Jesus is the Christ: Messianic Apologetics in the Gospel of Mark', *RTR* 64 (2005), pp. 1–15; idem, 'Obi-wan Kenobi, Neo, and Mark's Narrative Christology', in *On Eagles' Wings: An Exploration of Strength in the Midst of Weakness*, eds M. Parsons and D. Cohen (Eugene, OR: Wipf & Stock, 2008), pp. 51–62.

33. On the restoration of Israel in relation to Jesus, see Rom. 11.25-27.

34. On baptism as 'death', see Rom. 6.4; Col. 2.12.

35. On Pauline parallels with Mk. 10.45, see the sub-section on 'Salvation', p. 43.

36. On the rejection of Jesus by the Judaeans and Diaspora Jews, see Rom. 10.18-21; 1 Cor. 2.8; 1 Thess. 2.15.

him' (Mk 14.1-2); an anonymous woman anoints Jesus for burial, making a furtive connection between his messiahship and death (14.3-9); Judas agrees to betray Jesus (14.10-11), Jesus conveys his awareness of the conspiracy (14.18-21); Jesus institutes the new covenant through his death (14.22-25),[37] predicts his resurrection and Peter's betrayal (14.26-31) and waits in Gethsemane for his captors to seize him (14.32-51). When the arrest and crucifixion ensue, the only persons caught off guard are the disciples. Jesus has foreseen the event and freely embraced it. This is precisely what the reader is supposed to do as well.

In addition, there are a striking number of parallels between Mark's passion narrative and a Roman triumphal procession (note the *triumphus* imagery in 2 Cor. 4.9; Col. 2.15).[38] A triumphal procession celebrated the military victories of kings and generals who returned exultantly from a campaign with booty and captives. The triumphator would enter the city and lead a procession up the Sacra Via to the Jupiter Capitolinus amid accolades and much pomp and ceremony. From 20 BCE onwards, the ceremony was the exclusive right of the emperor, and its procedure sometimes culminated in his deification. This procession possesses several points of contact with Mark's passion narrative: the gathering of the whole Praetorian Guard, the purple ceremonial garb, the crowning of the triumphator, the accolades from the soldiers, the official who leads a sacrificial victim, the offer and refusal of a drink, the placard naming the conquered people, the accompaniment by two consuls or generals and the confession as a 'son of god' are all paralleled in the *triumphus*. Schmidt summarizes the parallels:

> The Praetorians gather early in the morning to proclaim the triumphator. He is dressed in the triumphal garb, and a crown of laurel is placed on his head. The soldiers then shout in acclamation of his Lordship and perform acts of homage to him. They accompany him from their camp through the streets of the city. The sacrificial victim is there in the procession, and alongside walks the official carrying the implement of his coming death. The procession ascends finally to the Place of the (Death's) Head, where the sacrifice is to take place. The triumphator is offered the ceremonial wine. He does not drink it, but it is poured out on the altar at the moment of sacrifice. Then, at the moment of being lifted up before the people, at the moment of the sacrifice, again the triumphator is acclaimed as Lord, and his vice-regents appear with him in confirmation of his glory. Following the lead of the soldiers, the

37. On Jesus' betrayal and the words of institution, see 1 Cor. 11.23-26.

38. T.E. Schmidt, 'Mark 15.16-32: The Crucifixion Narrative and the Roman Triumphal Procession', *NTS* 41 (1995), pp. 1–18; S.J. Hafemann, 'Roman Triumph', in *DNTB* (eds Craig A. Evans and Stanley E. Porter; Downers Grove, IL: InterVarsity Press, 2000), pp. 1004–8; Craig A. Evans, *Mark 8:27-16:20* (WBC; Nashville: Thomas Nelson, 2001), pp. lxxv–lxxxix.

> people together with their leads and the vice-regents themselves join in the acclamation. The epiphany is confirmed in portents by the gods: 'Truly this man is the Son of God!'[39]

Jesus' torturous walk along the Via Dolorosa is the anti-type to the triumphal procession along Rome's Sacra Via. The cascade of regal and triumphal imagery implies that what we have before us is no mere execution, but rather a coronation and epiphany of Israel's God. Schmidt comments: 'Mark designs this "anti-triumph" to suggest that the seeming scandal of the cross is actually an exaltation of Christ.'[40] This royal image of Jesus' crucifixion illuminates the reference to Jesus' death as an enthroned 'glory' in Mk 10.37. Similarly, Jesus' reply to Caiaphas in Mk 14.62 is perhaps a tacit threat that Caiaphas will see him exalted and enthroned in a position reserved exclusively for God amid his own execution. The crucifixion entwines together the scarlet threads of the Markan narrative, so that the themes of suffering, service, kingship, glory and vindication form a tapestry of poignancy and power.

In sum, Mark's narrative focus on the cross has several key points of intersection with Paul:[41] (1) the early intimation, literary focus and narrative climax of the Gospel on Jesus' death is conducive to Pauline proclamation. With the exception perhaps of the author of Hebrews, only Mark portrays the cross with a similar pathos and gravity to that of Paul. (2) The description of Jesus' death with the accompanying apocalyptic portents of cosmic darkness (Mk 15.33) and the rending of the veil in the temple (Mk 15.38) combined with early language in the Gospel about 'mystery' (Mk 4.11, 22) and 'this age' (Mk 10.30) likewise represent a Pauline apocalyptic perspective on Jesus' death and its divine revelation (Gal. 1.4, 6.14; 1 Cor. 2.7-9; Col. 1.12-14, 25-26).[42] (3) Mark and Paul share a perspective on Jesus' death as a means of power in weakness. It is precisely Jesus' lack of power in his death that expresses the power to save others (Mk 15.31-32).[43] Jesus preaches the kingdom of God and yet what we find at the end of the story is the announcement of the kingship of the crucified in the *titulus* (Mk 15.26), marking the moment when the kingdom of God comes with power (Mk 9.1).[44] Jesus' power is displayed in the zenith of degradation, death and disempowerment that has clear affinities with Paul's descriptions as Jesus of being humiliated, weak and yet triumphant (Phil. 2.5-11; 1 Cor. 2.8;

39. Schmidt, 'The Crucifixion Narrative', p. 16.

40. Schmidt, 'The Crucifixion Narrative', p. 1.

41. Cf. C. Clifton Black, 'Christ Crucified in Paul and in Mark: Reflections on an Intracanonical Conversation', in *Theology and Ehtics in Paul and His Interpreters*, eds E.H. Lovering and J.L. Sumney (FS V.P. Furnish; Nashville: Abingdon, 1996), pp. 201–6.

42. Cf. Black, 'Christ Crucified', p. 201.

43. Cf. Fenton, 'Paul and Mark', pp. 101–3.

44. Cf. Michael F. Bird, 'The Crucifixion of Jesus as the Fulfillment of Mark 9:1', *TrinJ* 24 (2003), pp. 23–36.

2 Cor. 8.9; 13.4; Col. 2.15). (4) The cross is also the apex of Christological revelation since it is only at the cross that Jesus is heralded as the Son of God by the centurion (Mk 15.29), which is a distinctly Pauline idea (Gal. 2.19-20; 4.4-5; cf. Rom. 5.10; 8.3). (5) Only Mark and Paul portray Jesus' crucifixion as a royal triumph (Mark 14–15; Rom. 8.37; Col. 2.15). Overall, it looks as if Mark incorporated the Jesus tradition into the Pauline kerygma of the cross.[45]

All of this suggests that a primary purpose of Mark's Gospel was to be an apology for the cross.[46] The apology is necessitated by Jewish and Graeco-Roman aversions to the veneration of a crucified person as a divine agent.[47] The drive behind Mark's Gospel is to persuade his readers to believe that Jesus is the Messiah, not despite the cross but precisely because of it. Mark could be thought to be trying to explain why the 'foolishness of the cross' in Pauline proclamation is the manifestation of God's power. I speculate that Mark's Gospel might even have been designed or at least utilized as a *Missionsschrift* for several communities that shared Paul's view of the centrality of the cross.

b. *Salvation*

The various expressions of early Christianity found in the New Testament all attribute God's act of deliverance to the events surrounding Jesus' life, death, resurrection and exaltation. Mark and Paul share a number of things in common with Christian groups, including the importance of faith in Jesus and following Jesus for salvation. What they also appear to share, more acutely with each other than with other Christian groups, is the heightened usage of the word 'gospel', a reference to 'redemption', and a similar salvation-historical scheme about the inclusion of the Gentiles.

The message about Jesus as a εὐαγγέλιον ('gospel') seems to have been widespread by the end of the first century.[48] Yet usage of the word did not always correspond precisely to Paul's employment of the term; there is mention of an 'eternal gospel' (εὐαγγέλιον αἰώνιον) in Rev. 14.6 that refers to God's intention from eternity past to provide salvation for the world in Jesus Christ. Also, by 70 CE Mark was probably the first person to describe a biography of

45. Cf. Rudolf Bultmann, *History of the Synoptic Tradition* (trans. J. Marsh; New York: Harper & Row, 1963), pp. 370–1; Willi Marxsen, *Mark the Evangelist* (trans. R. Harrisville; Nashville: Abingdon: 1969), p. 147; Joel B. Marcus, 'Mark – Interpreter of Paul', *NTS* 46 (2000), p. 477.

46. Robert H. Gundry, *Mark: A Commentary on His Apology for the Cross* (Grand Rapids, MI: Eerdmans, 1993), pp. 1022–6; Evans, *Mark 8:27-16:20*, pp. xciii; Joel F. Williams, 'Is Mark's Gospel an Apology for the Cross?', *BBR* 12 (2002), pp. 97–122; Robert H. Gundry, 'A Rejoinder to Joel F. Williams' "Is Mark's Gospel an Apology for the Cross?"', *BBR* 12 (2002), pp. 123–40.

47. Cf. Martin Hengel, *Crucifixion in the Ancient World and the Folly of the Message of the Cross* (Philadelphia: Fortress, 1977); David W. Chapman, *Ancient Jewish and Christian Perceptions of Crucifixion* (Tübingen: Mohr/Siebeck, 2008).

48. Cf. *TDNT*, vol. 2, pp. 707–37; *EDNT*, vol. 2, pp. 69–74.

Jesus as a 'Gospel' and so invented a new distinctive Christian literary form. Preaching a 'gospel' was also a feature of Jesus' ministry prior to Paul.[49] The narration of Jesus as preaching a gospel is not necessarily an anachronism that Christianizes Jesus. I would point out that Jesus' announcement of a 'gospel' is multiply attested in the Gospels (e.g. Mk 1.14; Lk. 4.18; Lk. 7.22/Mt. 11.5). Jesus' gospel is dissimilar to the early church in that his announcement is theocentric and focused on the kingdom with no reference to atonement theology. And yet Jesus' preaching remains concurrently similar to the early church who evidently took up his announcement but infused it with their post-Easter Christological narrative. Jesus' announcement of good news about God's reign is entirely conceivable within Judaism in light of the glad tidings of Isaiah about YHWH coming as king (40.9-11; 52.7; 61.1). There are similar hopes expressed in the *Psalms of Solomon* about the end of exile (11.1-5) and at Qumran with the anticipation of eschatological deliverance (11Q13; 4Q521 2.14; 1QH 18.14). Knowledge of a gospel with relatively consistent fixtures can be found in the preaching and teaching of the early church (e.g. Acts 5.42; 8.4; Rom. 1.3-4; 1 Cor. 15.3-5; Gal. 2.12; Col. 1.5; 2 Tim. 2.8; Heb. 4.2, 6; 1 Pet. 1.12). Paul's unique construal of the gospel included his resolute focus on Jesus' death and resurrection in relation to Jesus' identity as Lord and Messiah. It is essential for Paul that the person whom Christians confess as *Kyrios* is the same person who was also 'crucified' for sins. Mark only uses εὐαγγέλιον seven times (Mk 1.1, 14-15; 8.35; 10.29; 13.10; 14.9), but each occurrence can be correlated with Paul's employment of the term to varying degrees.[50]

Mark	*Paul*
Mk 1.1: 'The beginning of the gospel of Jesus the Messiah'	Paul commences Romans with references to the gospel (Rom. 1.1), including Jesus' messianic status as David's Son (Rom. 1.3). Paul also mentions the 'beginning of the gospel' as the commencement of a new stage of his evangelistic ministry in Philippi (Phil. 4.15).

49. Steve Mason, *Josephus, Judea, and Christian Origins: Methods and Categories* (Peabody, MA: Hendrickson, 2009), pp. 283–302, advocates that εὐαγγελιον was introduced into Christian usage by Paul (esp. pp. 284–85), but he clearly overstates his case in light of evidence from the epistles (Gal. 2.7-9; 1 Cor. 15.3-4) and the speeches in Acts that 'gospel' was part of the tradition that Paul himself received.

50. Cf. Peter Stuhlmacher, *Das paulinische Evangelium I* (FRLANT 95; Göttingen: Vandenhoeck & Ruprecht, 1968) argues for a strong connection between Mark's use of the term 'gospel' and Paul's understanding of the content of the 'gospel'. Mason (*Josephus, Judea, and Christian Origins*, p. 297) thinks that Mark's use of 'gospel' is just as distinctive as Paul's was. I would add that Luke and John do not use the noun εὐαγγέλιον at all and Matthew picks it up from Mark. Mark, for the most part, seems to use the term following on the coat-tails of Paul.

Mark	*Paul*
Mk 1.14-15: 'After John was put in prison, Jesus went into Galilee, proclaiming the gospel of God. "The time has come," he said. "The kingdom of God has come near. Repent and believe the gospel!"'	Paul also preached the 'gospel of God' (Rom. 1.1; 15.16; 1 Thess. 2.2, 8-9; 2 Cor. 11.7) and makes reference to the 'preaching of Christ' or the 'word of Christ' which are perhaps subjective genitives (Rom. 10.17; 16.25; Col. 3.16). Jesus' gospel of the kingdom is analogous to Paul's correlation of the gospel with the 'power of God' (Rom. 1.16).
Mk 8.35: 'For whoever wants to save his life will lose it, but whoever loses his life for me and for the gospel will save it.' Mk 10.29-30: 'Jesus said, "Truly, I say to you, there is no one who has left house or brothers or sisters or mother or father or children or lands, for my sake and for the gospel, who will not receive a hundredfold now in this time, houses and brothers and sisters and mothers and children and lands, with persecutions, and in the age to come eternal life."'	Paul connects the gospel to discipleship in several ways. Paul himself is not ashamed of the gospel (Rom. 1.16), he is a 'servant' of the gospel or 'serves' in the gospel (Rom. 1.9; 15.16; Phil. 2.22), he has lost all things so that he may gain Christ (Phil. 3.8-9) and he suffers imprisonment so that he might advance the gospel (Phil. 1.12; Phlm. 1.13). Paul preaches the gospel so that he might share in its blessings (1 Cor. 9.23) and Paul begat children in the gospel (1 Cor. 4.15). The gospel calls for submission and confession (2 Cor. 9.13). Paul cites the words of the Lord that it is possible to get one's living from the gospel (1 Cor. 9.14). Paul finds himself on trial for the gospel (Phil. 1.7, 16) and he expects persecution for the gospel (1 Thess. 3.2-3).
Mk 13.10: 'And the gospel must first be proclaimed to all nations.'	Paul believes that the Gentiles/nations are the particular objects of his gospel work (Rom. 15.16; 2 Cor. 10.14) and he notes the fruitfulness of the gospel among the nations (Rom. 15.19; Col. 1.23).
Mk 14.9: 'And truly, I say to you, wherever the gospel is proclaimed in the whole world, what she has done will be told in memory of her."'	Paul can highlight the role of particular individuals for preaching the gospel such as Titus (2 Cor. 8.18), Timothy (Phil. 2.22; 1 Thess. 3.2) and Euodia/Syntyche (Phil. 4.2-3).

Proclamation and publication of a 'gospel' was part and parcel of the kerygmatic discourse of the early church and centred on the life, death and resurrection of Jesus Christ. But Paul seems to have developed his own particular web of ideas associated with the gospel, which find suitable parallel in the Gospel of Mark. In particular we might point to the connection of 'gospel' with a narrative that culminates in Jesus' death, the theocentric dimension of the gospel, its connection to Christian service – all of these can be safely connected to Paul's distinctive conceptualizing of the meaning and application of the gospel that he proclaimed.

A second point of consideration is the reference to 'redemption' in Mk 10.45. The text reads:

For even the Son of Man came not to be served but to serve, and to give his life as a ransom for many.	Καὶ γὰρ ὁ υἱὸς ἀνθρώπου οὐκ ἦλθεν διακονηθῆναι ἀλλὰ διακονῆσαι καὶ δοῦναι την ψθχὴν αὐτοῦ λύτρον ἀντὶ πολλῶν

The authenticity of the logion is moot, though I remain more confident of its authenticity than most.[51] The question is whether it reflects a particular Pauline terminology for salvation. The word ἀπολύτρωσις is Paul's preferred term and it means release or redemption and is employed most frequently for the manumission of slaves (Rom. 3.24; 8.23; 1 Cor. 1.30; Col. 1.14; Eph. 1.7, 14; 4.30).[52] Outside of Paul's letters, ἀπολύτρωσις only occurs in Luke (21.28) and Hebrews (9.15; 11.35), and the cognate λύτρωσις is, again, used only by the same two authors (Lk. 1.68; 2.38; Heb. 9.12). Furthermore, Mark's λύτρον in 10.45 is shared only by the parallel version in Mt. 20.28. If we regard Luke and Hebrews as pro-Pauline writings, a fairly uncontroversial observation, then the metaphor for salvation as redemption seems to be limited to the circle of Pauline influence.[53] In addition, the phrase λύτρον ἀντὶ πολλῶν, is probably equivalent to Paul's Χριστὸς ὑπὲρ ἡμῶν ἀπέθανεν (Rom. 5.8; cf. Rom. 8.32; 1 Cor. 15.3; 2 Cor. 5.21; Gal. 1.4; 3.13) with connotations of interchange, representation and substitution.[54]

David Seeley argued that Mark uses Paul language only under duress. He argued that Mark cited Paul 'indirectly acknowledging a theologian he could not completely ignore, but whose theology he did not fully approve of'.[55] I suspect that such a remark probably tells us more about Seeley's negative assessment of Paul's atonement theology rather than Mark's reluctant need to

51. Cf. Peter Stuhlmacher, 'Vicariously Giving His Life for Many, Mark 10:45 (Matt. 20:28)', in *Reconciliation, Law, and Righteousness: Essays in Biblical Theology* (Philadelphia: Fortress, 1986), pp. 16–29; S. Page, 'Ransom Saying', in *DJG*, eds J.B. Green, S. McKnight and I.H. Marshall (Downers Grove, IL: InterVarsity Press, 1991), pp. 660–2. Scot McKnight, *Jesus and His Death* (Waco, TX: Baylor University Press, 2005), pp. 159–71.

52. Cf. analogous words such as ἐξαγοράζω (Gal. 3.13; 4.5; Col. 4.5; Eph. 5.16); ἀντίλυτρον (1 Tim. 2.6); and λύτρόομαι (Tit. 2.14).

53. The book of Revelation uses the word ἀγοράζω in Rev. 14.3-4, which means 'payment' or 'purchase' (BDAG, p. 14) and is often translated as 'redeem' (NRSV, ESV, NJB).

54. On the parity of the prepositions ὑπέρ and ἀντί for denoting 'in the place of' see Dan Wallace, *Greek Grammar Beyond the Basics* (Grand Rapids, MI: Zondervan, 1996), pp. 383–9. See also Bolt, *Cross*, pp. 71–5.

55. David Seeley, 'Rulership and Service in Mark 10:41-45', *NovT* 35 (1993), p. 249.

recognize Paul. Mark's picturing of Jesus' death as a ransom for others seems indebted to Jewish martyrological traditions, Jewish Christian appropriations of Isaiah 53 and, most important, is influenced by Paul's image of salvation as 'redemption'.

A further area of similarity between Mark and Paul is about the place of Gentiles in the church's mission.[56] The episode about Jesus and the food laws is followed by the unit detailing Jesus' encounter with the Syro-Phoenician woman in Mk 7.24-30, where the supplicant of healing is initially turned away as a 'dog' but eventually is able to cajole Jesus to help her by way of her witty reply to his rebuke. Joel Marcus states: 'Our story is thus about transcendence of Jewish particularism, and looks forward to the increasingly Gentile church of Mark's own day.'[57] While the unit is I believe based on authentic material,[58] Mark's redactional hand is discernible by the inclusion of the messianic secret in 7.24 and with the reference to 'first' (πρῶτον) in 7.27. In fact, Mark's use of the adverb πρῶτον appears again in Mk 13.10 with reference to the Gentile mission, 'And the gospel first must be preached to all the nations' (καὶ εἰς πάντα τὰ ἔθνη πρῶτον δεῖ κηρυχθῆναι τὸ εὐαγγέλιον). Although Jesus very likely annunciated the view that the inclusion of the Gentiles in God's salvation was bound up with the restoration of Israel, the language and perspective in Mk 13.10 is undoubtedly Christian and, more specifically, Pauline.[59] Brian Incigneri calls Mk 13.9-10 'Pauline in both language and sequence' (see Rom. 10.18, which includes witness and proclamation).[60] The resonance of Mk 7.27 and 13.10 with Paul is striking as both exhibit the view of the priority of Israel in God's salvation (i.e. Rom. 1.16, the gospel is 'to the Jew first and then to the Greek' [Ἰουδαίῳ τε πρῶτον καὶ Ἕλληνι]) and the necessity of preaching to the Gentiles before the final consummation (see Rom. 11.25). This suggests that the Pauline mission to the nations is the social context of Mark's Gospel.[61]

56. Cf. on mission in Mark: Ferdinand Hahn, *Mission in the New Testament* (London: SCM, 1965), pp. 95–103; Klemens Stock, 'Theologie der Mission bei Markus', in *Mission im Neuen Testament*, ed. K. Kertelge (Freiburg: Herder, 1982), pp. 130–44; Zenji Kato, *Die Völkermission im Markusevangelium: Eine redaktionsgeschichtliche Untersuchung* (Frankfurt and Bern: Peter Land, 1986); David Rhoads, 'Networks for Missions: The Social System of the Jesus Movement in the Narrative of the Gospel of Mark', *ANRW* II.26.2 (1995), pp. 1692–729; Florian Wilk, *Jesus und die Völker in der Sicht der Synoptiker* (BZNW, 109; Berlin: Walter de Gruyter, 2002); Eckhard Schnabel, *Early Christian Mission* (2 vols; Downers Grove, IL: InterVarsity Press, 2004), vol. 2, pp. 1496–7.

57. Marcus, *Mark 1–8*, p. 466.

58. Cf. Michael F. Bird, *Jesus and the Origins of the Gentile Mission* (LNTS 331; London: T&T Clark, 2006), pp. 112–16.

59. Cf. Bird, *Jesus*, pp. 168–72; Evans, *Mark*, p. 310.

60. Brian Incigneri, *The Gospel to the Romans: The Setting and Rhetoric of Mark's Gospel* (BIS, 65; Leiden: Brill, 2003), pp. 295–6.

61. John Painter, *Mark's Gospel: Worlds in Conflict* (NTR; London: Routledge, 1997), pp. 4–6, 213.

c. *Attitude to the Law*

There is surely no topic of Pauline theology so perplexing and so baffling as the puzzle of Paul and the Law. Paul is often assumed to have a perspective that places Christ and the Law in a sharp antithesis. However, Paul's 'Law-free gospel' is really a 'proselytism-free gospel' since his antithetical remarks about the Law pertain primarily to instances where Gentile believers are compelled to be circumcised and to adopt a Jewish way of life (e.g. Gal. 2.11-21). What is more, the Law still figures very prominently in Paul's moral exhortations to Gentile Christians (e.g. Rom. 13.9-10; 1 Cor. 7.19; 9.8-10; 10.7; 14.21, 34; 2 Cor. 6.16). However, Paul's rejection of the proselyte model of conversion is anchored in a fundamental disjunction between the epoch of Law and the epoch of the Messiah. The Law is bound up with the powers of the evil age (Gal. 1.4; 4.3-9), the curse of the Mosaic covenant (Gal. 3.10-13), and it forms a triumvirate of Law–sin–death (Rom. 5.12-21; 8.2-3; 1 Cor. 15.56; 2 Cor. 3.6). Instead of restraining sin, the Law contributed and even magnified human bondage to it (Rom. 7.7; Gal. 6.13; Col. 2.23). By entering into the Lordship of Jesus Christ, believers have died to the Law and are free from its power (Gal. 2.19; 5.18; Rom. 7.1-6). The Law was only ever a temporary holding pattern that cocooned God's purposes around Israel until the promised seed of Abraham came (Gal. 3.19) and it is fundamentally terminated in the revelation of the Messiah (Rom. 10.4; 2 Cor. 3.11). It is evident from 1 Cor. 9.20-23 that Paul considered 'becoming' (γινόμαι) a Jew (i.e. living like a Jew) just as much a compromise as becoming one 'without law' (ἄνομος) or 'weak' (ἀσθενής) for the sake of his missionary call to herald the gospel.

For Paul, the Law continues to exist and have relevance in two ways. First, because the Law is holy and good (Rom. 7.12) it retains a *consultative* role in genuinely informing one's 'walk' (Rom. 8.4). Second, the Law endures as a *cultural* pattern that Jewish or Judaistic believers may happily continue to follow and that must be respected (1 Cor. 10.22; Rom. 14.1-23). Yet it is not *constitutive* for the identity, salvation and behaviour of believers. The primary basis for upright living for Paul is the example of Christ, the teaching of Christ, the law of love, and life in the Spirit, which are thought to fulfill the Law.[62] In which case, according to Paul, the Law holds a different place for Jesus-believers than it does for Jews.[63]

The Gospel of Mark and the Law is a complex topic because we have in Mark a mix of authentic Jesus traditions and his own redactional handling of

62. Cf. Michael F. Bird, *A Bird's-Eye View of Paul: The Man, His Mission, and His Message* (Nottingham: InterVarsity Press, 2008), pp. 143–9.

63. Cf. Brian S. Rosner, 'Paul and the Law: What He Does Not Say', *JSNT* 32 (2010), pp. 405–19.

his material.[64] From a Jewish perspective, I think that the Markan Jesus might have been regarded as controversial, but nothing that Jesus says or does in the Gospel could be said to outright abrogate the Law of Moses. The relaxation of some commands and intensification of other commands was common in Jewish renewal movements in the first century.[65] Jesus' debates are more about *halakhah* than the continuing validity of the Torah, though not necessarily perceived that way by his contemporaries. One episode that stands out is the discussion of food laws in Mk 7.1-23.[66] At the level of the historical Jesus, Mk 7.1-23 (and par. in Mt. 15.1-20) is most likely a debate about the necessity or lack thereof for eating food with washed hands contra pharisaic tradition (hence Mt. 15.20, 'but to eat with unwashed hands does not defile a person' which aptly re-judaizes the story).[67] However, Mark frames the dispute in a rather stark and even crass manner in Mk 7.15, 19c. Even at the theological horizon of Mark's Gospel it can scarcely be a broad-blanket abrogation of the Mosaic Law, for it would be contradictory to have Jesus critique the Pharisees for nullifying the Laws of *Corban* only to have Jesus then declare the Levitical food laws defunct and void a few verses after. The controversial comment in 7.19c ('And he declared all founds clean' [καθαρίζων πάντα τὰ βρώματα, lit. 'cleansing all the foods']) is most likely an editorial aside designed for Gentile readers, hence the explanation of pharisaic customs in Mk 7.3-5. Mark is implying, *for you Gentiles*, this means all foods are clean or, I would say, the food laws are optional (and for Jewish Christians it remains an ambivalent matter).

What is interesting is that Mk 7.19c is very much like Rom. 14.14, and the latter reads:

I know and am persuaded in the Lord Jesus that nothing is unclean in itself; but it is unclean for anyone who thinks it unclean.	οἶδα καὶ πέπεισμαι ἐν κυρίῳ Ἰησοῦ ὅτι οὐδὲν κοινὸν δι' ἑαυτοῦ, εἰ μὴ τῷ λογιζομένῳ τι κοινὸν εἶναι, ἐκεινῳ κοινόν

64. Cf. Klaus Berger, *Die Gesetzauslegung Jesu. Ihr historischer Hintergrund im Judentum und im Alten Testament. Teil I: Markus und Parallelen* (Neukirchen: Neukirchener Verlage, 1972); Heikki Sariola, *Markus und das Gesetz: eine redaktionskritische Untersuchung* (AASF; Helsinki: Suomalainen Tiedeakatemia, 1990); William Loader, *Jesus' Attitude to the Law: A Study of the Gospels* (Tübingen: Mohr/Siebeck, 1997), pp. 9–135; Crossley, *Date of Mark's Gospel*, pp. 82–98.

65. Gerd Theissen, *The Sociology of Palestinian Christianity* (Philadelphia: Fortress, 1978), pp. 75–9; Markus Bockmuehl, *Jewish Law in Gentile Churches: Halakhah and the Beginning of Christian Public Ethics* (Edinburgh: T&T Clark, 2000), p. 10.

66. Cf. more extensive treatment of Mk. 7.1-23 in Michael F. Bird, 'Jesus the Law-Breaker', in *Who Do My Opponents Say that I Am? An Investigation of the Accusations against Jesus*, eds Joseph B. Modica and Scot McKnight (LHJS; London: T&T Clark, 2008), pp. 16–24.

67. Cf. Richard P. Booth, *Jesus and the Laws of Purity: Tradition History and Legal History in Mark 7* (Sheffield: JSOT Press, 1986), pp. 155–203; Crossley, *Date of Mark's Gospel*, pp. 191–3.

Several scholars see this passage in Romans 14 as a deliberate reference to dominical tradition and with good reason.[68] (1) The invocation of the 'Lord' is similar to the appeal to dominical tradition in 1 Cor. 7.10. (2) The coordinating conjunction ὅτι may be recitative and introduce a citation of the Jesus tradition, rather than comprise a dependent clause that gives Paul's ruling as one inspired within the sphere of the Lord's authority. (3) How could Paul say that 'nothing is unclean in itself' to a cluster of congregations that he did not know with diverse sympathies to the Law based on nothing more than his own authority? More likely, just as Paul uses traditional material elsewhere in Romans (e.g. Rom. 1.3-4; 4.25; 6.3-5), so now he appeals to the Jesus tradition to make his remark sure-footed.[69] If that is the case, then Mark's editorial comment in Mk 7.19c follows Paul's line that for Jesus-believers the food laws are *adiaphora*. Thus, while Mk. 7.15 is probably a *Jesu logia*, Mk 7.19c is Pauline *halakhah*. Overall, then, the coherence of Mk 7.15, 19c with Rom. 14.14, 20 would see Mark adopting a Pauline perspective on the food laws in relation to Gentile Jesus-believers.[70]

Crossley objects to the association of Mk 7.19c with Paul's view espoused in Rom. 14.14.[71] In Crossley's opinion, Mk 7.15, 19 may be an independent dominical tradition known to both Paul and Mark. The influence on Mark may be Petrine rather than Pauline, considering Peter's vision of the descending sheet with the unclean foods in Acts 10.9-17. I think that this scenario is certainly plausible given that the Jesus tradition circulated widely in the early church. It also corresponds to the agreement between Peter and Paul at the Jerusalem council to the effect that eating unclean food does not make a person 'unclean' (though I suspect that how Peter and Paul applied this observation to mixed Jewish/Gentile meal fellowship was considerably different [see Gal. 2.11-14]).

Yet Crossley's objections still do not eliminate the Pauline perspective in Mk 7.19c. First, Peter's vision in Acts 10 nowhere indicates that the food laws are done away with or that any Jesus-believer may henceforth eat unclean foods.

68. Cf. e.g. Michael B. Thompson, *Clothed with Christ: The Example and Teaching of Jesus in Romans 12.1–15.13* (JSNTSup, 59; Sheffield: JSOT Press, 1991), pp. 185–99; James D.G. Dunn, 'Jesus Tradition in Paul', in *Studying the Historical Jesus*, eds B.D. Chilton and C.A. Evans (Leiden: Brill, 1994), pp. 162–3; David Wenham, *Paul: Follower of Jesus or Founder of Christianity* (Grand Rapids, MI: Eerdmans, 1995), pp. 92–5; Seyoon Kim, *Paul and the New Perspective: Second Thoughts on the Origin of Paul's Gospel* (Grand Rapids, MI: Eerdmans, 2002), pp. 264–5; Robert Jewett, *Romans* (Hermeneia; Minneapolis: Fortress, 2008), p. 859.

69. Thompson, *Clothed with Christ*, pp. 196–8.

70. Cf. Bacon, *Gospel*, pp. 263–4; Taylor, *St. Mark*, pp. 346–7; Jesper Svartvik, *Mark and Mission: Mk 7:1-23 in its Narrative and Historical Contexts* (ConBNTS, 32; Stockholm: Almqvist & Wiksell, 2000), pp. 344–47; R.T. France, *The Gospel of Mark* (NIGTC; Grand Rapids, MI: Eerdmans, 2002), p. 278; David J. Rudolph, 'Jesus and the Food Laws: A Reassessment of Mark 7:19b', *EQ* 74 (2002), pp. 304–8; Leander E. Keck, *Romans* (ANTC; Nashville: Abingdon, 2005), pp. 344–5.

71. Crossley, *Date of Mark's Gospel*, pp. 49–50.

The episode is parabolic and interpreted that way by Peter in Acts 10.34-35, 11.12. The vision does not legitimate culinary licence, but shows that God is impartial, he accepts all those who fear him and believers should not make 'distinctions' between 'them' and 'us'. Indeed, the consternation at his visit to a Gentile's house by a party of circumcised believers assumes that the laws of purity (whether Torah or *halakhah*) were still very much thought to be operative and prescriptive (Acts 11.2-3). In contrast, Mark's presentation in 7.15, 19c certainly opens up the possibility of *some* persons eating foods that *some* others considered unclean. Second, if the matter that Mark's Jesus criticizes is merely the priority of washing hands before eating, then we are left explaining why Matthew chose to omit Mk 7.19c in his account of the story since he holds more explicitly than Mark the view that only hand washing was at stake (Mt. 15.20).[72] More likely, Matthew's omission was deliberate because he recognized the potential consequence that Mk 7.19c could promote a far looser attitude to the food laws by some of his audience. Paul clearly allows believers to eat any food they wish only on the proviso that it does not promote communal discord (e.g. Rom. 14.1-20; 1 Cor. 8.8-13; 10.25-33; Acts 21.21). I surmise that Matthew omitted the material in order to prevent Jewish Christians from taking up a Pauline view of the food laws. Third, the similarities between Mk 7.1-23 and Paul on the Law are as follows. (1) Both apply the principle of the cleanness of food in the context of a mission to Gentiles. Paul is concerned in Romans 14.1–15.13 with relations between the 'strong' and the 'weak' in the Roman churches, while Mk 7.1-23 heads up a Gentile section including the healing of the Syro-Phoenician woman's daughter (7.24-30), Jesus' journey to Tyre, Sidon and into the Decapolis (7.31-37) and the feeding of the 4,000 on the Gentile side of the Sea of Galilee (8.1-13). (2) The critique of 'human traditions' in Mk 7.8-9 is similar to the negative remarks about tradition in Gal. 1.14 and Col. 2.8. (3) The upholding of the Decalogue commandment about parents in Mk 7.10 is in accordance with positive references to the Decalogue in Rom. 13.9, Col. 3.20 and Eph. 6.2.

I would not go so far as Joel Marcus by saying that '[n]ot everyone agreed with Paul that the Law was passé for Christians – but Mark did'.[73] I think Paul's view is a lot more complex than that and Mark never portrays Jesus as anti-Law or flagrantly disobedient to its precepts. What can be said with more

72. Jesper Svartvik ('Matthew and Mark', in *Matthew and His Christian Contemporaries*, eds D.C. Sim and B. Repschinski [LNTS, 333; London: T&T Clark, 2008], pp. 40–1) goes so far as to state: 'Matthew has recast the Markan pericope in such a way that the antinomian flavor can no longer be detected. He has managed to rewrite the Gospel tradition to such an extent that the Markan upheaval of the food laws . . . is transformed into an inner-*halakhic* discussion on how to apply the regulations in terms of the washing of hands before meals.'

73. Marcus, 'Mark', p. 486.

conviction is that Mark follows Paul's *halakhah* that consuming unclean food does not render one unclean. There is no expectation for Gentiles to follow customs about Jewish food laws. Even for Jewish Christians like Paul and Mark, who can be counted among the 'strong', adherence to the food laws is optional precisely because of Jesus' teachings on the matter of what constitutes something that is unclean.

IV. *Conclusion*

Even if the Gospel of Mark was not written by the Cyprian Jewish Christian John Mark, the document is very probably indebted to Petrine tradition and exhibits a pro-Pauline theological texture. The marrying of the Jesus tradition and the Pauline kerygma was quite likely a necessity within the earliest churches who felt the influence, to varying degrees, of both apostles. I suggest that Mark was written generally to narrate the story of Jesus for Christians in the Graeco-Roman world. I contend further that it was composed more specifically to be an apology for the cross as the revelatory mechanism through which God's salvation came through his Messiah and this latter point would have had great utility in Pauline or Pauline-sympathetic groups. Mark has not been slavishly bound to Paul, nor does he use the story of Jesus to write a commentary on debates that affected the Pauline communities (hence the absence of reference to circumcision, apostleship, food offered to idols, etc.). Mark is very much his 'own man' with his own Gospel. Still, the interface of Petrine perspective at the literary and tradition-historical levels combined with the pro-Pauline stance on matters such as the cross, salvation and food laws is perhaps indicative of a conscious attempt to bring the two towering personalities of the pre-70 CE church into fruitful dialogue and co-operative engagement. Indeed, Paul's influence upon Mark cannot be adequately grasped or appreciated unless it is seen as part of Mark's concurrent appropriation of the Petrine tradition as well. Mark is engaging in a complex literary synthesis to harness what he finds useful from both Pauline and Petrine perspectives. Awareness of this helps us avoid characterizing Mark as either a strict Paulinist or simply dependent upon a number of Hellenistic traditions that parallel Paul. Though admittedly conjectural, if Mark was written in the aftermath of the martyrdoms of Paul and Peter in Rome, then the desire for a rapprochement between two schools, parties or clusters of adherents to the two apostles would be increased in the face of swelling opposition against Christians. Normally Luke has been attributed the role of the reconciler between Pauline Christianity and Petrine Christianity with his *via media* of 'early catholicism' in the late first or early second century. Yet, if this study is correct, the attempt to synthesize

Petrine and Pauline perspectives was first undertaken by Mark sometime around 70 CE.[74]

Appendix: The title and authorship of the Gospel of Mark

Among the various question concerning the origin of Mark's Gospel, we have to ask, when was the title ΚΑΤΑ ΜΑΡΚΟΝ first joined to the document and on what basis? Then, second, whether it was John Mark who was in fact the 'Mark' who authored this Gospel?

First, on the title, Rudolf Pesch writes, 'alle Inskriptionen und Subscriptionen in den Evangeliuenhandschriften sind spät'.[75] However, that claim is strenuously contested by Martin Hengel, who argued:[76]

1. There is no evidence that shorter readings like ΚΑΤΑ ΜΑΡΚΟΝ found in codex Vaticanus were more primitive than the longer readings like ΕΥΑΓΓΕΛΙΟΝ ΚΑΤΑ ΜΑΡΚΟΝ, since the earliest papyri all attest the longer reading (P^{64}, P^{66}, P^{67}, P^{75}).
2. The title ΕΥΑΓΓΕΛΙΟΝ ΚΑΤΑ ΜΑΡΚΟΝ etc. cannot be attributed to the fixing of the fourfold Gospel canon in middle to late second century in order to differentiate the books from each other because Aristides (*Apol.* 2; 16) and Justin (*Apol.* 66.3) both know of εὐαγγέλια ('Gospels' in the plural) and in the case of Justin there is an awareness that the Gospels derive from the apostles and their followers (*Dial.* 103.8).
3. Marcion's preference for Luke (c.144 CE) was perhaps based on his agreement with its title and tradition that already attributed it to a disciple of Paul as opposed to the judaizing Gospels of Matthew and John.
4. The statement attributed to Papias about the origins of the Gospels assumes a titular distinction between the Gospels because he explicitly names the authors as Mark and Matthew.
5. The titles of the non-canonical Gospels, some of which can be dated to the early or mid-second century (e.g. *Gospel of Thomas*, *Gospel of Peter*, *Gospel of the Ebionites*, etc.), are to be understood as a deliberate imitation of the titles of the canonical Gospels. Likewise, Basilides, the Alexandrian Gnostic in the early second century, wrote a twenty-four

74. For a similar perspective see Corley, 'Seminar', pp. 166–7.

75. Rudolf Pesch, *Das Markusevangelium 1,1-8,26* (HTKNT; Freiburg: Herder, 1976), p. 4.

76. Martin Hengel, *Studies in the Gospel of Mark* (trans. J. Bowden; London: SCM, 1985), pp. 64–85; idem, *The Four Gospels and the One Gospel of Jesus Christ* (trans. J. Bowden; Harrisburg, PA: Trinity Press International, 2000), pp. 48–56. Cf. Bo Reicke, *The Roots of the Synoptic Gospels* (Philadelphia: Fortress, 1986), pp. 150–5.

volume Gospel commentary (*Exegetica*) that perhaps included a titular distinction between the Gospels known to him.[77]

6. The longer ending of Mk 16.9-20 and the *Epistula Apostolorum*, dated to the first half of the second century, presupposes the widespread circulation and knowledge of the individual Gospels and Acts.
7. While the Gospels are strictly anonymous at the literary level that was possible only because their authorship and origin would have been known in its immediate setting.[78] Anonymous works were rare in antiquity and regarded with suspicion, hence the rise of pseudepigraphy. Tertullian (*Adv. Marc.* 4.2.3) went so far as to say that a Gospel not bearing the name of its author was not to be received, evidently because he knew of some Gospels that had titles (the canonical Gospels and perhaps others too) and some that did not (like Marcion's Gospel). Yet the titles were probably added to the Gospels very early on in order to identify the origin of the work when the Gospels were used in liturgical practice, disseminated further afield, or arranged in Christian libraries. If the Gospels were utterly anonymous (in terms of author and provenance) and circulated with no knowledge of their origins, then, this would have led to a multiplicity of titles that we simply do not find.[79] Thus, the titles were not added at the final redaction

77. Francois Bovon ('The Synoptic Gospels and the Non-Canonical Acts of the Apostles', *HTR* 81 [1988], pp. 22–3) and Helmut Koester (*From Jesus to the Gospels* [Minneapolis: Fortress, 2007], p. 64, n. 55) note that the titles of the NT Apocrypha were not stable, and thus their fittingness as an analogy for their canonical counterparts breaks down in part. However, Koester's claim (*Jesus to the Gospels*, p. 65) that the incipits were originally similar to those preserved in the Gospels from the Nag Hammadi Codices (e.g. *Apocryphon of James*) suffers from a sheer absence of evidence for such an analogy altogether. Papias' *Logia of the Lord* can refer to a mixture of sayings and stories about Jesus (U. H. J. Körtner, *Papias von Hierapolis: ein Beitrag zur Geschichte des fruhen Christentum* [Göttingen: Vandenhoeck & Ruprecht, 1988], pp. 151–67; J. Kürzinger, *Papias von Hierapolis und die Evangelien des Neuen Testaments* [Regensburg: Putset, 1983], pp. 50–1) meaning that it could, indeed, describe a document called a 'Gospel'.

78. One model of book production was that an author would compose a rough draft and have it reviewed by others. Once a final version was formulated it was then circulated among a wider group of friends and associates (Raymond J. Starr, 'The Circulation of Literary Texts in the Roman World', *CQ* 37 [1989], pp. 313–16; Harry Y. Gamble, *Books and Readers in the Early Church: A History of Early Christian Texts* [New Haven: Yale University Press, 1995], p. 85). Books could be circulated a number of ways in the ancient world. Authors themselves were often involved in the publication and dissemination of their own works. There was the copying and exchanging of books by scribes (Loveday Alexander, 'Ancient Book Production and the Circulation of the Gospels', in *The Gospels for All Christians: Rethinking the Gospel Audiences*, ed. R. Bauckham [Grand Rapids, MI: Eerdmans, 1998], pp. 88–99). In other words, the publication and initial dissemination of books meant that knowledge of a book's authorship and origins would have been commonplace in the acquisition and copying of the book in the first place.

79. A.Y. Collins (*Mark* [Hermeneia; Minneapolis: Fortress, 2007], pp. 2–3) is helpful as she points to an analogy with Galen who used to write books without a title and give them to pupils and friends who asked for written works to help them to remember what they had heard. In his book on his own books (*De libris propriis liber*) he states that he did not give any of his works titles, but that, as they began to circulate, the same work could be given different titles according to its various circumstances. This suggests that if the Gospel of Mark had circulated without a title it probably would have acquired various titles in the course of its transmission.

of the Fourfold Gospel collection in the middle of the second century, but were probably given during the dissemination of the Gospels to other communities when Christian scribes added the names based on collective knowledge about their authorship and origins.

8. In sum, Mark's incipit Ἀρχὴ τοῦ εὐαγγελίου Ἰησου Χριστοῦ led to the giving of the title εὐαγγελιον κατὰ Μαρκον, which led respectively to εὐαγγέλιον κατὰ Μαθθαῖον, εὐαγγέλιον κατὰ Λυκαν and εὐαγγελιον κατὰ Ἰωαννην.

Second, with regard to the attribution of authorship of the second Gospel to John Mark, scholarly opinion is divided. Consider the following remarks: 'There can be no doubt that the author of the Gospel was Mark, the attendant of Peter'[80] and 'The tradition that Mk was written by John Mark is therefore scarcely reliable.'[81] On the evidential side of things:

1. Internal evidence for the author being John Mark is admittedly weak. The most we can say from the text is that the author was obviously a devotee of Jesus who he acclaimed climactically as the Son of God. The focus on following Jesus in the 'way' looms large, especially in conjunction with the emphasis on the cross. The author was perhaps experiencing or anticipating persecution. He composed a Graeco-Roman biography of Jesus written through the lens of an apocalyptic worldview. He believed that the book would reach Gentile readers, hence the explanation of Judaean customs and translated Aramaism. Lastly, he writes in a simple and inelegant Greek suggesting that Greek was not his first language. This could describe any number of Christians in the Graeco-Roman world c.70 CE.
2. The case for John Mark's authorship rides very much on the evaluation of a fragment from Papias preserved by Eusebius of Caesarea.[82] Papias was

80. Taylor, *St. Mark*, p. 26.

81. W.G. Kümmel, *Introduction to the New Testament* (NTL; rev. edn; trans. H.C. Kee; London: SCM, 1975), p. 97.

82. Cf. Robert M. Grant, 'Papias and the Gospels', *HTR* 25 (1943), pp. 208–22; H.A. Rigg, Jr., 'Papias on Mark', *NovT* 1 (1956), pp. 161–83; Terence Y. Mullins, 'Papias on Mark's Gospel', *VC* 14 (1960), pp. 116–24; idem, 'Papias and Clement and Mark's Two Gospels', *VC* 30 (1976), pp. 189–92; K. Niederwimmer, 'Johannes Markus und die Frage nach dem Verfasser des zweiten Evangeliums', *ZNW* 58 (1967), pp. 172–88; U.H.J. Körtner, 'Markus der Mitarbeiter des Petrus', *ZNW* 71 (1980), pp. 160–73; idem, *Papias von Hierapolis: Ein Beitrag zur Geschichte des frühen Christentums* (FRLANT 133; Göttingen: 1983); J. Kürzinger, 'Der Aussage des Papias von Hierapolis zur literischen Form des Markusevangeliums', *BZ* 21 (1977), pp. 245–64; idem, *Papias von Hierapolis und die Evangelien des Neuen Testaments* (Regensburgh: Putset, 1983); Robert W. Yarbrough, 'The Date of Papias: A Reassessment', *JETS* 26 (1983), pp. 181–91; Bo Reicke, *The Roots of the Synoptic Gospels* (Philadelphia: Fortress, 1986), pp. 155–66; Robert H. Gundry, *Mark: A Commentary on His Apology for the Cross* (Grand Rapids, MI: Baker, 1993), pp. 1026–45; Samuel Byrskog, *Story as History, History as Story: The Gospel Tradition in the Context of Ancient Oral History* (Tübingen: Mohr/Siebeck, 2000), pp. 272–97; Richard Bauckham, *Jesus and the Eyewitnesses*, pp. 12–38; Charles E. Hill, 'Papias of Hierapolis', *ExpT* 117.8 (2006), pp. 309–15.

the bishop of Hierapolis in the Lycus valley. A contemporary of Polycarp, he lived until the early second century, and claimed to have had access to the 'living and enduring voice' of oral traditions about Jesus from elders who knew the apostles (Eusebius, *Hist. Eccl.* 3.39.3-4). His major work, *Exposition of Logia of the Lord*, was probably a five-volume commentary on extant sayings of Jesus. His comments concerning the origins of the Gospel of Mark are:

And the elder used to say this: 'Mark, having become Peter's interpreter, wrote down accurately everything he remembered, though not in order, of the things either said or done by Christ. For he neither heard the Lord nor followed him, but afterwards, as I said, followed Peter, who adapted his teachings as needed but had no intention of giving an ordered account of the Lord's sayings. Consequently Mark did nothing wrong in writing down some things as he remembered them, for he made it his one concern not to omit anything that he heard or take any false statement in them'. (Eusebius, *Hist. Eccl.* 3.39.15)	Καὶ τοῦτο ὁ πρεσβύτερος ἔλεγε· Μάρκος μὲν ἑρμηνευτὴς Πέτρου γενόμενος, ὅσα ἐμνημόνευσεν, ἀ κριβῶς ἔγραψεν, οὐ μέντοι τάξει, τὰ ὑπὸ του Χριστοῦ ἢ λεχθέντα ἢ πραχθέντα. οὔτε γὰρ ἤκουσε τοῦ κυρίου, οὔτε παρηκολούθησεν αὐτῷ, ὕστερον δέ, ὡς ἔφην, Πέτρῳ, ὅς πρὸς τὰς χρείας ἐποιεῖτο τὰς διδασκαλί ας, ἀλλ' οὐχ ὥσπερ σύνταξιν τῶν κυριακῶν ποιούμενος λογίων, ὥστε οὐδὲν ἥμαρτε Μάρκος, οὕτως ἔνια γράψας ὡς ἀπεμνημόνευσεν. ἑνος γάρ ἐποιήσατο πρόνοιαν, τοῦ μηδὲν ὧν ἤκουσε παραλιπεῖν ἢ ψεύσασθαί τι ἐν αὐτοῖς."

Niederwimmer rejects the Papian testimony to the Mark-Peter relationship as 'eine Fiktion darstellt' and contends that 'nicht nur die Petrus-Konstrucktion ist ungeschichtlich, sondern auch die Heleitung des Evangeliums von dem Jerusalemer Johannes Markus'.[84] Byrskog states that rejection of Papias' statement as an apologetic fiction has become almost a 'scholarly dogma'.[85] But as we will see this tradition is far more credible than often alleged. *First*, scholars ordinarily date this tradition to c.130 CE, yet it is possible to date this tradition even earlier, to c.100–110 CE.[86] Eusebius locates Papias during the time of Polycarp and Ignatius, whom he also associates with Clement of Rome, and these persons were all active from the late first century and into the early second century (*Hist. Eccl.* 3.36.1-2; 3.39.1). The description of Papias comes before book 4 of Eusebius' *Ecclesiastical History* with the discussion

83. Michael W. Holmes, *The Apostolic Fathers: Greek Texts and English Translations* (3rd edn; Grand Rapids, MI: Baker, 2007), pp. 738–41.

84. Niederwimmer, 'Verfasser des zweiten Evangeliums', p. 185.

85. Byrskog, *Story as History*, p. 275.

86. Reicke, *Roots*, p. 155; Yarbrough, 'Date of Papias', pp. 186–90.

of the persecution under Trajan c.110 CE, meaning that Papias came from a period prior to that. Eusebius' *Chronicon* lays out an order of Apostle John, Papias, Polycarp and Ignatius, which edges forward to a date c.100 CE. Irenaeus refers to him as an 'ancient man' who knew the Apostle John and Polycarp and he was a primitive witness to the faith (*Adv. Haer*. 5.33.4). There is also no attempt by Eusebius or Irenaeus to cite Papias against later Gnostic beliefs, probably because he wrote long before Gnosticism became an issue in the wider church.[87] Obviously early does not require authentic, but we have here a tradition that on a plain reading reaches into the latter decades of the first century. *Second*, Papias writes as a third-generation Christian and here I take it that the statement has three tiers of transmission rather than four (Lord's Disciples → Elders→ Papias).[88] However, with respect to *Hist. Eccl*. 3.39.3-4, not too much should be made of the present tense of λέγουσιν as this is simply a historical-present rather than proof that the elders were still living during the time of Papias.[89] *Third*, it is unclear who the elder is,[90] but given the differentiation between the Apostle John and the elder John in *Hist. Eccl*. 3.39.3-4 it is probable that the 'elder' in *Hist. Eccl*. 3.39.15 is John the elder. *Fourth*, that Mark functioned as Peter's ἑρμηνευτὴς means something like translator or expositor.[91] *Fifth*, Papias' statement appears to be an apologetic defence of Mark's Gospel, but precisely what the alleged problem with Mark is remains opaque. Most likely, Papias appeals to a tradition that explains Mark's lack of rhetorical sophistication, οὐ μέντοι τάξις (perhaps vis-à-vis Luke's rhetorical complexity) and Mark's brevity, οὕτως ἔνια γράψας (perhaps vis-à-vis Matthew's comprehensiveness). Peter gave his teaching about Jesus in the form of χρεία (a pointed saying or short narrative), and did not arrange the sayings of the Lord as σύνταξις (rhetorically ordered). Thus, Mark's lack of order and gappiness is attributed to his dependence on Peter and Peter himself was anecdotal rather than refined in his teaching. Papias is not defending the

87. Cf. Hengel (*Studies in the Gospel of Mark*, p. 152, n. 61) against the view of W. Bauer and K. Niederwimmer (see similarly Philipp Vielhauer, *Geschichte der urchirstlichen Literatur* [Berlin: Walter de Gruyter, 1975], p. 762; R.P. Martin, *Mark: Evangelist and Theologian* [Grand Rapids, MI: Zondervan, 1978], pp. 80–3; Marcus, *Mark 1–8*, p. 23) that Papias' statement was to defend the Gospel of Mark against Gnostic usage of it. See similar to Hengel, Körtner, *Papias von Hierapolis*, pp. 154–59.

88. Cf. Yarbrough, 'Date of Papias', p. 184; Bauckham, *Eyewitnesses*, pp. 16–21, 32–3; Hill, 'Papias', p. 310.

89. *Contra* Yarbrough, 'Date of Papias', p. 185; Gundry, *Mark*, pp. 1029–31; Bauckham, *Eyewitnesses*, p. 17.

90. Although Irenaeus claims that Papias was a hearer of the Apostle John (*Hist. Eccl*. 3.39.1) and Eusebius could have had a motivation for separating John the elder from the Apostle John and making the former rather than the later responsible for Revelation, the fact remains that Eusebius clearly distinguishes John the elder and the Apostle John in *Hist. Eccl*. 3.39.14 (see Gundry, *Mark*, pp. 1029–31; Bauckham, *Eyewitnesses*, pp. 417–37).

91. Cf. Kürzinger, *Papias von Hierapolis*, pp. 45–6; Bauckham, *Eyewitnesses*, pp. 205–10.

Gospels against Gnostic usage, as much as he appears to be accounting for the differences among the Gospels.

Some argue that the appeal to Mark as the interpreter of Peter is a deliberate rejoinder to the Gnostic claim that Basilides was taught by Glaucias the interpreter of Peter (Clement, *Strom.* 7.106). Yet this is implausible for four reasons: (a) imitation is hardly an effective form of refutation; (b) the Peter-Glaucias tradition itself may have been influenced by the Peter-Mark tradition rather than vice versa;[92] (c) the aetiological stories of the genetic relationship between 'heretics' recorded by Heresiologists are chiefly polemical rather than historical; and (d) Irenaeus connects Basilides with a different Gnostic genealogy that is traced through Simon Magus and Menander (*Adv. Haer.* 1.24.3-7), while the Basilidians themselves laid claim to the teachings of the apostle Matthias (Clement, *Strom.* 7.108; Hippolytus, *Haer.* 7.20.1). *Sixth*, the Papian statement about the Peter-Mark link may be genuine and independent of 1 Pet. 5.13. John Mark probably had an 'evolving'[93] relationship with Peter from the days of the early Jerusalem church (Acts 12.12), to his exit from the Pauline mission (Acts 13.13; 15.37-40), his reconciliation with Paul in Ephesus (Phlm. 24; Col. 4.10) and finally his recapitulation of his role as 'helper' to Paul and Barnabas (Acts 13.5) by becoming an 'interpreter' of Peter (*Hist.* 3.39.16). Furthermore, although Papias knew 1 Peter (*Hist. Eccl.* 2.15.2; 3.39.17) it does not follow that Papias derived the Mark-Peter tradition from 1 Pet. 5.13.[94] The Papian statement does not show any distinctive features of the Petrine text such as Mark figuratively being Peter's 'son' or that they were in Rome (i.e. Babylon) as 1 Pet. 5.13 records.[95] We can note a further dissimilarity since Papias implies that Mark wrote after Peter's death, whereas subsequent traditions that follow

92. Cf. Birger A. Pearson ('Basilides the Gnostic', in *A Companion to Second-Century Christian 'Heretics'*, eds A. Marjanen and P. Luomanen Leiden: Brill, 2005, p. 4): 'The Peter-Glaukias tradition (whoever Glaukias was) can possibly be seen as a Basilidian counter to the Peter-Mark tradition current in Alexandrian ecclesiastical circles'. Winrich A. Löhr (*Basilides und seine Schule: eine Studie zur Theologie – und Kirchengeschichte des zweiten Jahrehunders* [Tübingen: Mohr/Siebeck, 1996], p. 22): 'Vielleicht gehört die basilidianische Petrus-Glaukias-Tradition in einem spezifich alexandrinischen Kontext, in dem die basilidianische Gemeinde sich gegen die entstehende, großkirkliche Legende von Markus als dem Gründer der christlichen Gemeinde in Alexandrien behaupte mußte. Triffte diese Vermutung zu, so, wäre die Notiz über die basilidianische Petrus-Glaukias Tradition bereits ein Zeichen für ein Ablösung der basilidiaschen Gemeinde von der Großkirche'.

93. Byrskog, *Eyewitnesses*, 279–90.

94. Cf. Niederwimmer ('Verfasser des zweiten Evangeliums', p. 186): 'Ein Blick in die dem Papias (oder schon seiner Tradition) vertrauten Schriften ließ diesen Markus prompt in I Petr 5_{13} finder, Durch den Begriff eines ἑρμηνευτὴς Πέτρου wurde das Verhältnis des Markus zu Petrus näherhin bestimmt'; see similarly Marcus, *Mark 1–8*, p. 22.

95. Note the words of Byrskog (*Eyewitnesses*, p. 278): 'The chronological connection between 1 Peter and the repeated view of the presbyter thus becomes too tight to allow any genetic relationship between the two. Instead, one finds, it seems, a synchronous and reciprocal confirmation of a tradition closely connecting Mark and Peter, speaking of Mark in one case as Peter's "son" and in the other case as his "interpreter"'.

1 Pet. 5.13 in linking Mark with Peter typically state that Mark wrote during Peter's lifetime such as the Old Latin prologue to Mark:

> Mark made his assertion, who was also named stubby-fingers, because he had in comparison to the length of the rest of his body shorter fingers. He was a disciple and interpreter of Peter, whom he followed just as he heard him report. When he was requested at Rome by the brothers and sisters, he briefly wrote this gospel in parts of Italy. When Peter heard this, he approved and affirmed it by his own authority for the reading of the church [though some of the Old Latin Anti-Marcionite prologues read *post excessionem ipsius Petri* ('After the death of Peter') and Irenaeus also (*Adv. Haer.* 3.1.1) places the composition of Mark after Peter's death].[96]

The tendency of some traditions about the origins of the Gospel was to posit the Apostles as still alive when their respective Gospels were composed (e.g. Clement cited in Eusebius, *Hist. Eccl.* 2.15.1-2; 6.14.5-7). In which case, the Papian testimony shows no signs of the distinctive elements of 1 Pet. 5.13 and is different from the developing tradition about the origin of the Gospel of Mark that was inferred from 1 Pet. 5.13 by Christian authors in the second and third centuries.[97]

The authenticity of the statement in 1 Pet. 5.13 that locates Peter and Mark together in Rome is understandably contested.[98] First, that the 'Mark' is 'John Mark' seems most likely as the link between the two figures is attested by the Papian testimony which, as we have seen, is probably independent of 1 Pet. 5.13. A second matter is whether the authorship of 1 Peter is pseudepigraphical or

96. Cf. discussion in France, *Mark*, pp. 37–8.

97. Cf. Gundry, *Mark*, 1043.

98. On the traditions about Peter in Rome (e.g. 1 Pet. 5.13; Irenaeus, *Adv. Haer.* 3.1.1; Eusebius, *Hist. Eccl.* 2.25.8; 3.3.1-3; with possible allusions in *1 Clem.* 5.3-4 and *Asc. Isa.* 4.2-3) see Richard Bauckham, 'The Martyrdom of Peter in Early Christian Literature', *ANRW* 2.26.1 (1992), pp. 539–95; Markus Bockmuehl, 'Peter's Death in Rome? Back to Front and Upside Down', *SJT* 60 (2007), pp. 1–27. Note the comment of Raymond Brown and John Meier (*Antioch and Rome: New Testament Cradles of Christianity* [New York: Paulist, 1983], p. 98): 'As for Peter, we have no knowledge at all of when he came to Rome and what he did there before he was martyred. Certainly he was *not* the original missionary who brought Christianity to Rome (and therefore *not* the founder of the church of Rome in that sense). There is no serious proof that he was the bishop (or local ecclesiastical officer) of the Roman church – a claim not made till the third century. Most likely he did not spend any major time at Rome before 58 when Paul wrote to the Romans, and so it may have been only in the 60s and relatively shortly before his martyrdom that Peter came to the capital.' On the strong possibility of the Roman provenance for the Gospel of Mark see Hengel, *Studies in the Gospel of Mark*, pp. 1–30; C. Clifton Black, 'Was Mark a Roman Gospel?', *ExpT* 105 (1993), pp. 36–40; Brian Incigneri, *The Gospel to the Romans: The Setting and Rhetoric of Mark's Gospel* (Leiden: Brill, 2003); Ivan Head, 'Mark as a Roman Document from the Year 69', *JRH* 28 (2004), pp. 240–59; Adam Winn, *The Purpose of Mark's Gospel: Early Christian Response to Roman Imperial Propaganda* (WUNT 2.245; Tübingen: Mohr/Siebeck, 2008).

authentic.[99] While the Greek literary style of 1 Peter is certainly above par in the New Testament epistles, even a well-travelled fisherman could gain proficiency in Greek with enough time. Canvassing the role of Silvanus as an amanuensis (1 Pet. 5.12), though often derided as fortress retreat for authenticity, is still a realistic possibility. The omission of reminiscences of Jesus' life as a mark against Petrine authorship, especially in relation to reflection on suffering and atonement in 1 Pet. 2.20-26, is only valid if this epistle were the only written discourse that Peter intended to leave behind as a testament, which as far as we know it is not. Evidence for dependence on Paul's letters is heavily overstated.[100] We should expect to find similarities between writings of the two as Paul and Peter both drew on a common tradition (see the 'we' language of Gal. 2.15-16, the 'I or they' who proclaim the same gospel in 1 Cor. 15.11, and Paul's endorsement of Cephas' itinerant ministry accompanied by a wife in 1 Cor. 9.5). Also, though the *Sitz im Leben* of 1 Peter might reflect a late first-century date, the exhortations are broad enough to accommodate and address any number of potential settings (hence 1 Peter's 'catholic' nature!). Most likely, 1 Peter constitutes a homiletic exhortation to Jewish Christians in Asia Minor experiencing harassment from local authorities, a notion that is hardly implausible pre-70 CE given the travails of Paul's own ministry in Asia (1 Cor. 15.32; 2 Cor. 1.8-12; cf. Col. 4.3) and accounts of opposition to Christians in Asia described in Acts (19.23-41). I concur with James Dunn: 'All in all, then, the issue of authorship is a good deal more intangible, and the possibility that Peter was himself the author of 1 Peter a good deal more open than has often been thought to be the case.'[101] That means that the reference to Mark in 1 Pet. 5.13, assuming that it is John Mark, is not an element of the 'fictive apparatus of pseudonymous letters'[102] but an actual person in close relationship with Peter (i.e. 'my son Mark').

Finally, if the thesis of the study is correct, that the Gospel of Mark contains a mixture of Petrine tradition and Pauline theological perspective, then the list

99. Cf. discussion in Peter Achtemeier, *1 Peter* (Hermeneia; Minneapolis: Fortress, 1996), pp. 1–43; John H. Elliott, *1 Peter* (AB; New York: Doubleday, 2000), pp. 118–30; F. Lapham, *Peter: The Myth, the Man and the Writings: A Study of Early Petrine Text and Tradition* (London: T&T Clark, 2003), pp. 141–7.

100. J. Herzer (*Petrus oder Paulus? Studien üben das Verhältnis des Ersten Petrusbriefs zuer paulinischen Tradition* [WUNT 103; Tübingen: Mohr/Siebeck, 1998], pp. 268–9) points out the problem: 'Literarische Vergleiche können nur erste Schritte sein, die den Weg der christlichen Überlieferungen zurückverfolgen, um schließlich unter Berücksichtigung historischer Konstellationen und Warhscheinlichkeiten eine Geschichte der frühchristichen Gemeinden und der für sie jeweils maßgeblichen Traditionen darstellen zu können.' His own study focuses on the letter opening in comparison with the Pauline letters, the 'in-Christ' language, concept of revelation, soteriology and Christology, ecclesiology and *charisma*, baptism, community exhortation and parallels between 1 Peter and Romans 12. In the end he finds no reason to postulate Pauline dependence and concludes that 1 Peter does not derive from a 'Schüler des Paulus'.

101. James D.G. Dunn, *Beginning from Jerusalem* (CITM 2; Grand Rapids, MI: Eerdmans, 2009), p. 1153.

102. Achtemeier, *1 Peter*, p. 355.

contain intractable interpretative issues. Both personalities, if we may be right to call them that, are complex and multilayered.[2]

Thus, one inevitably must conclude pessimistically that it is nearly impossible to present a *convincing* comparison of the two authors within contemporary New Testament scholarship because, in order to do so, one has to first take sides on so many controversial interpretative issues. One's view of Paul, for example, will no doubt disappoint some, anger others and please only very few. My own recent assessment of David Sim's work is a case in point.[3] If anything is clear within the murk of Pauline studies today it is that the field is now in what might be referred to as a post-consensus (my term); the discipline is so fragmented and polarized that a scholarly consensus, on which to build a comparison, is simply out of the question.

When one places his or her peculiar version of Paul in conversation with a Matthew that is perhaps only slightly less controversial the potential for scholarly disagreement multiplies exponentially. If I sound agnostic about the ability of modern scholarly comparison of the two figures, the impression will only be reinforced when I come to consider Paul and Matthew's historical settings and genres. The problem of comparison, then, is not only, or even mostly, at the level of modern scholarship. Rather, the problem goes to the very documents themselves.

Sim's work evinces just the kind of difficulty I am suggesting. In the aforementioned article (see Note 3) I attempted to address one element of Sim's onslaught of scholarly activity attempting to resurrect S. G. F. Brandon's old argument that Matthew's Gospel contains an aggressive anti-Paulinism. While Sim is apparently making it fashionable again to claim that Matthew was directly attacking Paul, his revision of the argument stumbles over the same obstacles Brandon's did, however much it may have been improved.[4]

For Sim's comparison to convince a reader, one has to agree to several controversial conclusions – built on a growing mound of educated guesses – about both Paul and Matthew. Putting his idiosyncratic view of Matthew aside, one can criticize Sim's perspective for its interpretation of Paul that is at the very least contestable. I say in my previous essay: 'Sim's interpretation of an anti-Pauline Matthew rises or falls on the question of who the historical Paul was.'[5] If Paul turns out to be different than the one Sim envisages, Matthew's

2. I use the term 'personality' as a figure of speech to represent the mind inculcated in the literature of the New Testament ascribed to these individuals.

3. Joel Willitts, 'The Friendship of Matthew and Paul: A Response to a Recent Trend in the Interpretation of Matthew's Gospel', *TS* 65.1 (2009), pp. 1–8 (61).

4. Ibid.

5. Ibid., p. 2.

enemy disappears like the Wicked Witch of the West, leaving only a vestige of itself in the ink of his published books.

The current state of Pauline studies was captured well recently by Magnus Zetterholm:

> Scholars, who traditionally have found an almost absolute opposition between Paul and Judaism, have during recent decades been profoundly challenged by those who argue that Paul remained faithful to the Torah, but believed that non-Jews should refrain from involving themselves in Torah observance.[6]

He then justifiably asserted: 'Since the same texts have given rise to both the idea that Paul opposed Judaism and that he lived and died as a Torah-observant Jew, it is obvious that Paul is being read from *different perspectives.*'[7] *Approaches to Paul,* Zetterholm's book-length study of this phenomenon, concludes:

> There is evidently a strong connection between the *overarching perspective* shared among scholars within each of these schools and the results that are produced. Within the traditional perspective, the normal assumption is that Paul opposed Judaism, whereas within the radical new perspective, scholars read Paul assuming the he did not break with Judaism.[8]

Sim needs to admit that his view of the relationship between Matthew and Paul is possible only within a certain Baurian framework of interpretation – one Zetterholm refers to as 'traditional'.[9] If the framework is rejected, and there are good reasons for this, than the whole speculative reconstruction falls down flat.

I have elsewhere discussed the methodological challenges involved in a comparison of Matthew and Paul.[10] It is legitimate to be severely sceptical of any interpretation that offers a direct comparison of Matthew and Paul given the complexity of the issues involved. It is one thing to *describe* each author's particular presentation of a topic they share in common and compare them; it is another thing entirely to draw definitive conclusions about their relationship based on the comparison; or, as some have done, to assume some kind of direct engagement by Matthew against Paul's theology. I concluded:

6. Magnus Zetterholm, 'The Didache, Matthew, James – and Paul: Reconstructing Historical Developments in Antioch', in *Matthew, James, and Didache: Three Related Documents in their Jewish and Christian Settings* (Huub van de Sandt and Jürgen Zangenberg [eds], SBL Symposium Series, 45; Leiden: Brill, 2008), pp. 73–90 (74).

7. Ibid., emphasis added.

8. Zetterholm, 'Paul', p. 233, emphasis added.

9. Ibid., p. 231.

10. Willitts, 'Matthew and Paul'.

> It would be one thing if Matthew and Paul shared a common social context – which they did not – if they dealt with similar rhetorical concerns – which they did not – or if they wrote in a similar genre – which they did not. Because Matthew and Paul shared none of these, claims of stark theological difference and, certainly, claims of explicit refutation are highly speculative and therefore unconvincing.[11]

Since writing this paragraph I have changed my mind on the first of these points as will become evident, but the other two remain significant obstacles.

Yet, I do think comparison can be instructive if its limits are appropriately appreciated. Perhaps an analogy from Source and Redaction criticism of the Gospels would be instructive. Scholars have spent a good deal of time and toner speculating on why Matthew and Luke are different in the details of a shared tradition only to find in the end the question is ultimately unanswerable. We simply do not have the evidence necessary for certain kinds of judgements. This notwithstanding, Synoptic comparison remains an important procedure for interpreting a Gospel's message. However, its usefulness has proven limited after nearly three-quarters of a century of practice.

At most the procedure helps to expose the unique contribution of a particular gospel by showing its distinct presentation of the words and works of Jesus through painstaking comparison with the others. Anyone who has colour-coded a synopsis knows what I mean. So, as far as it goes, Gospel criticism is a necessary tool for interpretation. But when descriptive comparison turns into imaginative speculation about the sources behind the Synoptic Gospels and what an Evangelist did or did not do to them the procedure proves only marginally useful for interpretation.

Similarly, it can be constructive to compare Paul and Matthew on topics they have in common – areas where they are discussing the same thing. Such comparisons can illuminate the distinct resonance of an author within the larger symphony that is the New Testament. Here's the crucial methodological principle: *the interpreter must limit herself primarily to the descriptive task and resist the urge to draw speculative conclusions.*

Some less cautious than I will think this to be an unnecessary restriction, asserting that educated guesses are the warp and woof of the scholarly task. While this point is conceded to a degree, we must be careful because at the point of interpretation where this sort of comparison takes place the educated guesses begin to pile up so high that one wonders if there is even an ounce of truth left in the hundred pounds of speculation.

Admittedly, this analogy with Gospel criticism breaks down because a comparison between Paul and Matthew is nothing like comparing Matthew with

11. Ibid., p. 6.

Luke. With the former, the issue of genre and rhetorical interests particularly undermine direct comparison. For even when we are considering a shared topic, theme or tradition we must, nevertheless, assume that (1) their respective discussions do not represent their whole mind on a given issue, (2) they are restrained by some unique rhetorical concern that dictates how they address the issue and (3) the different genres control the manner and, in some instances, the content of communication.

Thus, I think the wisest course of action methodologically is to take a descriptive approach and then only very cautiously draw conclusions about things, such as the type of Christianity represented by both, or whether and to what extent Paul's influence is felt in Matthew or Matthew is a reaction to Paul.[12] Additionally, in light of Zetterholm's accurate depiction of the situation within Pauline studies at the moment (and something similar could be said of Matthaean studies) and the example of Sim's most recent work, I believe it is necessary to be straightforward about the 'school' to which one belongs and unapologetically present an interpretation of Matthew and Paul within the overarching framework that the school presupposes. If this approach in the end limits the contribution of comparative projects then so be it. However, I see no other path to take.

My interpretation of the relationship of Paul and Matthew and the larger framework on which that interpretation is dependent will need to be judged as to whether they are a more convincing hypothesis than that of, say, Sim. In this way, the debate is not in the details but rather between the larger synthetic hypotheses. The hypothesis that prevails is the one that fits in more of the evidence, is clearest and the most simple and convincingly explains data in other related areas.

b. *Paul and Matthew within 'apostolic Judaism': An alternative interpretative framework*

Delineating as accurately as possible what we know about the socio-historical settings of the authors and documents in question is a crucial *first step* in any historical comparison. This is perhaps too obvious a point to even mention, but it's a step that if done poorly or improperly will invalidate any conclusion about early Christianity(ies) one might draw from the comparison. The historical Paul must be reasonably reconstructed if he is to be compared with Matthew, otherwise the comparison is useless.

Characterizations of Paul, however, are polarized in contemporary scholarship, as noted earlier. Thus, it is necessary today in this post-consensus era

12. I think D. Harrington's essay exemplifies this approach quite well (Daniel J. Harrington, 'Matthew and Paul', in *Matthew and His Christian Contemporaries* [David C. Sim and Boris Repschinski (eds); London; New York: T&T Clark, 2008], pp. 11–26).

to state where one's interpretation begins. I will be conducting the study on Matthew and Paul with the assumption that *both* were *Torah-observant Jews and members of a new form of Judaism that has recently been labelled 'apostolic Judaism'*.[13] As with any particular form of ancient Judaism at the time, whether we're speaking of the Pharisees or Essenes, this was not a homogeneous body. But neither would it be accurate to label it heterogeneous, since all its expressions shared the conviction that the Messiah had come in the person of Jesus of Nazareth. One might say the varieties were nevertheless of the same species. Obviously there was something of an essential unity amid the diversity. Thus, apostolic Judaism was *allogeneic*. Drawing an analogy from immunology, elements of the movement were genetically dissimilar but belonged to the same species. As will become evident, the communities represented by Paul and Matthew were at once different and the same. The similarity was basic, but the differences were consequential.

We need, therefore, to discuss further the distinctive elements of the constituency to which the authors were writing. In order to avoid an overly speculative reconstruction that depends on specific assumptions about geographical location and date, we attune our ear to what the texts themselves presupposed about the readers. While one cannot assume an absolute correspondence between the implied reader (or, better, the authorial audience) and the real reader,[14] at least we are allowing the text itself to be determinative.

Broadly speaking, the social location of both Matthew and Paul seem most reasonably to be the Jewish synagogue in the Graeco-Roman world of the middle to late first century. While this assertion will not be all that controversial for Matthew's social location, it may seem counter-intuitive to many with regard to Paul, especially to those who have written on the subject of Paul and Matthew. However, I am among the growing number of scholars today who think that Paul's letters make the most sense when read *within* a Diaspora Jewish institutional context rather than outside it.[15] This brief section is not the place to argue for this; nor is it necessary to do so, as others have done it adequately. It will suffice to point out that Paul's apostolic work was conducted at a stage in the development of the Messiah-believing community when believers in Jesus had yet to move out from under the umbrella of Judaism. Thus, some of the

13. See Anders Runesson, 'Inventing Christian Identity: Paul, Ignatius, and Theodosius I', in *Exploring Early Christian Identity* (Bengt Holmberg [ed.]; WUNT, 226; Tübingen: Mohr Siebeck, 2008), pp. 59–92; idem, 'Rethinking Early Jewish-Christian Relations: Matthean Community History as Pharisaic Intragroup Conflict', *JBL* 127.1 (2008), pp. 95–132.

14. For a definition of authorial audience see Peter J. Rabinowitz, *Before Reading: Narrative Conventions and the Politics of Interpretation* (Columbus, OH: Ohio State University Press, 1987).

15. As I stated, I have changed my view on this point since writing the previous essay; see Willitts, 'Matthew and Paul'.

most significant challenges Paul's fledgling communities faced, at least in his view, were those posed by the Jewish institutional structures within which the churches lived. As M. Nanos has observed concerning the situation in Paul's Galatian churches: 'Paul's letter implies that the situations of the addresses in Galatia are intra-Jewish.'[16]

On the other hand, few scholars today would disagree with the assumption that Matthew's social location remained within something of a Jewish context, even if one thinks, as G. Stanton did, that they had very recently separated from their parent.[17] Thus, I am convinced with A. Runesson that it is best to think of both Pauline and Matthaean communities as Graeco-Roman associations under the umbrella of common Judaism, the Judaism of the Temple.[18]

Establishing this foundation of similarity, however, is certainly not the full story. The documents reveal very distinct communities within the same institutional structure. On the one hand, Matthew in my view represents an exclusively Jewish ethnic community and his intentions perceived through the Gospel's narrative seem narrowly ethnically Jewish.[19] On the other hand, Paul's communities were mixed ethnically and his rhetorical concerns or 'target' audience by contrast seem narrowly focused on the Gentiles within these communities.[20]

Options for the Social Setting of Matthew and Paul

	Matthew's Gospel	*Paul's letters*
1	**Written to Jewish believers in Jesus within an ethnically restricted Jewish social context.**	Written to Gentile believers in Jesus within an ethnically restricted Gentile social context – that is, outside the synagogue.

16. Mark D. Nanos, *The Irony of Galatians: Paul's Letter in First-Century Context* (Minneapolis: Fortress Press, 2002), p. 7. See also idem, *The Mystery of Romans: The Jewish Context of Paul's Letter* (Minneapolis: Fortress Press, 1996) and Runesson, 'Inventing'.

17. A Jewish context for Matthew is most strongly argued today by Sim (David C. Sim, 'Matthew, Paul and the Origin and Nature of the Gentile Mission: The Great Commission in Matthew 28:16-20 as an Anti-Pauline Tradition', *HTS* 64.1 [2008], pp. 377–92; idem, *The Gospel of Matthew and Christian Judaism: The History and Social Setting of the Matthean Community* [SNTW; Edinburgh: T &T Clark, 1998]). See also A. Runesson, 'Rethinking the Parting(s) of the Ways', paper presented at the annual meeting of the Society of Biblical Literature, Philadelphia, 19 November 2005. A. Runesson, 'Inventing', pp. 59–92. For an alternative view see Paul Foster, *Community, Law and Mission in Matthew's Gospel* (WUNT 2, 177; Tübingen: Mohr Siebeck, 2004); Graham Stanton, *A Gospel for a New People: Studies in Matthew* (Louisville: Westminster John Knox Press, 1993).

18. Runesson, 'Inventing'; idem, 'Rethinking'.

19. For a very persuasive argument for Matthew's ethnically Jewish interests see Runesson, 'Rethinking'.

20. See Nanos, *Irony*; idem, *The Mystery of Romans: The Jewish Context of Paul's Letter* (Minneapolis: Fortress Press, 1996); Peter J. Tomson, *Paul and the Jewish Law: Halakha in the Letters of the Apostle to the Gentiles* (Minneapolis: Fortress Press, 1990), pp. 58–62.

Options for the Social Setting of Matthew and Paul

	Matthew's Gospel	*Paul's letters*
2	Written to Jewish believers in Jesus within an ethnically diverse yet Jewish social setting of the synagogue; this means that it was written to Jews but heard by both Jews and Gentiles.	**Written to Gentile believers in Jesus within an ethnically diverse yet Jewish social setting of the synagogue; this means that they were written to Gentiles but heard by both Gentiles and Jews.**
3	Written to a mixed audience of both Jewish and Gentile believers in Jesus within an ethnically diverse yet Jewish social setting like a synagogue.	Written to a mixed audience of both Gentile and Jewish believers in Jesus within an ethnically diverse yet Jewish social setting like a synagogue.
4	Written to a mixed audience of both Jewish and Gentile believers in Jesus within an ethnically restricted Gentile social context – that is, outside the synagogue.	Written to a mixed audience of both Gentile and Jewish believers in Jesus within an ethnically restricted Gentile social context – that is, outside the synagogue.

In sum, Paul's letters were written to Gentile believers in Jesus within an ethnically diverse yet Jewish social setting (option 2), while Matthew's Gospel was written to Jewish believers in Jesus within an ethnically restricted Jewish social context (option 1).

These distinctions of social context and audience are not inconsequential for interpreting the two authors. The immediately relevant implication from these observations is our appreciation of the *ethnic limitations* of elements of the theological and practical instruction found in them. Matthew and Paul rarely discussed a topic from an ethnically neutral or universal perspective. In other words, they seldom addressed issues that were not *directly* related to a specific ethnic group. This is not to say that they never discussed topics of universal scope, or they would not have appreciated the full ethnic ramifications of their theological positions. Instead, it is to admit that very often a discussion had a much narrower reach. Paul, for example, did not write a treatise on the 'Jewish question' or the 'Gentile question' or 'Torah' or 'salvation' or 'ethics' or 'eschatology' or 'the church' or 'Christ'. He wrote letters to deal with *historically contingent situations* pertaining primarily to *ethnically non-Jewish believers* in Jesus.

This is admittedly a more important observation for Paul since he is writing letters directly addressing problems in his churches. More will be said about genre in a moment, but Matthew had less freedom to directly address his contemporary situation since he was telling a story about Jesus.[21] Stating

21. See Eugene E. Lemcio, *The Past of Jesus in the Gospels* (Cambridge: Cambridge University Press, 1991).

it straightforwardly, we know very little, on the one hand, of Paul's mind on halakic issues for Jews who believed in Jesus. Or, on the other hand, what Matthew thought to be a Gentile's relationship to the Torah. These concerns were simply out of the purview of Paul's and Matthew's purposes for writing.

Inextricably linked to the question of social location and rhetorical purposes is the question of genre. What is the implication of differing genres in the interpretation of the relationship between Matthew and Paul? As R. Mohrlang pointed out, the issue of genre 'provides perhaps the single greatest difficulty for any attempt to compare the two writers' thought comprehensively'.[22] Two points can be made – both of which are restrictive factors. First, the question of Matthew's genre has been largely settled in the pioneering work of R. Burridge.[23] If the 'new consensus' on the question is correct that the Gospel of Matthew is a form of Graeco-Roman βίος, then it is much more difficult to use the Gospel as a window into the so-called Matthaean community.[24] This would be one of my only criticisms of Runesson's recent article, which I referred to approvingly earlier. Second, the epistolary genre of Paul's correspondence restricts the scope of application of his instructions in the ways we have articulated. In light of the constraints of genre, one must be extremely cautious when universalizing Paul's statements beyond their Gentile horizon. This is of course unless Paul has explicitly signalled to the reader the universality of the instruction as he does 1 Cor. 7.17, where he states of an instruction: 'This is my rule in all the churches.'[25]

The discussion in this section leaves us with two propositions. First, because Paul and Matthew share a general context within first-century Judaism – namely, apostolic Judaism – and because they both function within the same Jewish social location in the Graeco-Roman world a comparison is theoretically possible and the present study justified. Furthermore, if this assumption is correct, one should expect a greater degree of agreement than has been typically assumed.

Second, the first point notwithstanding, the differences between the specific expressions of both apostolic Judaism and synagogue life mean that extreme caution must be exercised when formulating conclusions about the relationship

22. Roger Mohrlang, *Matthew and Paul: A Comparison of Ethical Perspectives* (Cambridge: Cambridge University Press, 1984), p. 130.

23. Richard A. Burridge, 'About People, by People, for People: Gospel Genre and Audiences', *The Gospels for All Christians: Rethinking the Gospel Audiences* (Richard Bauckham [ed.]; Grand Rapids: Eerdmans, 1998), pp. 113–45; idem, *Four Gospels, One Jesus? A Symbolic Reading* (Grand Rapids: Eerdmans, 2nd edn, 2005); idem, *What Are the Gospels?: A Comparison with Graeco-Roman Biography* (Grand Rapids: Eerdmans, 2nd edn, 2004).

24. Burridge, 'About People'; idem, *Gospels*, pp. 269, 306.

25. For a hermeneutical reflection on this topic written for a lay audience see Joel Willitts, 'Weighing the Words of Paul: How Do We Understand His Instructions Today?', *Covenant Companion* 108.3 (2009), pp. 28–30.

between Matthew and Paul based on the topics discussed. *There is a high probability when Matthew and Paul address the same topic that they deal with it for different reasons and to accomplish different ends*. Thus, their different approaches to or perspectives on a given topic do *not* necessarily represent a contrary or adversarial posture towards the other.[26] While it is not inconceivable that Matthew was intended as a response to Paul, the claim's central nerve is bruised by its speculative foundation. Our position is largely in agreement with Mohrlang, who stated, 'we must . . . be careful not to assume that the different outlooks expressed in the two writers can be adequately accounted for in terms of the differences of their individual perspectives alone'.[27]

The previous sections have accomplished two things. First we have raised the awareness of the major weakness of recent attempts at comparing Matthew and Paul. What's more, we have suggested the way forward for constructive comparison. As for the weakness, simply put it is the failure to adequately acknowledge the place of one's overarching framework in the interpretation of the relationship. The debate is not in the details of exegesis because these are contestable almost at every point; rather the debate should be of larger hypotheses. 'Which hypothesis is superior?' should be the question. Furthermore, the comparison is most productively left at the level of description, resisting the temptation to provide overly speculative reconstructions of relationships and influences.

Second, we presented a recent – and for me a much more satisfying – alterative framework for an interpretative comparison of Matthew and Paul. The framework is based on a reconsideration of Paul's relationship to Judaism, a fresh understanding of the social location of Matthew and Paul and a more concrete appreciation of the audiences and contingent rhetorical concerns of the authors. From these considerations I generated two significant assumptions that will guide the comparison of Matthew and Paul in the next section.

c. *Case studies*

We now turn to two case studies exploring topics common to both Mathew and Paul in light of the foregoing discussion. The purpose of this section is to merely illustrate a descriptive approach within a post-New Perspective

26. Perhaps the most critical topic where this phenomenon is likely is the Torah. N. Dahl (Nils Alstrup Dahl, *The Crucified Messiah, and Other Essays* [Minneapolis: Augsburg, 1974], p. 41) notes that the same thing might be said of Paul's use of the term 'Christ', stating: 'One must be aware that the epistles may provide a somewhat one-sided view of the apostle's usage. To Jews he might have spoken in another manner . . . This means that we must also reckon with the probability that the messiahship of Jesus had for Paul himself a much greater significance than emerges directly from the usage of the name 'Christ' in his epistles'.

27. Mohrlang, *Matthew*, p. 71.

framework. I've chosen to consider two themes that Matthew and Paul have employed from a common Jewish tradition. The two topics were chosen because: (1) both authors unmistakably use the traditions considered and (2) the traditions become readily apparent when reading the texts within a post-New Perspective structure. This latter criterion is important because I have found that authors have not appreciated enough how their choice (or omission) of topics in comparisons like this are informed by the overarching framework that govern their interpretation. Thus, for this purpose I've chosen the themes of Davidic Messianism and judgement according to works. Neither topic often, if ever, appears in comparative discussions. More by accident than by direct intention, Paul's letter to the Romans receives the primary focus in the discussion. This was a welcomed happenstance given the entrenched scepticism of the authenticity of the Deutero-Pauline and Pastoral Epistles.[28]

Before moving on, a qualification seems necessary at this point. I am acutely aware of the brevity of the foregoing analysis. I do not attempt any detailed exegetical arguments in the following discussion. Since this study is a synthetic enterprise, I believe such detailed arguments are counterproductive and unnecessary. No argument I make will depend on my own detailed exegesis in this chapter. Appeals will be made to exegetical work already available. I intend here to use the work of others to describe Paul's and Matthew's employment of common Jewish traditions.

1. *Davidic Messianism*

We begin the comparison between Paul and Matthew with a discussion of their employment of the Davidic promise tradition founded on 2 Samuel 7.[29] The presence and significance of the tradition is unquestioned in Matthew's case, but many scholars today deny its importance for Paul, although admitting that it is present.

The opening line of Matthew's Gospel reveals the centrality of Davidic Messianism in its understanding of the Gospel of the Kingdom: 'An account of the genealogy of Jesus the Messiah, the son of David, the son of Abraham' (Mt. 1.1).[30] L. Novakovic, speaking of the genealogy as a whole, states:

28. A notable, albeit extreme, position is the recent book by M. Borg and J. D. Crossan (Marcus J. Borg and John Dominic Crossan, *The First Paul* [New York: HarperOne, 2009]), which suggests that there are three Pauls in the canon: (1) the 'Radical Paul' of the undisputed letters, (2) the 'Conservative Paul' of the three disputed letters and (3) the 'Reactionary Paul' of the three inauthentic letters.

29. The Davidic promise is further developed by the Chronicler, the Psalms and the Prophets. For discussion see Yuzuru Miura, *David in Luke-Acts: His Portrayal in the Light of Early Judaism* (WUNT 2.232; Tübingen: Mohr Siebeck, 2007); Lidija Novakovic, *Messiah, the Healer of the Sick: A Study of Jesus as the Son of David in the Gospel of Matthew* (WUNT, 2.170; Tübingen: Mohr Siebeck, 2003).

30. See Joel Willitts, *Matthew's Messianic Shepherd-King: In Search of the Lost Sheep of the House of Israel* (BNZW, 147; Berlin; New York: Walter de Gruyter, 2007), pp. 1–2.

> On the one hand it demonstrates that Jesus, as any other member of the genealogy, is David's descendant and therefore rightly called the son of David. On the other hand, its numeric structure indicates that Jesus is not only *a* son of David . . . but that he is *the* Son of David. As the last member of the series of three times fourteen generations Jesus is the goal of history – the long-awaited Davidic Messiah.[31]

This opening salvo is nicely matched with the conclusion of the First Gospel, which recently R. T. France has noted reverberates with a similar Davidic royal tone: 'And Jesus came and said to them, "All authority in heaven and on earth has been given to me"' (Mt. 28.18). As France has rightly noted, this passage reveals that Matthew's narrative culminates with the 'theme of kingship which was introduced by the Davidic royal genealogy . . . It is the universal kingship of the Son of Man which has emerged as a distinctive feature of Matthew's presentation of Jesus'.[32] While there is no need to develop the argument here, Matthew presents Jesus' person, mission and contribution in a way that exploits the Davidic significance.[33]

To what degree does the Davidic Messianism inform Paul's understanding of Jesus' significance and accomplishments? Ask most scholars today and Andrew Chester's recent comment will capture the widespread opinion: 'Paul takes for granted that Jesus is the true Jewish Messiah, but that is *not* at all the main focus of his writings and theology.'[34] The opinion reveals an ambivalent estimation of the extent of Paul's employment of Davidic Messianism. This ambivalence is especially visible in Nils Dahl's important work. He wrote:

> Paul apparently attached little importance to teaching pagans the meaning of the name 'Christ'. But his entire work as an apostle is conditioned by the messiahship of Jesus. Paul could become the apostle to the Gentiles because the crucified and risen Jesus was the Messiah of Israel; his work as the apostle to the Gentiles aimed, in turn, at the salvation of Israel (Rom. 11.11ff). In the end shall 'all Israel be saved'; for Jesus continues to be Israel's Messiah. For Paul the parousia is connected with Jerusalem: 'From Zion shall come the deliverer; he shall banish godlessness from Jacob' (Rom. 11.26; cf. also 2 Thess. 4.4,8). This non-spiritualized, Old Testament messianic expectation cannot be regarded as an isolated and inconsequential

31. Novakovic, *Messiah*, p. 42.

32. R. T. France, *The Gospel of Matthew* (NICNT; Grand Rapids: Eerdmans, 2007), p. 1113.

33. There is an element of Davidic Messianism in Matthew that has largely been overlooked by Matthaean scholars; yet it seems to this writer that the territorial implications of Matthew's use of the Davidic promise tradition is significant. Matthew's unique territorial interests (e.g. Mt. 4.15; 5.5; and 15.21) and his mission to the 'lost sheep of the house of Israel' may be suggestive of an abiding interest in the territorial restoration of Israel. For a discussion of this see chs 6–8 of Willitts, *Shepherd-King*.

34. Andrew Chester, 'The Christ of Paul', in *Redemption and Resistance: The Messianic Hopes of Jews and Christians in Antiquity* (Markus N. A. Bockmuehl and James Carleton Paget [eds]; London; New York: T&T Clark, 2007), pp. 109–21, p. 110, emphasis added.

> rudiment in the Son of God and kyrios Christology. On the contrary, it is confirmed here that Jesus' messiahship actually had a *basic significance for the total structure of Paul's Christology.*[35]

Thus, while generally agreeing that Messianism provided the basic structure of Paul's theological outlook, scholars deny Jesus' Davidic ancestry played any role in Paul's theology.[36] What makes such an apparent contradictory position possible is the combination of significant factors: (1) Paul's pervasive use of the term Χριστός, which leaves the impression that the term has no titular force, (2) the rare mention of Jesus' ancestry[37] and (3) the complete lack of attempt by Paul to prove that Jesus was the Messiah, as Matthew had, by appeal to Davidic passages from the Jewish Scriptures.

Yet, these points notwithstanding, scholars must explain the key position of Paul's references to the Davidic ancestry of Jesus in his letter to the Romans. It is these references that have led some scholars recently to question the prevailing assumption about the place of Davidic promise tradition in Paul's theology.[38]

Paul's opening to Romans (1.1-6) affords him the opportunity to explain the gospel he proclaims in the briefest of terms. It is in the delineation of the 'gospel of God' (1.1) that Paul refers to Jesus' Davidic ancestry. Jesus' identity as the son of David is a central element of the gospel Paul proclaims and fundamental to his apostolic commission to the Gentiles. In declaring that the gospel of God is about God's Son, Paul defines the term with three assertions. First, Paul states God's Son means a descendant of David (ἐκ σπέρματος Δαυὶδ κατὰ σάρκα) according to the Scriptures (1.3). Second, Paul states the Davidic son has been 'installed' (ὁρισθέντος) Son of God, ruler of the world, on the basis of the resurrection (1.4). Third, Paul states that the enthroned Messiah, then, is the authority behind his apostleship to the nations in order to bring about

35. Dahl, *Messiah*, pp. 46–7, emphasis added.

36. See, for example, Chester, 'Christ'; Martin Hengel, *Between Jesus and Paul: Studies in the Earliest History of Christianity* (Philadelphia: Fortress Press, 1983); idem, *Studies in Early Christology* (Edinburgh: T&T Clark, 1995), pp. 213–14; Werner R. Kramer, *Christ, Lord, Son of God* (Studies in Biblical Theology, 50; London: SCM. Press, 1966); George MacRae, 'Messiah and Gospel', in *Judaisms and Their Messiahs at the Turn of the Christian Era* (Jacob Neusner, *et al.* [eds]; Cambridge; New York: Cambridge University Press, 1987), pp. 169–85.

37. Robert Jewett, *Romans: A Commentary* (Hermeneia; Minneapolis: Fortress Press, 2007), pp. 98, n. 21.

38. See, most notably, R. B. Hays and N. T. Wright: Richard B. Hays, *The Conversion of the Imagination: Paul as Interpreter of Israel's Scripture* (Grand Rapids: Eerdmans, 2005), pp. 101–18; N. T. Wright, *The Climax of the Covenant: Christ and the Law in Pauline Theology* (Minneapolis: Fortress Press, 1991), pp. 41–55; idem, 'The Letter to the Romans', *NIB* (Leander Keck [ed.];10; Nashville: Abingdon Press, 2002), pp. 395–770; idem, *The Resurrection of the Son of God* (Christian Origins and the Question of God, 3; Minneapolis: Fortress Press, 2003), pp. 242, 554.

the 'obedience of faith' among them (1.5-6). Jesus' sonship, then, involves his Davidic ancestry, his heavenly enthronement and his authority to commission Paul's apostolic work among the Gentiles. All three points, when considered against the backdrop of Davidic promise tradition, reveal the significance of Davidic Messianism for Paul's theology and mission.

The significance is paralleled at the end of the letter (Rom. 15.8-12), where Paul quotes LXX Isa. 11.10 referring to the 'root of Jesse' (ἡ ῥίζα τοῦ Ἰεσσαί), the arrival of the messianic Son of David,[39] at the end of a catena of five Scripture passages from all three parts of the Hebrew Bible.[40] As J. Wagner and others have pointed out, the verbal links tie this passage to the opening of Paul's theological argument of ch. 1, especially on the point of the Messiah's Davidic ancestry.[41] In this text Paul explained the unique implications of Jesus' Davidic messiahship for Jew and Gentile respectively.[42] In the case of the former, the coming of the Messiah represented God's faithfulness to his promises to the patriarchs. I see no reason to limit this stated fulfilment only to the element of blessing of the nations as most do. Rather, given the argument of Romans 9–11, it seems more suitable to take this as a comprehensive statement about Israel's restoration including land, descendants and worldly position.[43] In the case of the last of these, Jesus' messiahship revealed God's mercy to the Gentiles. God's mercy results in the praise of God by all the nations of the earth, thereby reversing the idolatrous nature of humanity (cf. 1.21).[44] This duality of significance for the messiahship of Jesus presents the essence of Paul's gospel.

A good many interpreters will no doubt have wished for a much more nuanced argument with a greater amount of detail in the footnotes. This fault of course I readily admit. It seems evident enough, however, that the pre-eminent position of the Davidic Messianism in Paul's most theologically comprehensive letter cannot easily be pushed to the side and certainly not by appealing to a hypothetically reconstructed redaction of a pre-Pauline tradition in Rom. 1.3-4.[45] Thus, while Paul's rhetorical purposes are likely the reason Davidic Messianism is not as explicit in this letter as in Matthew's Gospel, it is no less the basic presumption of his theology, as Dahl noted:

39. C. E. B. Cranfield, *Romans 9-16* (J. A. Emerton, *et al.* [eds]; ICC, 2; Edinburgh: T&T Clark, 1979), p. 747.

40. See Wright's comment (Wright, 'Romans', pp. 745, 748): the 'letter comes full circle'; see also Jewett, *Romans*, p. 891; J. Ross Wagner, 'The Christ, Servant of Jew and Gentile: A Fresh Approach to Romans 15:8-9', *JBL* 116. 3 (1997), pp. 473–85 (473); Wright, *The Climax of the Covenant*, p. 235.

41. J. Ross Wagner, *Heralds of the Good News: Isaiah and Paul 'In Concert' in the Letter to the Romans* (NovTSup, 101; Leiden: Brill, 2002), p. 319; Wagner, 'Christ', p. 473.

42. See Jewett, *Romans*, p. 892; Wright, 'Romans', p. 747, but especially Wagner, 'Christ', p. 481, with whose structural understanding of Rom. 15.8-9 I'm in agreement.

43. See J. Wagner for a somewhat similar perspective on Israel: Wagner, *Heralds*, pp. 317–27.

44. James D. G. Dunn, *Romans 9-16* (David A. Hubbard, *et al.* [eds]; WBC, 38b; Dallas: Word, 1988), p. 845; Jewett, *Romans*, p. 893.

45. For such an attempt see Jewett, *Romans*, pp. 103–8.

> Of Christology, eschatology, ecclesiology, soteriology including justification and the 'with Christ' and 'in Christ' phrases, Jesus' messiahship is the latent presupposition for all of this.[46]

In concluding the discussion one potential parallel between Paul and Matthew should be highlighted. Both seem to have employed LXX Isa. 11.10 in their descriptions of the universalistic vocation of Jesus. Paul quotes the text as the final passage in his catena of citations in Rom. 15.9-12, while Matthew appears to conflate it with Isa. 42.1-4 in Mt. 12.18-21.[47] One possible implication of this observation is that both writers see the Davidic Messianism as the basis of a universal dimension to Jesus' work.

Textual Comparison[48]

LXX Isaiah 42.4	*LXX Isaiah 11.10*	*Matthew 12.21*	*Romans 15.12*
καὶ ἐπὶ τῷ ὀ νόματι αὐτοῦ ἔθνη ἐλπιοῦσιν and nations will hope in his name	καὶ ἔσται ἐν τῇ ἡμέρᾳ ἐκείνῃ ἡ ῥίζα τοῦ Ιεσσαι καὶ ὁ ἀνιστάμενος ἄρχειν ἐθνῶν ἐπ᾽ αὐτῷ ἔθνη ἐλπιοῦσιν καὶ ἔσται ἡ ἀ νάπαυσις αὐτοῦ τιμή And there shall be on that day the root of Jesse, even the one who stands up to rule nations; nations shall hope in him, and his rest shall be honor.	καὶ τῷ ὀνόματι αὐτοῦ ἔθνη ἐλπιοῦσιν And in his name the Gentiles will hope	καὶ πάλιν Ἠσαΐας λέγει· ἔσται ἡ ῥίζα τοῦ Ἰεσσαὶ καὶ ὁ ἀνιστάμενος ἄρχειν ἐθνῶν, ἐπ᾽ αὐτῷ ἔθνη ἐλπιοῦσιν The root of Jesse shall come, the one who rises to rule the Gentiles; in him the Gentiles shall hope.

In the end, it is reasonable to conclude that Davidic Messianism was basic to both Matthew and Paul. While the point will be hotly contested, I think both (although Matthew more apparently than Paul) were in general continuity with their first-century contemporaries who employed a Davidic Messianism. I think there are significant and underappreciated parallels between Matthew (and to a

46. Dahl, *Messiah*, p. 45. I would only add the word 'Davidic' before 'messiahship'.

47. For the suggestion see Frank J. Matera, 'The Plot of Matthew's Gospel', *CBQ* 49 (1987), pp. 233–53 (250). R. Beaton (Richard Beaton, *Isaiah's Christ in Matthew's Gospel* [SNTSMS, 123; Cambridge: Cambridge University Press, 2002], p. 138) finds the suggestion possible, but is more cautious, noting that the quotation can be explained solely from the context of Isaiah 42. In addition, Wagner (Wagner, *Heralds*, pp. 319, n. 46) notes the similarities between Isa. 42.4 and 11.10.

48. According to Nestle-Aland 27th, the only other NT allusions to Isa. 11.10 are Rev. 5.5; 22.16, with the title ἡ ῥίζα καὶ τὸ γένος Δαυίδ.

much lesser degree Paul) and a text like *Psalms of Solomon* 17.[49] The difference between Matthew and Paul and their use of Davidic Messianism is most likely the result of genre and audience constraints.

Given our assumption that Paul wrote specifically to Gentiles within the synagogue communities of the Diaspora, one should expect the universal element of the David promise tradition emphasized to the exclusion of the more nationalistic-territorial elements. This cannot be taken to mean, however, that Paul now rejected these connotations of Davidic Messianism or thought the coming of Jesus rendered these Jewish nationalistic elements obsolete. Paul's letters are silent. Since Paul did not write a Gospel as an apology for the identity of Jesus to a Jewish audience, it is impossible to know if he would have written something altogether different than Matthew did. My suspicion is that he would have used Davidic Messianism as Matthew did, if he had written to the same audience for the same reason using the same genre.

2. *Judgement according to works*

We now turn to the question of the use of the Jewish tradition of eschatological judgement according to works. The view that God will judge humanity according to their works is a deeply rooted Jewish viewpoint based on the Scriptures. There are numerous places across the three parts of the Bible where the Scriptures teach implicitly or explicitly that God's judgement will be according to works.[50] For example, Ps. 61.13 and Prov. 24.12 say something very similar:[51]

Textual Comparison[52]

Psalm 61.13 [LXX]	*Proverbs 24.12 [LXX]*
ὅτι τὸ κράτος τοῦ θεοῦ καὶ σοί κύριε τὸ ἔλεος ὅτι σὺ ἀποδώσεις ἑκάστῳ κατὰ τὰ ἔργα αὐτοῦ that might is God's, and to you, O Lord, belongs mercy, because you will repay to each according to his works	ἐὰν δὲ εἴπῃς οὐκ οἶδα τοῦτον γίνωσκε ὅτι κύριος καρδίας πάντων γινώσκει καὶ ὁ πλάσας πνοὴν πᾶσιν αὐτὸς οἶδεν πάντα ὃς ἀποδίδωσιν ἑκάστῳ κατὰ τὰ ἔργα αὐτοῦ If you say: 'I do not know this person', be aware that the Lord is familiar with the heart of everyone, and he who formed breath for all, he knows everything, he who will render to each according to his deeds

49. See Novakovic, *Messiah*, pp. 12–76; Willitts, *Shepherd-King*; also Joel Willitts, 'Matthew and Psalms of Solomon's Messianism: A Comparative Study in First-Century Messianology', *BBR* (forthcoming 2012).

50. See summary in Kent L. Yinger, *Paul, Judaism, and Judgment according to Deeds* (SNTSMS, 105; Cambridge: Cambridge University Press, 1999), pp. 19–63: 'This widespread use of the motif along with its flexible application to a broad range of rhetorical situations also suggests that divine recompense according to deeds has already become in the OT an important theological axiom for Judaism' (p. 60).

51. See also Ps. 27.4 [LXX].

52. See similarly Sir. 35.22: ἕως ἀνταποδῷ ἀνθρώπῳ κατὰ τὰς πράξεις αὐτοῦ καὶ τὰ ἔργα τῶν ἀνθρώπων κατὰ τὰ ἐνθυμήματα αὐτῶν.

In addition, Simon Gathercole, in critiquing both traditional [Lutheran] and New Perspective views on Jewish soteriology, has convincingly shown that the Judaism of Matthew and Paul continued this perspective, holding that eschatological vindication was based on *both* election and obedience. While this resembles K. Yinger's earlier argument,[53] Gathercole thinks Yinger and other New Perspective scholars have not properly represented the perspective from the texts of the Second Temple period, ignoring or underappreciating the *function* the texts attribute to works in the final judgement. Gathercole summarizes the evidence thus:

> While there is considerable emphasis on gracious election in Jewish literature, this was by no means incompatible with obedience also being a basis for vindication at the eschaton . . . Texts from both Palestine (e.g., *Psalms of Solomon*, Pseudo-Philo, the Qumran literature) and the diaspora (Wisdom of Solomon, *Testament of Job, Apocalypse of Zephaniah*) witness to a theology of the final vindication of God's people on the basis of their obedience.[54]

According to Gathercole, works do not function in these texts simply as 'observable manifestations of covenant loyalty' as Yinger thinks; rather, they are part of the very *basis* of the divine verdict.[55] Gathercole takes the view that a person is saved by both elective grace and good works.

Turning to Matthew and Paul, while it would be less of a surprise that Matthew alone among the Synoptics employed the Jewish tradition of judgement according to works with little revision, such a viewpoint would appear to be completely at odds with Paul's gospel of *sola fide*. However, while other New Testament passages echo this Jewish proverb,[56] only Matthew and Paul appear to cite the final clause of the passages listed earlier, with minor alterations.[57]

53. Yinger, *Paul.*

54. Simon J. Gathercole, *Where is Boasting?: Early Jewish Soteriology and Paul's Response in Romans 1-5* (Grand Rapids: Eerdmans, 2002), pp. 263–64.

55. Yinger, *Paul*, p. 285. Yinger's wording in places can be misleading, as he states in one place 'Obedience cannot earn life or salvation, but it remains nevertheless the *evidentiary basis* or norm for the final verdict' (p. 202, emphasis added).

56. See Rom. 14.12; 1 Cor. 3.10-15; 2 Cor. 5.10; 11.15; 2 Tim. 4.14; 1 Pet. 1.17; Rev. 20.12; 22.12).

57. R. Gundry (Robert H. Gundry, *Matthew: A Commentary on His Handbook for a Mixed Church under Persecution* [Grand Rapids: Eerdmans, 2nd edn, 1994], p. 341) refers to this as an 'allusive quotation'. There is disagreement among commentators as to whether Matthew can be said to be quoting Ps. 63.13/ Prov. 24.12. Among those who think it is a quotation is Joachim Gnilka, *Das Matthäusevangelium: II. Teil* (HTKNT; Freiburg: Herder, 1992), pp. 88–9.

I think Luz's characterization of the Matthaean citation as 'reminiscent' is extremely understated; cf. Ulrich Luz, *Matthew 8-20* (trans. James E. Crouch; Hermeneia; Minneapolis: Fortress, 2001), pp. 385, n. 44; see also W. D. Davies and Dale C. Allison, *The Gospel According to Saint Matthew* (ICC, 2; Edinburgh: T&T Clark, 1991), p. 676.

By contrast, interestingly, there is little doubt among commentators of Romans 2 that Paul was

Textual Comparison

Matthew 16.24-27	*Romans 2.6-11*
Then Jesus told his disciples, "If any want to become my followers, let them deny themselves and take up their cross and follow me. For those who want to save their life will lose it, and those who lose their life for my sake will find it. For what will it profit them if they gain the whole world but forfeit their life? Or what will they give in return for their life? For the Son of Man is to come with his angels in the glory of his Father, and then ***he will repay everyone for what has been done***" (ἀποδώσει ἑκάστῳ κατὰ τὴν πρᾶξιν αὐτοῦ).	For ***he will repay according to each one's deeds*** (ὃς ἀποδώσει ἑκάστῳ κατὰ τὰ ἔργα αὐτοῦ): to those who by patiently doing good seek for glory and honour and immortality, he will give eternal life; while for those who are self-seeking and who obey not the truth but wickedness, there will be wrath and fury. There will be anguish and distress for everyone who does evil, the Jew first and also the Greek, but glory and honour and peace for everyone who does good, the Jew first and also the Greek. For God shows no partiality.

Gathercole is correct to stress that, given the fact that Matthew's quotation 'follows straight on from Jesus' description of those wishing to save their lives losing them', the 'recompense *cannot* be for individual deeds *within* the future kingdom', i.e. Christian rewards.[58] Rather, in view of the parallel in Mt. 25.31-46, Matthew sees deeds (in this case deeds of hospitality) as a criterion for eschatological judgement (25.46).[59] Mohrlang similarly characterizes Matthew's ethic as 'teleological', by which he means 'everything is done with a view to its consequences (cf. 5.44f, 46; 6.1-6, 16-18), especially the eschatological consequences; for God judges people on the basis of how they live'.[60] Mohrlang reasons that Matthew believed 'the threat of eschatological judgment [was] the strongest and most effective means that the evangelist [knew] of reinforcing his stringent demands for a life of absolute obedience'.[61]

In discussing Matthew's view of the place of works in eschatological

directly quoting. R. B. Hays (Richard B. Hays, *Echoes of Scripture in the Letters of Paul* [New Haven: Yale University Press, 1989], p. 42) refers to it as a 'virtual quotation'; see James D. G. Dunn, *Romans 1-8* (David A. Hubbard, *et al.* [eds]; WBC, 38a; Dallas: Word, 1988), p. 85; Otto Michel, *Der Brief an die Römer übersetzt und erklärt* (Göttingen: Vandenhoeck & Ruprecht, 1963), p. 75; Thomas R. Schreiner, *Romans* (BECNT 6; Grand Rapids: Baker, 1998), p. 112; Peter Stuhlmacher, *Paul's Letter to the Romans: A Commentary* (trans. Scott J. Hafemann; Louisville: Westminster John Knox Press, 1994), p. 41. Dissenters include Roman Heiligenthal, *Werke als Zeichen: Untersuchungen zur Bedeutung der menschlichen Taten im Fruhjudentum, Neuen Testament und Fruchristentum* (WUNT, 2.9; Tübingen: Mohr Siebeck, 1983), p. 174; Douglas J. Moo, *The Epistle to the Romans* (NICNT; Grand Rapids: Eerdmans, 1996), p. 136. Even if one is not convinced that Matthew and Paul are in fact quoting, this likely means, as Yinger has pointed out, that the tradition is so proverbial that direct quotation is unnecessary.

58. Gathercole, *Boasting*, p. 113, emphasis added.

59. See France, *Matthew*, p. 959; Benno Przybylski, *Righteousness in Matthew and his World of Thought* (R. McL. Wilson [ed.]; SNTSMS, 41; Cambridge: Cambridge University Press, 1980), p. 111.

60. Mohrlang, *Matthew*, p. 54.

61. Ibid., p. 57.

judgement one has to also factor into the equation his equally clear stress on the role of election and grace, as the parable of the Labourers in Mt. 20.1-6 illustrates. However, even here the point of the parable does not escape the presumption of work. Those who are the benefactors of the unequal pay are still characterized as working in the vineyard even if only briefly (20.7). Matthew reveals, then, that God's gracious election and a person's obedience together form the basis for vindication at the eschaton. Matthew is in direct continuity with the Jewish tradition, although the obedience now required is to the teaching of Jesus (Mt. 28.19-20), which, for Matthew, there is every reason to think, included the Torah (perhaps the messianic Torah) in view of Mt. 5.17-19.

E. P. Sanders, in his groundbreaking work *Paul and Palestinian Judaism*, described Romans 2 as 'aberrant' and sought to mitigate the apparent contradiction to Paul's soteriology by arguing that Paul makes a distinction between being saved 'by God's grace' and being judged 'according to deeds'.[62] Sanders thinks the righteousness to which Paul is referring here in Romans 2 'has to do with whether or not one is punished on the day of judgment'.[63] He concludes: 'Once we see that here the righteousness terminology refers to the question of punishment, and not to whether or not one is saved, the difficulty vanishes'; and, typical of Sanders, he writes that: 'good deeds are the *condition* of remaining "in", but they do not *earn* salvation'.[64]

Mohrlang's important work on Paul and Matthew was completed in the same year Jimmy Dunn proclaimed a New Perspective on Paul, nearly three decades ago.[65] Mohrlang's appreciation of the New Perspective is felt here as he depended squarely on Sanders's argument. Mohrlang reveals the shift that was taking place in Pauline scholarship by attempting to show that Paul *did* have a concept of future judgement by works.

In Mohrlang's view, however, the end-time judgement is *not* salvific. One's salvation is secured by the gracious work of God in Jesus Christ. The future judgement in Paul's soteriology is confirmatory in its function. Mohrlang asserted that works for Paul, while not being the *basis* of justification, could nevertheless determine a person's eschatological destiny. Paul believed that certain works could *disqualify* you from salvation, according to Mohrlang. Works then function so that, having gotten *in* by grace – notice Sanders's

62. E. P. Sanders, *Paul and Palestinian Judaism: A Comparison of Patterns of Religion* (Philadelphia: Fortress Press, 1977), p. 516.

63. Ibid.

64. Ibid., p. 517, emphasis his.

65. James D. G. Dunn, 'The New Perpsective on Paul', *BJRL* 65.2 (1983), pp. 95–122.

influence here – one stays in. As Mohrlang puts it, 'it is one of the conditions of remaining within that grace':[66] 'salvation by grace and judgment by works'.[67]

Eschatologically speaking, Mohrlang believes Paul has two aspects to his view of divine judgement on believers. The first is drawn from the repeated instances where Paul warns of ultimate condemnation, which some Christians are in danger of falling into. There are certain kinds of behaviour that can rob someone of their salvation. Mohrlang puts it this way: 'though moral living in itself does not earn salvation, the lack of moral living may exclude one from it'.[68] On the other hand, certain references in Paul refer rather to *rewards or loss of rewards* for believers. The warning of judgement in these cases is *not* put in terms of a loss of salvation *but* of a loss of reward. Mohrlang summarizes his two points:

> It is apparent that the apostle thinks of judgment on an eschatological level in two quite different senses: (1) as threat of ultimate condemnation, for unbelievers and those who either theologically or morally fall away from their secure position in God's grace in Christ . . . and (2) as the expectation of reward or loss of reward in the new age for those who remain securely within that grace.[69]

The strength of Mohrlang's argument is the acknowledgement in Paul of works as a criterion in the eschatological judgement. Nevertheless, its weaknesses are more clearly evident now than they were in 1983 at the rise of the New Perspective. Two points need to be levelled against Mohrlang's view. First, insofar as Mohrlang's theory is dependent on Sanders, Gathercole's critique mentioned earlier – although he is by no means alone[70] – against the New Perspective's tendency to either ignore, underplay or redefine the function of works at the final judgement applies.[71]

Second, Mohrlang provides *no* discussion of Romans 2, which is the one place where Paul most expressly presents his view of the function of works at the final judgement. Mohrlang is another example of K. Snodgrass's observation that 'it is not uncommon to find explanations of these verses completely omitted'.[72] Thus, it appears that Mohrlang's understanding of the theme of

66. Mohrlang, *Matthew*, p. 63.

67. Ibid., p. 60. See likewise Yinger, *Paul*, p. 202.

68. Mohrlang, *Matthew*, p. 61.

69. Ibid., pp. 62–3. See similarly more recently Yinger, *Paul*. Yinger states, 'Both entry into and continued (and final) enjoyment of salvation find their cause in God's grace and mercy; the condition for the maintenance and final enjoyment of the same human obedience' (p. 4).

70. See, for example, Klyne R. Snodgrass, 'Justification by Grace – to the Doers: An Analysis of the Place of Romans 2 in the Theology of Paul', *NTS* 32 (1986), pp. 72–93.

71. Yinger, *Paul*.

72. Snodgrass, 'Justification', p. 73.

judgement according to works in Paul lacks a careful assessment and approbation of teaching on Romans 2. We might be right to assume that Mohrlang would agree with Sanders's interpretation of Romans 2, which, by taking its cues from the future tense of the verb δικαιωθήσονται in 2.13, drew a distinction between two different kinds of righteousness: one that is based on faith, which is soteriological, and one based on deeds, which is retributive.[73]

Romans 2.6-11 is the crux of the issue although in no way is it an isolated teaching in the Pauline corpus.[74] Unless one attempts to explain the passage away,[75] the text asserts three ideas: (1) God judges impartially, (2) God's judgement is according to works and (3) Jew and Gentile will receive the same standard of judgement. That Paul saw this perspective of eschatological judgement as not in tension with his strong statements concerning justification apart from the Torah in Rom. 3.21-31 is seen in Rom. 2.16, where Paul gives the manner, agency and basis of the judgement: 'on the day when, according to my gospel, God, through Jesus Christ, will judge the secret thoughts of all'. The judgement according to works is 'according to my gospel'. Snodgrass, then, is correct:

> The belief in judgment according to works is not an inferior theology to be set aside. It is the assumption of Paul elsewhere and indeed it is the assumption of the entire Biblical tradition. To argue that Paul did not accept the statements in 2:6-16 not only sets him at odds with Judaism, the Old Testament, Jesus and the rest of Christianity, and indeed himself, but it makes difficult any thought of seeing Romans in the light of his intended trip to Jerusalem. Paul's defence of his mission would not have had the slightest chance with Jews or Jewish Christians had he rejected this cardinal belief of the Biblical and Jewish tradition.[76]

From this very brief sketch of Matthew and Paul one can conclude the following: (1) both Matthew and Paul employed the Jewish tradition of judgement according to works and (2) both reveal a strong continuity with the Jewish tradition. The primary discontinuity with their Jewish tradition relates to the 'Christocentric nature' (in Gathercole's words) of the obedience, although we will not address this here.[77] Thus, in the words of Zetterholm, Matthew and

73. Sanders, *Paul*, p. 518.

74. See especially Rom. 14.10-12; 1 Cor. 3.13-15; 2 Cor. 5.10; 9.6; 11.15; Gal 6.7-8; and Col. 3.23-25; Eph. 6.8; 1 Tim. 5.24-25; 2 Tim. 4.14. See also Yinger, *Paul*, pp. 178, n. 109.

75. See the most recent attempt by D. Campbell (Douglas Campbell, *The Deliverance of God: An Apocalyptic Rereading of Justification in Paul* [Grand Rapids: Eerdmans, 2009], p. 529) to argue that the perspective contained in Rom. 1.18–3.20 is 'a reproduction of the [false] Teacher's rhetoric and not Paul's', such that 'very little within this extended demonstration now represents the thinking of Paul directly'.

76. Snodgrass, 'Justification' (79).

77. See Gathercole, *Boasting*, pp. 131–4. Consult also Michael Bird, *The Saving Righteousness of God: Studies on Paul, Justification and the New Perspective* (Milton Keynes: Paternoster, 2006),

Paul show 'continuity with Jewish tradition in regarding obedience to be a vital criterion for the judgment, and discontinuity with regard to the character of obedience'.[78]

I conclude with Gathercole's words about the 'common ground' between the traditions of early Christianity and ancient Judaism: 'It is not that both consist in initial grace that fully accomplishes salvation, followed by works which are evidence of that; rather, both share an elective grace and also assign a determinative role to works at the final judgment.'[79] Matthew and Paul, then, seem to line up perfectly on this point, although their appeal to it might be made in different ways given their unique rhetorical purposes.

d. *The relationship between Matthew and Paul*

Finally we come to the question of the relationship between Matthew and Paul. The answer will be dependent on the overarching framework within which one reads the data as we have contended. In addition, discussions of their relationship have also largely depended on historical reconstructions of the respective writings.

In the main, those that have recently discussed the relationship between Matthew and Paul (e.g. Sim and Harrington) agree that Paul's undisputed letters were composed in the 50s of the first century CE from mostly Ephesus and Corinth. What's more, they place a significant amount of weight on Paul's time in Syrian Antioch and particularly focus on the Antioch Incident recorded in Gal. 2.11-14. There is also agreement that Matthew was written in the late 80s or early 90s CE, also in Syrian Antioch.[80] Thus, the Antiochean connection between Paul and Matthew has proved crucial and is used as a vital warrant for relating Matthew and Paul. Furthermore, the Antioch Incident becomes paradigmatic of the relationship between the Jewish Christianity of Matthew and the Gentile Christianity of Paul.[81]

There are a number of points to dispute in this historical reconstruction, although more so in this case with Matthew than with Paul. Two points in particular undermine the use of both the Antiochean provenance and Antioch Incident in ascertaining the relationship between Paul and Matthew. They will be redressed briefly here. First, with respect to Matthew, the assumption of an Antiochean provenance has been critically reassessed recently. This reconsideration has seriously undermined the former Antiochean consensus.

pp. 155–78. Bird writes: 'Works as Christologically conceived, pneumatically empowered, and divinely endowed are necessary for salvation' (p. 178).

78. Zetterholm, *Paul*, p. 181; cf. also Gathercole, *Boasting*, p. 133.

79. Gathercole, *Boasting*, p. 135.

80. Harrington, 'Matthew and Paul', pp. 12–13.

81. See especially Sim, *Gospel of Matthew*.

Many now believe that it is more likely that Matthew's Gospel was composed in the Land of Israel and more particularly in Galilee. The obvious impact of Paul's legacy, which would be palpable in an antiochean context, on Matthew is adumbrated. If Matthew was written instead in Galilee, Paul's direct influence could be minimal.

The Antioch Incident is also problematic as a foundation for a discussion of the relationship between Matthew and Paul. Recent discussions of the passage in Galatians have raised questions about (1) the nature of the conflict between Peter and Paul, (2) the source of the conflict, and (3) the players involved. It now seems more likely that the conflict was not at all between the Jewish-Christian church based in Jerusalem and the frontiers of the Gentile mission, i.e. an intra-Christian one. Instead the incident revealed an *inter-Jewish* conflict among Jewish groups about the status and privilege of Gentile God-fearers versus Jewish proselytes.[82] If the Incident recorded in Galatians 2 is not intra-Christian, it cannot be used to interpret relationships between Jewish Christians and Gentile Christians in early Christianity.

So to discuss the relationship between Paul and Matthew one will need both (1) an interpretative framework and (2) a historically reconstructed date and provenance for the documents. This squares with what I have discussed in the opening sections of this essay. In light of these considerations and their obvious import I have advocated a descriptive methodology, which I illustrated with the topics of Davidic Messianism and judgement according to works. Having addressed two test cases within the particular framework I adopted – namely, a post-New Perspective framework – what might we suggest about the relationship between Paul and Matthew?

Three positions have been suggested for the First Gospel's relationship to the Pauline corpus: Matthew is (1) anti-Pauline,[83] (2) un-Pauline[84] or (3) pro-Pauline.[85] While I think we can reject the anti-Pauline stance for Matthew,[86] the other two are more difficult to assess. The difficulty is related to how one defines the prefixes 'un-' and 'pro-'. On the one hand, for the former, if 'un-' is meant to imply that Matthew and Paul do not have a common theological

82. For example, see Nanos, *Irony*; Mark D. Nanos, 'What was at Stake in Peter's "Eating with Gentiles" at Antioch', in *The Galatians Debate: Contemporary Issues in Rhetorical and Historical Interpretation* (Mark D. Nanos [ed.]; Peabody, MA: Hendrickson 2002), pp. 282–318. For other alternative readings of the Antioch Incident see Markus Bockmuehl, *Jewish Law in Gentile Churches: Halakhah and the Beginning of Christian Public Ethics* (Grand Rapids: Baker, 2003), pp. 49–83; Philip F. Esler, *Galatians* (John Court [ed.]; NTR; New York: Routledge, 1998); Tomson, *Paul*, pp. 222–30.

83. David C. Sim, 'Matthew's Anti-Paulinism: A Neglected Feature of Matthean Studies', *HTS* 58.2 (2002), pp. 767–83.

84. Stanton, *A Gospel*, p. 314.

85. W. D. Davies, *The Setting of the Sermon on the Mount* (Cambridge: Cambridge University Press, 1964), pp. 325–32.

86. See Willitts, 'Matthew and Paul'.

foundation, that they represented 'two different, parallel traditions' of early Christianity, then I think this view should also be rejected. Alternatively, if by 'un-' one means Paul's rhetorical concerns are not Matthew's and that Matthew seems wholly disinterested in Paul then the prefix seems appropriate. On the other hand, for the prefix 'pro-', if by this one means that Matthew is a Pauline advocate explicitly supporting Paul then this too must be rejected. However, if the 'pro-' has a more restricted sense, referring to a shared theological outlook, then I think this term is also appropriate.

In sum, I think one can justifiably conclude that Matthew was either pro-Pauline in the Davies sense or un-Pauline in the Stanton sense.

4

Paul and Matthew: Two Strands of the Early Jesus Movement with Little Sign of Connection

Paul Foster

I. *Introduction*

At one level the question concerning how the 'Christianity' of the Gospel of Matthew relates to that of Paul and the Pauline writings is both anachronistic and a *non sequitur*. The enquiry is anachronistic because the term 'Christianity' is not used by either Paul or Matthew, and a non sequitur because the temporal distance between the death of Paul and the composition of the First Gospel means there is no direct relationship between these two advocates of faith in Jesus. Even in a less direct way, the writing of the later figure – the Gospel of Matthew – presents no obvious citation of the Pauline epistles. Nor is there any unambiguous use of concepts drawn from Paul's thought, either in the form of positive appropriation or negative critique of Paul himself, or the ideas that were circulating in his name. This differs from certain other later New Testament writings. For instance, Acts explicitly presents a type of 'life of Paul'; the author of one of the Petrine epistles refers to both 'our beloved brother Paul' and his writings (2 Pet. 3.15); and in a more veiled manner the author of the epistle of James critiques a 'faith without works' theology, which probably is a reaction against ideas stemming from Paulinist circles, if not directly from Paul. By contrast, the Gospel of Matthew offers nowhere such levels of transparency that would allow one to construe its outlook as being influenced by Paul's teaching. Perhaps the obvious needs to be restated: Matthew's Gospel is primarily written to tell the story of Jesus in order to commend faith in that person as God's Messiah.[1] It does not reveal its support for or opposition to Pauline perspectives in any unambiguous way.

1. Speaking of the canonical Gospels generally, in their introduction describing the purpose of the Gospel of Matthew, Davies and Allison comment that the Gospel writers 'intend to point to the manifold

What then is the purpose of this discussion? It needs to be stated that because Matthew's agenda was not to write a polemical tractate in relation to Paul, nor to pen a positive statement concerning the Pauline theology, the possibility for establishing a definitive answer concerning that relationship is minimal. Instead, it is possible to compare and contrast respective outlooks in relation to similar themes, and consequently it may be possible to tentatively account for any similarity or dissonance that may exist between their respective perspectives. However, what is not possible, due to the limitations of the evidence, is to postulate whether Matthew was aware of the Pauline mission and the teachings enshrined in his writings. Furthermore, it is not possible to advance a hypothesis with evidential support, which would go beyond mere speculation as to whether Matthew was in support of Paul's teaching, or whether he would have been a strident opponent of the Pauline message. Beyond the confines of this study, it may be potentially helpful to discuss how both writings are appropriated by Christian figures in the second century.[2]

II. *Themes for comparison*

If the surviving documentary data does not permit the proposal of theories of direct conflict or influence,[3] it is nonetheless possible to look for similar thematic concerns that may exist between the Gospel of Matthew and the corpora of Pauline writings. Yet once again, a caveat is necessary. If thematic similarities are found, this does not establish contact or direct influence. It must be remembered that both Matthew and Paul were members of the same relatively small religious movement centred on the person of Jesus. The size of the entire movement, and the fact that its separate communities and strands were not hermetically sealed entities, would suggest that there was exchange of ideas, engagement in debates surrounding similar issues and the use of shared linguistic expressions to articulate core religious beliefs. Such points of similarity should not be reified as proofs of direct linear dependence. Rather,

significance of Jesus of Nazareth for the communities within which they wrote and for humankind and his *mysterium tremendum*'. W.D. Davies and D.C. Allison, *The Gospel According to Saint Matthew*, vol. I (Edinburgh: T&T Clark, 1988), 5.

2. A possible starting point would be to consider the reception of both Matthew's Gospel and the Pauline epistles in the writings of Ignatius of Antioch. See P. Foster, 'The Use of the Writings that Later Formed the New Testament in the Epistles of Ignatius of Antioch', in A. Gregory and C.M. Tuckett (eds), *The Reception of the New Testament in the Apostolic Fathers* (Oxford: OUP, 2005), 159–186.

3. Admittedly, not all would agree that it is not possible to posit the direct dependence of Matthew upon Paul. One scholar who argues that Matthew was writing directly with a positive appreciation of Pauline theology is M.D. Goulder, *Midrash and Lection in Matthew* (London: SPCK, 1974). He seeks to argue that 'time and again we find Paul's teaching reappearing, if not actually echoed, in Matthew' (156). More recently, a larger group of scholars have suggested that Matthew is writing in opposition to Paul. Their ideas will be discussed in this study.

they reflect the cross-pollination and interpenetration of theological concepts, liturgical expressions and communal structures within the embryonic Jesus movement.

Notwithstanding these limitations, both the Gospel of Matthew and the Pauline writings discuss a number of related thematic issues, albeit in generically distinct forms. The Gospel presents a historical narrative of events that predate the time of composition by approximately half a century, and while more contemporary concerns may intrude on the historical events; nevertheless, the narrative does purport to relate controversies and incidents drawn primarily from the setting of the life of Jesus. By contrast, the Pauline epistles, while written closer to the time of Jesus, are not directly concerned with the same historical vista. Instead they are discursive, didactical and paraenetic letters written to instruct and encourage communities or recent converts in their new-found faith. However, since Pauline communities are related (at least in some way) to the foundational figure of Jesus and his message, there are still points of intersection between Paul's epistolary correspondence and Matthew's gospel account of Jesus.

Overlapping topics that will be explored in this discussion to situate the Matthaean and Pauline writings both within the emergent Jesus movement and vis-à-vis Judaism will include (a) the way in which the Hebrew Scriptures are utilized; (b) attitudes towards the role of Torah; (c) Christological perspectives; (d) participation in Gentile mission and (e) reflections on community structures. The purpose is not to provide an exhaustive discussion of each of these topics, since to do so would require a monograph for each on a single text alone. Instead, the aim is to highlight areas of convergence or divergence and then, if possible, to attempt to account for the factors that may have generated points of contact or areas of dissimilarity.

a. *The use of the Hebrew Scriptures*

Both Paul and Matthew are steeped in the Scriptures of first-century Judaism. It is important to assess the way the two authors deploy Scripture and to attempt to ascertain their reasons for drawing upon this repository of religious tradition. Turning first to Paul, although Christopher Stanley's magisterial study focuses primarily on the technical aspects of Paul's citational techniques, he advances the following observation concerning Paul's attitude towards Scripture.

> Though he quotes his ancestral Scriptures for a variety of purposes, there is no questioning the fact that Paul regards the words of Scripture as having absolute authority for his predominantly Gentile congregations. How this is to be reconciled with his insistence that the Jewish Torah is no longer in force for these same Gentile Christians has perplexed numerous

> investigators, and cannot be resolved here. The important point for now is that, however, his theological pronouncements are understood, Paul's reliance on the authority of Scripture is wholly in line with contemporary Jewish practice.[4]

While Stanley is correct that Paul feels no incongruity in claiming that Scripture has an abiding authority for Gentiles, there is another key function that Paul derives from citation of the Hebrew Bible. Paul's Christological claims are seen as having been established and confirmed through the prophetic promises contained in the corpus of Jewish scriptural writings, and his use of these writings is seen as a proclamation of the fulfilment of Scripture in the person of Jesus as the promised Messiah. As Seifrid recognizes, '[t]he incarnate, crucified, and risen Christ is the center and end of Scripture. Paul's interpretation of Scripture arises from this confession.'[5] It is helpful to consider a couple of concrete examples of Paul's use of Scripture both to elucidate the technical aspects of his citations and to explore the specific examples of his purpose.

Taking Paul's largest letter, which arguably contains the most self-reflective insights into the apostle's theology, it is helpful to consider the first explicit citation of Scripture contained in that epistle. In Rom. 1.17, Paul cites Hab. 2.4 with an introductory formula and in the form κὰθως γέγραπται ὁ δὲ δίκαιος ἐκ πίστεως ζήσεται.[6] The introductory formula is used here, as frequently in the Pauline writings, 'as an appeal to Scripture to document or prove an assertion just made'.[7] The assertion presented by Paul is that the gospel with which he has been entrusted is the means by which God reveals righteousness on the basis of faith. The Habakkuk citation is particularly apposite to Paul since it resonates so strongly with his own preceding formulation in which he states that in the gospel 'the righteousness of God is revealed from faith to faith' (Rom. 1.17a). It is perhaps a false dichotomy to enquire whether Paul's formulation was framed prior to considering the scriptural support of Hab. 2.4 or whether he designed his own formulation to parallel the prophetic proof-text. As somebody both immersed and trained in the Jewish Scriptures, any paralleling between his formulation and Hab. 2.4 may have taken place at an almost subconscious level,

4. Christopher D. Stanley, *Paul and the Language of Scripture: Citational Technique in the Pauline Epistles and Contemporary Literature*, SNTSMS 74 (Cambridge: CUP, 1992), 338–339.

5. Mark A. Seifrid, 'Romans', in G.K. Beale and D.A. Carson, *Commentary on the New Testament Use of the Old Testament* (Grand Rapids/Nottingham: Baker Academic/Apollos, 2007), 607.

6. Apart from the form cited by Paul, at least three other slightly variant forms are known to be in circulation during the first century: the Hebrew tradition as reflected in the MT and 1QpHab; the LXX; and the citation in Heb. 10.38. Paul offers a form without any possessive pronoun, thereby rendering it ambiguous as to whether the faith belongs to God or to the righteous person; in Heb. 10.38 it is the righteous one that belongs to God.

7. See J.D.G. Dunn, *Romans 1-8*, WBC 38A (Dallas: Word, 1988) 44. As further examples of this tendency Dunn cites Rom. 2.24; 3.4, 10; 4.17; 8.36; 9.13, 33; 10.15; 11.8, 26; 15.3, 21.

which only became crystallized in his thought processes when he 'searched' for a scriptural text to support his assertion. Setting aside the specific exegetical issues that attend this verse, in general terms it can be observed that for Paul the revelation of God's salvific plan aligns with the message of Scripture.[8] Moyise engages in a detailed study of the hermeneutical principle that might undergird Paul's citation of Hab. 2.4. Drawing a contrast with the use of this text in the Qumran pesher (4QpHab 2.4), Moyise argues that the opposing interpretations of these texts

> can either be explained as: (1) the needs of the readers were different (i.e. they had different rhetorical purposes); or (2) they held different convictions. Though the first is undoubtedly true, it is difficult to imagine any circumstances where Paul would have interpreted the verse as applying to 'those who observe the law in the house of Judah.' It must therefore be due to their very different prior convictions.[9]

If this is correct, while there is a complex dialectic between prior insights and textual interpretation, Paul's purpose in citing this Scripture is to claim that his own soteriological outline of the plan of God aligns with the message of the prophet.

Paul engages in a more direct Christological application of Scripture in other passages. In Rom. 10.6-9, Paul glosses the text of Deut. 30.11-14 in various ways to introduce a strongly Christological reading.[10] However, there is another way in which Paul invokes scriptural support for his messianic claims without recourse to direct citation. In Romans 5, his Adam Christology, most clearly presented in vv. 14-15, refers to the fallen state of Adam prior to the revelation of Torah, in order to equate the restoration with a new Adamic figure who is identified as 'the one Man, Jesus Christ' (Rom. 5.15). Here the technique that is employed depends upon the perceived typological fulfilment or completion of what are seen by Paul as stories or soteriological events that were lacking their ending until they found messianic fulfilment in Christ. To achieve this hermeneutic, the role of Torah is redefined. 'The entrance of the law significantly changes the situation of humanity, but it does not undo Adam's deed. Its role is entirely subordinate: in multiplying Adam's transgression (5:20), the law provides the "place" in which the grace of God in Christ may exercise its reign.'[11]

8. Seifrid, 'Romans', 608.

9. S. Moyise, *Evoking Scripture: Seeing the Old Testament in the New* (London: T&T Clark, 2008), 62.

10. As Jewett observes, 'This passage is a classic instance of Paul's interpretation of Scripture to make his point about the promise of the gospel.' R. Jewett, *Romans*, Hermeneia (Minneapolis: Fortress, 2007), 624.

11. Seifrid, 'Romans', 628.

The use of Scripture in the First Gospel appears to have many broad similarities and shared aims when compared with Pauline usage. Matthew appears to use Scripture also for Christological and salvation-historical purposes. The fulfilment motif has been widely recognized in the so-called 'fulfilment quotations'.[12] There are over sixty explicit citations from the Jewish Scriptures in the First Gospel. Hagner comments upon the salvation-historical emphasis noting that this 'heavy dependence on the OT reflects Matthew's interest in the kingdom as the fulfilment of OT expectations'.[13] Thus, for Matthew there is a certain interconnectedness between the events or prophecies of the Jewish Scriptures and the person of Jesus. While Matthew's precise understanding of Scripture may be open to debate, for the evangelist these citations help establish the case that Jesus is the promised Messiah. Consideration of Matthew's longest formula citation, Mt. 12.17-21, is instructive for appreciating some factors in the evangelist's thinking. First, the text drawn from Isa. 42.1-4 resonates with a number of key Matthaean themes. These include the bestowal of the spirit on God's servant, proclamation to the Gentiles and the trust they place in the servant figure, the meek and gentle approach of this figure, combined with his eventual victory. Therefore, as Davies and Allison observe,

> [c]oncerning the use of Isa. 42 in Mt. 12.18-21: the quotation . . . is linked in several intriguing ways with its present context and its 'targumized' text shows it to be the product of much care and reflection. These facts give us to understand the great importance for Matthew of Jesus' role as servant. . . . Matthew's emphasis upon the love commandment goes hand in hand with his desire to interpret Jesus with the christological category of servant. As the perfect embodiment of God's moral demand, Jesus the servant lives the commandment to love.[14]

Here one sees careful selection and shaping of scriptural texts not only to argue for the messianic fulfilment of Scripture in the person of Jesus but also in a highly nuanced fashion Matthew emphasizes the type of messiahship he envisages through the careful deployment of scriptural texts.

Apart from finding scriptural texts to speak about his vision of Jesus as servant, Matthew also taps into contemporary Jewish scriptural debates. Although not presented with an introductory formula, the combined citation of Isa. 26.19; 29.18; 35.5-6; 42.7, 18; and 61.1 placed on the lips of Jesus resonates with a similar catena of citations found among Qumran texts. The Messianic Apocalypse (4Q521), which is admittedly a fragmentary and brief

12. For an extensive discussion see G.M. Soares-Prabhu, *The Formula Quotations in the Infancy Narrative of Matthew* (Rome: Biblical Institute Press, 1976).

13. D.A. Hagner, *Matthew 1-13*, WBC 33A (Dallas: Word, 1993), liv.

14. W.D. Davies and D.C. Allison, *The Gospel According to Saint Matthew*, vol. II (Edinburgh: T&T Clark, 1991), 328–329.

text, opens its extant portion with a declaration that 'the heavens and earth will listen to his Messiah'. It then describes the role of the Messiah in the following terms: 'upon the poor he will place his spirit . . . freeing prisoners, giving sight to the blind, straightening out the twisted . . . for he will heal the badly wounded and will make the dead live, he will proclaim good news to the meek' (4Q521 frag. 2, col. II, lines 5-12).[15] The similarity between 4Q521 and Mt. 12.18-21 raises questions of the mechanism by which the Qumran text and Matthew's Gospel both cite a similar catena of Scripture. However, regardless of the answer to that question, Matthew appears to tap into some wider Jewish repository of Messianic texts and apply those Scriptures to Jesus.

Typological fulfilment is also a shared feature of the approach to Scripture of both Paul and Matthew. Matthew's typological patterning of aspects of Jesus' life on that of Moses is well known and established.[16] There is no need to rehearse all of those arguments here. Suffice to observe that the typological technique has much in common with Paul's Adam Christology. The patterning of aspects of Jesus' life on Hebrew Bible figures is assumed to show that Jesus has salvific significance, which in some way aligns with the comparative figure from Jewish Scripture. Thus for Paul, Jesus, the new Adam, deals with the introduction of sin into the world by the first Adam. As the last Adam, he quashes and defeats sin. For Matthew, Jesus is the new Moses. On the mountain, he brings forth a new law based on his own authoritative pronouncements, and grounds his teaching in a mutual love ethic. Consequently both Paul and Matthew see Jesus closely linked to key figures from Jewish Scriptures: they understand Jesus as surpassing the significance of these figures since his actions have undone the negative effects of Adam's sin, or bring forth a new inclusive teaching for Matthew's community. The similarities around the technical use of Scripture or the interpretations derived from such citation do not establish dependence. Such techniques were widely known in contemporary Judaism, and as has been discussed through the example of 4Q521, other broadly contemporary Jewish groups could employ the same selection of scriptural texts also for the purpose of advancing specific messianic clams.

b. *Attitudes towards the role of Torah*

Once again, this topic has generated huge bodies of research and literature in relation to both the Pauline attitude towards the law[17] and the Matthaean outlook

15. The ellipses show both lacunae in the manuscript and omission of text in the citation.

16. See D.C. Allison, *The New Moses: A Matthean Typology* (Minneapolis: Fortress, 1993).

17. The treatments of the topic of 'Paul and the Law' are legion, and many different understandings have been proposed. One of the most influential recent studies proposes in relation to Paul's attitude to the Mosaic Law (in contrast to the new dispensation in Christ) that 'Paul found the former, glorious as it had been, to be worthless'. E.P. Sanders, *Paul, the Law, and the Jewish People* (Minneapolis: Fortress,

on Torah.[18] In Romans, Paul makes numerous statements concerning the law that are notoriously difficult to synthesize into a coherent or logically consistent perspective. Paul states that only doers of the law are justified before God, not hearers of the law. Although after these statements he immediately notes the possibility of Gentiles doing instinctively the things required of the law, and thereby being justified (Rom. 2.13-15). However, in the following chapter, Paul states that performance of works of the law is not able to justify (Rom. 3.20) and that a man is 'justified by faith apart from works of the law' (Rom. 3.28). However, as Dunn has argued, it may be a mistake to try to emphasize an apparent discord between these sentiments. In relation to the material in ch. 2, Dunn argues that Paul's primary purpose is 'to puncture a Jewish assurance falsely based on the fact of having the law, of being the chosen people of God', and moreover what negates this nationalistic self-confidence is that 'there are many Gentiles who show more evidence in themselves of what the law points to than many Jews'.[19] Again, for Dunn, the obvious contrast in perspective between Rom. 2.13 and 3.20 must be read as forming part of Paul's larger purpose in negating claims of Jewish particularism or superiority based on possession and performance of Torah. Thus he states, 'Paul's purpose throughout the preceding paragraphs was to show that the Jewish particular should be merged with the human universal as "all alike are under sin".'[20]

The Matthaean perspective has been the focus of scholarly debate which has resulted in diametrically opposing positions being defended. For those who advocate that the Matthaean community observed the law, the usual starting point is seen as Mt. 5.17-19, which portrays Jesus as making three explicit statements concerning the law. According to Sim, these statements are 'plain and unambiguous'.[21] In regard to the first statement Sim suggests that Jesus' fulfilment of the law 'must in some manner entail continuity' and

1983), 144. From a different perspective, N.T. Wright argues that Paul's statements about Torah are more situationally generated. See N.T. Wright, *The Climax of the Covenant: Christ and the Law in Pauline Theology* (Edinburgh: T&T Clark, 1991).

18. For those who advocate that Matthew and his community were Torah-observant see A.J. Saldarini, *Matthew's Christian-Jewish Community* (Chicago: University of Chicago Press, 1994); J.A. Overman, *Church and Community in Crisis: The Gospel according to Matthew* (Valley Forge, PA: Trinity Press International, 1996); D.C. Sim, *The Gospel of Matthew and Christian Judaism: The History and Social Setting of the Matthean Community* (Edinburgh: T&T Clark, 1999). The perspective that Matthew and his community were at some stage of transformation that weakened the degree of law observance is advocated by J.P. Meier, *Law and History in Matthew's Gospel: A Redactional Study of Mt 5:17-48*, Analecta Biblica 71 (Rome: Biblical Institute Press, 1976); G.N. Stanton, *A Gospel for a New People – Studies in Matthew* (Edinburgh: T&T Clark, 1992); P. Foster, *Community, Law and Mission in Matthew's Gospel*, WUNT 2.177 (Tübingen: Mohr Siebeck, 2004).

19. J.D.G. Dunn, *Romans 1-8*, WBC 38A (Dallas: Word, 1988), 106.

20. Dunn, *Romans 1-8*, 153.

21. Sim, *The Gospel of Matthew and Christian Judaism*, 124.

that Jesus 'fulfils the law by bringing out its original intention and meaning'.[22] Leaving aside the vexed question of how one might know the original meaning and intention of Torah, Sim sees the second statement (Mt. 5.18) as offering an eschatological time limit on the validity of the law. The third statement (Mt. 5.19) in this sequence is seen as being consequential to the previous two. Therefore, Sim asserts that '[s]ince the Torah remains valid until the parousia, the Matthean Jesus states unequivocally that it must be obeyed in full until that time.'[23] Sim's description is extremely helpful in providing one of the clearest statements of the case by those who would argue that Matthew advocates complete observance of the Jewish law.

Not all scholars find such arguments compelling. Bringing Mt. 5.20 into the debate, Moule noted that the emphasis on possessing a righteousness that exceeded that of Jewish interlocutors might suggest that this is a constructed defence against the charge that Matthew's community had abandoned the law.[24] Similarly, discussing a parallel in *Test. Lev.* 16.3 where Jesus is said to renew the law, Stanton highlights what is the obvious weakness in the proposal advanced by Sim and those others who advocate a law-observant Matthaean community. Discussing the Greek term underlying the description of the renewal of the law, Stanton states that the 'verb used, ἀνακαιονποιέω might be taken simply as a re-affirmation of the law or it might mean that Jesus brings a new perspective on the law; the verb is just about as ambiguous as πληρόω in Mt. 5.17!'[25] Furthermore, in a previous study, I have argued that the interpretation of the notion of fulfilment in Mt. 5.17 must be interpreted in concert with the concrete examples of Torah interpretation given by the Matthaean Jesus in the antitheses of Mt. 5.21-48.[26] Therefore, '[i]n terms of their position in the Matthean macronarrative, this sequence of six antitheses constitutes an interpretative explanation of the programmatic statement in 5.17-20 concerning the law.'[27] These antithetical statements do not redefine previous legal stipulations in the same way. The first and second on murder and adultery provide an intensification based on a higher standard of righteousness. The third, dealing with divorce, revokes a practice permitted in the Torah. The fourth, on oaths, provides a ruling directly in opposition to the positive injunction in the Torah to use oaths on certain occasions (Exod. 22.6-7, 10; Numbers 19–22; Deut. 6.13; 10.20). Therefore, in this instance, the Matthaean Jesus appears to categorically

22. Sim, *The Gospel of Matthew and Christian Judaism*, 124.

23. Sim, *The Gospel of Matthew and Christian Judaism*, 126.

24. C.F.D. Moule, 'St Matthew's Gospel: Some Neglected Features', reprinted in his *Essays in New Testament Interpretation* (Cambridge: CUP, 1982), 69.

25. Stanton, *A Gospel for a New People*, 247.

26. Foster, *Community, Law and Mission in Matthew's Gospel*, 94–143.

27. Foster, *Community, Law and Mission in Matthew's Gospel*, 94.

reject a Torah injunction. This sense of rejection is even stronger in the fifth antithesis dealing with retribution. Interestingly, in the thesis statement of this fifth antithesis (Mt. 5.38) the form cited is the closest of the six antitheses to the text form contained in the Torah (cf. Exod. 21.24; Lev. 24.20; Deut. 19.21), although this is still a highly abbreviated form. This suggests that the author was aware of the Torah stipulation that the Matthaean Jesus is presented as intentionally revoking.

No doubt there are significant differences in the ways in which Paul and Matthew handle the subject of the law. Paul's understanding can be unhelpfully oversimplified as a wholesale rejection of the law. However, at a deeper level one can recognize the strong internal struggle Paul had in relation to working out the place of Torah in God's salvation purposes and, consequently, Paul's understanding of the connectedness of the divine plan may account for his unwillingness to reject it as having been utterly worthless. Matthew does, likewise, appear to wrestle with an appropriate way to affirm the abiding validity of the law, yet does this in a manner markedly different from that of Paul. In part, this difference in approach may reflect the divergent social settings of their communities. However, it would be wrong to infer from such divergence that Matthew was in dispute with Pauline understandings of the Torah. As France comments on this issue, 'difference is not opposition'.[28] And neither of course could it be construed as similarity. Therefore, in relation to attitudes towards the law, Paul and Matthew display some marked differences in understanding, but these differences should not be polarized to argue that their positions reflected extreme libertinism on Paul's part and hard-line conservatism by Matthew. Both writers are far more nuanced in their treatments. As has been discussed, Matthew's presentation of Jesus' actual handling of Torah stipulations in the antitheses (Mt. 5.21-48) appears to offer a somewhat surprisingly subversive reading of the programmatic statements on the law in Mt. 5.17-20. This does not transform Matthew into a disciple of Paul. Rather, it reveals the complexity of Matthaean theology, and shows that the Gospel only gives fleeting and partial insights into what was presumably a sensitive issue for Matthew's community.

c. *Christological perspectives*

It has long been recognized that an author's Christological outlook does not simply reside in the titles that are employed to describe Jesus.[29] The actions

28. R.T. France, *Matthew – Evangelist and Teacher* (Exeter: Paternoster, 1989), 110.

29. Specifically in relation to Pauline Christology (which will be a focus of this discussion), Tuckett makes the following pertinent point: 'In trying to assess the significance of the person of Jesus for someone like Paul, it is probably somewhat artificial to isolate this from what Paul regards as having been achieved by Paul's life and death. In terms of technical theological jargon, we cannot easily separate Christology

attributed to Jesus reveal much concerning an author's understandings of Jesus, and even at a deeper level the structure of a literary work, be it narrative or epistolary paraenesis, may contain embedded within its deep structure insights into an author's central commitment to and understanding of the figure of Jesus. Notwithstanding these important insights, a titular approach to Christology still provides a basic and probably fundamental appreciation of the broad contours of the respective authors' outlooks and beliefs concerning Jesus. For this reason consideration of Paul and Matthaean Christological titles will serve as a starting point, but will be supplemented with wider aspects of character portrayal and authorial commitments to probe similarities and differences that may exist between the two authors.

Paul's Christological understandings have been the focus of both studies into that specific area, and occupying the attention of numerous commentators on his epistles. Mere word statistics are striking in consideration of Paul's prime Christological outlook. Among the seven letters widely accepted as authentically written by Paul, the term χριστός is used to describe Jesus on approximately 270 occasions, κύριος some 184 times, whereas there are only about fifteen usages of 'Son of God'.[30] Precisely what the term χριστός denoted for Paul, and also what his multiple readers understood by this title, is a problematic issue. Within the LXX the term χριστός is used to translate מָשִׁיחַ. This term has a range of rich sacred and religio-political overtones.[31] Whether Paul contemplated the full range of meanings of this term and intended his readers to pick up such associations is probably unknowable. However, he appears to have at the very least chosen to use a term employed in the wider Jesus movement that had a background in Second Temple Judaism for referring to a promised liberator and restorer of religious and political status for the Jewish people. As E.P. Sanders comments in relation to the expectation of an eschatological deliverer described in Rom. 11.26,

> "The Deliverer," as most scholars agree, is almost certainly Christ in Paul's understanding. It is Christ who is God's end-time agent in 1 Cor. 15:20-28 . . . it is likely that he thought of Christ as coming at the end, before the kingdom was handed over to God (1 Cor. 15:24).[32]

from soteriology.' C.M. Tuckett, *Christology and the New Testament: Jesus and His Earliest Followers* (Edinburgh: EUP, 2001), 42.

30. Again, see Tuckett, *Christology and the New Testament*, 46.

31. In terms of its priestly or sacred sense, when used adjectivally the term denoted a priest anointed for office, whereas in 1 and 2 Samuel the term refers to the possessor of the kingly office. Obviously there is no hermetically sealed division between religious and political roles, but for heuristic purposes it is helpfully to see the term at least encompassing both these aspects.

32. E.P. Sanders, *Paul, the Law, and the Jewish People* (Minneapolis: Fortress, 1983), 194.

In this sense Paul saw Christ language as a means of succinctly summarizing Jewish expectations concerning an eschatological deliverer, and equating this figure with the person of Jesus.

There are, however, times when the title has become so standardized, especially when used in conjunction with the name Jesus, that one may wonder if readers would have recognized it as being anything more than a two-part name. However, regardless of the way the title functions in each instance the joint use of the Greek translation of the term Messiah coupled with Paul's attribution to Jesus of the future expectations that were part of Jewish messianic theologies reveals that Paul viewed Jesus as the promised deliverer, yet saw the salvific hope transcending national boundaries.

The term κύριος perhaps resonated more easily with both Jewish and Gentile audiences due to the polyvalence of the term. For Greek-speaking Jews, the term was employed in the LXX as the primary translation of the Tetragrammaton. In the Gentile world, particularly in the eastern Mediterranean part of the Roman Empire, the term 'Lord' was used as an expression of imperial devotion. Deissmann recognized that there was a subversive element in Paul's application of the term 'Lord' to the crucified Jew Jesus. He stated that there was an 'early establishment of a polemical parallelism between the cult of Christ and the cult of Caesar in the application of the term *kyrios*, "Lord"'.[33] Paul uses the term κύριος in numerous ways. When citing the LXX, he continues the use of the term as the translational equivalent of the divine name (e.g. Rom. 4.8; 9.28). Paul is capable of using κύριος as a term of respect for earthly masters (e.g. Rom. 14.4). In a widespread and frequent usage it is combined with 'Ιησους or χριστός, or both (1 Cor. 1.2; 1 Thess. 1.1). With these examples of co-ordinated Christological terms, it is perhaps more difficult to discern any specific emphasis that Paul might be making by using the title κύριος. There are, however, a number of uses of κύριος in isolation from other Christological titles. Potentially these reveal some of the unique emphases Paul sees in this term.

Interestingly, although in Romans κύριος is used in isolation on numerous occasions as either a citation of the LXX or in commentary on a passage just cited from the LXX, when unambiguously referring to Jesus it is rarely used in an uncombined manner. There are perhaps two types of exceptions. The first occurs in Romans 14, a passage where Paul initially uses κύριος language to refer to an earthly master (Rom. 14.4). Next he shifts the reference of the terminology to denote 'God', which is used synonymously with κύριος in Rom. 14.6. By the time the argument has moved to Rom 14.8 it is perhaps most

33. G.A. Deissmann, *Light from the Ancient East: The New Testament Illustrated by Recently Discovered Texts of the Graeco-Roman World* (trans. William E. Wilson; Grand Rapids: Baker, 1965), 349.

natural to understand the κύριος language as probably still referring to 'God', at least initially. The participatory clause at the end of the verse, 'we are the Lord's', however, may suggest that Paul's thinking has shifted.[34] This is reinforced in the following verse, where Paul uses the conjunctive phrase εἰς τοῦτο γάρ to argue that it is Christ who died that 'he might be Lord' (κυριεύσῃ) 'both of the living and the dead'. Here the singular usage of κυριεύσῃ in the final clause of Rom. 14.9 is obviously a back-reference to Christ in the previous clause. His death and living again is claimed as being the basis of his 'lordship' of the dead and the living. Thus in a convoluted manner in Rom. 14.8 it appears at least in the final clause of that verse Paul is referring to Jesus as κύριος, which in this context demonstrates dominion over death and the pastoral comfort to believers that neither life nor death ends the state of belonging to the Lord. Here, as Jewett notes, Paul has exploited the household language of masters possessing slaves (Rom. 14.3-4);[35] however, the line of argument progresses to reveal that the Lordship of Jesus encompasses the power of life and death itself.

The second sequence of κύριος language in Romans which is not closely connected with other Christological titles occurs in the greetings section of Romans 16, where a number of figures are stated as being 'in the Lord' and the recipients of the letter are instructed to greet or receive certain people 'in the Lord'.[36] Six or seven individuals are to be the recipients of such recognition: Phoebe (Rom. 16.1-2); Ampliatus (Rom. 16.8); Tryphaena, Tryphosa and Persis (Rom. 16.12); Rufus and presumably his mother also are seen as 'in the Lord' (Rom. 16.13).[37] Given that these verses are interspersed with references

34. Moo also notes the difficulty in determining the shifts in usage of κύριος in this passage. He states, '[t]he referent of "lord" (κύριος) throughout this passage is not easy to determine.' He goes on to note that 'the verb "lord it over" in v. 9 must have Christ as its subject; and this, in turn, suggests that "Lord" in the closely related v. 8 must also refer to Christ'. Moo also suggests, although far more tentatively, that the references in vv. 4c and 6 'both probably also refer to Christ'. This is, indeed, far less certain. See D.J. Moo, *The Epistle to the Romans* (NICNT; Grand Rapids: Eerdmans, 1996), 840.

35. Jewett does, however, note the important ways in which this household language is qualified. First, this 'lordship is a gracious rather than a domineering one', and '[a]lthough all the members of the Roman house and tenement churches belong to Christ, they are not to be treated as menial slaves.' R. Jewett, *Romans* (Minneapolis: Fortress, 2007), 848.

36. The relationship of Romans 16 to the rest of the letter has been an important textual and theoretical issue for a number of scholars. The theory that 16.1-20 was initially addressed to Ephesus and later appended to an original version of the letter that concluded at 15.33 (see T.W. Manson, 'St Paul's Letter to the Romans – and Others', in M. Black (ed.), *Studies in the Gospels and Epistles* [Manchester: MUP, 1962], 225–241) lacks support among the Greek manuscript tradition. Certain Vulgate and Old Latin manuscripts preserve a fourteen-chapter text, with the grace and doxology appended. That Rom. 16.1-20 is an authentic element of Paul's letter is strongly supported by the extant manuscript evidence. For further discussion see H.Y. Gamble, *The Textual History of the Letter to the Romans: A Study in Textual and Literary Criticism* (SD 42; Grand Rapids: Eerdmans, 1977).

37. The same woman, Rufus' mother, appears to have functioned as a mother to Paul. It is unlikely that the phrase 'his mother and mine' is denoting two separate mothers.

to other figures such as Prisca and Aquila being 'in Christ Jesus' (Rom. 16.3), or simply in Christ (Urbanus, Rom. 16.9), there can be little doubt that κύ ριος is a Christological referent here. While Fee states of Rom. 16.1-16, 18 that the 'final set of κύριος texts in this letter have very little christological import', they do perhaps do more than emphasize the Christocentric nature of the new life of believers.[38] Dunn argues that the ἐν κυρίῳ formula may perhaps express 'a degree of intimacy', or 'bring out the more authoritative force of κύριος' or be used for 'exhortation'.[39] Jewett, however, emphasizes the mystical dimension encapsulated in this phrase.[40] The participatory nature of Paul's κύριος Christology needs to be recognized here in this greetings list, as well as elsewhere throughout the epistle.

Another important aspect of Paul's κύριος Christology is the eschatological dimension. Paul speaks of the parousia of the Lord (1 Thess. 4.15) although more frequently he employs a combined referent such as 'the parousia of our Lord Jesus' (cf. 1 Thess. 2.19; 3.13; 5.23). Therefore, Paul's understanding of the teleological goal is the coming of the imminent divine presence. In this way Pauline Christology envisages believers being fully with the Lord, when the Lord comes to be with them. In 1 Thess. 4.15, Paul is assuring believers that death does not disadvantage those who have died. Those believers who have died will, according to Paul, share the same fate as believers who are alive at the parousia. Thus for Paul physical life and death are no longer ultimate ontological categories. Rather, being 'in the Lord' is what Paul considers to be the ultimate life-sustaining category. It is for this reason that Paul can assert that the power of life and death does not stem from any earthly lord but is found in the one who has been made 'Lord of the living and the dead' (Rom. 14.9).

Matthew's Christology is obviously different from that of Paul, but it may be wrong to see such differences as either compatible or conflicting. While certain scholars have stressed the importance of a 'wisdom Christology' in Matthew,[41] it may be the case that this strand is not a central aspect of the Matthaean understanding of Jesus.[42] Occupying a far more central role are the various 'son' categories Matthew employs to describe Jesus. In terms of his salvation-history schema, in the opening verse of the Gospel Matthew affirms Jesus both as son of David and as son of Abraham. While the description of Jesus as son of David

38. G.D. Fee, *Pauline Christology: An Exegetical-Theological Study* (Peabody, MA: Hendrickson, 2007). 267.

39. J.D.G. Dunn, *Romans 9-16* (WBC 38B; Dallas: Word, 1988), 887–888.

40. Jewett, *Romans*, 858.

41. M.J. Suggs, *Wisdom, Christology and Law in Matthew's Gospel* (Cambridge, MA: HUP, 1970); B. Witherington III, *Jesus the Sage: The Pilgrimage of Wisdom* (Edinburgh: T&T Clark, 1994).

42. For a similar perspective on the somewhat marginal nature of 'wisdom Christology' in Matthew see Tuckett, *Christology and the New Testament*, 128.

is a recurring theme in the First Gospel (Mt. 1.1; 9.27; 12.23; 15.22; 20.30, 31; 21.9, 15; 22.42), the description 'son of Abraham' occurs only once (Mt. 1.1). Matthew may be exploiting, and potentially redefining, popular expectations concerning the coming of a Davidic Messiah. Kingsbury sees both theological and apologetic purposes in Matthew's use of this term.

> Theologically, Matthew takes great care, particularly 1:1-2:6, 15:24, and 21:1-9, to portray Jesus as Israel's royal Messiah in whom OT prophecy concerning David is fulfilled. At the same time, Matthew does not honor popular notions of the Davidic Messiah according to which he is to be a political and military figure, but instead shows him to be a humble King and attributes to him the activity of healing. . . . Apologetically. Matthew utilizes the title Son of David in order to underline the guilt that devolves on Israel for not receiving its Messiah.[43]

Paul also makes use of the notion of Davidic sonship, yet presents such an understanding of Jesus' identity as incomplete (Rom. 1.3). Therefore, Matthew and Paul appear to share a similar outlook in seeing this description of Jesus as an inadequate Christological understanding in isolation.

Perhaps the central Christological affirmation in Matthew's Gospel is that of Jesus as Son of God. It may appear strange to assert that the 'Son of God' concept is more important for Matthew than Paul, when the former uses it only on nine occasions, whereas the latter has fifteen occurrences.[44] However, significance is not always proportional to numerical occurrence. Disclosure of Jesus' identity as Son of God occurs at key moments in the Gospel. Moreover, Matthew affirms Jesus divine sonship not only through explicit use of the title 'Son of God' but also by declaring that Jesus was conceived by the Holy Spirit, and through the reciprocal language Jesus employs to describe the unique paternal relationship he enjoys with his heavenly Father. The confession made by Peter that Jesus is 'the Christ, the Son of the living God' (Mt. 16.16) not only combines 'Christ' and 'Son of God' titles but also evokes an affirmation that also acknowledges Jesus' divine filiation: this was revealed by 'my Father who is in heaven'. Regardless of any debates surrounding the historicity of the Caesarea Philippi incident in the ministry of Jesus, given that Matthew places this in a context that emphasizes establishment of ἐκκλησία, this would appear to support Kingsbury's observation that 'the most exalted confession of Matthew's church is that Jesus is the Son of God'.[45]

43. J.D. Kingsbury, *Matthew: Structure, Christology, Kingdom* (Philadelphia: Fortress, 1975), 103.

44. Matthew's nine uses occur at Mt. 4.3, 6; 8.29; 14.33; 16.16; 26.63; 27.40, 43, 54. Paul's fifteen occurrences, including those referring to Jesus absolutely as 'Son' when the context makes clear that this is divine sonship, are Rom. 1.3, 4, 9; 5.10, 8.3, 29, 32; 1 Cor. 1.9; 15.28; 2 Cor. 1.19; Gal 1.16; 2.20; 4.4, 6; 1 Thess. 1.10.

45. Kingsbury, *Matthew: Structure, Christology, Kingdom*, 67.

The use of κύριος language is prominent is Matthew's Gospel. The riddle Jesus presents to the Pharisees in Mt. 21.41-45 concerning whose son the Christ is (Mt. 22.42) results in the unanswered question, 'If David calls him Lord, how is he his son?' Here the affirmation is that the Christ is both David's Lord and the son of one superior to David. Thus Matthew combines his central commitment to Jesus as Son of God, with an affirmation Jesus is indeed David's 'Lord'. Consequently, as Davies and Allison note, this text, 'rightly understood, in no way denigrates Davidic Christology, but instead presupposes its truth. The tension between "Son of David" and "Lord" is creative, not diminishing.'[46] It is the creative aspect of this tension, which for Matthew leads to his highest Christological confession – namely, that Jesus is God's son. Such usage of κύριος language in this same context, while not identical with Pauline use of the term, does have many points of contact and, moreover, does not appear to reveal a major divergence in thinking.

However, there is another aspect of Matthew's use of κύριος language that may be perceived as being more critical of Pauline Christology. These are the two occasions when Matthew presents the double vocative κύριε, κύριε (Mt. 7.21-22; 25.11). This plaintive cry appears to belie an inadequate and false form of discipleship. The first instance occurs in a section of the Sermon on the Mount that warns against false prophecy. The theme of false prophets is explicitly announced in Mt. 7.15, and the connection of 7.21-23 with 7.15-20 is apparent in v. 22, where those who utter the Christological cry of κύριε, κύριε also claim to have prophesied in that name.[47] The Matthaean version of this tradition is both expanded and appears to have a harder and more specific polemical edge. Fleddermann argues that the Lukan form stands much closer to the origin wording of the underlying Q saying, and that 'Matthew changed the two main verbs into participles, introduced the concept of entering the kingdom of heaven, and changed the original "do what I say" to "doing the will of my father in heaven"'.[48] Although there is little precise information in this passage, one of the more popular among the myriad of views on the identity of these 'false-prophets' is that they were antinomian libertine Hellenists, and perhaps Paulinists or even ultra-Paulinists.[49] There are, however, a number of problems with seeing Matthew reacting against Pauline teaching, especially in the area of Christology. First, the problem is not that of the use of the title κύριος but,

46. W.D. Davies and D.C. Allison, *The Gospel According to Saint Matthew*, vol. III (Edinburgh: T&T Clark, 1997). 250–251.

47. For a more extended discussion of the unity of 7.15-23 see Davies and Allison, *The Gospel According to Saint Matthew*, vol. I, 701–702.

48. H.T. Fleddermann, *Q: A Reconstruction and Commentary* (Leuven: Peeters, 2005), 306.

49. J. Weiss, *Earliest Christianity*, trans. F.C. Grant; 2 vols (New York: Harper & Brothers, 1959), vol. II, 753.

rather, the use of it without what is deemed to be appropriate matching behaviour. Furthermore, while much of the perspective of Mt. 7.21-23 must be seen as stemming from Matthew's redactional activity, the double vocative κύριε, κύ ριε is derived from double-tradition material that Matthew develops to address some problem surrounding false prophecy, not a perceived Christological error. Finally, given the lack of transparency concerning the situation behind this pericope, the chronological distance between Matthew and Paul and the lack of any specific anti-Pauline focus in the text, the case for reading it as a critique of Paulinism or more specifically Pauline Christology cannot be sustained.

It is apparent that Matthew and Paul use similar Christological formulations. No doubt this is due in major part to the fact that both are representatives of the wider Jesus movement, with the use of certain titles gaining currency as an appropriate linguistic vocabulary emerged to describe the perceived elevated status of Jesus. Notwithstanding these similarities, there are differences in the frequency of use of certain titles between Matthew and Paul, as well as potentially different understandings. Paul's use of the terms χριστός and κύριος predominate his references to Jesus, but he can also affirm the filial role of Jesus to the father. Matthew highlights the status of Jesus as 'Son of God' at key junctures in his Gospel, and this appears to be the key Christological affirmation in the First Gospel. Such differences of emphasis should not be read as implied critiques of Pauline theology by Matthew. If this were the case, one would have to conclude that it has been undertaken in such a subtle manner that the critique has in fact failed. Rather, it is perhaps fairest to observe that because of the different genres of their works, and because of different emphases in their theologies, Paul and Matthew formulate their Christology in ways that are indeed different, but not antithetical.

d. *Participation in Gentile mission*

If there is one certain fact in early Christianity it is that Paul radically embraced the proclamation of the gospel to Gentiles and inclusion of non-Jewish believers in the new movement as co-religionists without any diminution of status for Gentile believers. The controversial aspect of Paul's Gentile mission was his stance that these non-Jewish converts who become members of a Jewish messianic movement centred on Jesus of Nazareth could become full members without adherence to some of the boundary-marking aspects of Torah observation. In particular, male members were not required to be circumcised, dietary laws were not mandatory and observance of Sabbath was unnecessary. The tensions this caused with certain members of the movement are well documented in both Paul's epistles and the secondary literature that discusses these issues. In terms of his self-understanding, Paul viewed his experience on the Damascus Road not as a generalized call to apostleship but as a specific call to be the apostle to the Gentiles (Rom. 11.13). Taking Gal. 1.16 in conjunction with Rom. 1.14, Schnabel argues that 'Paul understands himself as directed by the risen Lord to preach the gospel to the Gentiles in particular – that is, non-Jews, polytheists, including proselytes and God-fearers whom he would encounter in the Diaspora synagogues.'[50] It is, however, this last statement, which correctly refers to Paul's strategy of entering Diaspora synagogues, that reveals that he understood his mission to the Gentiles in a non-exclusivist way. Thus, contrary to the apparent implications of Gal. 2.7-8, Paul did not take either his call to be apostle to the Gentiles nor the division of mission in Gal. 2.7-8 between his mission to the uncircumcised and Peter's to the circumcised as limiting him from entering synagogues or preaching the gospel to circumcised Jews.

Strategically, Paul's use of Antioch as a missionary base provided a community setting that was sympathetic to Gentile mission, helpfully distant from the more traditional Torah-based forms of the Jesus movement based in Jerusalem and Judaea, and geographically convenient for outreach to Gentiles in major population centres of the eastern Mediterranean. In what may probably be his earliest extant epistle, Paul commends the Thessalonian believers for turning from idols to serve God. Such language confirms that the addressees were indeed Gentile polytheists. Moreover it appears likely that Paul formulated his Christology and teaching in a way that would resonate with Gentile understanding. Therefore, to 'Gentile audiences Paul argued that Jesus is the Kyrios, the Lord of the world, who is in the process of establishing his kingdom'.[51] Paul's teaching concerning his newly founded Gentile or mixed communities was that they constituted the eschatological people of God without any need for circumcision or Torah observance.

While acknowledging Matthew's statements concerning mission, a number of recent studies argue that the First Gospel envisages a Torah-observant mission to Gentiles often as a prelude to the eschaton. Among these studies it is sometimes suggested that Matthew's hypothetical commitment to mission was conceived in direct opposition to Paul.[52] While there is widespread agreement on a number of central aspects of the Pauline mission – its reality, its focus on Gentiles, its non-compulsion of Torah observance – the discussion concerning Matthew's attitude to mission is far more contested. This makes comparisons between the missionary outlook of Matthew and Paul potentially insecure. Since scholars take diametrically opposing views on Matthew's attitude towards mission, many will view whichever position is taken on the Matthaean

50. E. Schnabel, *Early Christian Mission, vol. 2: Paul and the Early Church* (Leicester: Apollos [InterVarsity Press], 2004), 935.

51. Schnabel, *Early Christian Mission*, 1483.

52. In particular, see Sim, *The Gospel of Matthew and Christian Judaism*, 188–213.

perspective towards mission as invalidating the comparison. If one adopts Sim's position that for the Matthaean community mission was an ethnically and temporally differentiated task, then a sharp distinction emerges between Paul and Matthew. First, Sim rejects the participation of the Matthaean community in any proselytizing activity towards non-Jews.

> In view of this, there is no necessity to attribute any role for Matthew's community in the Gentile mission which needed to take place before the arrival of the end (Mt. 24:14). This church would continue to take responsibility for the Gospel to the Jews, while other Christian groups which had taken responsibility for the Gentile mission would fulfill this role in the eschatological plan.[53]

Yet what Sim envisages is no division of missionary labour between a Jewish mission and an equally valid Pauline mission to Gentiles, as suggested in Gal. 2.7-8. Rather, he views Matthew and his community as intentionally and aggressively anti-Pauline. He argues that in articulating a Christian-Jewish ideology Matthew rejected a law-free mission to Gentiles and purposefully sought to undermine Pauline Christianity. Thus Sim states that 'Matthew's Jewish Christian perspective, his support for a Law-observant Gentile mission and the presence of anti-Paul texts in his Gospel . . . pointed inevitably to the conclusion that Matthew was engaged in a bitter and sustained polemic against Paul himself.'[54]

By contrast, it is possible to represent Matthew's outlook on mission as more positive to the inclusion of Gentiles. The passage that is usually seen as most problematic for those who suggest that Matthew held an inclusive view of mission is Mt. 10.5b-6. Here the prohibition placed on the lips of Jesus and addressed to the Twelve stipulates 'Do not go in a way of the Gentiles, and do not enter into a city of the Samaritans, but rather go to the lost sheep of the house of Israel' (Mt. 10.5b-6). Before considering the meaning of this verse and its overall significance for determining the Matthaean view of Gentile mission, it is first helpful to survey other statements Matthew makes that impinge on the theme of mission.[55] In the second half of the Gospel there appears to be a shift to a more positive attitude to Gentiles, which, if not triggered by the encounter with the Canaanite woman (Mt. 15.21-28), at least becomes apparent after it. France takes this transition as a deliberate thematic strategy on the part of Matthew. 'This section at the close of the Galilean phase of Matthew's

53. D.C. Sim, 'The Gospel of Matthew and the Gentiles', *JSNT* 57 (1995), 42.

54. D.C. Sim, 'Matthew's anti-Paulinism: A neglected feature of Matthean studies', *HTS Teologiese Studies/Theological Studies* 58 (2002), 777.

55. The following discussion draws on my larger treatment of this topic in ch. 6 of Foster, *Community, Law and Mission in Matthew's Gospel*, 218–252.

story thus marks a decisive break from the previous pattern of Jesus' ministry, a deliberate extension of the Messiah of Israel to the surrounding non-Jewish peoples.'[56] While Sim emphasizes Jesus' statement 'I was not sent except to the lost sheep of the house of Israel' (Mt. 15.24),[57] this approach fails to allow the pericope to govern its own concluding emphasis – namely, the commendation of the Canaanite woman's faith and the concomitant attitudinal change on Jesus' part towards this Gentile.

Another passage that is relevant to this discussion, but also fraught with highly contested interpretation, is Mt. 21.43. At the conclusion of the parable of the rented vineyard, Jesus, addressing Jewish leaders, makes the following declaration: '[T]herefore I say to you, the kingdom of God will be taken from you and given to a nation producing the fruits of it' (Mt. 21.43). The meaning and significance of the term ἔθνει (here translated as 'a nation') is hotly debated. Sim claims that here the term is self-referential for Matthew's community. He states, 'it demonstrates that Matthew's Christian Jewish group claimed (albeit unsuccessfully) a leadership role within the Jewish community and within the Jewish religion'.[58] While it needs to be noted that here Matthew uses a singular form, whereas it occurs elsewhere in the plural (apart from Mt. 24.7) in all other Matthaean usages of this term, elsewhere it unambiguously refers to non-Jews.[59] On certain occasions it is employed as a pejorative term (Mt. 6.32; 18.19), while for the most part it is used descriptively to denote non-Jewish humanity. Hence, wider Matthaean use does not appear to support Sim's interpretation. Alternatively, to varying degrees other commentators have seen this passage as envisaging some form of replacement theology whereby the representative Jewish leaders are told that their salvation-historical privileges would be transferred to a different nation. This appears to be more clearly the case when it is recognized that this parable is second in a triadic sequence of parables: one son responding to a call, which another son rejects (Mt. 21.28-32);[60] a nation being given the salvation-historical privileges that are taken from Jewish leaders (Mt. 21.33-46); and those who reject their invitation to the wedding banquet being replaced by the most unexpected guests (22.1-14). There is obviously a danger of this theme being overplayed and being used to feed into some highly unpalatable theological interpretations that need to be resisted in the strongest terms. Nonetheless, Stanton appears correct in his reading of

56. R.T. France, *The Gospel of Matthew* (NICNT; Grand Rapids: Eerdmans, 2007), 588.

57. Sim, *The Gospel of Matthew and Christian Judaism*, 224.

58. Sim, *The Gospel of Matthew and Christian Judaism*, 149.

59. See Mt. 4.15; 6.32; 10.5, 18; 12.18, 21; 20.19, 25; 24.7, 9, 14; 25.32; 28.19.

60. There are significant text-critical problems with the form of the parable of the two sons. For a discussion of these see P. Foster, 'A Tale of Two Sons: But Which One Did the Far, Far Better Thing? A Study of Matt 21:28-32', *NTS* 47 (2001), 26–37.

this verse in its first-century context when he states, '[t]he verse is certainly one of the most significant in the whole Gospel, for it confirms that Matthew's Christian community had parted company with Judaism.'[61] It is striking that two diametrically opposed understandings of the social setting of the Matthaean community can be derived from the same verse. Given the context of the triad of three parables with some form of replacement theme, the wider usage of the term ἔθνος in Matthew's Gospel, and the positive outlook on Gentile mission in the second half of the Gospel, it would appear that the evidence aligns with Stanton's proposed interpretation.

In Matthew's eschatological discourse, the proclamation of the gospel to the nations is seen as part of a sequence of events leading to the consummation of this age (Mt. 24.14). However, when read in light of Mt. 24.7, Luz interprets both verses taken together as implying that 'the Gentile mission already seems to be underway in the present'.[62] Sometimes the perspective of this verse is also combined with the perspective enshrined in the commendation of the woman who anoints Jesus. She is promised that she will be remembered 'wherever this gospel is preached in the whole world' (Mt. 26.13). Thus France explains:

> The blessings of Israel are not for Israel alone. The mission of the disciples which Jesus had initially limited to Israel (10:5-6, 23) is soon to be 'preached throughout the whole world, as a testimony to all nations' (24:14), and the devotion of the woman who anoints Jesus' head before the passion will be remembered 'wherever this gospel is preached in the whole world' (26.13).[63]

While most aspects in France's comments are correct, there are perhaps two slight nuances that could be suggested. First, in relation to Mt. 26.13, it needs to be acknowledged that Gentile mission is not explicitly mentioned. However, as France appears to suggest, this verse is at best a corroboration of the wider perspectives in the Gospel, such as Mt. 14.14 and 28.16-20, that there will be a universal proclamation of the gospel and this will include Gentiles. The second slight corrective is perhaps more substantive. Whereas France feels the mission to the nations is 'soon' to occur, it is perhaps better to understand it as having already commenced. Matthew retrojects these predictions back to the time of Jesus, thereby historicizing the coming of the universal mission. However, that historicized future prospect is likely to be the present reality for the Matthaean community. Given the discussion of Mt. 18.1-22, which is replete with ecclesial themes, it is not impossible that the warning against causing the little ones

61. G.N. Stanton, *A Gospel for a New People – Studies in Matthew* (Edinburgh: T&T Clark, 1992), 7.
62. U. Luz, *The Theology of the Gospel of Matthew* (Cambridge: CUP, 1995), 16.
63. France, *Matthew – Evangelist and Teacher*, 234.

to stumble (Mt. 18.6, 10) is in fact a veiled admonition to long-term Jewish-Christian community members against marginalizing and despising more recent Gentile members of the community. The complex of material in Mt. 18.10-14 consists of two framing verses (18.10, 14), which provide the interpretative matrix for the Q parable of the lost sheep (Mt. 18.12-13//Lk. 15.4-7).[64] Both the framing material with its more communally oriented address and the re-wording of the Matthaean form, which speaks of wandering (πλανάω) in place of being lost (ἀπόλλυμι), may plausibly suggest that Matthew has given this tradition a pastoral focus, which may in turn address tensions in his community concerning neophyte Gentile members who are being caused to stumble and are consequently in danger of wandering away from the flock.

Without doubt the climax of the Gospel, Mt. 28.16-20, is potentially the most transparent statement concerning the Matthaean attitude towards Gentile mission. Yet here again the interpretation of these verses has recently become highly contested. Much of the debate revolves around not the geographical but rather the ethnic scope of the phrase πάντα τὰ ἔθνα (Mt. 28.19). Overman develops an argument that broadly aligns with the positions of other scholars who deny that Matthew envisaged the possibility of a law-free mission to Gentiles. Initially Overman affirms that Matthew had awareness of Diaspora Jewish communities and that 'he would have believed that they, too, needed to embrace Matthean Judaism in order to "fulfill all righteousness"'.[65] Overman also advances the opinion that Matthew was not hostile to Gentiles, although this would be contested by scholars who hold an even more exclusive interpretation of the ethnic scope of the Matthaean mission. Thus, according to Overman, the Matthaean perspective on Gentile mission is that '[t]hey may have been an afterthought, but Gentiles, along with diaspora Jews, should hear the message of the Gospel.'[66] This, however, according to Overman, is within the context of observance of Matthaean Torah-based piety. In agreement with Sim's perspective,[67] Overman sees a strong apocalyptic dimension, that universal mission was a prelude to the end. Therefore Overman concludes that 'Matthew believed that all people should be able to understand and to live out Matthean Judaism. He believed it was for all people. The Matthean community

64. On text-critical grounds Mt. 18.11 appears to be a later addition to the text. The verse is omitted in a wide range of early and significant manuscripts and is unknown to certain early church fathers, ℵ B L* Θ* $f^{1.13}$ 33. 892* *pc* e ff^{1} sy^{s} sa mae bo^{pt}; Or Eus.

65. Overman, *Church and Community in Crisis*, 407.

66. Overman, *Church and Community in Crisis*, 407.

67. See D.C. Sim, *Apocalyptic Eschatology in the Gospel of Matthew*, SNTSMS 88 (Cambridge: CUP, 1996), esp. 99–109.

. . . appears to be lacking in enthusiastic missionaries.'[68] Sim is somewhat more rebarbative in his reading of this text. First, he states:

> There is no doubt that 28.19 accepts without question the validity of the Gentile mission; it is no less an authority than the risen Jesus himself who instigates it. But accepting the legitimacy of the Gentile mission does not necessarily mean that the Matthean community had any active involvement in it. There is a distinction here which scholars have not sufficiently appreciated.[69]

Yet one must ask whether such an interpretation is plausible. Can the final climactic imperative given to disciples on a mountain top be considered an 'optional extra' by the Matthaean evangelist? One would also have to consider the injunctions to disciples contained in the Sermon on the Mount to be optional. However, for Sim this constructed distinction is necessary. He must insist upon 'a law-observant mission to Gentiles' supported by the Matthaean community,[70] for this allows him to formulate the following proposal concerning Matthew's attitude to Paul: 'The strong anti-Pauline perspective in the Gospel is evidence enough that Matthew deemed Pauline mission to be completely illegitimate.'[71] The reality, however, is that the Gospel provides very few insights (if any) into inner-Christian tensions. Given that Paul may have been dead for two decades when Matthew wrote, and that the Gospel makes no explicit reference to Paul, one wonders whether the apostle was a real issue for the Matthaean evangelist. Given that he is primarily writing the story of the ministry of Jesus, later developments in the Jesus movement seem to have little impact on his narrative. That is not to deny that the Gospel is written in such a way as to have certain pastoral concerns and behaviour-forming imperatives that were of contemporary relevance, but there is very little to suggest any critique of Paul, implicit or otherwise, within the actual text of the Gospel.

In place of this proposal of hypothetical commitment to a law-observant mission, it appears that the final words of the Matthaean Jesus were intended to have some real impact on the first hearers of the Gospel. It may be the case that some long-term Jewish-Christian members of Matthew's community resisted Gentile mission. If that were the case, then Matthew invokes the authority of the risen Jesus to change such attitudes with a countermand, which legitimates Gentile mission. As Hooker argues,

68. Overman, *Church and Community in Crisis*, 408.
69. Sim, *The Gospel of Matthew and Christian Judaism*, 245.
70. Sim, *The Gospel of Matthew and Christian Judaism*, 246.
71. Sim, *The Gospel of Matthew and Christian Judaism*, 246.

> The ministry of Jesus was limited to Israel, and the work of his disciples was similarly circumscribed; but now the authority of the risen and ascended Lord is without bounds – and the mission of his followers is equally extensive . . . Matthew sees the limitation of 10.5b-6 as a temporary one, no longer applicable in the post-resurrection situation.[72]

The flow of the Matthaean macronarrative in relation to the whole topic concerning Gentiles and mission to them appears to be carefully structured in the Gospel to initially affirm the dominical saying that limited mission during the ministry of Jesus (Mt. 10.5b-6), and then to legitimate the universal scope of mission in Matthew's contemporary setting by portraying shifts in Jesus' own attitude and through the climactic affirmation of mission.[73]

There is absolutely no doubt that Paul, the self-styled apostle to the Gentiles, was actively and unrelentingly engaged in Gentile mission. Nor is there any doubt that certain Jewish believers in Jesus opposed his proclamation of a law-free version of the gospel (Gal. 2.11-14; 5.2-11). The contested issue for this discussion is where Matthew stood in relation to Gentile mission and, more specifically, in regard to Paul's missionary activities. Whether Matthew's community was actively participating in mission of any kind is an open issue; there is simply no clear evidence in the Gospel. There are, however, hints in Mt. 24.9-10 that due to public proclamation of the gospel community members would face the prospect of ostracism. Perhaps public proclamation of the gospel may be equated with at least some form of mission. Despite suggestions to the contrary, the most straightforward reading of Mt. 28.19-20 would appear to suggest that at least for the author of the Gospel participation in Gentile mission was at the very least seen as a positive aspiration for the community in its contemporary setting, and not simply something that they should hope would be done by others on an indefinite eschatological horizon. The degree of law observance that the evangelist would wish to lay on Gentile converts is unknown. For Sim it is self-evident that male converts to the Matthaean community would be required to undergo circumcision. Consequently he states, '[o]n the much debated questions whether the male gentiles were circumcised and whether all of them were expected to follow the whole Torah, the evidence

72. M.D. Hooker, 'Uncomfortable Words X: The Prohibition of Foreign Missions (Mt 10.5-6)', *ExpT* 82 (1971), 363.

73. Another approach has been to refute the idea that Mt. 10.5b-6 and Mt. 28.19 actually create a tension. Thus, LaGrand argues that understood within contemporary Judaism the term 'Israel' was a 'designation for the people of God' and consequently this was theologically a broader and more inclusive term than is often recognized. J. LaGrand, *The Earliest Christian Mission to 'All Nations': In the Light of Matthew's Gospel* (Atlanta: Scholars Press, 1995), 64. However, given that in part his conclusions are based on the decision to date Matthew to the pre-70 CE period, the supposed context may invalidate the evidential basis that he invokes.

implies that they were on both counts.'[74] At best this is an inference (and a highly contested one at that) that is extrapolated from Matthaean texts that make no explicit pronouncements on this subject. It therefore remains beyond the available evidence to determine whether Matthew envisaged a law-free or law-observant mission to Gentiles, although some passages in the Gospel might point perhaps more strongly to the possibility of a law-free mission, or at least a slightly relaxed outlook. However, on the issue of similarity with or difference from Pauline perspectives on mission, apart from acknowledging that both affirmed Gentile mission in some form, there is little more that can be said.

e. *Community structures*

Much like the previous topic of Gentile mission, in Paul's letters there are statements that deal directly and quite extensively with community structures, whereas in Matthew's Gospel there are some elusive statements that may or may not refer to the contemporary situation of the evangelist. Again the genre problem of comparing a Gospel account set during the life of Jesus with epistles written several decades after the death of Jesus, written to fledgling communities of believers to regulate those groups, needs to be acknowledged. Furthermore, with the Pauline epistles in the widest sense of the term, there is development in thinking on church structure and a plurality of scenarios reflecting the situational nature of these writings, but despite the range of texts information can be tantalizingly obscure. The situation with Matthew is more difficult due to the lack of direct textual attestation concerning the organization of Matthew's community. In order to provide a somewhat useful comparison, the discussion will be limited to leadership roles in Pauline and Matthaean communities, since the latter may give some clues concerning this topic.

Matthew may provide a glimpse of community structure in the ecclesial material in Mt. 18.1-22, as well as when critiquing the synagogue practices of scribes and Pharisees (Mt. 23.1-12). In the former, Matthew calls for mutuality and equality among community members based on childlike status. The description moves from a dominical teaching about children to a discussion of 'little ones' in the community (Mt. 18.6-9), with the concern that such people may be given cause to stumble. The passage then discusses an ethic of generous forgiveness, but regulated by ecclesial accountability and authority (Mt. 18.15-20). Having identified the 'little ones' as disciples who believe in Jesus (Mt. 18.6), Bornkamm advances the following observation:

> The term ['little ones'] is more especially accented in 18:10ff. as it is applied to those members of the congregation who are in danger of straying and perishing (18:10 and 14). Thus, in this

74. Sim, *Apocalyptic Eschatology in the Gospel of Matthew*, 209.

> context, the parable does not serve primarily for the proclamation of divine grace towards the lost; rather it serves to impress upon the congregation their duty to care for the straying.[75]

While some of these points were made earlier in this discussion, the significant point here is that Matthew promotes an ethic of corporate pastoral care and responsibility in his community. This may point away from considering the group to have had a highly developed and clearly delineated hierarchical leadership. Although employing different terminology, Paul speaks of the imperative to consider the pastoral needs of the weaker brother (1 Cor. 8.7-12). Given the lack of shared terminology, perhaps all that should be inferred is that two leading figures in the wider Jesus movement understood that the community structures are not to result in the dominance of weaker group members. However, for Matthew group discipline is a corporate responsibility for recalcitrant members (Mt. 18.17), in certain cases potentially resulting in exclusion from the group.[76] Similarly, Paul, on occasion, seems to deal with matters of community discipline in the same manner. In relation to the case of sexual irregularity in 1 Cor. 5.1-8, he advises the Corinthian believers as an assembled body to deliver the man concerned 'over to Satan for the destruction of his flesh' (1 Cor. 5.5). Therefore, for both Paul and Matthew, it appears that pastoral care and group discipline are community responsibilities and not entrusted to certain officials in the respective communities.

For Matthew, his apparently anti-hierarchical vision of leadership appears to be, at least in part, formed in reaction against synagogue structures. After the possibly somewhat caricatured portrayal of Jewish scribal and Pharisaic leaders, the Matthaean Jesus addresses both crowds and his disciples employing the contrastive construction ὑμεῖς δέ (Mt. 23.8). Davies and Allison observe the function of the contrast formed by this phrase, stating 'vv. 1-7 (a polemical portrait of vanity) and vv. 8-12 (a little community rule on humility) portray antithetical behaviour'.[77] In relation to the so-called 'little community rule' it may be possible to infer some indication of community structure and leadership. First, the use of status-forming titles is eschewed, both to acknowledge that leadership of the community belongs to Christ alone and also to maintain the egalitarian nature of inner-group relations. Therefore, humility and self-abasement are the qualities that Matthew seeks to promote among his co-religionists. Such self-abasement is a the theme taken up by Paul

75. G. Bornkamm, 'The Authority to "Bind" and "Loose" in the Church in Matthew's Gospel', in G.N. Stanton, *The Interpretation of Matthew* (2nd edn; Edinburgh: T&T Clark, 1995), 106.

76. France notes that exclusion from the group is not portrayed as the desired outcome; rather, the 'object of the gathering is not to pronounce judgment but to strengthen the pastoral appeal'. France, *The Gospel of Matthew*, 693.

77. Davies and Allison, *The Gospel According to Saint Matthew*, vol. III, 265.

in the Christological hymn of Phil. 2.8-9, as well as being the quality that he says depicts his ministry among the Corinthians (2 Cor. 11.7).[78] Once again, however, the similarities in these values should not be seen as evidence of direct dependence. Rather, it is more plausible that Paul and Matthew either share common perspectives of the wider early church or may be drawing on dominical teaching.

While acknowledging such conceptual affinities, one may wonder how the ethic of egalitarianism played out in practice. In Paul's epistles, on occasions, a fairly autocratic and self-referential form of leadership comes out. Paul parades his apostolic status before those who question it, claiming both equal status with the most eminent apostles and to have performed 'signs and wonders and miracles' among the Corinthians (2 Cor. 12.11-12).[79] Paul claims the right to discipline the Corinthian community, issuing the ultimatum 'shall I come to you with a rod or with love and a spirit of gentleness?' (1 Cor. 4.21). Moreover, Paul advocates a degree of uniformity of practice among his communities that is expressed in the form of his so-called ecclesial argument (1 Cor. 4.17; 7.17; 11.16; 14.33; cf. 2 Thess. 2.15). Thiselton may over-interpret what looks like a not-too-veiled apostolic threat with the language of arbitration and mediation when he states: 'Only after all this does Paul reach a point where, if all else fails, he must resort to a declarative speech-act, or an illocutionary act of apostolic pronouncement, which presupposes the importance of tradition or "catholicity" among Paul's congregations.'[80] What this seems to mean is that if Paul cannot convince members of his newly formed communities by debate he will then invoke apostolic authority. This may undercut some of the claims concerning the equality of members. Hence, Paul may not emphasize egalitarian status to the same degree as Matthew. However, the reality is that there are no insights into how the Matthaean commitment to egalitarianism was realized in practice. The centrality of the authority of Peter to 'bind and loose' (Mt. 16.19) somehow appears to have been accrued to the Matthaean community (Mt. 18.18), but what this actually meant in practice or what leadership structure was in place to yield such power is now beyond historical recovery.

III. *Conclusion*

The purpose of this discussion was twofold. The first aim was to attempt to situate Paul and his writings, along with Matthew's Gospel, within the context

78. See D.A. Hagner, *Matthew 14-28*, WBC 33B (Dallas: Word, 1995), 662.

79. Here Barnett brings out the force of the Pauline rhetoric: '[I]n saying that he is nothing, at the same time he is saying he is everything'. P. Barnett, *The Second Epistle to the Corinthians* (Grand Rapids: Eerdmans, 1997), 579.

80. A.C. Thiselton, *The First Epistle to the Corinthians*, NIGTC (Grand Rapids: Eerdmans, 2000), 848.

of early Christianity by considering a set of issues that may be common to both. The second aim was to consider the extent to which Paul influenced Matthew's Gospel, and to assess in what way Matthew's Gospel might be a reaction to Paul and his legacy.

In relation to the first aim, the five topics for comparison have revealed some striking similarities between the theological outlooks of Paul and Matthew as well as some notable differences. For both, there is a rich use of the Hebrew Scriptures, which are understood to contain prophetic attestation of the claim that Jesus is the promised Messiah. The topic of ongoing Torah observance has been seen by some as marking a dividing line between Matthew and Paul, with the former being understood as calling for a continued commitment to all the requirements of the law. For example, on Sim's reading of the Gospel he concludes that 'the Matthean community comprised Christian Jews who believed that the coming of Jesus had not in any way invalidated the ancient laws of Moses. The Torah remained valid and authoritative in the present age and faithful followers of Jesus Christ were expected to keep all parts of it.'[81] However, as has been discussed, this is not a view that is uniformly held, and in fact the Matthaean characterization of Jesus as giving a new law from a mountain top directly contrasted his own pronouncements with what the ancient authorities proclaimed (Mt. 5.21, 27, 31, 33, 38, 43). This suggests a far more nuanced understanding of the Torah than that suggested by Sim.[82]

The Matthaean and Pauline Christological titles were seen to demonstrate significant overlap, although their respective preferred ways of referring to Jesus did not coincide. With regard to attitudes to Gentile mission, unsurprisingly Paul with shown to be fully engaged in a law-free mission to Gentiles. The specific details concerning Matthew's attitude to mission to non-Jews are, again, a topic of debate. The position that Matthew did not feel his community had any role in mission to Gentiles was seen to be implausible given the climactic words of the risen Jesus at the end of the Gospel. There is simply not sufficient information to state whether Matthew would have advocated a law-free or law-observant mission. Finally, with the structure and leadership of the respective communities, whereas the Pauline epistles supply much information that is not entirely consistent, at best Matthew supplies partial glimpses into the organization of his community. It would be reckless to extrapolate too much from a comparison of Pauline and Matthaean ecclesial structures when the former is varied and the latter poorly known. These five themes for comparison reveal that there are multiple points of similarity in areas of theology,

81. See Sim, *The Gospel of Matthew and Christian Judaism*, 138–139.

82. For further discussion on this see Foster, *Community, Law and Mission in Matthew's Gospel*, 94–143.

Christology and ecclesiology between Paul and Matthew. However, it appears that this is primarily due to both sharing some of the core commitments, beliefs and affirmations in common with the wider early Jesus movement.

In relation to the second aim, gauging the extent to which Paul influenced Matthew's Gospel, and assessing how Matthew's Gospel might be a reaction to Paul and his legacy, the results are largely negative. Chronologically Matthew's Gospel is later than the Pauline epistles.[83] So if there is influence it must be Matthew who would be dependent upon Paul. However, the Gospel contains no explicit reference to Paul or his writings; the points of contact between the two bodies of literature appear so general that there is no way of establishing the case of dependence. In fact, from the available evidence one could not even infer that Matthew had significant awareness of Paul. This may leave modern readers bemused. Was the community that produced what was to become the most widely used Gospel so theologically isolated that it was unaware of the significance of Paul? Or was Paul deemed far less significant in some Christian circles towards the end of the first century that it was considered unnecessary to mention him? Alternatively, perhaps Matthew had knowledge of Paul but felt this later phase of the Jesus movement was irrelevant to his own literary project which narrated the earlier period of the ministry of Jesus. These are all unknowns of history.[84] The responsible conclusion is to squarely acknowledge the limitations of the historical sources, and not to force the data to address modern questions to which the sources actually make no contribution. Did Matthew know of Paul? Who knows? What is clear is that Paul and his writings left no significant imprint on Matthew's Gospel.

83. This is certainly the case for any epistles that are deemed authentically Pauline. Admittedly, for deutero-Pauline letters there is the hypothetical possibility that these were written after the composition of the First Gospel and consequently drew upon it as a source. However, no evidence of this is detected in reality.

84. Here it may be best to follow Stanton's comment that 'Matthew's gospel as a whole is neither anti-Pauline, nor has it been strongly influenced by Paul's writings; it is simply un-Pauline.' Stanton, *A Gospel for a New People*, 314.

5

Luke and Paul on Repentance

David Morlan

I. *Introduction*

According to early Christian tradition, the relationship between Paul, the famed Apostle to the Gentiles, and Luke, a physician and supposed writer of Luke-Acts,[1] displayed unity in mission (Phlm. 1.24) and closeness of friendship (Col. 4.14). Only Luke remained loyal to Paul when others abandoned him, ashamed of his chains (2 Tim. 4.11). Likewise, Paul's 'Gospel' (Rom. 2.16; 16.25; cf. 2 Tim. 2.8) referred not to his *own* Gospel, but to his friend's Gospel – the Gospel written by *Luke* (*Eccl. Hist.* 3.4).[2] Similarly, Luke held Paul in high regard in Acts as *the* key figure in the spread of 'the way'. Eusebius noted that for Luke, Paul's actions in Acts were 'demonstrated before his [Luke's] own eyes' (*Eccl. Hist.* 3.4).[3] Luke witnessed his friend in action and wrote about it so others could know. Paul and Luke showed genuine closeness and exhibited a true Christian alliance.

Such was the relationship of Paul and Luke before the dawn of the critical era. In 1831, however, Baur wrote the now famous essay on the Christ party in the Corinthian church in which he argued that early Christianity was divided bitterly along Jewish/Hellenistic lines.[4] Among other things,[5] Baur laid the

1. According to the early church historian Eusebius, Luke was a physician and wrote 'inspired' books that exemplified his 'art of healing souls' (*Eccl. Hist.* 3.4).

2. A. Just (ed.), *Luke* (Ancient Christian Commentary on Scripture, Downers Grove: InterVarsity Press, 2003), p. 3.

3. That is, if one believes the 'we' passages in Acts to be Luke's eyewitness account.

4. F. Baur 'Die Christuspartei in der korinthischen Gemeinde, der Gegensatz des petrinischen und paulinischen Christenthums in der ältesten Kirche, der Apostel Petrus in Rom', *TZTh* 4 (1831), pp. 61–206.

5. Baur suggested that division characterized the early church rather than harmony. The four identified parties in Paul's first letter to the church in Corinth (1 Cor. 1.12) represented a sharp divide between two factions in the early church. This separation, which ran along Hellenistic and Jewish lines, lurked behind the texts of the NT. Paul represented the Hellenistic Christian church while Peter, James and the 'Christ party' represented the Jewish faction of Christianity. The former rallied around the radical universal

foundation for what was later to be called *Tendenzkritik*, a method of reading the NT, which had this historical situation as its fundamental assumption. This 'tendency criticism' deciphered the particular theological viewpoint of each NT writer in the effort to determine if the writer was on Paul's side or on Peter's side of the early church. NT scholars tried to get behind the glossed-over text to discover the real historical and theological position of the individual writers. The theological fallout from Baur's essay and his *Tendenzkritik* is multifaceted. However, for the purpose of this essay, I call the reader's attention to the ramifications Baur's essay had on the unity, congruence and compatibility of Luke and Paul. Using legal jargon, Baur's essay 'filed the paperwork' that would lead to the permanent divorce of Paul and Luke.[6]

Questions continue to surround the historical and theological relationship between Luke and Paul as scholars seek to discover if Paul had any meaningful influence on Luke. To what extent scholars can have confidence that Luke knew Paul's letters and was shaped by them is difficult to judge. Some scholars assume that due to their apparently different theologies Luke must not have been familiar with Paul's letters.[7] Walker argues vigorously, however, that Luke *was* familiar with Paul's letters but that Luke placed Paul's theology in the preaching of Peter rather than Paul (except in Acts 13.39).[8] Yet, whether

doctrine of justification by faith while the latter held on tightly to the particularism of the law and ties to the historical Jesus. The former emphasized the work of the spirit in the progress of history (i.e. following Hegel's *Phänomenologie des Geistes*) and knew Christ according to the spirit, while the latter insisted on their relationship with Jesus according to the flesh. This bitter and basically irreconcilable split lay at the centre of the early Christian movement.

6. Most serious modern works that compare Luke and Paul note, to varying degrees, the obvious differences between them: (1) Paul and Luke wrote different types of literature: Paul wrote epistles while Luke wrote a story. (2) Paul and Luke had very different audiences: Paul wrote to churches, some of which he started himself, while Luke addressed both of his volumes (Lk. 1.3; Acts 1.1) to the frustratingly mysterious Theophilus. (3) Paul addressed theological and social issues directly. Luke wrote a story, which reflected theological assumptions and pictured social issues, but his medium of narrative prevented him from dealing with them as directly as Paul's medium did. (4) Luke pulled together resources in order to give a putatively reliable account of the origin and growth of the early church (Lk. 1.1-4). Paul relied primarily on his personal source, the revelation of Christ (Gal. 1.1, 12; 1 Cor. 15.8), and leaned very little on other sources in comparison with Luke (cf., however, 1 Cor. 15.3).

These differences alone point to drastically different purposes in writing, which may have caused them to highlight different aspects of their theologies. Despite these difficulties, however, discovering the extent of the differences and similarities between the theologies of Luke and Paul is an important task that must not be ignored. Together the writings of Luke and Paul comprise the majority of the NT and, as such, theological interpretations of their writings have enormous influence in the world today. For the Christian church worldwide, theologies derived from the writings of Paul and Luke not only set the course of direction for numerous denominations but also help shape the actual religious beliefs of untold millions. For scholars of the NT, understanding better the theological beliefs of Luke and Paul helps to untangle how each of these lofty figures accounted for the numerical growth of the Christian movement. Furthermore, understanding the extent of their theological relationship helps scholars to be conscious of the unity and diversity within the NT itself.

7. e.g. W. Kümmel, *Introduction to the New Testament* (New York: Abingdon, 1975).

8. W. Walker, 'Acts and the Pauline Corpus Reconsidered', *JSNT* 24 (1985), pp. 3–23. Luke did

or not Luke knew Paul personally or had read his letters, it is clear that Luke's writings are fundamentally his own. Hence, the comparison between Luke and Paul in the following essay is one that represents two largely independent thinkers of the early Christian movement.

In this chapter I will compare Luke and Paul's notion of repentance, especially as it fits within their wider theologies of conversion and as it relates to issues of human and divine agency. My hope is that a focused study on this concept will provide a sharp theological profile of Luke and Paul based on what they actually articulated regarding this concept. While this essay will highlight more the *contrast* between these twin towers of early Christianity, I believe this actually lays a foundation for important similarities between them.[9]

II. *Luke and repentance*

Repentance for the forgiveness of sins is a major theme in Luke's two-volume narrative[10] as is the auditors' response to its proclamation.[11] Luke wrote about repentance more extensively than the other Synoptic authors, and repentance continued as a dominant theme in Acts as well. Méndez-Moratalla points out that Luke's *repeated* usage of repentance shows it to be central to his theology.[12] As such, understanding the meaning of repentance according to Luke is vital in order to grasp his theology of conversion. While Méndez-Moratalla argues that Luke's intended meaning of repentance was 'fairly traditional', simply because a belief may be 'traditional' or 'inherited' does not make it any more or less important in an individual writer's theological construct.[13]

Luke celebrated the hope of repentance and portrayed it to be an integral part of Jesus' message. In Luke's 'Great Commission', 'repentance for the forgiveness of sins' was the central message of the Risen Christ (Lk. 24.44) in contrast to the Matthaean version in which repentance is totally absent (Mt. 28.18-20). In Luke's second volume this commission to call sinners to repentance was followed both forcefully and fearlessly in the preaching of Peter (Acts 2.38; 3.19),

this for the sake of Paul's reputation – if Peter was really the originator of the Gentile mission, then Paul's missionary journeys and churches he planted were legitimized. Thus Luke's depiction of the early church is one in which the original Apostles and Paul were in fundamental congruence (Walker, 'Acts', p. 17).

9. D. Morlan, 'Conversion in Luke and Paul' (unpublished doctoral dissertation, Durham University, 2010).

10. e.g. Lk. 17.3-4; 24.47; Acts 2.38; 3.19; 5.31; 8.22.

11. e.g. Lk. 10.13; 11.32; 13.3; 16.30; Acts 11.18; 17.30.

12. F. Méndez-Moratalla, *The Paradigm of Conversion in Luke* (London: T&T Clark, 2004).

13. Moreover, this aspect of conversion contrasts with Paul who rarely mentioned the common terms for repentance (Rom. 2.4; 2 Cor. 7.9-10; 12.21). While some may argue that *concepts* of repentance can be found in Paul, the fact remains that repentance *language* was not used by Paul and that this is thus an area of contrast with Luke. Of course, there is a possibility that Paul and Luke have similar concepts of conversion while using different vocabulary to express them.

the Apostles (5.29-31) and Paul (17.30; 20.21; 26.20). Luke bracketed his two-volume narrative with messages of repentance: John the Baptist's imperative in Lk. 3.8, ποιήσατε οὖν καρποὺς ἀξίους τῆς μετανοίας,[14] and Luke's Paul in Acts 26.20 urging both Jews and Gentiles, μετανοεῖν καὶ ἐπιστρέφειν ἐπὶ τὸν θεόν, ἄξια τῆς μετανοίας ἔργα πράσσοντας.[15] Only Luke's Gospel included Jesus forgiving a repentant criminal even in the 'eleventh hour' after the criminal's admission of guilt and request to Jesus to remember him in paradise (Lk. 23.39-43). It is only in Luke's Gospel that we discover explicitly that Jesus' mission was not just calling sinners (Mt. 9.13; Mk 2.17) but calling sinners to repentance (Lk. 5.32).[16] Using the most basic tools of redaction criticism, scholars deduce that Luke's addition of repentance here points to a theology in Luke which is, in some ways, different from Matthew and Mark – a theology in which repentance is held in unusually high esteem.

Perhaps the most explicit depiction of repentance in Luke is the parable of the so-called 'prodigal son' – a story famously unique to Luke. The setting of this story, Jesus being criticized for eating with notorious sinners, launches into a series of three parables each ending in a celebration. The last and most detailed story, the return of the lost son, ends with a celebratory homecoming given by his father. As an explanation, Jesus says that, likewise, the angels in heaven celebrate when just one sinner repents (Lk. 15.10, 22-23).

a. *Luke, repentance and the Hebrew Scriptures*

Traditionally scholars have understood the verb שׁוב to stand behind the concept of repentance as found in the NT, including Luke-Acts.[17] The purpose of this section is to explore how שׁוב was used in the Hebrew Scriptures (OT) and to extrapolate the relationship, if any, between it and Luke's notion of repentance. An effective place to start such a study is with the groundbreaking work on repentance by Holladay.[18]

14. 'bear fruit worthy of repentance'.

15. 'to repent and turn to God, performing deeds in keeping with their repentance'.

16. That Luke added repentance in this context led Witherup to conclude that repentance is necessary along with forgiveness of sins in order for conversion to occur. R. Witherup, *Conversion in the New Testament* (Collegeville: Liturgical Press, 1994), pp. 46–56.

17. 'The NT . . . employs μετανοέω to express the force of שׁוב, turn around.' J. Goetzmann, 'Repentance', *NIDNTT* (ed. C. Brown; Grand Rapids: Zondervan, 1975), pp. 354–360. Healey points out, however, that the LXX translates שׁוב as ἐπιστρέφω most of the time. This indicates that a possible shift in the covenantal understanding of repentance as expressed in the term μετάνοια 'took place during the Intertestamental Period, perhaps under Hellenistic influence'. J. Healey, 'Repentance', *The Anchor Bible Dictionary, Vol. 5 O–Sh* (ed. D. Freedman; New York: Doubleday, 1992), p. 673. While this is difficult to prove, this underscores the importance of exploring the concept of repentance rather than just the terms.

18. W. Holladay, *The Root SUBH in the Old Testament* (Leiden: Brill, 1958). נָחַם is also a very important term describing repentance in the OT. However, because it usually refers to God rather than humanity, I will not engage with it in this essay.

In his Herculean work, Holladay provides an analysis of each occurrence of שׁוב in the OT – a total of 1,064 occurrences. One of the results of his study was a 'bare-bones' definition of שׁוב as expressed in the OT. He states that שׁוב indicates movement 'in an opposite direction in which one was going with the assumption that one will arrive again at the initial point of departure'.[19] In other words, he concluded that the basic meaning of שׁוב was 'to return'. The fruit of Holladay's analysis was the compilation of distinct categories of שׁוב, most of which refer to the physical movement of returning to a particular location or simply the act of turning around. However, Holladay observed a way שׁוב was used that is particularly germane to this investigation. He pointed out that שׁוב was used in a unique way to refer to the relationship between Israel and God, and as such identified a new category of שׁוב called the 'Covenant usage of שׁוב'.[20]

Holladay shows that there are 164 usages of שׁוב that explicitly refer to the covenant relationship between Israel and God. Of these usages, Israel is the subject 123 times. In other words, שׁוב is used in this context almost exclusively to picture Israel as 'returning' or being called upon to 'return' to God. Only six of the 164 usages refer to God as returning to Israel, yet five of these six usages state that God's return to Israel was contingent upon what Israel did in reference to her relationship with God. Thus שׁוב was used in the OT to refer to the explicitly religious return of a people to their deity.

Holladay finds the bulk of his evidence in the books of Jeremiah and Deuteronomy. Holladay's thesis is that Jeremiah should be credited as the first ancient writer who carved a clear concept of repentance using שׁוב. While his *historical* argument is not important in this essay, the *theology* of repentance he argues Jeremiah inaugurated, and its possible impact on the thinking of NT writers and Luke in particular, does have a bearing on this essay. Holladay proposed that Jeremiah 'saw apostasy and repentance as correlative . . . he saw them as aspects of the same act; a changeable people must change: it has changed enough, it must change'.[21]

With the context of Jeremiah being that of the exile of Israel because of her 'apostasy' (Jer. 31.32, 'my covenant that they broke, though I was their husband'), the notion of return from exile is combined and, at times, is almost

19. Holladay, *Root*, p. 53.

20. Ibid., pp. 116–157. The connection between the covenant and repentance has long been acknowledged by NT scholars as enormously influential. Cf. J. Lunde, who stated 'repentance is associated in the OT with God's chosen people. Thus one should understand the concept, usually expressed metaphorically by the Hebrew verb שׁוב, to be grounded in the gracious covenant that God had previously established with Israel . . .' J. Lunde, 'Repentance', *New Dictionary of Biblical Theology* (ed. B. Rosner; Downers Grove: InterVarsity Press, 2000), p. 726.

21. Holladay, *Root*, p. 157.

indistinguishable from a more spiritual return to God. See, for example, Jer. 31.21b:

> שׁוּבִי בְּתוּלַ ת יִשְׂרָאֵל
> □
> שֻׁ□ בִי אֶל־עָרַ□יִךְ אֵלֶּה
>
> *Return, O virgin Israel*
> *Return to these your cities*

In this text Jeremiah refers to Israel's obedient return to God while at the same time indicating a physical return from exile. As Huey points out, 'the return was to have a spiritual aspect as well'.[22]

This idea of a 'changeable people called to change' became an important aspect of the corporate identity of the Jews. The very thing that had caused them to move away from God is what is called upon for them to return to God. Both the source of their problem and the hope that their problem can be remedied stemmed from their fundamental changeableness. Furthermore, it is not hard to see how this may have paved the way for them increasingly to cherish the concept of repentance. However, could such a concept of repentance, which emphasizes the 'changeable' and fickle character of human beings, have been in the mind of Luke while he wrote his two volumes?

That Luke was familiar with Jeremiah and used Jeremiah in his Gospel is unquestioned. There are at least nine passages in Luke's Gospel that either directly refer or allude to Jeremiah.[23] The most notable example is found in Luke 15: in particular, Jesus' parable of the man who finds a lost sheep (Lk. 15.3-5). This Lukan story is likely derived from Jer. 31.10 in which God promises to gather Israel and 'keep him as a shepherd keeps his flock'.[24] As a result of experiencing discipline, Israel is *returning* (וְשָׁבוּ) back to the land while at the same time asking God to restore her relationship with him (31.17-18). Israel's restoration is then described in terms of her return to God (וְאָשׁוּבָה) and a feeling of remorse for her disobedience (נִחַמְתִּי).

In a very limited sense, Jeremiah's twin themes of repentance and shepherding mirror the notion of repentance and shepherding in Lk. 15.3-5. Both characterize God as the shepherd and describe the disobedient as repenting

22. F. Huey, *Jeremiah, Lamentations* (Nashville: Broadman Press, 1993), p. 277.

23. Lk. 1.15=Jer. 1.5; Lk. 1.70=Jer. 23.5; Lk. 1.77=Jer. 31.34; Lk. 12.20=Jer. 17.11; Lk. 13.35=Jer. 12.17, 22.5; Lk. 15.4=Jer. 31.10, 19, 20; Lk. 18.13=Jer. 31.19; Lk. 19.46=Jer. 7.11; Lk. 22.20=Jer. 31.31-34.

24. Culpepper states that the repentance image of a sheep returning to the shepherd appears 'frequently in the post-exilic prophets as well as the Psalms'. R. Culpepper, *Luke* (Nashville: Abingdon Press, 1995), p. 296; cf. Ps. 23.1-6. As such, in addition to Jeremiah it also likely evokes Ezek. 35.15, 'I myself will be the shepherd of my sheep . . . I will seek that which was lost.'

and turning back to God. Yet, in a broader sense, can the double entendre of Israel's return, being both physical and spiritual, be seen in the narrative of the prodigal son? His return home is also both physical and spiritual. He confesses his sin against his father and God and initiates an actual return back home. Furthermore, the initial act of his coming to his senses mirrors a fundamental 'changeableness' as seen in Jeremiah. The son had experienced apostasy (he was dead) but later experienced repentance (he is now alive) – does this point to an aspect in Luke's anthropology that mirrors that of Jeremiah stated earlier?

Deuteronomy is another book in which the author(s) employs the so-called covenant use of שׁוב extensively. The Sinai covenant was 'wholeheartedly' received by Israel in Exod. 19.7-8, but by the end of Deuteronomy Israel's inability to keep this covenant was obvious (e.g. Exodus 32–34; Numbers 14; Deuteronomy 9). Indeed, the exile of Israel from the land would be 'inevitable apart from their full and pre-emptive repentance'.[25] For Israel judgement would come, but would it come and leave them with no hope for future redemption? C. Wright argues that Moses here actually looks beyond exile to a time of restoration. 'However, with great amazement and wonderful rhetoric (esp. Deut 30), Moses points beyond that Judgment to offer the sure and certain hope of restoration and new life if the people would return and seek God once more.'[26]

In Deut. 30.1-10, the author uses שׁוב six times, leading some OT scholars to consider this the most revealing use of שׁוב in all the OT.[27] The writer also uses a chiasmus, which I have highlighted by my arrangement of the text.[28] The chiasm shows poetically what is at the centre of an effective return to God – namely, that God is enabling a wholehearted love of himself.

A Recall these words and return (וְשַׁבְתָּ) to the Lord (30.1-2)

B The Lord will restore you (וְשׁב) and He will return (וְשָׁב) (30.3)

C The Lord will bring you back to the land of your fathers (30.4-5)

X The Lord will circumcise your heart which will enable you to love the Lord will all your heart and with all your soul (30.6-7)

C You will return (תָשׁוּב) and heed the voice of the Lord (30.8)

B The Lord will return (יָשׁוּב) to take delight in you (30.9)

A You will heed the Lord's voice when you return (תָשׁוּב) to him (30.10).

25. E. Merrill, *Deuteronomy* (Nashville: Broadman & Holman, 1994), p. 387.

26. C. Wright, *The Mission of God: Unlocking the Bible's Grand Narrative* (Grand Rapids: InterVarsity Press, 2006), p. 341.

27. Merrill, *Deuteronomy*, p. 387.

28. My arrangement is a modified 'menorah pattern' done by Christensen. D. Christensen, *Deuteronomy 21.10-34.12* (Nashville: Thomas Nelson, 2002), p. 736.

שׁוב in the text shown here was key to avoiding God's judgement exemplified in exile from the land. שׁוב was also Israel's way of restoration once under God's judgement. Repentance was key if Israel's fortunes were ever to be restored.

But if Israel already proved herself incapable of living obediently, what confidence does this text provide that, if she did repent, she would not just fall into disobedience once again? Merrill writes that God promised 'Israel to make them his people forever, [He] would bring about a spirit of repentance and obedience among them'.[29] In other words, the key to successful repentance (i.e. heart and soul devoted to God) was God enabling such an act (i.e. circumcising the heart).[30]

Deuteronomy is also a book that Luke relies upon heavily.[31] For example, Luke quotes Deut. 6.5 twice, which refers to loving 'the Lord your God with all your heart and with all your soul and with all your strength' (Lk. 10.27; cf. Lk. 11.42), the language of which is nearly identical to the repentance passage of Deuteronomy 30 given earlier. Indeed, recent scholarship points out that Luke uses Deuteronomy 30 explicitly. In his article on restoration in Luke-Acts, Bauckham points to Lk. 1.6, 'He will turn many of the children of Israel to the Lord their God', and argues that this 'looks like an allusion to Deut. 30.2 "[if you] return to YHWH your God"'.[32]

In his monograph, *Jesus and the Victory of God*, Wright argues that the story of the prodigal son is precisely the story of Israel's return from exile and that Jesus is the agent of this return. He states:

> Exile and restoration: this is the central drama that Israel believed herself to be acting out. And the story of the prodigal says, quite simply: this hope is now being fulfilled – but it does not look like what was expected. Israel went into exile because of her own folly and disobedience, and is now returning simply because of the fantastically generous, indeed prodigal, love of her god.[33]

29. Merrill, *Deuteronomy*, p. 387.

30. Cf. Milgrom's argument that personal heart change, felt repentance, is also at the centre of the Jewish cult. He points out the numerous occasions when God berates Israel's sacrifices because her heart was actually far from him. Such treatment from God shows the importance of internal repentance along with external sacrifices. J. Milgrom, *Cult and Conscience: The Asham and the Priestly Doctrine of Repentance* (Leiden: Brill, 1976), pp. 782–784.

31. Lk. 1.6=Deut. 5.33; Lk. 2.41=Deut. 16.1-8; Lk. 4.8=Deut. 6.13; Lk. 4.12=Deut. 6.16; Lk. 6.1=Deut. 23.25; Lk. 6.30=Deut. 15.7, 8, 10; Lk. 9.41=Deut. 32.5; Lk. 10.27=Deut. 6.5; Lk. 11.42=Deut. 6.5; Lk. 15.12=Deut. 21.17; Lk. 18.20=Deut. 5.16-20; Lk. 20.28=Deut. 25.5; Lk. 22.7=Deut. 16.5-8; Lk. 24.27=Deut. 18.15.

32. R. Bauckham. 'The Restoration of Israel in Luke-Acts', *Restoration: Old Testament, Jewish and Christian Perspectives* (ed. J. Scott, Leiden: Brill, 2001), pp. 435–487.

33. N.T. Wright, *Jesus and the Victory of God* (London: SPCK, 1996), p. 133. Wright then suggests that Jesus casts himself as the prodigal son who is returning home. 'Thus, in a nutshell, the parable of the prodigal father points to the hypothesis of the prophetic son: the son, Israel-in-person, who will himself go into the far country, who will take upon himself the shame of Israel's exile, so that the kingdom may

Of course, we cannot now determine whether or not Wright and Bauckham are correct in their arguments, but we can begin to observe that some influential scholars have drawn a line not only between Deuteronomy 30 and Luke's theology of repentance but also between the conception of restoration and specifically Luke's story of the prodigal son.

The stated evidence suggests that repentance was an important aspect of the relationship between God and Israel. In Jeremiah, we see that repentance and apostasy both stem from a core human changeableness. Thus no matter how far Israel was from God, she generally possessed within herself an ability to change direction.[34] Likewise, walking with her God was no guarantee that she could not return in disobedience. Thus the key to lasting repentance was not gaining the ability to repent, which Israel clearly already had, but rather was in the hands of God himself. While repentance was a change of heart and soul, according to Deuteronomy, *successful* and *lasting* repentance is pictured as ultimately God-given – he must circumcise the heart and soul. We also see that both Jeremiah and Deuteronomy are influences in Luke's writing.

b. *Repentance and the prodigal son*

While there is a plethora of historical Jesus scholarship regarding repentance and Luke 15, my purpose here is to judge how Luke himself described repentance and conversion in this parable[35] – but to do so we must be equipped with some interpretative tools. In his extensive work on the parables of Jesus, Blomberg shows that the story of the prodigal son is a 'simple three-point parable'.[36]

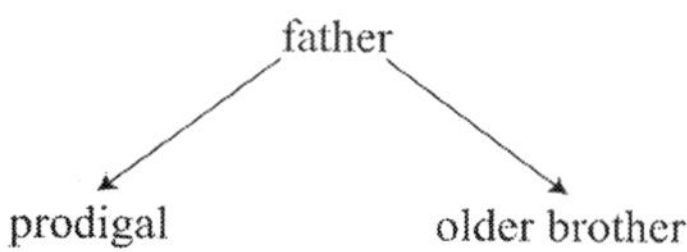

come, the covenant be renewed, and the prodigal welcome of Israel's god, the creator, be extended to the ends of the earth' (Wright, *Jesus*, p. 133). Yet Bailey helpfully points out that Israel is not just pictured as the prodigal son but *also* as the son who remained home. He concedes that 'exile and return is the main theme of the parable of the two lost sons' but cautions that 'any attempt at finding too close a parallel (or a set of parallels) between the exodus, the exile and the parable creates problems for interpretation' (K. Baily, *Jacob and the Prodigal* [Downers Grove: InterVarsity Press, 2003], p. 197).

34. The exception is when God explicitly denies the repentance of Israel or an individual (e.g. Jer. 15.1).

35. Barton warned that attempts to get to the 'real message' of Luke 15, whether from the historical Jesus or just from Luke, are in danger of becoming 'rationalistic and reductionist'. S. Barton, 'Parables on God's Love and Forgiveness', in *The Challenge of Jesus Parables* (ed. R. Longenecker; Grand Rapids: Eerdmans, 2000), pp. 199–216 (200). My purpose in focusing on Luke's thinking is not to reduce the meaning of the text but rather to sharpen our attention so as to fit within the aims of this essay, which are ideological/theological rather than historical.

36. C. Blomberg, *Interpreting the Parables* (Grand Rapids: InterVarsity Press), p. 172.

This type of parable fits within a 'monarchic' parable pattern in which a key authority figure (king, master or father) presided over two subordinates (servant, worker or son) who then, in turn, behave differently from each other.[37] Oftentimes the underling who acted in an apparently shameful way was deemed by the authority figure to be better off than the other 'more righteous' subordinate – these were 'parables of reversal'.[38] Blomberg helpfully subdivides this passage into three episodes, each one focusing on a particular aspect of the meaning of the prodigal's repentance:

> 11-20a: 'Even as the prodigal had the option of repenting and returning home, so also all sinners, however wicked, may confess their sins and turn to God in contrition.'
>
> 20b-24: 'Even as the father went to elaborate lengths to offer reconciliation to the prodigal, so also God offers all people, however undeserving, lavish forgiveness of sins if they are willing to accept it.'
>
> 25-32: 'Even as the older brother should not have begrudged his brother's reinstatement but rather rejoiced in it, so those who claim to be God's people should be glad and not mad that he extends his grace even to the most undeserving.' (1990, 174)

Thus, depending on the particular members of Luke's audience, the meaning for them would be slightly different, which is, of course, part of the genius of using parables as a tool for communication.

But how exactly do the three stories in Luke 15 relate to one another? While the story of the lost sheep (Lk. 15.4-7) and the lost coin (Lk. 15.8-10) are 'three-point parables' in and of themselves,[39] how are they to be read in light of the story of the prodigal son? Are they to be read as three different units or as a single unit? Bailey argues that they are to be understood as 'three stories, one parable'.[40] They are clearly three different stories in that the characters and settings are all different in each section and narrative tools are used to show a division between each section (v. 8 h1 τίς, v. 11 εἶπεν δέ). However, they represent a single parable because Jesus used the singular παραβολήν rather than the plural (v. 3).[41]

37. e.g. Lk. 7.41-43; 12.42-48; 16.19-31.

38. J. Crossan, *In Parables: The Challenge of the Historical Jesus* (New York: Harper & Row, 1973), pp. 53–78; Blomberg, *Parables*, p. 172.

39. Blomberg, *Parables*, p. 179.

40. Bailey, *Jacob*, p. 54.

41. Ibid., pp. 54–57. I will refer to Luke 15 and the parable of the prodigal son as the same teaching even though, technically, Luke 15 has the story of the coin and the lost sheep in addition to the prodigal son.

The narrative context begins with Jesus' acceptance of sinners and tax-collectors – a strong Lukan motif that runs throughout his narrative (7.36-50; 10.38-42; 11.37-54; 14.1-24; 15.1-2; 19.1-10). More specifically, Jesus draws the ire of the Pharisees and scribes for allowing the τελῶναι and the ἁμαρτωλοί to draw near to listen to him (15.1-2a). Jesus responds to this accusation by telling three stories of lost items (a sheep in v. 4; a coin in v. 8; a son in v. 13) that were eventually found by their rightful owners (a man in v. 5; a woman in v. 9; the father in v. 24). Jesus then twice compares the joyful reunion of the lost item to the rightful owner (vv. 7, 10) to that of angelic joy, which erupts in heaven when one sinner (ἁμαρτωλός) repents (μετανοέω). The implication, then, of Jesus' eating with these sinners is that they are like the items that have been lost, but are now found. Tannehill points out that the table fellowship of the reconciled father and son is a 'parabolic mirroring' of the actual situation between Jesus and the sinners.[42] Sinners have repented and are in fellowship with God,[43] who is pictured as the loving, forgiving father.[44]

This story of the prodigal son starts with the younger of two sons asking his father for his inheritance. But to what extent, if any, the son's request is an insult to his father is open to debate. Bailey has argued that the son's request treats the father as if he were dead,[45] but this has been vigorously opposed in more recent scholarship.[46] However, in light of the context, Bock is quite right to assert that the 'son clearly looks to sever his relationship to his father and go away'.[47] The key point, however, of this whole interchange is that the 'son's request is graciously granted' by the father.[48] Schrenk points out that this is Luke's way of picturing God's 'letting go' of a sinner who desires to leave him.[49]

The son takes his inheritance and his life crumbles shortly thereafter. He travels to a distant land and quickly squanders the inheritance from his father (v. 13). If the accusation of the older brother is any hint (v. 30), the younger son's 'wild living' was considered sinful for any Jew. After he spent his money, a famine struck the land and for the first time in this story the son was in need

42. R. Tannehill, *The Narrative Unity of Luke-Acts: A Literary Interpretation* (vol. 1; Philadelphia: Fortress, 1986), p. 171.

43. How these new converts are then treated by 'those who need no repentance' (i.e. the Pharisees and scribes) is then the question left for the 'older son' (v. 32) to answer.

44. S. Kistemaker, *The Parables of Jesus* (Grand Rapids: Baker, 1980), p. 216.

45. K. Bailey, *Poet and Peasant: A Literary Cultural Approach to the Parables in Luke* (Grand Rapids: Eerdmans, 1976), p. 165.

46. Donahue counters Bailey by arguing that four million Jews were in the Diaspora at this time while a paltry half million were in Palestine. Thus, because of the economic situation, that a son would ask for his inheritance before his father's death was 'an ordinary request at the time'. J. Donahue, *The Gospel in Parable* (Minneapolis: Fortress Press, 1988), p. 153. Méndez-Moratalla, *Paradigm*, p. 135.

47. D. L. Bock, *Luke 9:52–24:53* (BECNT; Grand Rapids, MI: Baker, 2007), p. 1310.

48. Ibid.

49. *TDNT* 5.983-84.

(v. 14, lit. he began to lack, ἤρξατο ὑστερεῖσθαι). The young son who once had a family, homeland and money now had nothing.

The son finds a job working for a Gentile who managed a pig farm (v. 15). The son is sent out to feed pigs, which as a Jew is highly dishonourable (Lev. 11.7; Deut. 14.8; Isa. 65.4; 66.17). As Bock states, '[i]n effect, the son has taken the lowest job possible – one that no Jew would even want'.[50] Evidently, the son is not treated well by his employer because he is on the brink of starvation (v. 17). Indeed, the son 'longed' to be fed with the pigs (v. 16). Moreover, *no one* gave him anything as he was too low to be worth giving to (v. 16b).

He begins to consider the irony that his father's hired servants have plenty of bread while he is starving. The son, in despair, acknowledges that he has sinned against both God and his father. Eastman suggests that '[t]here is nothing here about repentance as a moral turn-around',[51] yet the internal dialogue of the son given by Luke does seem to suggest that the son was beginning a process of such 'turn-around'. However, Eastman's main point is well taken that the 'initial key to the son's "repentance" is the father's abundance, and the means of their reconciliation is the free gift of relationship that the father gives as he runs to meet his son'.[52]

The son *resolves* to confess his disqualification as a son to his father (v. 18). Strikingly, even when his father acted as if he would accept his wayward son *without* a confession, the son confesses his sin and declares his disqualification as a son nevertheless (v. 21). The reunion of the son and his father, which I will address more extensively in my explanation of 'divine initiative' to come, was characterized by the father's enthusiastic acceptance of his son. He considered his son to have died but now, by his return, he is alive. The son's older brother, however, was upset at his father's generous treatment of the prodigal. The parable ends with the father repeating to the older son that the prodigal was lost but has now been found – was dead but has now been made alive.[53]

Now that we have met the prodigal, we will seek to see to what extent this parable is paradigmatic in the thinking of Luke.

c. *The prodigal as paradigmatic*

In his monograph, *The Paradigm of Conversion in Luke*, Méndez-Moratalla conducts an analysis of the conversion stories in Luke including Levi (5.27-32), the Woman of the City (7.36-50), the Prodigal Son (15.11-32), Zacchaeus (19.1-10),

50. Bock, *Luke*, p. 1311.

51. S. Eastman, 'The Foolish Father and the Economics of Grace', *ExpT* 117.10 (2006), pp. 402–405 (403).

52. Ibid.

53. In an interesting article, Landmesser suggests that both sons actually turn away from the father, who was the source of life, yet he offers to both the gift of repentance and forgiveness. C. Landmesser, 'Die Rückkehr ins Leben nach dem Gleichnis vom verlorenen Sohn', *ZTK* 99 (2002), pp. 239–261.

the Criminal (23.39-43) and, finally, the non-conversion of a ruler (18.18-30). The most significant outcome of his research, as the title of his book suggests, is that 'it is legitimate to speak of a *Lukan paradigm* of conversion'.[54] He notes ten elements that are most common in Luke's conversion stories. I will briefly highlight them and then show in what ways they do and do not relate to the conversion story of Luke 15.

1. *Divine Initiative*: He notes that '[t]he theme of God's salvific plan is a central motif in the Lukan narrative and, as part of that purpose, divine initiative becomes a relevant Lukan emphasis. To express such a salvific plan at work in and through Jesus, Luke uses the language of necessity (cf. 2.49; 4.43; 9.22; 13.33; 17.25; 19.5; 22.37; 24.7, 44 all unique to Luke except for 9.22), as it is the divine initiative that prompts the action.' Especially when it regards the low status of tax-collectors and sinners, 'Luke makes acceptance of them a consequence of the gracious divine purpose and initiative at work in his ministry which goes beyond both any social or religious claim and any predetermined boundaries'.[55]
2. *Conflict*: He notes that because Jesus accepted those who were outside of 'conventional socio-religious values', this then became a major cause for conflict and opposition to his ministry from those who were portrayed as within the social and religious norms (5.30; 7.39; 15.2; 19.7). Indeed, 'in line with the polarized responses to God's salvific plan, those converting are considered outside the margins of acceptability according to both social and religious conventions, while those sitting and living within those margins do not convert but oppose the divine salvific plan'.[56]
3. *Sinner*: He notes that '[s]inners are the goal of Jesus' ministry. This is what Jesus tells his critics, that he has come to call them to repentance (5.32). Divine initiative works in favour of those on the fringes of social and religious acceptability who, in turn, are depicted as those ready to acknowledge their sin and receptive [*sic*] towards the ministry of God's envoy.'[57]
4. *Repentance*: He states that '[r]epentance becomes in Luke's conversion accounts both the expected consequence of the divine initiative and also the sole condition for forgiveness.' Furthermore, 'those despised as sinners are the ones depicted as repenting, while those who see themselves as righteous remain unaltered'.[58]
5. *Wealth/Possessions*: He notes that Luke's emphasis on the proper use of wealth 'signals whether repentance is present or not (cf. 3.11, 13-14; 5.28;

54. Méndez-Moratalla, *Paradigm*, p. 217.
55. Ibid., p. 218.
56. Ibid.
57. Ibid., p. 219.
58. Ibid.

8.1-3; 15.12-14, 29-30; 19.2, 8)'.[59] He states that '[b]ehind the Lukan stress on repentance manifested in the attitude towards possessions lies the struggle between opposing and mutually excluding allegiances, not a plea for poverty. At stake is who becomes the master of people's lives, either mammon or God.'[60]

6. *Forgiveness*: While he admits that forgiveness in Lukan conversion stories is rarely offered, it is clear through the 'attitudes and actions of Jesus towards people that forgiveness has happened (cf. 5.29; 7.47-49; 15.20, 22-24; 19.5, 7; 23.43)'.[61]
7. *Table-Fellowship and Joy*: He states that 'it is at the table that both the joy of salvation is celebrated and Jesus' forgiveness is granted to those who repent'.[62]
8. *Reversal*: He argues that since Jesus welcomed in those considered outside of the social and religious norms, Jesus 'reformulates values held by leading socio-religious groups. Honour and community acceptance are now attained through repentance'. Furthermore, he states, 'Lukan conversion stories have become not simply a challenge and reinterpretation of generally accepted socio-religious values but their reversal for those who convert'.[63]
9. *Climactic Pronouncement*: He states that '[a]ll conversion stories conclude with a pronouncement by Jesus, linking the main scope of ministry and the main theological emphasis of the story.'[64]
10. *Christological Emphasis*: He states that '[i]n sum, it has been in the encounter with Jesus that forgiveness has been granted and salvation bestowed. It is in the way people favourably respond to God's initiative towards them in Jesus that salvation is obtained. He is acknowledged as saviour.'[65]

In Luke 15 all ten of these elements of conversion are at play, while some are more explicit than others. The first element, divine initiative, is perhaps the most complex in the story of the prodigal son. In some ways the son is the initiator: while the son is in a far-off place, he 'comes to his senses',[66] realizing that he would be better off as a servant of his father because at least he would be fed (Lk. 15.17). The son resolves to return home, rehearses his

59. Ibid.
60. Ibid.
61. Ibid., p. 220.
62. Ibid.
63. Ibid., pp. 220–221.
64. Ibid., p. 221; cf. Lk. 15.7.
65. Méndez-Moratalla, *Paradigm*, p. 221.; Lk. 15.1-32.
66. For the connection between this phase and repentance see the discussion of element #4 on p. 129.

confession of sin and then takes the journey. Thus, up to a point, the son is the initiator of the action – he is the initial driving force behind his own eventual conversion. In v. 20, however, the father jarringly becomes the central figure in the narrative. When the boy is still at a great distance, it is the *father* who instigates their reconciliation. The agenda of the son is instantly overtaken by the agenda of his father. On two occasions the father interrupts the plans of the son (v. 20 '*but* while he was still a long way off'; v. 22 '*but* the father said to the servants'). 'The father's compassion outruns the son's repentance, and the speech of repentance is cut off mid-sentence.'[67] The father wanted his *son*, not another servant. Then he emotionally runs towards his son, and in so doing he casts aside all cultural norms of proper behaviour for a Middle Eastern father. He then calls for a celebration: they would kill the fatted calf to express his joy (v. 23). Thus there appears to be both human and divine agency in the prodigal son. In some ways, the son is the initiator in that he must first acknowledge that he is lost and needs to go home. However, the father is the initiator of the process that actualizes his reconciliation. Moreover, only the father can pronounce that his son is back from the dead (cf. element #9).

Méndez-Moratalla's second element of conversion in Luke is the role of conflict. The story begins with conflict between Jesus and the Pharisees and scribes over his generous treatment of sinners (15.2).[68] It ends with unresolved conflict between the father and the older son.

The third element of conversion is the notion of sinners. As we see in Luke 15, Jesus deals with sinners twice. The first mention of sinners is in that Jesus' crowd were considered sinners by the religious elite (15.2). Second, the final story of the prodigal depicts the son describing himself as one who 'sinned against heaven' (15.18, 21).

The fourth element of conversion is the use of repentance. The notion of repentance is explicitly mentioned by Jesus (15.7, 10), which is easily connected to the repentance of the sinners and tax-collectors. But what can we make of the prodigal son's 'repentance'? Starving, alone and longing to be fed as a pig, the son, at last, begins to consider a return home (v. 17) as he literally 'came to himself' (εἰς ἑαυτὸν δὲ ἐλθών), which is a counterpart to the English idiom 'coming to one's senses'.[69] But what exactly is meant by the phrase εἰς ἑαυτὸν δὲ ἐλθών? Three basic options are (1) the son did not really repent, (2) the son did repent and (3) the son engaged in a pre-repentance. With respect to (1), Donahue argues that the point of Luke 15 is not to emphasize repentance

67. S. Ringe, *Luke* (Louisville: Westminster John Knox, 1995), p. 208.

68. That Jesus would eat with them shows a willingness to defy the Jewish purity code for membership in some Jewish sects. Indeed, οὗτος ἁμαρτωλοὺς προσδέχεται καὶ συνεσθίει αὐτοῖς (15.2b).

69. Bock, *Luke*, p. 1312. Interestingly, for Luke, returning to the Father is a result of doing what is most natural – in one's *right* mind, one will return home.

but rather to show 'the joy of finding and of being found'.[70] He continues that 'neither the sheep nor the coin "repents". The one who is seeking provides all the dramatic action in the parable.'[71] Thus Luke does not depict the son as repenting as much as he is showing a son being found. Regarding (2), Stein suggests, in contrast, that coming to one's senses is a 'Hebrew/Aramaic expression for "repented"'.[72] Thus Luke shows the son to have clearly repented. Arguing for (3), Bailey counters that Luke's oddly worded phrase suggests that typical repentance was *not* what he had in mind. Since Luke never before hesitates to use common language for repentance, this likely indicates that there is some variation of meaning at work here. Bailey states that it is rather a statement that at some point he would repent but has not yet repented.[73] Likewise, Green says that 'shades of repentance are clearly evident'.[74] Hence repentance was in play for the son but it did not culminate with 'conversion' until he reengaged with his father.

The third option is preferred because it shows the complexity of the story: it *is* a story about being found (Donahue), but it is not *just* a story of being found, as it shows the complexity of the son's thinking regarding his desire to return home. Likewise, this *is* a story about repentance (vv. 7, 10); yet, the son's repentance could, at best, win his acceptance as a hired servant, *not* as a son. It was not until the father received him (taking over the narrative in the process) that the son learned of his *full* reconciliation – his father deemed him to have returned from the dead.

The fifth element of conversion relates to change in attitude regarding wealth and possessions. The son's confession to the father that he would be a servant and not require any money fits with Méndez-Moratalla's element #5. The son who wanted money and left home (15.12-13) then returned home, asking not for money but to be a servant (15.19): this is a sign of real conversion.

The loving response of the father indicates that forgiveness (element #6) occurred (15.20, 22). The father's full acceptance of the son is obvious as the son is given a robe, shoes and a ring (v. 22). The context in which Jesus told these parables was that of table-fellowship (element #7) and each parable concludes with a celebratory meal and great joy (15.6, 9, 23).

In Luke 15 there is at least a partial reversal (element #8): the Pharisees and scribes are told that the sinners and tax-collectors are actually repentant and in fellowship with God. The *inclusion* of the 'outsider' did not necessarily mean the *exclusion* of the 'insider'. The 'older son' is not asked to leave the

70. Donahue, *Gospel*, p. 151.
71. Ibid.
72. R. Stein, *Luke* (Nashville: Broadman Press, 1992), p. 406.
73. K. Bailey, *Poet and Peasant* (Grand Rapids: Eerdmans, 1983), p. 175.
74. J. Green, *The Gospel of Luke* (Grand Rapids: Eerdmans, 1997), p. 581.

family, but rather is asked *to join* in the party and rejoice in the inclusion of his younger brother.

There is also a final pronouncement (element #9) given by Jesus through the words of the father. Indeed, the father's explanation for the celebration is perhaps the most insightful comment regarding Luke's notion of repentance and conversion: the father's son was dead, but now, by his return home, is alive (vv. 24, 32). The tenth element of conversion, Christology, is seen from the outset of the narrative: it is explicitly though their relationship with Jesus that he deems the sinners to have repented and come home to the Father.

d. *The prodigal and Luke's theology of repentance*

Given the evidence stated, it is certainly plausible that the story of the prodigal son is representative of Luke's thinking regarding repentance. Whether or not Méndez-Moratalla's paradigm of conversion is totally sustainable, it is striking to read ch. 15 in line with all of the elements of conversion as categorized by Méndez-Moratalla. Thus, I think he is justified in renaming this parable 'A Parable of Conversion'. Furthermore, I think it is reasonable that if we extract Luke's notion of repentance as expressed in this parable, then it will go a long way in building our profile of Luke's theology of conversion. We now turn our attention to Paul's notion of repentance and we will begin to see the contrast between him and Luke emerge.

III. *Paul and repentance*

A conundrum exists in the guild of NT studies regarding the precise perspective Paul takes on repentance. This dilemma is not primarily about what Paul *says* regarding repentance as much as it is about his unusual silence. As Enslin aptly puts it, it is the *lack* of repentance in Paul that is 'a conspicuous silence'.[75] Paul mentions repentance only three times in his unquestioned letters. First, Rom. 2.4 in the form of a question, which will be the subject of our investigation in this chapter: ἢ τοῦ πλούτου τῆς χρηστότητος αὐτοῦ καὶ τῆς ἀνοχῆς καὶ τῆς μακροθυμίας καταφρονεῖς, ἀγνοῶν ὅτι τὸ χρηστόν τοῦ θεοῦ εἰς *μετάνοιάν* σε ἄγει. The second and third times are in 2 Cor. 7.10/12.21, addressing the restoration of wayward Christians: ἡ γὰρ κατὰ θεὸν λύπη μετά νοιαν εἰς σωτηρίαν ἀμεταμέλητον ἐργάζεται / καὶ πενθήσω πολλοὺς τῶν προημαρτηκότων καὶ μὴ μετανοησάντων ἐπὶ τῇ ἀκαθαρσίᾳ καὶ ἀσελγείᾳ ᾗ ἔπραξαν.[76] Due to this lack of data, there is no consensus in scholarship as to *where* this important aspect of first-century CE Jewish/Christian

75. M. Enslin, 'Paul and Repentance: A Conspicuous Silence', *Eretz-Israel* 16 (1982), pp. 37–42.

76. 'For godly grief produces a repentance that leads to salvation without regret/and I may have to

conversion theology – preached by John the Baptist,[77] Jesus[78] and the early church[79] – fits in with Paul's theology of conversion, if at all.

In her brief article penned in the first half of the twentieth century, Andrews observed this phenomenon of the relationship between Paul and repentance.[80] Given the increasing centrality of repentance in the Second Temple Judaism of his day, she notes the remarkable fact that Paul, though 'a Hebrew of Hebrews' (Phil. 3.5), basically ignored it in his letters. Andrews concluded that '[w]ith emphasis on repentance so clear in his ancestral faith, and his letters revealing such abundant opportunity for exhortation to repentance, his almost total neglect of the idea invites study'.[81] With this I agree. Moreover, considering the two-part historical reality that (1) the religious movement, which became known as Christianity, did so by *converting* Jews and Gentiles and (2) that no other adherent of whom we know was more successful at converting others than Paul (and the missionary endeavours he spearheaded), it is all the more curious that he opted not to use the *primary* conversion language of his day or culture.

The methodological pitfalls of *argumentum ex silentio* are well known and I do *not* plan to fall into one here. To the contrary, what Paul *says* about repentance in Romans 2 provides the foundation for my ensuing argument. A study of Paul's usage of repentance in Rom. 2.4-5 gives insight into both what he believed about repentance and why he used other terms such as ἐπικαλέω (e.g. Rom. 10.12, 13, 14) and πιστεύω (Rom. 10.9, 10) to describe conversion. The result of this study will reveal a sharper profile of Paul's theology of conversion by showing where the concept of repentance, as he understood it, actually fits.

There are several options available regarding how repentance was utilized by Paul in Romans 2. We will begin with Sanders, not just because his is currently the most famous approach to Paul and repentance but also because his is the most provocative and, as such, has advanced the discussion of the relationship between Paul and repentance.[82] Sanders suggests that Paul, in Romans 2, splices

mourn over many of those who sinned earlier and have not repented of the impurity, sexual immorality, and sensuality that they have practised.'

77. Cf. Mt. 3.2, 8, 11; Mk 1.4; Lk. 3.3, 4; Acts 13.24; 19.4.

78. There is much speculation about whether or not the historical Jesus preached repentance and, if he did, what sort of repentance it was that Jesus actually required. I mention it here because the early church evidently believed Jesus taught repentance (Mt. 4.17; Mk 1.15; Lk. 5.32; 15.7; 24.47), thus making Paul's silence about it all the more interesting.

79. Cf. Acts 2.38; 3.19; 5.31; 8.22; 11.18; 26.20.

80. M. Andrews, 'Paul and Repentance', *JBL* 54.2 (1935), p. 125. Of course, Andrews was not the first to notice this tension regarding repentance. Indeed, in his recent article, Brecht argues that it is precisely Luther's shift in understanding repentance (that it must be based on grace) that was the foundation of his initial argument against indulgences. M. Brecht, 'Luthers neues Verständnis der Busse und die reformatorische Entdeckung', *ZTK* 101.3 (2004), pp. 281–291.

81. Andrews, 'Paul', p. 125.

82. E. P. Sanders, *Paul, the Law, and the Jewish People* (Minneapolis: Fortress Press, 1983).

a previously existing synagogue sermon into his letter to the Romans. Paul then fails to integrate theologically this sermon with the whole of his letter. Sanders maintains that Paul clings to repentance in the Jewish Pharisaical tradition: 'Pharisees and rabbis of all schools and all periods strongly believed in repentance and other means of atonement in the case of transgression.'[83] Thus, 'Paul takes over to an unusual degree homiletical material from Diaspora Judaism', which he changes only in an 'insubstantial way'.[84] Due to this 'Jewish' understanding of repentance, Paul entertains the possibility that some will be saved by their works. Hence, Paul's understanding of repentance is inconsistent with his overall argument in Romans regarding universal sinfulness. Romans 2 according to Sanders means little more than 'repent and obey the law from the bottom of your heart, so that you will be a true Jew'.[85]

Sanders's characterization of 'Jewish' repentance does not reflect the widely divergent views of repentance within Judaism in Paul's day and adds support to the accusation against him of oversimplifying Judaism. However, while many rightly criticize Sanders's view of repentance, as we will see, most 'alternatives' to Sanders's position actually land very close to his view.[86] The only real difference is that these 'alternatives' do not see the inconsistency as Sanders does between Paul's greater argument of sinful humanity and his straightforward call to repentance.[87]

The works of Kirk, Cranfield, Barrett, Harper and Moo all suggest that Paul's accusation in vv. 1-3 leads to a straightforward call for repentance in v. 4. According to this reading, God's kindness puts pressure on Paul's audience to repent *and* Paul evidently hopes (perhaps even expects) that they will do so. Moo comments only on the 'surprisingly small part in Paul's teaching' that

83. Ibid., p. 28.

84. Ibid., p. 123.

85. Ibid., p. 129.

86. Even in Seifrid's critique of Sanders's view of Romans 2, he concedes, 'In a narrow and facile sense, Sanders is correct'. M. Seifrid, 'Unrighteousness by Faith: Apostolic Proclamation in Romans 1.18-3.20', in *Justification and Variegated Nomism Vol. 2.* (eds D. Carson, P. O'Brien and M. Seifrid; Tübingen: Mohr Siebeck, 2004), pp. 105–145 (126).

87. In his recent massive monograph, *The Deliverance of God*, Campbell offers a strikingly original reading of Romans 1–3. He suggests that Rom. 1.18-32 is *not* Pauline but, by use of 'speech and character', Paul is characterizing a judgemental Jewish 'Teacher' who Paul fears will arrive in Rome and corrupt the church there. Repentance in Romans 2 then functions as a way for Paul to condemn this 'Teacher' by using the same standard used by the Teacher against Gentiles. While this is an original thesis regarding the function of repentance in Romans 2, the basis of it (i.e. Campbell's mysterious 'Teacher' theory) is too tenuous to be seriously considered. His evidence for 'speech and character' in Rom. 1.18-32 is so scant that even those who are sympathetic to Campbell's overall reading remain totally unconvinced. D. Campbell, *The Deliverance of God* (Grand Rapids: Eerdmans, 2009). Cf. Gorman's review of Campbell read at SBL in New Orleans, 2009 as well as Watson's review, which states that only time will tell if anyone will be persuaded by Campbell's thesis. F. Watson 'Review of The Deliverance of God by Douglas Campbell'. EC 2010, 1: 1-8.

repentance plays and does not attempt to ask why Paul uses it here.[88] Hence there is surprisingly little difference in these readings of Paul's notion of repentance from what Sanders has proposed. While some have a more sophisticated notion of how repentance functioned for Paul,[89] they all basically agree with Sanders that the point here is a straightforward call to repentance from the bottom of one's heart.

There are at least two other possible options besides Sanders. First, we have Käsemann.[90] He does not take the term 'repentance' at face value and insists that it is actually just a component of faith. Repentance is the 'integral element of faith', in which one submits oneself to the Judge rather than being the judge oneself. Hence Käsemann defines the meaning of repentance from what Paul means by faith. Second, we have Bultmann, who suggests that perhaps Paul reverts back to his style of preaching and calls for repentance just as he would do in a missionary evangelistic setting. Bultmann believed that μετάνοια was part of Paul's missionary preaching and that is how it ought to be understood here.[91]

While both Käsemann and Bultmann provide interesting alternatives to Sanders, neither explains *why* Paul decided to use the term 'repentance'. If Käsemann is correct, why is it that Paul explained only this important element of faith once in all his letters? If Bultmann is correct, why did Paul immediately abandon this language in favour of other terminology without explanation? Another problem in the readings offered by Bultmann and Käsemann is that neither explains *how* repentance fits in with Paul's broader argument. Hence according to their readings Paul would have been better off to use the term 'faith' than repentance.

In contrast to these readings of Paul and repentance, I suggest a reading of repentance that fits Paul's overall argument. I think it unlikely that Paul in Romans 2 flatly contradicts his broader argument in Romans 1–3 and I think it unlikely that he inexplicably reverted to his old preaching style. Neither

88. D. Moo, *The Epistle to the Romans* (Grand Rapids: Eerdmans, 1996), p. 134.

89. Cf. Yinger, who states that repentance here was intended by Paul on a dual level: first, for his 'imaginary dialogue partner', the call to repentance was to be understood 'generally as a *warning*' (K. Yinger, *Paul, Judaism and Judgment according to Deeds* [Cambridge: Cambridge University Press, 1999], p. 162; emphasis his). He explains further, 'The critic should recognize his/her presumptuous reasoning and hypocritical behavior (cf. verses 1-3), and allow God's kindness to produce repentance (cf. verse 4); otherwise wrathful judgment is threatened (verse 5)' (ibid., p. 162). On another level, the call to repentance was intended for his Jewish-Christian readers to 'challenge them in an indirect way to correct possibly faulty attitudes. Paul is not accusing them of impenitent sinning or apostasy; rather he is concerned lest their thinking mirror that of the diatribe partner' (ibid., p. 163).

90. E. Käsemann, *Commentary on Romans* (Grand Rapids: Eerdmanns, 1980), p. 55.

91. R. Bultmann, *The Second Letter to the Corinthians* (Minneapolis: Augsburg, 1985). It is a genuine prophetic call to repentance of the style of John the Baptist, Jesus and apostolic proclamation in Acts.

does it seem very Pauline for Paul to transfer what he meant by 'faith' into the term repentance without explanation or without ever replicating it in his unquestioned letters.

The problem with the majority of views about repentance in Romans 2 is the disconnection between what Paul says about repentance in v. 4 and what he says about it in v. 5.

> v. 4 – ἢ τοῦ πλούτου τῆς χρηστότητος αὐτοῦ καὶ τῆς ἀνοχῆς καὶ τῆς μακροθυμίας καταφρονεῖς, ἀγνοῶν ὅτι τὸ χρηστὸν τοῦ θεοῦ εἰς μετάνοιάν σε ἄγει;[92]

> v. 5 – κατὰ δὲ τὴν σκληρότητά σου καὶ ἀμετανόητον καρδίαν θησαυρίζεις σεαυτῷ ὀργὴν ἐν ἡμέρᾳ ὀργῆς καὶ ἀποκαλύψεως δικαιοκρισίας τοῦ θεοῦ[93]

The prospect of one's μετάνοια is immediately qualified (δέ) by their being 'hard' (σκληρότης; cf. Deut. 9.27) and having an impenitent (ἀμετανόητος) heart. While, on the one hand, God's kindness *ought* to lead them to repentance (v. 4), on the other hand, Paul diagnoses them with a bad heart that is unable to accomplish such an action. Paul used an ἀμετανόητος – μετάνοια wordplay to show that repentance, given the current conditions of their heart, is ineffective.[94] This then functions to set up the result of Paul's statement that God will render to each one according to what he had done (2.6). That is, because of man's heart, no one can 'do good' (cf. 3.12).

If this is the case, we may notice then how it affects Cranfield's argument, which is representative of most views of how Paul uses repentance: '[E]ven now, when God's wrath and His righteous judgment are actually being revealed as the gospel is preached, the person whom he is addressing cannot think of anything better to do than to go on storing up wrath for himself by his self-righteous, impenitent attitude'.[95] However, if Paul modified repentance with 'impenitent heart', it is precisely the capacity of the heart to repent that is the problem. It is not an attitude problem in which one has the ability to change but refuses to do so. Rather it is a καρδία problem that calls for a more radical procedure – one that is impossible to self-administer. Indeed, when Paul describes an 'inner Jew' later in this chapter (v. 29) it is precisely the καρδία

92. 'Or do you presume on the riches of his kindness and forbearance and patience, not knowing that God's kindness is meant to lead you to repentance?'

93. 'But because of your hard and impenitent heart you are storing up wrath for yourself on the day of wrath when God's righteous judgment will be revealed.'

94. While this dynamic has no obvious predecessor, we do see a similar wordplay in *Martyrdom of Polycarp* XI using a cognate of ἀμετανόητος, ἀμετάθετος. *Ἀμετάθετος* γὰρ ἡμῖν ἡ ἀπὸ τῶν κρειττόνων ἐπὶ τὰ *μετάνοια* 'a change of mind from better to worse is not a change that is an option for us' (cf. BDAG article 'ἀμετάθετος').

95. C. Cranfield, *Romans 1-8* (London: T&T Clark, 1975), pp. 145–146.

that is at issue – yet this time it has been circumcised *by the Spirit*. In vv. 4-5 Paul diagnoses the problem and in v. 29 previews what it takes to fix such a problem – surgery on the καρδία itself performed by the hands of God. Hence, I think the effect Paul wished to give to his readers is that the heart is not just unrepentant; it is, in reality, *unrepentable*.[96]

If this is a better reading of Rom. 2.4-5, then was Paul alone in believing in an unrepentable heart or did this fit within a pre-existing strand of Jewish thought? The term ἀμετανόητος was used rarely in ancient literature – only Rom. 2.4 and *Test. Gad* 7.5 use this term in a clearly understood way.[97] Interestingly, both use it to describe that the impenitent are subject to God's wrath (e.g. *Test. Gad* 7.5, '[the] unrepentant is reserved for eternal punishment' and Rom. 2.5, 'because of your hard and impenitent heart you are storing up wrath for yourself'). The concepts that comprise this reading of an unrepentable heart, however, were not totally original to Paul (while use of ἀμετανόητος to describe this may be original to him). These can be seen in texts such as 2 Esd. 9.10-13 and in *Sib. Or*. 4.166-170 that indicate effective repentance only occurs as it is given by God himself (e.g. 'God will grant repentance' *Sib. Or*. 4.168). By implication it is an impossible task to repent without God granting it.

a. *Paul's logic in negating repentance*

If my argument is right, then why did Paul choose to explain repentance in this way? Is it not odd to mention repentance just to show that one cannot repent? While Paul's arguments can be famously dense (cf. 2 Pet. 3.16), I argue that Paul's use of repentance here forms part of a larger pattern of logic seen in Romans 2–3.

Paul begins in vv. 4-5 with what I have suggested is a μετάνοια – ἀμετανόητος dynamic. This quickly leads into the concept of 'doing good' in v. 7 (τοίς μὲν καθ' ὑπομονὴν ἔργου ἀγαθοῦ) and v. 10 (εἰρήνη παντὶ τῷ ἐργαζομένῳ τὸ αγαθόν). Just as many scholars have been baffled at Paul's usage of repentance, even more have been confused as to Paul's apparent work-based approach to gaining peace (e.g. Sanders, as noted earlier). Once again scholars are left to interpret this either at face value – simply inconsistent with Paul's overall argument – or as that Paul himself was not quite sure what he was saying.[98]

96. By *unrepentable* I mean incapable of repentance.

97. Noting the *hapax legomena* in this verse, including ἀμετανόητος, Dunn states that this 'strongly suggests that Paul is striving to find words which will maximize the impact of what he is saying and not be shrugged off as merely formulaic or commonplace'. J. Dunn, *Romans 1-8* (Dallas: Word, 1988), p. 83. Cf. also Epictetus, frag. 25.

98. 'My suggestion is that Paul has not worked out in detail, and I think in fact nowhere works out in great detail, exactly what that "keeping the law" involves.' N. T. Wright, 'The Law in Romans 2', in *Paul and the Mosaic Law* (ed. J. Dunn; Grand Rapids: Eerdmans, 2001), pp. 131–150 (138).

However, just as Paul negated the possibility of repentance, so too, later in this argument, Paul negated the possibility of anyone 'doing good' (3.12, οὐκ ἔστιν ὁ ποιῶν χρηστότητα).

Paul then approached the concept of seeking eternal life (v. 7, ζητοῦσιν ζωὴν αἰώνιον) only to conclude that no one really seeks God (3.11, οὐκ ἔστιν ὁ ἐκζητῶν τὸν θεόν). It is possible to read Paul as simply contradicting himself in Romans 2 and 3 but reading these terms as foils to be negated makes better sense of what Paul seems to be suggesting in this section of Romans. While it may seem unusual that Paul waited so long to complete the negation of 'seeking' and 'doing', recent scholarship demonstrates that Paul was quite able to maintain a logical sequence while not necessarily using it in a 'point by point . . . linear fashion'.[99] Paul might have used a literary device that Bassler calls the 'postponed conclusion'.[100] This means that Paul sometimes gave the main conclusion to one argument after (and sometimes in the middle of) another argument. For example, both Myers and Bassler suggest that when Paul noted in Rom. 3.22-23 that 'there is no distinction since all have sinned', this is actually the postponed conclusion of his discussion in Rom. 3.9-20. Similarly, Paul's statement in Rom. 3.28 is actually the postponed conclusion of his discussion in Rom. 3.21-26. While the possibility of 'postponed conclusion' does not prove Paul was using it with 'doing good', and 'seeking', it does show the capacity in Paul to use unorthodox logical sequences in proving his point. As Seifrid helpfully points out, 'Paul does not work as a bricklayer adding piece upon piece, but as an artist, who covers the whole canvas quickly with very broad strokes and then returns to fill in the details.'[101]

This way of reading 'repentance', 'seeking' and 'doing good' actually fits Paul's overall argument of universal sinfulness in 1.18–3.26 and gives explanatory force as to *why* he uses them. Hence, if what I suggest is correct, some of the arguments that attempt to explain that Paul did not mean what it seems like he means can be put to rest. Paul means *real* repentance, *real* seeking God and *real* doing good – it is just that no one can do them.

b. *The law and conversion language*

Now, for Paul, the question becomes how exactly one describes a καρδία transformation. If the problem is the heart itself, how is it changed? Why is it that repentance is not the answer for Paul, even as it was the most common

99. C. Myers, 'Chiastic Inversion in the Argument of Romans 3-8', *NovT* 35.1 (1993), pp. 30–47 (32).

100. J. Bassler, *Divine Impartiality: Paul and a Theological Axiom* (Atlanta: Scholars Press, 1982), p. 59.

101. M. A. Seifrid, 'Unrighteaous by Faith: Apostolic Proclamation in Romans 1:18–3:20', in *Justification and Variegated Nomism: The Paradoxes of Paul* (eds D. A. Carson, M. A. Seifrid, P. T. O'Brien; Grand Rapids, MI: Baker, 2004), p. 107.

term for conversion? I suggest two basic reasons: (1) repentance was too closely associated with the law and as such forced him to create new conversion language and (2) Paul's radical understanding of sin rendered repentance, as it was commonly understood, useless.

The relationship between Paul and the law in Romans 2 is closely related to the relationship between Paul and repentance. Pedersen suggests that the fundamental difference between Paul's understanding of the law and his former way of understanding the law was whether or not the law-giving event itself was the primary salvation event. After his conversion, Paul understood the coming of Christ as the primary salvation event rather than the giving of the law. Thus he states, 'what at the deepest level divides Jews and Christians is the basic salvation event'.[102] In light of this, is it not to be expected that Paul would also craft a new 'response' to this salvation event?[103] If so, then he would be wary of using repentance language that recalled the common way of salvation and would look for something new to describe conversion. Moo is not too far off the mark when he states, regarding the lack of repentance in Paul, that 'this is because the coming of Christ has revealed to Paul that acceptance with God requires a stronger action than the word "repentance" often connoted at the time'.[104]

Repentance is no longer a useful term for Paul because of its heritage within Judaism, especially in light of its relationship with the law (e.g. Deuteronomy 30). Repentance, for some Jews, was another way of calling wayward Jews back to the *law*: '[W]hen you obey the voice of the Lord your God, to keep his commandments and his statutes that are written in this Book of the Law, when you turn (ἐπιστραφῇς) to the Lord your God with all your heart and with all your soul' (Deut. 30.10). Rather than turning his listeners to the law, Paul wanted them to turn to the Christ (Rom. 10.4). It therefore seems very logical that he would be careful not to confuse his readers on this point and would select other terms that did not have such a close connection with the law. Hence Paul does not use repentance because of preconceptions present in his Jewish audience.

In his article 'Romans 2: A Deuteronomistic Reading' Ito argues that the blessings and curses of Deuteronomy 27–30 function as Paul's interpretative framework in Romans 2.[105] He notes that vv. 7 and 10 promise a blessing to those who do good while vv. 8-9 declare curses on evil doers.[106] He also shows the similarity in language between v. 8 'wrath and fury' (ὀργὴ καὶ θυμός) and that of Deut. 29.27, 'in anger and fury and great wrath' (ἐν θυμῷ καὶ ὀργῇ καὶ παροξυσμῷ μεγάλῳ). Likewise v. 9, 'there will be tribulation and distress

102. S. Pedersen, 'Paul's Understanding of the Biblical Law', *NovT* 44.1 (2002), pp. 1–34 (12).

103. Pedersen, 'Paul', p. 5.

104. Moo, *Romans*, pp. 133–134.

105. A. Ito, 'Romans 2: A Deuteronomistic Reading', *JSNT*, 59 (1995), pp. 21–37.

106. Ibid., p. 25.

(θλῖψις καὶ στενοχωρία), matches Deut. 28.53, 55, 57, 'in the siege and in the distress' (ἐν τῇ στενοχωρίᾳ σου καὶ ἐν τῇ θλίψει σου). Furthermore, he notes that Paul's reference in v. 29 to the circumcision of the heart is a reference to Deut. 30.6, 'and the Lord your God will circumcise your heart (καρδίαν) and the heart (καρδίαν) of your offspring, so that you will love the Lord your God with all your heart (καρδίας) and with all your soul, that you may live'.

Interestingly, Ito does not factor in Paul's use of repentance in his argument, which is ironic because repentance was the key to restoration in Deuteronomy 30. Using Ito's insight, however, one can see even more clearly how Paul may be using repentance. He is drawing on a common understanding of Jewish soteriology derived from Deuteronomy and deconstructing it, having eliminated the power of repentance to save. Likewise, Paul previews another soteriology (2.29), also drawn from Deuteronomy (30.6 and 29.28), but one in which repentance is not the major emphasis.[107]

Following Ito is the recent work by White, who also argues that Paul has Deuteronomy in mind here; yet, unlike Ito, he connects Paul's use of repentance with the Deuteronomistic notion of repentance.[108] He states: '[T]he language of Rom. 2.5 shows clear linguistic parallels with the Moabic narrative. The verdict that the interlocutor has a hard heart . . . parallels the verdict of Moses on Israel (Deut. 9.6 LXX).'[109] Likewise, the summons for repentance recalls Deut. 30.1-10, yet as it is used in Rom. 2.4 it highlights Israel's stubborn refusal to repent.[110] White, however, fails to see the possibility that Paul may be alluding to this Deuteronomy passage for the purpose of showing that a return to the law is no longer effective in one's return to the Lord. In his monograph *No One Seeks for God* Bell admits that repentance, if taken at face value, may well have been considered a 'work' within Paul's Judaism.[111] Thus, in Bell's reading, 'the most important question' concerns how this notion of repentance 'can be reconciled to Paul's theology of justification sola fide, sola gratia'. However, if my reading is correct, the tension that Bell refers to is relieved.

In his recent article, Hägerland argues that Jesus, who preached to primarily Jewish audiences, saw a stark difference between repentance that implied ritual law and that which implied spiritual and moral change.[112] While his

107. A pattern Paul uses again in Romans 10.

108. Scott argues that Paul's thought flowed through a basic Deuteronomnic framework of sin-exile-restoration. J. Scott, 'Paul's use of Deuteronomic Tradition', *JBL* 112.4 (1993), pp. 645–665. I agree with his basic insight, yet, similar to White, I think he missed Paul's contrasting notions of repentance and faith in Deuteronomy (cf. Deut 30.14; Rom. 10.8).

109. P. White, 'An Intertextual Analysis of Romans 2:1-16', *ER* 1.2 (2009), pp. 2–39 (15).

110. White, 'Intertextual', p. 17.

111. R. Bell, *No One Seeks for God: An Exegetical and Theological Study of Romans 1.18-3.20* (Tübingen: Mohr Siebeck, 1998), p. 108.

112. T. Hägerland, 'Jesus and the Rites of Repentance', *NTS* 52 (2006), pp. 166–187 (169).

conclusion about how the historical Jesus viewed repentance is irrelevant to this investigation, his observation about the complex ways the call for repentance could have been understood, especially within Judaism, is relevant. If it is true that 'repentance was taken for granted as a characteristic of Jewish piety', then it might equally be true that the actual implications of 'repentance' could vary widely depending upon which strand of Jewish thought the auditor relied upon.[113] Thus, perhaps Paul, who claimed sensitivity to his audiences (1 Cor. 9.22), refrained from using it so as not to confuse his readership. Thus, while Bultmann might not be totally wrong to insist that Paul may have used repentance in his missionary preaching, in this reasoned letter to the Romans, Paul must be more careful with his words. Indeed, his polemic against repentance in 2.5 safeguarded his brief mention of it in v. 4 so as to erase any notion that one may have regarding human ability to orient oneself towards God via works of the law.[114]

c. *Repentance and the power of sin*

The second reason Paul did not use repentance was because of his radical understanding of sin.[115] In order to see how radical was Paul's view of sin, we first need to observe some similarities between him and other first-century Jews. Indeed, Paul was not the only Jew in the first century CE who questioned the effectiveness of repentance. Philo and the writer of *Jubilees* also had their reservations, but in different ways and for different reasons.

Philo noted that only God himself is without sin. However, if a man sins, a *wise* man will go forward in repentance. τὸ μὲν μηδὲν ἁμαρτεῖν ἴδιον θεοῦ, τὸ δὲ μετανοεῖν σοφοῦ (*Fug*. 157). But to achieve repentance is 'very difficult and very hard to attain to' (καὶ δυσεύρετον τοῦτό γε) (*Fug*. 157). Thus repentance remains a possibility but only for a select few who are already wise. However, for those who are not wise, repentance is never actually achieved even though there are claims that it has been. 'And that man is crazy who, speaking falsely instead of truly, while still committing iniquity, asserts that he has repented' (*Fug*. 160). While the wise actually repent, others continue on in sin claiming all the while they have repented. For this category of the unrepentant a 'storing up' of judgement awaits, just as it does for Paul. Philo said that it is as 'if

113. Bell, *Seeks*, p. 169.

114. This might make sense for Jewish audience members, but what about the Gentile ones? The simple answer to that is Gentile Christians felt great pressure in the early church to integrate Jewish practices into their Christianity. Thus Paul may well have wanted to avoid the Jewish aspect of this term so as not to confuse his Gentile Christians by suggesting they ought to revert to a Jewish way of atonement.

115. Vos argues that Paul, in his letter to the Romans, often brought up the notion of law for the express purpose of showing the nature of sin. J. Vos, 'Sophistische Argumentation im Romerbrief des Apostels Paulus', *NovT* 43.3 (2001), pp. 224–244.

one who had a disease were to pretend that he was in good health; for he, as it seems, will only get more sick, since he does not choose to apply any of the remedies which are conducive to health' (*Fug.* 160). Thus, like Paul, Philo saw death as the result of unrepentance; however, unlike what I am arguing Paul was saying, Philo does hold out the possibility that people have it within themselves to 'choose to apply' repentance.[116]

Lambert recently argued that the writer of *Jubilees* had his doubts not about who could repent, in contrast to Philo, but about the effectiveness of repentance. Instead, what *Jubilees* looked for was a '*divinely* initiated transformation of human nature – let us call it "new creation" or, perhaps better, "re-creation" – rather than *humanly* initiated repentance'.[117] The writer of *Jubilees* altered the biblical story recounting the conversation between Moses and God. Rather than God calling on Israel to repent in a Deuteronomistic fashion, Moses interrupts God and begs him to

> create for them a just spirit. May the spirit of Belial not rule them so as to bring charges against them before you and to trap them away from every proper path so that they may be destroyed from your presence. They are your people and your heritage whom you have rescued from Egyptian control by your great power. Create for them a pure mind and a holy spirit. May they not be trapped in their sins from now to eternity. (1.19-21)

According to *Jubilees*, in order for Israel to repent, it was incumbent upon God to change Israel's nature first (Deut. 10.16). Their mind and spirit needed to be recreated.[118]

In concert with Philo and *Jubilees*, Paul also had his doubts about repentance, not because it was too hard and not *just* because the human condition needed divine agency (certainly Paul believed it did)[119] but primarily because the overpowering role of sin in the heart of mankind had spoiled its effectiveness. Most Jewish thinkers believed that there were individual sins in a person's life that needed to be atoned for in some way. Indeed, part of the concept of

116. Cf. *Somn.* 2.292, 'giving ear to their new counsellor, which never flatters, and which cannot be corrupted, namely, repentance, having propitiated the merciful power of the living God by sacred hymns of repentance instead of profane songs, they will find entire forgiveness'.

117. D. Lambert, 'Did Israel believe that Redemption Awaited its Repentance? The Case of Jubilees 1', *CBQ* 68.4 (2006), pp. 631–650 (633).

118. Cf. Josephus' view of repentance in which he believed it could not undo the consequences of sin. In describing Joseph's refusal of the sexual advances of Potiphar's wife: 'He also put her in mind that she was a married woman, and that she ought to cohabit with her husband only; and desired her to suffer these considerations to have more weight with her than the short pleasure of lustful dalliance, which would bring her to repentance afterwards, would cause trouble to her, and yet would not amend what had been done amiss' (*Antiq.* 2.51).

119. Cf. *Divine and Human Agency in Paul and his Cultural Environment* (eds J. Barclay and S. Gathercole; London: T&T Clark, 2008).

repentance itself presupposes that there is sin to turn from. But sin was not seen as an agent that could negatively affect an individual in such a way as to make repentance itself useless.[120] For Jews repentance provided the *hope* of ultimate salvation. And it is this *hope* that I think Paul in Romans 2 wished to dash. For Paul, sin destroyed all human confidence to achieve salvation and any term that may conjure up such confidence in the flesh, such as repentance, he was careful to argue against.

d. *Repentance and Romans 2*

If what I have argued is correct regarding repentance in vv. 4-5 then how is the rest of Romans 2 to be read in the light of it? I suggest that the blessings and curses of vv. 6-11 are to be seen in an equally gloomy light now that the traditional means of restoration has been taken away.[121] In this section, which is bracketed by the statements 'He will render to each one according to his works' (v. 6) and 'for God shows no partiality' (v. 11), Paul stated that God will give the ultimate blessing of 'eternal life' (ζωὴν αἰώνιον) for those who earnestly seek for glory, honour and immortality (v. 7). Similarly, the blessing of glory, honour and peace await those who 'do good' (v. 10). Hence, for Paul it is the notion of eternal life for the individual (ἕκαστος) that is at stake in this section and, furthermore, this eternal life is based on what one does.

In v. 12, however, the power of sin comes into play once again: 'For all who have sinned without the law will also perish without the law, and all who have sinned under the law will be judged by the law.' For Gentiles, Paul shows that they will perish without the given Jewish law (v. 12), even though they have a law written on their hearts (v. 15) that will only work to condemn them (vv. 15b-16).[122]

Having the law written on the hearts of the Gentiles could indicate a Stoic notion of natural law as expressed in Cicero's statement: 'Law is the highest reason implanted in Nature, which commands what ought to be done and forbids the contrary. This reason, when firmly fixed and perfected in the human mind, is law' (*De legibus* 1.6.18). Martens argues, furthermore, that this Stoic notion of the law in the heart was a reflection of Zeus himself and only a 'sage'

120. But there is some question regarding Esau and whether or not God allowed him to repent as a result of his sin; see *Secrets of Enoch* 62.1-3; *Sib. Or.* 4.166-170.

121. Paul stated explicitly elsewhere his pessimism regarding the outcome of blessings and curses: 'For all who rely on works of the law are under a curse; for it is written, "Cursed be everyone who does not abide by all things written in the Book of the Law, and do them"' (Gal. 3.10). Thus, for Paul, 'Christ redeemed us from the curse of the law by becoming a curse for us – for it is written, "Cursed is everyone who is hanged on a tree"' (Gal. 3.13).

122. While Paul also holds out the possibility that their conscience might also excuse them (v. 16), this is to be read in light of the previous logic regarding 'doing' the law. This is not really an option in Paul's thinking.

could possibly fulfil this natural law. Yet, Martens suggests it was likely that it was only 'theoretically' possible to achieve this, and, indeed, highly unlikely that any mortal had ever fulfilled it. Hence, according to this reading, Paul refers to it here to show that, like the Jews, Gentiles also are self-condemned.[123] While it is difficult to know its origin for certain, it is plausible that Paul employed the notion of the law written on the heart to show that Gentiles 'can distinguish between good and bad' and thus will be held accountable on the day of judgement (v. 16).[124]

I consider these readings to make more sense in the context of what Paul is arguing than reading Paul as describing a Gentile Christian (vv. 14-15) who is actually justified by doing the law.[125] While Gathercole makes a compelling argument that connects v. 14 with v. 13, one could then demand that both vv. 13 and 14 ought to be read in the context of v. 12, which describes the condemning sinfulness of both Jew and Gentile.[126] Thus, despite some similarities between vv. 13-15 and Jer. 31.33,[127] it is still a better reading to understand this person as a non-Christian Gentile.

For Jews, they have the law and will thus be judged by the law (v. 12). Paul

123. J. Martens, 'Romans 2:14-16: A Stoic Reading', *NTS* 40 (1994), pp. 55–67. Or it could express a belief in a Noahic law to which Gentiles where held accountable. C. Talbert, *Romans* (Macon: Smyth & Helwys, 2002), p. 85.

124. M. Luther, *Commentary on Romans* (Grand Rapids: Kregel, 1954), p. 60.

125. e.g. S. Gathercole, *Where is Boasting? Early Jewish Soteriology and Paul's Response in Romans 1-5* (Grand Rapids: Eerdmans, 2002), p. 127 and F. Watson, *Paul, Judaism and the Gentiles: Beyond the New Perspective* (Cambridge: Eerdmans, 2007), pp. 205–215.

126. S. Gathercole, 'A Law unto Themselves: The Gentiles in Romans 2.14-15 Revisited', *JSNT*, 85 (2002), pp. 27–49 (33).

127. Cranfield has argued (in line with Augustine) that Paul has Gentile Christians in mind in v. 15 and connects it with Jer. 31.33. C. Cranfield, *Romans 9-16* (London, T & T Clark, 2004), pp. 158–159:

Rom. 2.15: 'They show that the work of the law is written on their hearts.'

Jer. 31.33: 'But this is the covenant that I will make with the house of Israel after those days, declares the Lord: I will put my law within them, and I will write it on their hearts. And I will be their God, and they shall be my people.'

There is of course an obvious similarity between these two passages: the 'work of the law' and the 'law' are both written on hearts in these verses. However, in the Romans passage Paul explicitly takes his aim off of the 'house of Israel' and focuses instead on 'the gentiles' (v. 14), whereas in the Jeremiah 31 passage it is precisely the 'house of Israel' who is foreseen as having the law written on the heart. It must be noted that there is no shortage of passages in the OT that predict an eschatological inclusion of the Gentiles that Paul could have used to refer to the Gentiles here (e.g. Isa. 42.6; 43.9; 49.6; 65.1; Jer. 3.17; 4.2) and, indeed, he uses them at other points in his letter (cf. Rom 10.20), yet he does *not* do so here. Cranfield's argument only works, as he himself acknowledges, if one *already* concedes that Paul is discussing specifically Gentile Christians. Furthermore, Cranfield is confident that Paul is talking about Gentile Christians because Cranfield is convinced that v. 15 refers to Jer. 31.33, which, to me, seems to fall victim to circular reasoning (Cranfield, *Romans*, p. 159). However, it does not do to follow Dunn, who, in contrast to Cranfield, not only sees these Gentiles as non-Christian Gentiles but also reads Paul at face value and states that Paul is open to 'the reality, not just hypothetical possibility of Gentile goodness' (Dunn, *Romans*, p. 99). Dunn's interpretation, then, is in direct conflict with Paul's major anthropological point in Romans 3 that no one does good. However, if the repentance-impenitent wordplay was intended by Paul as I propose it was, then what he describes in vv. 13-15 makes sense: he is describing non-Christian

outlined in vv. 17-24 specific occurrences of their breaking the law and thus their condemnation alongside the Gentiles. While it is true that Paul explained a final judgement by works elsewhere (Phil. 2.12-16; 1 Cor. 3.11-15), this is not the point Paul wishes to make here. Rather, Paul is making the case that the human heart is incapable of *doing* repentance and *doing* the law, whether it is the law known instinctively (v. 15) or by the letter (v. 17). It is in vv. 25-29 that Paul asserts how this heart is to be changed: only the heart that has been circumcised by the Spirit (Deut. 30.6) will be acceptable to God (v. 29).[128]

IV. *Conclusions*

For Luke, conversion was depicted primarily as a *return* to the Lord, the Creator and Father. The very notion of return (repentance) assumed a fundamental changeability in humanity that is absent in Paul. While we have noted that *successful* repentance, for Luke, was never achieved without the agency of God, Luke was much more comfortable expanding the boundaries of human agency than Paul was.

For Paul, the notion of human changeability was no longer valid because of the power of sin in the heart of humanity. Effective human turning to God was rendered impossible because the heart was, itself, unrepentable. Humanity could *not* change and its only hope was to encounter an outside rescuing force that could transform them into something new. For Paul, the hope of conversion rested in an understanding of God whose call and gifts are unchanging, not in an understanding of humanity whose nature is changeable.

A key text that both Luke and Paul referred to in these important passages was Deuteronomy 30. I argued that the repentance used by Paul in Rom. 2.4-5 evoked the type of repentance expressed in Deuteronomy 30. The function of this repentance for Paul was to show humanity to be in a more desperate situation than a simple *return* to the Lord conveyed. Moreover, the repentance mentioned in Deuteronomy 30 was a return *to the law*; the very action Paul was arguing against. Hence he used this sort of repentance to show it was not useful towards restoration with God.

In contrast, Luke used Deuteronomy 30 positively to evoke one's desire to return to God. However, Luke suggested that *effective* and *lasting* repentance did not, in the end, rest on the quality of the repentance of the individual. Regardless of the sincerity of one's repentance, it was God – the one who

Gentiles who, like Jews, have a law, but who, also like the Jews, are guilty of breaking it and are therefore subject to God's wrath.

128. Cf. Moo, who concurs that it is vv. 28-29 that '[f]or the first time . . . alludes to Christians' (Moo, *Romans*, p. 175).

circumcises the heart – who would enact final restoration. As Luke showed in Luke 15, the repentance of the prodigal could, at best, earn the status of a servant. Only the father had the power to declare the prodigal to be fully restored as a *son*, not just as a servant.

6

LUKE: COMPANION OR DISCIPLE OF PAUL?

Stanley E. Porter

I. *Introduction*

There are currently two major streams of thought regarding the question of the relationship of Paul to the Gospel of Luke. On the one hand, there are those, like I. Howard Marshall, who argue that there is a clear affinity between the writings of Luke and those of Paul. As Marshall states: 'Luke's work, for example, should not be dismissed as typical of "early Catholicism" with the implication that it is somehow inferior to that of Paul. On the contrary, there are grounds for believing that his grasp of the gospel is in essential harmony with that of Paul, even if he has his own individual understanding of it.'[1] On the other hand, there are those, like Werner Georg Kümmel, who argue directly against such a position. As Kümmel states: 'It has been asserted that Lk. shows a striking affinity with the theology of Paul and so must have originated with a pupil of Paul.' Kümmel is willing to admit that there is common ground between Luke and Paul over such topics as 'universalism', 'stress on faith', 'God's love for sinners', 'the gospel of joy' and 'such common concepts [*sic*] as σωτηρία . . ., κύριος for the earthly Jesus . . ., δικαιόω'.[2] However, after citing this list of purported examples, he continues: 'all these instances involve general Gentile-Christian concepts and words, and the specifically Pauline *theologumena* are lacking. . . . [I]n Lk. the author is obviously a total stranger to the theology of Paul.'[3] He notes further that major distinctions are found, especially in the view of the death of Jesus. 'In view of this different interpretation of the death of Jesus by Luke nothing can be said about the proximity of Lk. to the theology

1. I. Howard Marshall, *Luke: Historian and Theologian* (Grand Rapids: Zondervan, 1970), p. 10.
2. Werner Georg Kümmel, *Introduction to the New Testament* (trans. Howard Clark Kee; Nashville: Abingdon, 1975), p. 149. Words are not concepts, as James Barr has so ably indicated (*Semantics of Biblical Language* [Oxford: Oxford University Press, 1961], p. 207).
3. Kümmel, *Introduction*, p. 149.

of Paul; indeed, it only raises the question about the tradition that Luke is the author of Lk.'[4] Kümmel focuses upon purported differences between the Lukan and Pauline views of Jesus' death not only as a means of dismissing similarities in their theology but also to go as far as to call into question Lukan authorship of the Gospel.

Such a situation requires that we examine a number of different dimensions of Luke's Gospel and Paul's letters in order to examine and perhaps even to establish their relationship. In this essay, I will examine these topics from a number of different angles. I will begin with discussion of the issue of authorship of Luke's Gospel, as a means of establishing a foundation for their mutual interaction and analysis. Then I will discuss a number of the major issues that have been raised here and elsewhere to try to establish the possible relationship between the two.

II. *Authorship of Luke's Gospel and of Paul's letters as a basis for further discussion*

In his comments cited earlier, Kümmel raises the issue of whether the differences between Luke's and Paul's theologies are sufficiently great so as to call into question Lukan authorship of the Gospel. Kümmel raises a legitimate point, because one of the major reasons for raising the issue of how Luke and Paul are intertwined results from the traditional view of authorship of Luke's Gospel (and Acts as well, though I will not address those issues here), and what expectations this position seems to raise regarding the interaction between the two. Whereas there is a more apparently obvious intersection between Paul and the book of Acts, with Paul being a major figure in the book, if Acts was written by the same author as Luke and they are relatively unified[5] then it stands to reason that there is a relationship between Paul and the Gospel of Luke as well. This has been the assumption of much previous scholarship.

The Gospel of Luke is formally anonymous and makes no attribution of authorship. The author claims in the cultivated literary preface to be one who has received traditions 'handed down' by those who were 'eyewitnesses and servants of the word' (Lk. 1.2).[6] The traditional ascription of authorship of the

4. Kümmel, *Introduction*, p. 149.

5. This is the view of most scholars. However, there has been some reaction to this in recent scholarship. See Mikeal C. Parsons and Richard I. Pervo, *Rethinking the Unity of Luke and Acts* (Minneapolis: Fortress, 1993), with a response in I. Howard Marshall, 'Acts and the "Former Treatise"', in ed. Bruce W. Winter and Andrew D. Clarke, *The Book of Acts in its First Century Setting*. Vol. 1: *Ancient Literary Setting* (Grand Rapids: Eerdmans, 1993), pp. 163–82.

6. For a recent view of the preface, which takes it as consonant with other literary prefaces, rather than simply as a preface found in the common literature of the day, see Sean A. Adams, 'Luke's Preface

Third Gospel is to Luke, the physician and sometime travelling companion of Paul (see Phlm. 1.24; Col. 4.14; 2 Tim. 4.11), an understandable if not also appropriate attribution in light of the claims of the preface and other features of the Gospel.[7] Luke's Gospel was known early on, as we see from its being alluded to at the end of the first century in *1 Clement* (13.2; 48.4)[8] and then later in the second century by *2 Clement* (13.4) and Justin Martyr (*Dialogue with Trypho* 78, 88, 100, 103, 105, 106),[9] and from its use in the *Diatessaron*.[10] The direct evidence of Luke's authorship of the Gospel is later but virtually unanimous and unified in its assessment.[11] This includes the second-century ascriptions of the Gospels, including the ascription at the end of the Gospel by P^{75} (c. 175–225 CE),[12] the Muratorian canon (c. 170–180 CE, though some put this document in the fourth century), Irenaeus (175–195 CE) (*Against Heresies* 3.1.1, 3.14.1), an ancient prologue to Luke's Gospel (late second-century, which is often though perhaps unfairly referred to as the Anti-Marcionite prologue to Luke's Gospel),[13] Marcion (c. 150 CE), who used only one Gospel, Luke's, identified by Tertullian (early third-century) (*Against Marcion* 4.2, 5), Origen (c. 254 CE; cited by Eusebius, *Hist. Eccl.* 6.25.6), Eusebius himself (c. 303 CE) (*Hist. Eccl.* 3.4.6-7) and some other, later sources.

Some scholars have disputed the force and implications of this evidence,[14] however, often because some of the descriptions of Luke show no more knowledge of him than one can glean from the NT itself – such as his being a physician, a co-worker of Paul and a writer to the Gentiles. However, despite this, there are other statements made about Luke contained in the aforementioned sources that are not derived from the NT, such as his being from Syrian

and its Relationship to Greek Historiography: A Response to Loveday Alexander', *JGRChJ* 3 (2006), pp. 177–91.

7. See Donald Guthrie, *New Testament Introduction* (Downers Grove: InterVarsity Press, 3rd edn, 1970), pp. 98–99.

8. Darrell L. Bock, *Luke* (2 vols; BECNT; Grand Rapids: Baker, 1994), I, p. 5.

9. Alfred Plummer, *A Critical and Exegetical Commentary on the Gospel According to S. Luke* (ICC; Edinburgh: T&T Clark, n.d.), p. xv.

10. Plummer, *Luke*, p. xv. We do not have the Greek text of the *Diatessaron*, so this conclusion is based on a later translation of an Arabic manuscript.

11. Besides sources noted earlier, see especially Joseph A. Fitzmyer, *The Gospel According to Luke* (AB, 3AB; Garden City, NY: Doubleday, 1974), pp. 35–40; Henry J. Cadbury, 'The Tradition', in *The Beginnings of Christianity Part I The Acts of the Apostles*. Vol. II: *Prolegomena II, Criticism* (ed. F.J. Foakes Jackson and Kirsopp Lake; London: Macmillan, 1922), pp. 209–64; Kurt Aland, *Synopsis Quattuor Evangeliorum* (Stuttgart: Württembergische Bibelanstalt, 2nd edn, 1964), pp. 531–48.

12. Martin, Hengel, *The Four Gospels and the One Gospel of Jesus Christ* (trans. John Bowden; Harrisburg, PA: Trinity Press International, 2000), pp. 48–56; Philip W. Comfort and David P. Barrett, *The Text of the Earliest New Testament Greek Manuscripts* (Carol Stream, IL: Tyndale House, 2001).

13. See Fitzmyer, *Luke*, I, p. 39, for comments on this prologue's value; cf. Kümmel, *Introduction*, p. 147, who dismisses its value.

14. Besides Kümmel, these include Rudolf Bultmann, Henry Cadbury, Ernst Haenchen, Philip Vielhauer and especially other German scholars.

Antioch, his being unmarried and childless and his death in Boeotia at the age of 84. It is difficult to assess the reliability of individual elements of these descriptions, but their being found in several early and distinct sources and their being, if not necessarily consistent, uncontradictory, points to an independent and reliable tradition regarding Lukan authorship.[15] The evidence for Luke in the New Testament is relatively slight, including his not being identified as a disciple of Jesus, so it is unlikely that he of all possible NT figures would have been selected as the author of the Third Gospel, when there were other more likely candidates, if there were not some grounds for attribution. Therefore, apart from the issue of theology but simply on the basis of the earliest attested evidence, the vast majority of scholarship (apart possibly from that in Germany), including recent scholarship, has accepted the attribution of the Third Gospel to Luke, and accept that he was in some sense associated with Paul.[16] However, it is not uncommon in debates about the relationship of Luke and Paul to find an expectation that, because of Luke's association with Paul, his theological perspective would be very similar to if not identical with that of Paul. Such a perspective is apparently in evidence in Kümmel's disjunctive characterization of the relationship between Luke and Paul. In other words, being a sometime companion is translated into Luke's becoming a Pauline disciple. This does not necessarily follow. Even though the later sources tend to emphasize the closeness of the relationship between Luke and Paul, there is nothing substantive to indicate his being anything more than a companion, albeit a highly literate one who wrote the first major history of early Christianity. As Earle Ellis has pointed out, in citing the work of Adolf Harnack and B.H. Streeter, Luke is not necessarily the disciple of Paul,[17] and hence it is unreasonable to expect that Luke, albeit a travelling companion and in some ways collaborator with Paul in his work, would when he writes his own account of the events of early Christianity reflect an identical perspective to Paul's. In fact, this might be expecting far too much from one of such literary abilities.

A problem related to this discussion, but one that is often not raised, concerns authorship of the Pauline letters. This is certainly not the place to engage in a discussion of all of the issues regarding the history of debate over Pauline

15. Other evidence more relevant to Acts, such as the role of the 'we' passages, is not considered here, but does have a bearing on the wider issue of Lukan authorship of Luke and Acts. See Stanley E. Porter, *The Paul of Acts: Essays in Literary Criticism, Rhetoric, and Theology* (WUNT, 115; Tübingen: Mohr Siebeck, 1999), pp. 10–46.

16. Fitzmyer, *Luke*, I, pp. 40–1. Besides Marshall, other scholars who concur are Darrell Bock, Martin Dibelius, Earle Ellis, Alfred Harnack, Luke Timothy Johnson, Leon Morris, John Nolland, Robert Stein, B.H. Streeter.

17. Earle E. Ellis, *Luke* (NCB; Grand Rapids: Eerdmans, rev. edn, 1974), p. 42, citing Adolf Harnack, *Luke the Physician* (London: Williams & Norgate, 1907), pp. 142, 147; and B.H. Streeter, *The Four Gospels* (London: Macmillan, 1924), pp. 561–2.

authorship, except where matters in that debate have important implications for our discussion. One of these is that two of the three references to Luke in the Pauline letters occur in highly disputed letters: Col. 4.14 and 2 Tim. 4.11.[18] If these two references are discounted on the basis of their authorial uncertainty, this would leave only a single reference to Luke in the undisputedly authentic letters of Paul, as simply a fellow worker of Paul. However, 2 Tim. 4.11 does not provide much useful information of its own, apart from recognizing Luke as a companion of Paul. Most scholars, even if they dispute authorship of Colossians, would see it as sufficiently Pauline to use its evidence in a secondary way in discussion of Paul's theology. The larger question is not authorship but how to use disputed letters in such a discussion, especially where larger theological issues are involved. In some ways, restricting the Pauline corpus would make the task of comparison with Luke easier, because it limits the evidence and the scope for problematic comparisons within the disputed letters. However, I will take into consideration all of the Pauline letters. Whereas I appreciate the problems of determining ancient authorship, I remain convinced that Paul was the author of all of the letters attributed to him. Further, apparently so did the early Church writers, according to the evidence stated earlier, in their affirmation of Luke as physician. Finally, I believe that a comparison of Paul and Luke on theological grounds benefits from using the range of evidence available.

A final issue to consider is the date of composition of the books of the NT involved in this discussion as this has bearing on Luke's Gospel as a possible post-Pauline appropriation of Paul. There are three possible dates for composition of Luke's Gospel: before 70 CE, sometime relatively soon after 70 CE or 115–135 CE. The late date is rightly dismissed. The second or middle date is the consensus view of scholars, because there are a number of Gospel events, e.g. the fall of Jerusalem (Lk. 21.20-24), that scholars think were written about after the fact. The nature of Luke's Gospel as a narrative about Jesus makes it difficult to establish influence of Paul's letters upon the content of the Gospel. The opportunity for influence of the letters themselves is less likely with the early date, except as Luke was actually in contact with Paul and a visitor to any of the cities he addressed, and virtually impossible for any later inauthentic letters. In this scenario, the Gospel would probably have been written just before Acts, which would have been written around 64/65 CE, before Paul was killed. However, with the middle date, there is the possibility that Luke's

18. Fitzmyer, *Luke*, I, p. 36. Questions of authorship of these letters from my perspective are discussed in Lee Martin McDonald and Stanley E. Porter, *Early Christianity and Its Sacred Literature* (Peabody, MA: Hendrickson, 2000), pp. 471–6, 492–7.

Gospel, which still could have been written by the historical Luke,[19] may have been influenced by both authentic and even some early inauthentic letters. If this view is correct, it is more likely, therefore, that Luke's Gospel is in some ways a reaction to Paul's letters, especially his major undisputed letters. Only an assessment of major theological issues will help to determine this.

III. *Luke and Paul and the major theological issues*

As I have already noted, there are a number of areas where scholarship sees similar theological perspective between Luke and Paul. Kümmel attributes these to their being 'general Gentile-Christian concepts and words'.[20] I think it is debatable whether these commonalities are so easily explainable in such generalized terms. Nevertheless, I do not think it profitable to debate these issues here. What is more important is to focus upon those areas where there is agreed upon difference of opinion between Luke and Paul, and to examine the various scholarly viewpoints on these topics and how they might relate to each other, in order to try to describe further the relationship between Luke's Gospel and Paul. There are a number of areas that merit comparison and contrast between Luke and Paul, besides the ones noted by Kümmel. It is not possible here to treat all of the issues that are relevant. Instead, I have isolated several that are the most important for discussion.

a. *Use of Scripture*

Scripture plays a major role in both Luke and Paul, although their approach is different in a number of respects. Luke uses a number of explicit quotations of the OT in his Gospel, although not as many or frequently as quotations are used in Matthew or Mark. He also has a number of allusions, but these are much more difficult to quantify. The *UBSGNT* counts twenty-seven explicit quotations of the OT in Luke's Gospel.[21] The distribution is uneven throughout the Gospel, with the quotations bunching around the opening chapters (Lk. 1-4, with eight quotations, as well as a number of allusions)[22] and the Passion Week

19. See Luke Timothy Johnson, *The Gospel of Luke* (SP 3; Collegeville, MN: Liturgical, 1991), p. 2.

20. Kümmel, *Introduction*, p. 149.

21. *UBSGNT* (3rd edn), p. 901. On questions of method in determining quotations – a topic too complex to explore fully in this essay – see Stanley E. Porter, 'The Use of the Old Testament in the New Testament: A Brief Comment on Method and Terminology', in *Early Christian Interpretation of the Scriptures of Israel: Investigations and Proposals* (ed. Craig A. Evans and James A. Sanders; JSNTSup, 148; SSEJC, 5; Sheffield: Sheffield Academic Press, 1997), pp. 79–96; Porter, 'Further Comments on the Use of the Old Testament in the New Testament', in *The Intertextuality of the Epistles: Explorations of Theory and Practice* (ed. Thomas L. Brodie, Dennis R. MacDonald and Stanley E. Porter; NTM, 16; Sheffield: Sheffield Phoenix Press, 2006), pp. 98–112.

22. See Joel B. Green, 'The Problem of a Beginning: Israel's Scriptures in Luke 1–2', *BBR* 4 (1994), pp. 61–85.

(Lk. 19-23, with eleven quotations). There are fewer quotations in the central section, although several scholars have seen Luke's central section as being a midrashic interpretation of the book of Deuteronomy.[23] The most frequent text used by the author is the Septuagint, the Greek version of the Old Testament.[24] Luke frequently uses the word 'write' (γράφω), as in (but not exclusively) 'it stands written' (γέγραπται), to introduce OT quotations (ten times), followed by use of 'say' or 'speak' (with λέγω or λαλέω), as in 'God says' (four times), or simply some other introductory words (three times).[25] The rest of the quotations are simply embedded in the text in some way. Joseph Fitzmyer has drawn attention to a number of features of Luke's use of the OT and two are worth noting here. The first is that Luke does not normally cite lengthy passages from the OT. There are a few quotations that are as long as three verses (e.g. Isa. 40.3-5 in Lk. 3.4-6), but few this long, with most being a single verse in length, without stringing them together in midrashic form. The second is Luke's sources for his quotations are generally the Pentateuch, prophets and Psalms, but never the historical books of the OT.[26]

Paul is generally constrained in his use of OT quotations also, apart from the book of Romans. Of his eighty-five or so quotations, which can be expanded to over one hundred if one disentangles all of the overlapping texts, and which reflect a mix of textual traditions (Septuagint, MT and other),[27] forty-five of these appear in Romans, but the others of his letters have only relatively few quotations. First Corinthians has fifteen, 2 Corinthians seven, Galatians ten, Ephesians four, Philippians two, 1 Timothy one and 2 Timothy one. The rest of the letters do not have quotations.[28] The OT books drawn upon by Paul include the Pentateuch (esp. Genesis and Deuteronomy), the historical books, Psalms, and the prophets (esp. Isaiah). Apart from Romans, quotations often appear individually, but are strung together at a few places (e.g. 2 Cor. 6.16-18, with Lev. 26.12; Ezek. 37.27; Isa. 52.11; Ezek. 20.34; 2 Sam. 7.8, 14). In Romans, this practice is common, as found in Rom. 3.10-18; 9.12-29; 10.5-8, 11-21, and possibly other places.

23. C.F. Evans, 'The Central Section of St. Luke's Gospel', in *Studies in the Gospels* (R.H. Lightfoot Festschrift; ed. D. E. Nineham; Oxford: Blackwell, 1955), pp. 37–53; Craig A. Evans, 'Luke 16.1-18 and the Deuteronomy Hypothesis', in Evans and James. A. Sanders, *Luke and Scripture: The Function of Sacred Tradition in Luke–Acts* (Philadelphia: Fortress, 1993), pp. 121–39.

24. Joseph A. Fitzmyer, 'The Use of the Old Testament in Luke–Acts', in Fitzmyer, *To Advance the Gospel: New Testament Studies* (Grand Rapids: Eerdmans, 2nd edn, 1998), pp. 295–313 (304–6).

25. Fitzmyer, 'Use', pp. 296–8.

26. Fitzmyer, 'Use', pp. 302–4.

27. See Christopher D. Stanley, *Paul and the Language of Scripture: Citation Technique in the Pauline Epistles and Contemporary Literature* (SNTSMS, 74; Cambridge: Cambridge University Press, 1992).

28. See Richard N. Longenecker, *Studies in Paul, Exegetical and Theological* (NTM, 2; Sheffield: Sheffield Phoenix Press, 2004), pp. 67–93 (68), with references to Philippians added from Porter, 'Further Comments', p. 108.

The differences in use of the OT between Luke and Paul are accentuated when one examines not just the mechanics of their use of the OT but also their interpretations. In light of Luke's use of the Pentateuch, prophets and Psalms as the source of his quotations, it is logical that Lukan scholarship has found what appears to be a consensus in Luke's using a 'proof from prophecy' or 'promise and fulfilment' motif in his use of the OT.[29] By contrast, Pauline interpretation of the Old Testament, on the basis of his use of the range of Old Testament texts and his frequent stringing together of various citations, especially in Romans, has indicated to most interpreters some form of Jewish exegesis, especially midrash, which is seen as a literalistic form of interpretation.[30] So far as these broad analyses are accurate, they illustrate points of comparison and contrast between Luke's and Paul's use of Scripture. Luke's use of Scripture appears at key places in his narrative, such as the birth and early period of Jesus' ministry and the final week of his life, and draws upon passages with prophetic significance, to see their fulfilment in Jesus. Thus, the prophetic statement of Isa. 40.3-5 about one crying in the wilderness is fulfilled in the coming of John the Baptist (Lk. 3.4-6) and the prophetic enthronement in Ps. 110.1 is fulfilled in Lk. 22.69. By contrast, Paul uses OT citations selectively and not in every book. There are many places, as already noted, where Scripture is cited as a form of literalistic proof-text, often with one text strung together with another one in support of a particular point. Recent analyses of both Luke and Paul and their use of the Old Testament, often (unfortunately) under the term intertextuality,[31] have brought to our attention that such analysis may well be overly simplistic. Such an approach tends to focus upon isolated instances of use of the OT, but overlooks that any use of an OT text is an act of interpretative citation, and that the wider context of usage within the NT must be taken into account.[32] In that sense, both Luke and Paul are creative interpreters of the OT.

Luke 4.18-19 is not the first place in Luke's Gospel where an OT passage is

29. Stanley E. Porter, 'Scripture Justifies Mission', in *Hearing the Old Testament in the New Testament* (ed. Stanley E. Porter; Grand Rapids: Eerdmans, 2006), pp. 104–27 (105–7). See also Kenneth Duncan Litwak, *Echoes of Scripture in Luke–Acts: Telling the History of God's People Intertextually* (JSNTSup, 282; New York: Continuum, 2005), pp. 8–17. There have been other viewpoints on Luke's use of Scripture proposed, such as imitation or continuity, typology and intertextual interpretation (the last has been very popular lately), but none of these is as widely used as the 'proof from prophecy' notion.

30. See Richard N. Longenecker, *Biblical Exegesis in the Apostolic Period* (repr. Carlisle: Paternoster, 1975), pp. 114–32. The other interpretative forms are allegory and pesher – but the clear examples of these are relatively few. See also E. Earle Ellis, *Paul's Use of the Old Testament* (repr. Grand Rapids: Baker, 1957).

31. Intertextuality has come to refer to any type of interpretative use of the OT, and has thus lost all effective meaning as an interpretative strategy. It now is used to label a descriptive technique. See Richard B. Hays, *Echoes of Scripture in the Letters of Paul* (New Haven: Yale University Press, 1989).

32. See Francis Watson, *Paul and the Hermeneutics of Faith* (London: Continuum, 2004), pp. ix–x, and elsewhere.

cited or alluded to. There are several passages that precede it, both as citations and as allusions. However, I believe that this particular citation[33] is used by Luke to serve as a programmatic introduction to his book, and by doing this to introduce, promote, and confirm the ministry of Jesus. As Robert Tannehill states, 'By the scene at Nazareth with which he introduces his narrative of the ministry of Jesus, Luke intends to reveal to the reader certain fundamental aspects of the meaning of that ministry as a whole.'[34] This citation of Isa. 61.1-2 is the first extended use of the Old Testament specifically by Jesus after the beginning of his public ministry. To this point in Luke's narrative, the OT has been cited either by the author, by John the Baptist or by Jesus in staccato dialogue with the devil. This is also the first sermon of Jesus in this Gospel. As a result, this passage has the character of an inaugural address. Jesus' interpretation of the statement and the response by those who hear him are also recorded. All of these factors point to the significance of this initial sermon of Jesus, which is an exposition of an OT passage. Jesus interprets it as a proclamation of the coming of a messianic figure and as a proclamation of salvation being brought to the Gentiles. The interpretation is a good example of the 'proof from prophecy' or 'promise and fulfilment' motif, as the passage recounts tasks of the Messiah that Jesus claims are fulfilled that day in the hearing of the audience, including the inauguration and extension of his salvific ministry. There is more to the use of the passage than this, however, illustrating Luke's creative engagement with the text. Luke, and according to Luke, Jesus, is quite possibly making a veiled reference to Jesus' divinity by this quotation. In the Qumran document 4Q521 1 ii 1-13, which alludes to Isaiah 61, the figure who is speaking and appropriating for itself the actions of Isaiah 61 appears to be God. There is a shift in the text between the Messiah and God. This Qumran fragmentary text attests to a tradition in the Judaism of Jesus' time in which God himself was the one who was proclaiming and accomplishing the actions of Isaiah 61, with quite probably the Messiah also depicted as performing the same kinds of actions as God himself.[35] It is against this possible textual backdrop that Luke depicts Jesus making his instigatory proclamation. The rest of Luke's Gospel then serves as an exemplification through the ministry of Jesus of God acting through him to bring salvation to those in need of it. This is then confirmed when the Passion Week events again invoke the OT to bring the narrative to a close.

This same type of interpretative creativity and strategic placement of the OT

33. Similar to the way that Joel 2.28-32, Ps. 16.8-11, and Ps. 11.1 are used in Acts 2.14-36.

34. Robert Tannehill, 'The Mission of Jesus according to Luke', in *Jesus in Nazareth* (ed. Walter Eltester; BZNW, 40; Berlin: de Gruyter, 1972), pp. 51–75 (51).

35. The discussion of Isa. 61.1-2 and Lk. 4.18-19 is from Porter, 'Scripture Justifies Mission', pp. 109–19.

is found in Paul, in particular in his citation of Hab. 2.4 in Rom. 1.17. This is the first citation of an OT text in the book of Romans, the Pauline book with the largest number and concentration of OT citations. In a technique similar to that of Luke, Paul cites this quotation – though not a long one – in the 'thesis statement' of Romans to establish the thematic thrust of the book. Moisés Silva has noted the creativity with which Paul interprets Hab. 2.4 in Rom. 1.17, what Silva calls 'the programmatic verse in Romans'.[36] Silva describes several features of Paul's use of Hab. 2.4 (in Gal. 3.11 also) that appear to go beyond its original context. The first is that the word used for 'faith' in the Greek version of Hab. 2.4 translates a Hebrew word meaning 'steadiness, faithfulness', and thus implies 'obedience to the Law'. Paul, however, uses Hab. 2.4 'to attack the notion of justification by works of the law'. So, as Silva states, Paul uses 'this verse in a way not originally intended – namely, to propound a distinctively "Pauline" doctrine'. More than that, 'his meaning appears to be exactly the opposite of the original'.[37] The second feature is that the Hebrew Bible seems to interpret the verse as referring to the faithfulness of the Jewish people when opposed by the Babylonians, with the author of Habakkuk possibly interpreting living by faith as the maintaining of a life of faithfulness. The third feature is that other interpreters of this passage – such as the Septuagint (faithfulness), the Qumranites (faithfulness to the Teacher of Righteousness) and the author of Hebrews (perseverance) – interpret it differently than does Paul. As Silva states:

> After describing his gospel as the fulfillment of the OT promises (Rom 1:2) and appealing to Habakkuk 2:4 as a key to understanding that gospel (Rom 1:16-17), Paul spends considerable time elaborating on the significance of Abraham's faith (Rom 4 . . .), and then devotes a major section to the doctrine of the believer's sanctification (Rom 6–8 . . .). Paul was genuinely indebted to that text as a source for his teaching; moreover, his own theological formulations strengthened and advanced the prophetic message.[38]

Thus, there are a number of differences in use of the OT by Luke and Paul. However, they have in common their use of the OT in a creative interpretative way as the basis of their proclamation, Luke in his Gospel and Paul in Romans. There does not appear, however, to have been a significant or definable influence of Paul's interpretative technique or hermeneutical stance upon Luke.

36. Moisés Silva, 'Old Testament in Paul', in *Dictionary of Paul and his Letters* (ed. Gerald F. Hawthorne, Ralph P. Martin and Daniel G. Reid; Downers Grove, IL: InterVarsity Press, 1993), pp. 630–42 (640). See also Silva, *Explorations in Exegetical Method: Galatians as a Test Case* (Grand Rapids: Baker, 1996), pp. 165–7.

37. Silva, 'Old Testament', p. 641.

38. Silva, 'Old Testament', p. 641.

b. *Christology: Jesus and his identity in Luke and Paul*

Philip Vielhauer, in his now famous essay on the Paulinism of Acts, asserts, 'the distinction between Luke and Paul was in Christology'.[39] For Vielhauer, Pauline Christology apparently means that Paul understood Jesus' 'divine sonship' in metaphysical or pre-existent terms, whereas Luke's Christology is 'pre-Pauline' or 'closer to the Christology of the earliest congregation' and thus more like Peter's than Paul's.[40] Although there has been some disagreement among scholars regarding Pauline Christology, especially as it addresses the question of pre-existence, most have rejected views such as those of James Dunn who wish to see pre-existence as a later concept.[41] Instead, most scholars see Paul as promoting a clear pre-existence of Christ on the basis of such passages as Rom. 10.9 ('Jesus is Lord') and 13 ('call upon the name of the Lord and you will be saved'), 1 Cor. 12.3 ('Jesus is Lord'), and especially the great Christological formulation in Phil. 2.6-11.

By contrast, there are a number of different 'names' and 'titles' that are used of Jesus in Luke's Gospel. These include 'Messiah' (or Christ), 'saviour', 'son of God', 'son of man', 'servant', 'prophet', 'king', 'son of David', 'holy one', 'righteous one', 'teacher' and even possibly 'God'.[42] Insofar as these titles are unique to Luke's Gospel and not found in Paul, there is clearly a distinction in at least their expression of their view of Jesus' identity, if not the substance. Luke but not Paul uses the titles 'son of man', 'servant', 'prophet', 'king', 'holy one', 'teacher' and possibly 'God' of Jesus, and thus there are clearly differences in the depiction of Jesus between Luke's Gospel and Paul's letters. However, the question is not so much the titles used but the identity of Jesus as depicted, and how similar and divergent these pictures are. The standard view of Lukan Christology, following Vielhauer, is that Luke's is an adoptionist and not a pre-existence Christology, and hence a 'low' Christology.[43]

This view has recently been challenged by Kavin Rowe. He argues that, in

39. Philip Vielhauer, 'On the "Paulinism" in Acts', in *Studies in Luke–Acts* (ed. Leander E. Keck and J. Louis Martyn; Philadelphia: Fortress, 1980), p. 43.

40. Vielhauer, 'On the "Paulinism" in Acts', pp. 48, 45.

41. James D.G. Dunn, *Christology in the Making: A New Testament Inquiry into the Origins of the Doctrine of the Incarnation* (Philadelphia: Westminster, 1980).

42. Fitzmyer, *Luke*, I, pp. 197–219.

43. The standard view in Pauline scholarship is that Paul's use of 'Christ', especially in the phrasing 'Jesus Christ' or 'Christ Jesus' reflects a name, not a functional title, reflective of his high Christology. This was apparently established as a position by Nils A. Dahl in his 'Die Messianität Jesu bei Paulus', in *Studia Paulina in honorem Joahnnis de Zwaan septuagenarii* (Haarlem: Bohn, 1953), pp. 83–95; ET 'The Messiahship of Jesus in Paul', in *The Crucified Messiah* (Minneapolis: Augsburg, 1974), pp. 37–47. This position has recently been questioned by Matthew V. Novenson, 'Can the Messiahship of Jesus Be Read off Paul's Grammar? Nils Dahl's Criteria 50 Years Later', *NTS* 56 (2010), pp. 396–412. If Novenson is correct that the evidence is not as unambiguous as Dahl and others have supposed, then the potential increased functional rather than nominative use of Paul's language to refer to Jesus as Christ 'lowers' Paul's Christology in at least some instances to a position similar to Luke's purported view of Christ.

his use of the term κύριος ('Lord'), Luke 'positions κύριος within the movement of the narrative in such a way as to narrate the relation between God and Jesus as one of inseparability, to the point that they are bound together in a shared identity as κύριος'. Just as God is identified as Lord, so Jesus, in Luke's Gospel according to Rowe, is narratively identified as Lord, having a shared divine identity. Rowe argues that

> the development of κύριος throughout the entire Gospel narrative serves to tell the human or earthly story of the heavenly Lord. In other words, Luke uses κύριος to unify the earthly and resurrected Jesus at the point of his identity as Lord. There are not two figures, one Jesus of 'history', as it were, and another exalted Lord, but rather only one: the Lord who was κύριος even from the womb.[44]

As a result, Rowe believes that Luke's Christology is situated 'in closer proximity to Paul . . . than is usual in modern NT scholarship'.[45]

This is not to say, according to Rowe, that every use of κύριος in Luke's Gospel is Christological, but that the narrative takes the inherently ambiguous term, 'Lord', and depicts contexts in which Jesus is seen to be Lord in the same sense as is God, and creates a textual environment for the reader to grasp this meaning even in contexts that remain ambiguous. For instance, of the twenty-five uses of 'Lord' in the Lukan birth narrative, Rowe selects two instances as carrying 'such weight that they shape profoundly the interpretation of the rest of the narrative'.[46] The first is Lk. 1.43, where Elizabeth greets Mary as the 'mother of my Lord'. The second is Lk. 2.11, where the angels tell the shepherds that in Bethlehem is born a saviour, Christ the Lord. There are ambiguous instances in Lk. 1.17, 76 and 3.4. In Lk. 5.8, Peter addresses Jesus as 'Lord' with Christological identification in Luke's Gospel. This instance is important because it is in the vocative case in Greek. Traditional interpretation has seen the use of the vocative as simply a term of address, whereas Rowe sees it as establishing a pattern of Christological use of the vocative. This is followed by other similar uses of the vocative in Lk. 5.12, 6.46, 7.6, 9.54, 10.40, 14.22, 19.8 and 22.38, 49.[47] Further instances of non-vocative usage include: Lk. 5.17, with reference to the 'power of the Lord'; 6.5, where the Lord of the Sabbath is seen to be Jesus; 10.17, where Jesus is Lord of the harvest; 12.42,

44. C. Kavin Rowe, *Early Narrative Christology: The Lord in the Gospel of Luke* (repr. Grand Rapids: Baker, 2006), p. 27.

45. Rowe, *Early Narrative Christology*, p. 28.

46. Rowe, *Early Narrative Christology*, pp. 31–2.

47. Rowe (*Early Narrative Christology*, pp. 211–12) is correct that one cannot categorically exclude the vocative use, as does C.F.D. Moule in 'The Christology of Acts', in *Studies in Luke-Acts* (ed. Keck and Martyn), pp. 159–85 (160).

where Jesus responds as Lord; 19.31-34, regarding the colt; 19.38, about coming in the name of the Lord; 19.44, with Jesus' lament over Jerusalem; 20.42, quoting Pss. 110; 22.33, Peter's denial; 22.61, Jesus' response; 24.3, regarding the absent body of the Lord; and 24.34, speaking of the resurrection.

Rowe goes to elaborate lengths to prove that 'context' shows that, despite the other usage of this language, what he calls the double referent of κύριος (master and God) encompasses both Jesus and God. This pushes him to see such usage as indicating a shared identity for Jesus. If he is right, Luke's Christology is definitely higher than most have seen before, and much more like Paul's. However, the question is whether he is right. There are several reasons to question his conclusions. The first is that he admits that his argument is cumulative, and insists that his position can only be attacked by examining not individual instances but his overall narrative strategy.[48] This looks like special pleading. If an argument is cumulative of weak instances – and many of the instances are debatable, as Rowe admits as he discusses them – then the result can be no more certain than the strength of these tentative examples. Second, there is question about his narrative method. For example, he seems to think that lumping together instances of use of κύριος is in some sense more important than distinguishing meaningful units within a narrative.[49] Further, his notion of context is not well enough developed to provide guidance for interpretation. A third question concerns the inescapable sense – despite Rowe's protests to the contrary – that some of James Barr's critique of lexical study still has relevance. Rowe seems to confuse sense and reference, and performs his own form of illegitimate totality transfer by playing on the ambiguity of the use in Greek of a single word, κύριος, that has two distinct meanings (or it represents two homographs). Finally, there are numerous questions to be raised about individual interpretations. For example, Rowe takes Lk. 6.5 as better translated as 'the Lord of the Sabbath is the Son of Man', when 'Son of Man' has the article in a copulative construction. The grammar says otherwise.

If Rowe is correct in his analysis of the use of κύριος, then Luke's and Paul's views of Jesus' identity are clearly more consonant. However, the case remains unproven, and so the question remains of whether Luke and Paul had the same conception of Jesus as Lord.

c. *Jesus and his death and resurrection*

Scholarship has frequently emphasized the difference in understanding of Jesus' death and resurrection between Luke's Gospel and Paul. As Kümmel states, 'the death of Jesus is understood [in Luke's Gospel] as a transition

48. Rowe, *Early Narrative Christology*, p. 197.
49. Rowe, *Early Narrative Christology*, p. 158.

to heavenly glory in accordance with divine necessity (9:22; 17:25; 24:26) but only a single time is there mention of an expiatory death . . . Only in the Eucharistic word (22:19 f) is the death of Jesus said to be "for you".'[50] In other words, whereas Paul sees Jesus' death as expiatory and atoning,[51] apart from the wording in the Eucharistic words, Luke's Gospel is claimed not to demonstrate that understanding of Jesus' death. It is interesting to note that Marshall largely concurs in this assessment. As he states, 'the evidence of the Gospel has often been taken to imply that the death of Jesus had little significance for Luke. It should be observed, however, that the situation is not so very different from that in Mark and Matthew',[52] and thereby, by implication, admittedly different from Paul. Marshall then specifies that Mark and Matthew also have a relative 'silence about the death of Jesus'.[53] What little evidence there is in Matthew and Mark regarding Jesus' death appears to have been even further minimized by Luke. Luke does not include the statement on Jesus' death being a ransom for many found in Mk 10.45 when he cites similar wording, though in a different context, in his Gospel (Lk. 22.24-27). Jesus' cry of abandonment on the cross found in Mk 15.34 is not found in Luke's equivalent episode (Lk. 2.44-49). Most scholars see the death of Jesus in Luke as the innocent death of a martyr, rather than an atoning and expiatory one, as in Paul. Finally, even though Luke uses suffering servant language on one occasion (Lk. 22.37), he does not use it to explain Jesus' death. Despite some recent attempts to reassess the meaning of Jesus' death in Luke,[54] there has not been a significant shift in this overall understanding, especially in relation to Paul's thought.[55]

Before leaving this clear indication that Luke's Gospel is not a Pauline book, I think that something more must be said about Luke's Eucharistic words, found in Lk. 22.19-20. The significance of these words, especially for the role they might play in Luke's Gospel, has been downplayed by some scholars, some by seeing the meaning as less atoning and more covenantal, and others by attributing them to tradition.[56] However, these explanations may minimize their importance. There has been much discussion of the relationship between the various versions of the words of the Eucharist (Lk. 22.15-20; Mk 14.22-25;

50. Kümmel, *Introduction*, p. 149. Kümmel cites in agreement Hans Conzelmann, C.K. Barrett, Charles H. Talbert, Heinrich Schütz, Eduard Lohse, Siegfried Schulz and Gerhard Voss.

51. Still one of the best and most concise descriptions of Paul's theology of the atonement is J.K. Mozley, *The Doctrine of the Atonement* (London: Duckworth, 1915), pp. 64–83.

52. Marshall, *Luke*, p. 170.

53. Marshall, *Luke*, p. 171.

54. See, for example, Peter Doble, *The Paradox of Salvation: Luke's Theology of the Cross* (SNTSMS, 87; Cambridge: Cambridge University Press, 1996).

55. Kevin L. Anderson, *'But God Raised Him from the Dead': The Theology of Jesus' Resurrection in Luke–Acts* (PBM; Milton Keynes: Paternoster, 2006), pp. 37–9; Kümmel, *Introduction*, p. 149; Marshall, *Luke*, pp. 170–1.

56. Anderson, *'But God Raised Him'*, p. 38.

Mt. 26.26-29), the question whether Luke's longer or shorter version is to be accepted (Lk. 22.17-20 or 22.17-19a) and the relationship of Luke's words to Paul's (cf. 1 Cor. 11.23-25). Scholarship is divided on which version of the Eucharistic words is the earliest, with some accepting Mark's and others Luke's (and/or Paul's). The two Gospel versions are clearly distinct. The fact that Luke's wording is so similar to Paul's, and Paul's is the oldest literary version, probably indicates that Luke and Paul's similar wording follows a common, earlier tradition. The longer version is almost certainly to be accepted, as the shorter form is only found in Codex Bezae and the early Latin tradition, and was probably abbreviated in that textual tradition, possibly for theological or liturgical reasons.[57]

Two factors are important to note for our discussion. The first is the question of the possible dependence of Luke on Paul or vice versa. The two may have had independent access to the same earlier tradition, especially if they, at least for a time, moved in similar early ecclesial circles, possibly in Jerusalem. But there are other possibilities as well. If Paul is the earliest written source of the sayings, it is possible that Luke used Paul as his direct source, if he had access to Paul's letters. It is also possible that Luke had the information from his own research and, if he was an early travelling companion of Paul, passed it on to him. The second factor to note is that Luke, whatever his relationship to Paul, enhances the expiatory or atoning characteristic of the Eucharistic words. Luke says, first, regarding the body, that 'this is my body, the one give for (ὑπέρ) you' (Lk. 22.19). This wording is similar to Paul's statement, except that Paul does not have the verb for 'give' (διδόμενον) in 1 Cor. 11.24. Luke and Paul both have the statement regarding the body being given for you, whereas neither Mark (14.22) nor Matthew (26.26; Matthew follows Mark) has this statement. Some might attempt to tone down the significance of the use of the prepositional phrase 'for you', by interpreting the preposition as indicating benefit: 'given for your benefit'. I find it unlikely that Luke is using the phrase in a sense that mitigates its expiatory force, because the sacrificial element is present in the entire statement regarding his body being given for others. Certainly this would be the understanding, if not in the original context by the original hearers, in the literary context by Luke the author writing to his audience, who would have the benefit of knowing of Jesus' subsequent death.[58] Luke then, secondly, states regarding the cup that 'this cup is the new covenant in my blood, the one (cup) poured out for you' (Lk. 22.20). Paul does not have such a statement regarding the purpose of the cup, but simply states that 'this

57. See Joachim Jeremias, *Die Abendmahlsworte Jesu* (Göttingen: Vandenhoeck & Ruprecht, 1960), pp. 132–81, for a summary of these issues.

58. See Bock, *Luke*, II, p. 1725.

cup is the new covenant in my blood' (1 Cor. 11.25). Mark (14.24) and Matthew (26.27b-28) both have a statement regarding the purpose of the cup, but it is that the cup is poured out for many (and in Matthew for forgiveness of sins, with the same phrase as is found in Lk. 3.3 and Mk 1.4). The similar prepositional phrase is used as in the first saying. We see that there is an added expiatory, even if covenantally oriented, emphasis in Luke's Eucharistic words. Whereas these words may have been traditional or formulaic in origin, the way that he quotes them seems to indicate that he wishes to emphasize the expiatory dimension, in this instance more than does Paul, and more specifically than do Mark and Matthew. The usage may not be widespread throughout the Gospel, as it is in Paul, but it is significant nonetheless. Is it Pauline in nature? It is difficult to say whether Paul has influenced Luke, but it appears that, in a limited sense and in this context, Luke develops the atoning language further and in his own way.

When one takes the resurrection into account, however, one finds a closer relationship between Paul and Luke. Concerning the death and resurrection, Vielhauer states that, for Paul, by contrast to Luke, the '"cross" is judgment upon all mankind and at the same time reconciliation', and is closely linked to the resurrection, which signals Christ's 'dominion over the world', 'introduces the final drama of the general resurrection of the dead' and marks the 'turn of the aeons, the eschaton'. As a result, 'now' becomes 'the last hour' and the 'day of salvation', with those who believe being 'in Christ' and part of the new creation, which is only possible as part of the body of Christ.[59] I will treat the issue the aeons and eschatology in the next section, but wish to concentrate here on the resurrection, and along with it salvation. In his recent work on Jesus' resurrection in Luke-Acts, Kevin Anderson puts forward the hypothesis that 'salvation' is the major theme of Luke-Acts, on the basis of the prominence of salvific terminology and the emphasis upon salvation at crucial junctures in the narrative (e.g. Luke 1–2 and the fulfilment of God's salvific promises, and Jesus' programmatic statement in the Nazareth synagogue in Lk. 4.16-30),[60] and the resurrection is the focal point of Luke's salvation message.[61] The resurrection is central on the basis of the frequency of explicit reference to the resurrection (e.g. Lk. 16.31; 18.33; 24.7, 46; 24.6, 34), in which Luke's references are more frequent than those in any of the other Gospels, with only

59. Vielhauer, 'On the "Paulinism" of Acts', pp. 44–5.

60. Anderson, *'But God Raised Him'*, pp. 22–5. He is preceded in this assessment by Marshall, *Luke*, pp. 92–4.

61. Anderson, *'But God Raised Him'*, pp. 26–30. Anderson sees salvation in Luke-Acts as encompassing four major categories: theology (including the kingdom of God [Lk. 4.43; 6.20; 7.28; 8.1; etc.] and divine plan of history [Lk. 1.1; 4.21; 21.22, 24; 22.37; 24.44]), Christology (patterned after the examples of significant leaders such as Abraham, Moses and David), ecclesiology (covenant promises, Luke 1–2), and eschatology (e.g. Luke 10.23-24).

Paul having similar frequency of usage. Further, the resurrection is seen to play a prominent role in the Lukan narrative (e.g. Lk. 9.22; 18.31-33).[62] The one thing that Anderson does not fully develop is the supporting relationship of death and ascension to creating a single complex and meaningful event. He integrates the ascension with the resurrection, but distinguishes the death of Jesus, affirming the non-atonement view. Nevertheless, a larger conglomerate event, involving certainly death and resurrection, if not also ascension, is indicated by the evidence that Anderson himself marshals, with his emphasis upon salvation as a theme that entails the reality of death but also resurrection and ascension. Like Paul, who sees the resurrection in light of the death of Jesus (e.g. 1 Cor. 15.3-4, with the death and resurrection together as foundational), Luke, according to the evidence Anderson provides, can be seen similarly. Anderson's four major themes entailed by salvation – theology, Christology, ecclesiology and eschatology – overlap significantly with Vielhauer's characterization of Paul's thought as concerned with God's divine plan, the place of Jesus Christ as a deliverer figure, and ushering in the new age or eschaton. As noted in Anderson's own discussion, not all of the evidence is equally strong for both Luke and Acts, and in fact some of the evidence that he cites is stronger for Acts than it is for Luke. Anderson himself does not draw the close connection between death and resurrection that I do here. Nevertheless, his research has opened up a means of seeing a closer connection between Luke and Paul on the death and resurrection of Jesus than have many previous interpreters.

Luke clearly does not have the same view of the death of Jesus as does Paul. Nevertheless, Luke does indicate that he has in common with Paul a view of the death as in some way expiatory or 'for you', even if this is not a major emphasis. When the resurrection is taken into account, however, there is much more of a common view of the death and resurrection to be found in both Luke and Paul. The evidence is limited, so that only the Eucharistic words show possible signs of Pauline influence upon Luke, but even here Luke develops his ideas further independently of Paul.

d. *Eschatology and early Catholicism*

Scholarship has often endorsed the conclusion that Paul is an eschatological teacher who expected the imminent return of Jesus Christ, whereas Luke reflects a salvation-historical view, in which early Catholicism has replaced eschatological urgency. This view is largely accredited to Hanz Conzelmann, who argued that Luke's Gospel reflects what he termed *Heilsgeschichte* ('salvation history'). As Conzelmann states, the period of Jesus is seen by Luke to be different from the historical period in which he lives, and is characterized by

62. Anderson, *'But God Raised Him'*, pp. 32–4.

statements and commands for Jesus' contemporary situation. However, Luke confronts a number of theological problems, not least the delay of the immediate return of Christ or the parousia.[63] As a result, 'Luke is confronted by the situation in which the Church finds herself by the delay of the Parousia and her existence in secular history, and he tries to come to terms with the situation by his account of historical events'. Therefore, Luke makes a clear distinction between the 'period of Jesus' and the 'period of the Church', as two 'distinct, but systematically interrelated epochs'.[64] This results in a salvation history in three parts: the period of Israel, the period of Jesus and his ministry and the period from the ascension to the parousia.[65] This third segment Conzelmann attributes to the period of the Church. The Church is, according to him, the true Israel (Romans 9–11), and its place is located between the ascension and the parousia. The expected world of the future is now only a distant idea, and so one must find the Christian means to live within this time period until the parousia.[66] Luke's Gospel explicitly addresses this historical reality, in the form of what Conzelmann, following others, such as Vielhauer, calls *Frühkatholizismus* ('early Catholicism').[67] Features of the early Catholicism include the Church viewing itself as placed within the world and needing to function within that context, and hence to adapt traditions to suit the Church age. This marks the beginning of the growth of belief in historical revelation and various supportive practices, such as the regularization of traditions through teaching and church order, and the institutionalization of the Spirit and the sacraments, many of which developments are seen more clearly in the book of Acts than in Luke's Gospel.[68]

This is not the place to subject Conzelmann's form-critically based analysis to a thorough analysis. This has been done elsewhere.[69] Even within a salvation-historical framework, however, one can raise questions about Conzelmann's and similar analyses. By doing so, we can see that there may be more common ground between Paul and Luke than has been suggested within this purported

63. Hans Conzelmann, *The Theology of St Luke* (trans. Geoffrey Buswell; London: Faber & Faber, 1961), p. 13. The fullest treatment is probably Oscar Cullmann, *Salvation in History* (trans. Sidney G. Sowers; London: SCM Press, 1967).

64. Conzelmann, *Theology*, p. 14.

65. Conzelmann, *Theology*, pp. 16–17. Conzelmann emphasizes that this scheme is based upon Luke's two works, the Gospel and Acts, but I confine my discussion to the Gospel.

66. Hans Conzelmann, *Grundriss der Theologie des Neuen Testaments* (Munich: Kaiser, 1968), p. 170.

67. Conzelmann, *Grundriss*, p. 169. See Vielhauer, 'On the "Paulinism" of Acts', p. 49; E. Käsemann, *New Testament Questions of Today* (trans. W.J. Montague and Wilfred F. Bunge; London: SCM Press, 1969), pp. 21–2, 236–51.

68. Conzelmann, *Grundriss*, p. 169.

69. Good examples are Marshall, *Luke*, pp. 77–102, and John T. Carroll, *Response to the End of History: Eschatology and Situation in Luke–Acts* (SBLDS, 92; Atlanta: Scholars Press, 1988), esp. pp. 1–30.

theological framework. A.L. Moore wrote an important work on the parousia in the NT, in which he addresses the issue of the salvation-historical framework and expectation of the parousia. Working within salvation history, he makes a number of important observations. One is that the salvation-historical framework is typically drawn in too discrete categories, with periods of time that do not have overlap. Another is that there is disjunctive thinking on the part of those who do and do not follow the salvation-historical framework, with pressure to make biblical authors conform in particular ways or not. As a result, Moore re-examines the evidence and shows that there is much more room for common theological conception between Luke and Paul, especially around salvation history and expectation of the parousia.

Paul, for example, rather than simply having expectation of the imminent parousia, recognizes what has come to be known as an 'already and not yet' theology. Moore calls this the 'temporal tension between a "then" in the past and a "then" in the future (e.g. II Cor. 1, 10)'.[70] As he states, Paul recognizes that 'the new aeon has begun', as is shown in 2 Cor. 5.14-15, Gal. 6.14-15 and Col. 1.12-13, but he also recognizes that the 'old' aeon 'continues', when he recognizes that people 'continue to sin' (1 Cor. 1.11-12; 5.1ff.) and 'continue to die' (1 Cor. 11.30; 1 Thess. 4.13-14), as evil is still at work in this present time (2 Cor. 2.11; Gal. 4.8), so that humans continue to need to be 'admonished and encouraged to obedient behaviour' (Gal. 5.4; 6.6; Rom. 12.1ff.).[71] This time in which Paul is living, rather than being given over solely to eschatological expectation, is 'characterized by mission', so that he is concerned to continue his present mission (1 Cor. 9.23; 2 Cor. 10.16; Phil. 1.24-25), further the spread of the gospel (1 Cor. 9.13; 2 Cor. 6.3-4) and extend his mission further (Rom. 15.19ff.).[72] The Spirit is involved in this work (2 Cor. 1.22; 5.5; Rom. 8.23; Eph. 1.14).[73] Further, 'the present is not a mere phenomenon, nor simply a haphazard continuum, but has a definite content and progression fore-ordained and divinely directed', as is illustrated in Phil. 1.12-13, Romans 9–11 (see 11.13), 1 Cor. 9.16, 2 Thess. 2.6ff. and Col. 1.22-29.[74] I also add that even those passages that have often been used to justify the unqualified imminence of the parousia and hence its clear expectation in the early Church are not entirely univocal. Paul recognizes in 1 Thess. 4.17 that there are those alive and remaining who

70. A.L. Moore, *The Parousia in the New Testament* (NovTSup, 13; Leiden: Brill, 1966), p. 84.

71. Moore, *Parousia*, p. 84 and nn. 1, 2.

72. Moore, *Parousia*, p. 84 and n. 3. Moore does not differentiate between the present and extended mission in his discussion.

73. Moore, *Parousia*, p. 84 and n. 4.

74. Moore, p. 84 and n. 6.

are not part of those who have already died in Christ, and in 1 Thess. 5.1-11 he outlines numerous conditions before the day of the Lord.[75]

Moore recognizes that Conzelmann perhaps overdraws his categories when Conzelmann 'maintains that Luke departs from early eschatology and, under the pressure of the Parousia delay, alters the tradition in favour of his own historicizing'.[76] Moore cites five major examples that not only undermine Conzelmann's analysis but also illustrate the possibility of Luke and Paul having more in common regarding their salvation-historical and hence eschatological framework. The first is Luke's purported treatment of John the Baptist as an Israelite prophet (Lk. 3.10-14), not an eschatological figure.[77] Conzelmann says that, in Luke's depiction of John, 'the threat of judgment is now independent of the time when the judgment will take place . . . John does not declare that judgment is near'.[78] Moore points out two competing factors. The first is that Luke has not taken up the description of John in Mk 1.6 that would clearly have placed him among the prophets. The second is that Conzelmann does not address Lk. 3.8-9, where 'imminent judgment' seems to be at hand.[79] The second example is that, despite the claims of Conzelmann and others, Luke is not the first to write a 'history' of Jesus, as would be fitting in the kind of salvation-historical perspective he describes. Matthew 1–2 grounds the story of Jesus in a similar historical framework (even though it has different emphases), and the Lukan prologue (1.1-4) indicates that others had thought to do similarly.[80] The third example concerns Christian behaviour. Conzelmann stresses that Luke depicts the present time as an epoch, not an intermediate stage, and hence the need for emphasis upon Christian behaviour. Moore does not dispute that the Lukan parables – such as the Good Samaritan (Luke 10.29-37) or Prodigal Son (Luke 15.11-32), among others[81] – emphasize behaviour. He notes, however, that 'this concern represents rather an emphasis than a special theological standpoint',[82] especially as Mark also shows concern for ethical behaviour (Mk 3.35, about doing God's will; 7.6-8, about neglecting God's commands; 9.35, about being a servant; and 10.5-6, about the role of commandments).[83] The fourth example addresses Luke's supposed lack of a

75. For treatment of these and other eschatological passages, though not necessarily arriving at the same conclusions, see Joseph Plevnik, *Paul and the Parousia: An Exegetical and Theological Investigation* (Peabody, MA: Hendrickson, 1997).

76. Moore, *Parousia*, p. 84.

77. Moore, *Parousia*, p. 85.

78. Conzelmann, *Theology*, p. 102.

79. Moore, *Parousia*, p. 85.

80. Moore, *Parousia*, p. 85.

81. See Lk. 12.13-21 (proud farmer); 13.6-9 (fig tree); 16.1-13 (unjust steward); 16.19-31 (rich man and Lazarus); 18.1-8 (persistent widow); 18.9-14 (Pharisee and sinner).

82. Moore, *Parousia*, p. 85 and n. 9.

83. Moore, *Parousia*, p. 86 and n. 1.

sense of urgency, which is more typical of an established Church. This, Moore contends, simply is not true, as are illustrated in Lk. 13.6-9, in which the fig tree is given only a year to produce, and 18.8, where the son of man is said to be bringing justice quickly.[84] The fifth and final example is a comparison of Lk. 21 and Mark 13, the eschatological discourses of the two Gospels. Moore shows that at numerous points, where Conzelmann has indicated that there are distinct differences in which Luke minimizes the expectation of an imminent parousia, the near expectation remains. For example, Lk. 21.7-9 is not any less expectant than the Markan parallels (Mk 13.4-7); the Lukan pattern of persecution preceding proclamation is found in both (Lk. 21.12; Mk 13.10); both Luke (21.19) and Mark (13.13) advocate endurance; divine providence is seen to be at play in both (Lk. 21.6, 18; Mk 13.12-13); the destruction of the Temple is not merely historical but meant as a sign of the end (Lk. 21.20-21; Mk 13.20-26); and both have a phased implementation of the events surrounding the coming of the kingdom (Lk. 21.24-28, 29-31; Mk 13.20-22, 28-29).[85]

These examples illustrate that the position of Luke and Paul toward the parousia may have more in common than has often been thought. Whereas Paul is typically depicted as expecting an unqualified imminent return, he himself indicates his belief in an in-between stage, an already and not yet perspective on the parousia. Whereas Luke is typically depicted as having abandoned and even attempted to minimize an imminent return, he himself also indicates an in-between stage, an expectation of future events still present even during this Church age.[86]

IV. *Conclusion*

This essay has of necessity focused upon a few key issues regarding the relationship between Luke's Gospel and Paul as seen through his letters. I have not addressed a number of areas where scholars have recognized their convergence in order to concentrate on several major areas where there has been more widespread disagreement. These begin with the issue of authorship, where even the issue of authorship helps to discern and clarify some of the issues regarding the relationship between Luke and Paul. The relationship

84. Moore, *Parousia*, p. 86 and n. 3.

85. Moore, *Parousia*, pp. 86–8. To this might be added other passages that also indicate an imminent eschatological expectation. These include Luke 1–2 and the annunciation, with the announcement that the final period of history has begun; Luke's admonition for vigilance in Lk. 12.35-48; instructions regarding the day of the son of man in Lk. 17.20-18.8. See Carroll, *Response*, pp. 37–96.

86. This conclusion is similar to what Carroll calls the 'dichromatic approach', represented by Stephen Wilson, A.J. Mattill, Beverley R. Gaventa, E. Earle Ellis and J. Ernst, in which there are indications of both imminence and delay in the parousia (see Carroll, *Response*, pp. 13–16). However, my conclusion is not tied to documentary theories, as are some of these.

of the time of composition of the Gospel and the letters indicate that finding lines of convergence on the basis of the letters and the Gospel will be limited. Whatever view one takes of Lukan authorship of the Gospel, there is scope for understanding the range of potential difference of viewpoint on a number of major theological issues within the early Church. I have identified four of these. In all of these, I have discovered a common pattern regarding scholarly opinion and possibilities of interpretation. In all of them, there is a typical pattern of drawing the lines of divergence much more strongly than is necessary. That does not mean, however, that to dissolve such disjunctions one must find extensive commonality. However, there are a number of instances in which a more common viewpoint and even a similar theological stance is to be found.

Although Luke and Paul use various Old Testament Scriptures in various ways and with varying frequencies, they have the common interpretative practice of establishing the major theme or idea of a written text by means of an exemplary quotation. In Christology, an area where the lines of disagreement have often been the most firmly drawn between a high Christology in Paul and a low Christology in Luke, evidence based upon more nuanced reading of Luke's Gospel indicates that Luke's treatment of the 'Lord' may be higher than previously thought. One cannot say that Luke is responding to Paul in this instance, as the evidence is not nearly as assured as it is in Paul, but the evidence is worth considering, nevertheless. Luke is often said not to have an extensive view of the expiatory death of Jesus. However, when the limited evidence of the Eucharistic words are examined in more detail and when Luke's conglomerate view of salvation and the resurrection are brought into the discussion, Luke is seen to have a more complex view of the salvific significance of Jesus' death and resurrection. The Eucharistic words found in Luke and Paul probably originated with a common source, but it is possible that Paul had a direct influence upon Luke at this point. However, Luke has taken the words and developed the expiatory sense further than is even found in Paul in the equivalent sayings. Finally, one of the standard conceptions of the difference between Luke and Paul is around the role of salvation history and early Catholicism. Luke has been singled out by scholars for special treatment as illustrating a particularly well-defined and rigidly drawn scheme of salvation history that led to an institutionalization of teaching, even in Luke's Gospel, as a compensation for the delay of the parousia. Once more, an examination of the evidence opens up the possibility that such a distinction has been overdrawn, when we consider that Luke is less grounded in the Church age and Paul is less focused upon the imminent return, but that there is again a broad common ground where they can illustrate a tension between the immediate teaching of Jesus and expectation of his return.

There are many more issues that certainly could be treated in a chapter such as this. These, however, offer some insights into the possible theological relationship, as demonstrated through their writings, of Luke's Gospel and Paul. The results allow us to appreciate the individual view of each, recognizing a number of points of theological convergence around major issues in the early Church while maintaining their distinctive voices. In many ways, this is the kind of profile one might expect from missionary companions of the likes of Luke and Paul.[87]

87. I take Ellis's comment, following Harnack and Streeter, seriously that one does not need to see Luke as the disciple or conceptual servant of Paul, and that by not doing so one opens up more possibilities for seeing theological and historical rapprochement between their respective writings.

7

Kyrios Christos: Johannine and Pauline Perspectives on the Christ Event

Mark Harding

I. *The question of influence*

How does the Christianity represented by the Gospel of John relate to the Christianity represented by Paul and the Pauline writings? To what extent did Paul influence the Fourth Gospel (FG)? Is the FG a reaction to Paul and his legacy? These are questions that the editors of this volume have set for our investigation.

We would appear to be on safe ground in at least one respect – namely, that the letters of Paul, certainly the undisputed letters, predate the FG. Therefore the influence, if any, must flow from the letters to the Gospel. Even if the Gospel was completed very early, a minority view to be sure, the earliest date to which scholars have assigned it is the mid-60s CE.[1] The scholarly consensus decidedly favours a date in the last decade of the first century.[2] So, while we cannot

1. A date at the end of the first or the beginning of the second century has been often proposed. See, for example, B. F. Westcott, *The Gospel of According to St. John* (London/New York: Macmillan, 1901), p. lxxxii; Edwyn Hoskyns and Francis Noel Davey, *The Fourth Gospel*, rev. edn (London: Faber & Faber, 1947), p. 96; Craig S. Keener, *The Gospel of John: A Commentary, Volume One* (Peabody: Hendrickson, 2003), pp. 140–142. A date between 100 and 120 CE is proposed by John Marsh, *Saint John* (Harmondsworth: Penguin, 1968), pp. 27–28. By contrast, a date prior to 70 CE is argued by John A. T. Robinson, *Redating the New Testament* (London: SCM Press, 1976), pp. 254–311. That John was the fourth Gospel to be written, see Eusebius, *Hist. Eccl.* 6.14.5-7, for which the authority of Clement of Alexandria is cited. Clement is represented as observing that John, seeing that there were already three Gospels that presented the 'outward facts' (τά σωματικας), wrote a 'spiritual gospel' (πνευματικὸν εὐαγγέλιον).

2. Some scholars propose the pre-existence of sources and successive editions of the FG prior to its reaching its final form. For one such theory, one in five stages, see R. E. Brown, *John, Volume One* (New York: Doubleday, 1966), pp. xxxiv–xxxix. Brown argues that the historical tradition incorporated into the Gospel dates to 70 CE. The various editions of the FG may date to the years 75–110 CE, with a preferred date of c.100 CE for the final form of the Gospel (fifth stage). According to a Committee of the Oxford Society of Historical Theology, *The New Testament in the Apostolic Fathers* (Oxford: Clarendon, 1905), p. 83, the use by Ignatius (d. c.110 CE) of the FG is 'highly probable, but falls some way short of certainty'.

absolutely rule out the influence of the Gospel on Paul and his thought, it is highly likely that any traceable relationship flows in the direction from Paul to John – that is, from Paul and the undisputed letters, all of which were written by the early 60s CE, to the thought that comes to expression in the FG. However, that is not to say, with respect to the post-Pauline corpus of Colossians, Ephesians, 2 Thessalonians and the three Pastoral Epistles, all to be dated, in my view, to the generation after Paul's death, that these might have influenced the FG and vice versa given the fact these letters are more likely to be contemporaneous with the Gospel than the undisputed letters. The possibility of influence from the Pauline corpus to the FG, and perhaps from the post-Pauline letters to the Gospel, finds support in early evidence of the Gospel's Ephesian provenance.

That the FG was written by the apostle John in Ephesus is attested early.[3] Most modern scholars, while not fully accepting the ancient testimony that the apostle wrote the FG, regard the apostle as the authority behind the work.[4] Moreover, Ephesus, whose church was founded by Paul (Acts 19.8-10; cf. 20.31), was the city where Paul spent three years of his ministry. Ephesus was a centre of Paulinism and the headquarters of the Pauline mission during the 50s CE and after his death as his work and vision was promoted by second-generation Paulinists.[5] There is a strong case, therefore, that the Gospel reached its final form in the city where Paul had laboured and from where his successors continued his work. To an examination of the possibility of Paul's influence on the Gospel, and, if demonstrated, its extent and scope, we now turn.

The question of how influence might be determined and its extent assessed is a difficult one, especially with respect to the FG, which shows evidence that its thought can be paralleled in a diversity of religious trajectories.[6] There is

3. For the association of the apostle John, the FG and Ephesus, see Eusebius, *Hist. Eccl.* 3.1.1; 3.23.1-4 (citing Irenaeus, *Haer.* 2.22.5); 3.23.6; 3.31.3; 5.8.4. Eusebius cites Irenaeus (d. c.200 CE) for support and also appeals to Clement of Alexandria as a witness. For a recent discussion of the second-century evidence for the Ephesian provenance of the FG, see P. Trebilco, *The Early Christians in Ephesus from Paul to Ignatius* (Grand Rapids/Cambridge: Eerdmans, 2007), pp. 241–263.

4. See, for example, Keener, *John*, p. 83: 'whereas John the disciple ultimately "stands behind" the FG, others may have developed his tradition into the finished Gospel'.

5. For discussions of Paul's Ephesian ministry see George S. Duncan, *St. Paul's Ephesian Ministry* (London: Hodder & Stoughton, 1929); James D. G. Dunn, *Christianity in the Making, Volume 2: Beginning from Jerusalem* (Grand Rapids/Cambridge: Eerdmans, 2009), pp. 766–780. For the post-Pauline situation see H.-M. Schenke, 'Das Weiterwirken des Paulus und die Pflege seines Erbes durch die Paulus-Schule', *NTS* 21 (1975), pp. 505–518 (esp. p. 516); Trebilco, *Early Christians*, pp. 90–94. Timothy is placed in Ephesus according to 1 Tim. 1.3 (cf. Eusebius, *Hist. Eccl.* 3.3.5). There is also mention of an Onesimus as bishop of Ephesus in Ign. *Eph.* 2.1, though it is unlikely that this is the same person known to Paul (Phlm. 1.10) fifty years before.

6. The Gospel has links with the Dead Sea Scrolls corpus and the *Odes of Solomon*, of Syrian provenance. James H. Charlesworth notes the parallels between the *Odes* and the Dead Sea Scrolls (especially the Hodayot, 1QH) and the FG in his 'Odes of Solomon', in James H. Charlesworth (ed.), *The Old Testament Pseudepigrapha, Volume Two* (Garden City: Doubleday, 1985), p. 728 and throughout the introduction (pp. 725–734) to his translation.

evidence that Christian communities were not isolated and unaware of other communities. Paul actively sought to build relationships among his churches and to relate them to the church in Antioch and in Jerusalem. Paul has a wide network of fellow workers around the Aegean and the eastern Mediterranean. The letter to the Hebrews, certainly not by Paul, nevertheless knows of 'our brother Timothy' (13.23), Paul's co-worker. Though he did not found the church in Rome, Paul feels sufficiently acquainted with it, through associates like Priscilla and Aquila, to write and introduce himself and his message. Peter and other apostles were known to the church at Corinth. The author of 2 Peter is acquainted with Paul's letters (2 Pet. 3.15-16). At a later time, Ignatius is aware of believers in the cities through which he travelled to Rome and has fellowship with them on the way. Papias of Hierapolis seeks out any who had links with the apostles and other early believers.[7] Still later, Irenaeus is indebted to the Pauline and Johannine trajectories of Christian thought.

However, we know of no associates of Paul who had links to the Johannine community. And yet there are tantalizing possibilities here. Paul knew the work and reputation of the Alexandrian and former follower of John the Baptist, Apollos. He was active in Ephesus in the 50s CE, and had been converted by Priscilla and Aquila early in the decade. Apollos was a well-educated man, a rhetorician (Acts 18.24; ἀνὴρ λόγιος). He was co-opted into the Pauline circle, and was active in Corinth after Paul had founded the church.[8] It is possible that he might have influenced the FG. That the Gospel might have been written to convince the disciples of the Baptist to believe in Jesus is possible,[9] and, of course, Apollos had been such a disciple (Acts 18.24-28), whose subsequent ministry was to show the Jews that Jesus was the Messiah (18.28). Accordingly we should not be surprised to discover Pauline influences in the FG and even, perhaps, reactions to the Pauline legacy in the FG.

II. *Literary influence*

In the first forty years of the twentieth century several scholars proposed that there was a demonstrable literary relationship between the Pauline corpus and FG. In his 1904 book on Paul, William Wrede observed that Paul's letters were 'collected and circulated' such that after his death the apostle 'became a literary

7. Eusebius, *Hist. Eccl.* 3.39.4.

8. See Acts 18.24-28; 1 Cor. 1.12; 3.4-6, 22; 4.6; 16.12. For a recent study of Apollos, see Patrick. J. Hartin, *Apollos: Paul's Partner or Rival?* (Collegeville: Liturgical Press, 2009). Hartin does not discuss the possibility that Apollos might have links to the FG. However, a century earlier, E. F. Scott had proposed this. See his *The Fourth Gospel: Its Purpose and Theology* (Edinburgh: T &T Clark, 1908), pp. 53–54.

9. See Marsh, *Saint John*, p. 42.

entity'.[10] In 1908 E. F. Scott noted parallels of wording and thought between Paul and the FG.[11] Edgar Goodspeed argued that an early circulating collection of Paul's letters exercised an influence over most of the books of the NT. The collection was prefaced by the letter to the Ephesians, specially written by the collector, as a summary of the Paulinism of the collection that followed. This collection contained ten letters but did not include the Pastorals. Goodspeed publicized his theory in several books and an influential article.[12] He argued that the publication of Luke-Acts in the 80s of the first century CE aroused interest in Paul and led to the collection of his letters. No NT document earlier than Luke-Acts seems aware of the letters, whereas subsequent to the circulation of Luke-Acts Paul's influence is ubiquitous.

Goodspeed's theory provided the impetus for a thorough analysis by Albert E. Barnett of the literary relationship between Paul's letters and the rest of the NT and early Christian literature, including the Apostolic Fathers and a number of later second-century works (including *2 Clement*, and works by Justin and Melito).[13] The reader of the FG, Barnett observes, is 'constantly reminded of Pauline ideas and phrases' and that 'the fundamental conception of Christianity expressed by Paul and the author of the Gospel is largely the same'.[14] Barnett rated the degree of certainty of the literary relationship between passages from 'practical certainty' (A) to a 'high degree of probability' (B) and a 'reasonable degree of probability' (C). Allusions were classified under the heading 'unclassed'. There was 'no painful copying' on the part of the author(s), Barnett claims, though 'the actual expressions of the letters are occasionally reproduced'.[15] Barnett's list of results shows seven passages in the ten-letter

10. See William Wrede, *Paul* (Eugene, OR: Wipf and Stock, 2001 [orig. 1904; Eng. 1907]), pp. 169–170. The apostle's influence on the FG was foundational, Wrede wrote (*Paul*, p. 171). Note also B. H. Streeter, *The Four Gospels*, rev. edn (London: Macmillan, 1951), pp. 371, 372.

11. In his *Fourth Gospel* Scott does not expect to see evidence of literal reproduction of Pauline theology but rather its echoes. Two articles of B. W. Bacon – 'Pauline Elements in the Fourth Gospel: I. A Study of John i-iv', *ATR* 11.3 [1929], pp. 199–223, and 'Pauline Elements in the Fourth Gospel: II. Parables of the Shepherd, John X. 1-39', *ATR* 11.4 [1929], pp. 305–320 – engage with Scott. Bacon argues that Pauline influence on the FG is most in evidence in those places where the text of the Gospel has been displaced. He nominates Jn. 2.12–3.21, 31-36 in the first article and Jn. 10.1-39 in the second. In the former Paul's teaching on new birth by the Spirit and justification by the blood of Christ are encountered. In the latter warnings from the Pauline tradition (see Acts 20.28-31 and the Pastoral Epistles) regarding the depredations of false teachers are met.

12. *New Solutions of New Testament Problems* (Chicago: Chicago University Press, 1927); *The Meaning of Ephesians* (Chicago: Chicago University Press, 1930); 'The Place of Ephesians in the First Pauline Collection', *ATR* 12 (1930), pp. 189–212; *An Introduction to the New Testament* (Chicago: Chicago University Press, 1937).

13. *Paul Becomes a Literary Influence* (Chicago: Chicago University Press, 1941). Note Barnett's debt to Goodspeed on p. ix. Goodspeed wrote the brief Foreword (pp. vii–viii) commending Barnett's research as 'indispensable to any serious literary study of the New Testament and early Christian literature' (p. vii).

14. Barnett, *Literary Influence*, p. 104.

15. Ibid., p. 105.

Pauline corpus that are ranked A, 52 are ranked in the B category, 79 are ranked in the C category and 81 are 'unclassed'. There are seven passages in the FG that correspond to the seven Pauline passages in Barnett's A category.[16]

These seven Johannine passages relate to three broad themes. First, grace comes through Christ and not through the law. 'The law was given through Moses', the evangelist writes in 1.17, 'Grace and truth came through Jesus Christ'. In Rom. 4.16 Paul expresses a similar thought, though negatively: 'Grace did not come through the law'. Second, in Jn 8.34-36 there are three statements about slavery to sin for which Barnett finds parallels in Rom. 6.16-18; Gal. 4.30 and 5.1. For Barnett both the FG and Paul are agreed that the Son provides freedom from the law. Third, the theme of unity of Jew and Gentile in Christ that is expressed in Jn 10.16 and 11.52 and 'implied' in 17.11, 21 and 23 is paralleled in Ephesians, especially in 2.13-18.

Barnett is right to underscore the theme of the unity of believers common to the FG and found in Ephesians. The Johannine Jesus speaks of 'other sheep not of this fold' that he will gather so there will be one flock, one shepherd (10.16). That Jesus has been sent not just for the nation of Israel but also to gather into one the dispersed people of God, Jews and Gentiles, I contend, is expressed in Jn 11.52 (cf. 12.32).[17] Ephesians 2.11-22 is the classic Pauline passage celebrating the unity of Jew and Gentile in Christ through the breaking down of barriers of hostility between the two.

Nevertheless, the evidence for literary relationships is overstated. The putative parallels in wording and expression are not as compelling as the case for allusions to certain themes of the Pauline corpus that are also found in the FG. Evidence of the shortcoming of Barnett's method is found in his discussion of Jn 12.37-40, which deals with the failure of the Jews to accept Christ. Barnett observes that both Paul and John cite Isa. 53.1 (see Jn 12.38; Rom. 10.16). He draws a literary parallel between the blindness and hard-heartedness of the Jews expressed by their lack of faith in Christ in Jn 12.37-40 and Rom. 9.30-31. But although the thematic link between Paul and John would appear to be a substantial one, Barnett, focused on literary relationships (parallels of wording), assigns a C rating.[18] We will have cause to return to this theme shortly (section Vb) since, in my view, it marks a legitimate thematic parallel between

16. Ibid., p. 142. The relevant passages are Rom. 1.17 (Rom. 4.16; Gal. 1.13); 8.34 (Rom. 6.16-18), 35 (Gal. 4.30), 36 (Gal. 5.1); 10.16 (Eph. 2.14-17); 11.52 (Eph. 2.13-18; 3.6; 4.4-6); 17.11, 21, 23 (Eph. 2.14-18; 3.6; 4.4-6).

17. Note the discussion of the unity of believers in J. Ferreira, *Johannine Ecclesiology* (JSNTSup 160; Sheffield: Sheffield Academic Press, 1998), pp. 132–134. Note that Ferreira argues that the ecclesial oneness of Jews and Gentiles in Paul for its own sake is not the focus of the Johannine ecclesiology. For the FG the unity of believers grows out of divine oneness between Father and Son and the believers' 'solidarity' with the salvific mission of the Son of God.

18. Barnett, *Literary Influence*, p. 129.

Paul and the FG, albeit one with a significant disjunctive element, as we shall see.

Scholars have not been persuaded by Barnett's data in support of *literary* dependence, and there appears no support for the theories of Scott, Goodspeed and Barnett today.[19] The lack of evidence for an early circulating Pauline letter corpus is a major objection, especially if 2 Pet. 3.15-16, the one non-Pauline NT passage in which there is an undoubted awareness of Paul's letters, is to be dated late. The establishment of literary influence is always a task fraught with difficulty unless, as in the case for the dependence of Matthew and Luke on Mark and Q, there are undeniable parallels in wording and narrative order that strongly imply a literary relationship.

Having expressed doubt that there exist sustained literary parallels between Paul and the FG and affirmed the likelihood of the presence of thematic parallels, other scholars have sought to establish the essential unity and coherence of Paul and the FG that stems from their being grounded in the one message of Jesus. In a recent monograph Larry R. Helyer appeals to the work of the Holy Spirit (the 'one Spirit') guaranteeing the unity and coherence, not of just Jesus, Paul and John but of the whole biblical deposit.[20] He is critical of Eduard Lohse's commonplace observation that 'historical-critical exegesis of the New Testament writings forces us to conclude that they . . . do not develop a unified teaching but different theological presentations'.[21] By contrast he mounts a case for the unity of Jesus, Paul and John. 'Paul and John', he writes, 'simply elaborate what is found in Jesus'.[22] He is undaunted by appearances to the contrary, such as the fact that the theme of the Kingdom of God, common in the Synoptic Gospels, is rarely encountered in Paul and John. Helyer argues

19. Three more recent investigations of Pauline parallels operate under different methodologies. In their investigation of similarities of letter structure, form and theme or image, Fred O. Francis and J. Paul Sampley, *Pauline Parallels* (Philadelphia: Fortress Press, 1975) confine themselves to the Pauline corpus, and note in passing a mere three Gospel parallels (Mk 10.2-12//1 Cor. 7.10-11; Mk 10.10-12//1 Cor. 7.12-16; and Mk 14.22-25//1 Cor. 11.23-26). Walter T. Wilson, *Pauline Parallels: A Comprehensive Guide* (Louisville: Westminster John Knox Press, 2009) lists thirty-four passages from the Pauline corpus that have Johannine parallels in terms of similarity of specific terms, concepts, and images. For many of these the parallels are slight. Patricia Elyse Terrell's, *Paul's Parallels: An Echoes Synopsis* (New York/London: Continuum, 2009) is an ambitious project of some 963 pages in which echoes of Paul are provided from the Bible, Second Temple Jewish texts and Graeco-Roman writers. The author of the foreword, Christopher Rowland, lists this resource's many 'features' on pp. xxxiv–xxxv. Among them is the following: 'Paul made scholarly contributions to the gospel writers, which can be tested through this material. The educated Jewish Pharisee, Paul, showed the gospel writers which Jewish material mattered and ways to organize it' (p. xxxv). Terrell provides no analysis of her own, but trusts that that *Paul's Parallels* will prompt students and scholars to follow where the echoes lead.

20. Larry R. Helyer, *The Witness of Jesus, Paul and John* (Downers Grove: InterVarsity Press Academic, 2008).

21. Cited in Helyer, *Witness*, p. 381, without identifying the source.

22. Ibid., p. 383.

that all that Jesus meant by this term is found in Paul and John under other ideas and themes. For example, Col. 1.15-20 and the ideas found there about the supreme role of Christ in effecting cosmic redemption express the essence of the Kingdom of God and demonstrate that the Kingdom is 'one of the fundamental sub-structures of Pauline thought'.[23] The Kingdom also appears in John under the metaphors of light, truth, love, knowledge and life. Paul and John alike are focused on the cross as the supreme moment of redemptive history. Both agree that human sin is the fundamental reason for the coming of Christ and explain his death. The eschatology of Paul and John are elaborating the teaching of Jesus on this theme. In short, the Spirit has ensured the coherence of the message preached by and about Christ.

Helyer's thesis is boldly driven by theological concerns such that differences between the Pauline corpus and the FG become chimerical. Real differences, discontinuities and distinct perspectives are all levelled and reduced to a theologically coherent bedrock. However, I believe that the reality is otherwise. The remainder of this essay will be devoted to analysis of scholars who perceive varying degrees of continuity and discontinuity in Paul and John.

III. *Paul and John as products of Hellenistic Christianity*

In 1913, building on the research of his contemporaries, Wilhelm Bousset published an influential, large-scale defence of the view that both Paul and the FG represent the Hellenization of an original Palestinian Christology that is expressed in the Synoptic Gospels and Acts. Paul and John wrote for communities that moved in the wider Hellenistic world and, because they too were products of that world, naturally articulated their understanding of the Christ event in Hellenistic religious categories.[24] By contrast, the early Palestinian communities spoke of Jesus of Nazareth as the Son of Man who, by virtue of the resurrection, was raised by God to the status of Messiah. Acts 2.36 is the definitive Palestinian confession of the apotheosis of Jesus, a view that also finds expression in Rom. 1.3.[25] As a title, 'Son of Man' originated in eschatologically focused Jewish apocalypses (Daniel 7 and *1 Enoch* 37–71) emanating from Palestine. According to Bousset, Jesus of Nazareth did not claim Messianic status. Neither was he a pre-existent being nor had he come down from above, and nor did he claim to be the Son of Man. But, under the Palestinian church's confession of Jesus as Son of Man he came to be endowed with the title

23. Ibid., p. 382.

24. This is a summary of the thesis of Wilhelm Bousset, *Kyrios Christos* (Nashville/New York: Abingdon, 1970 [1913]).

25. Bousset, *Kyrios Christos*, pp. 33, 115.

and status of Messiah since the Son of Man was identified with that figure.[26] Paul was the thinker who decisively transposed Palestinian Christology into Hellenistic religious categories. Eschewing Son of Man Christology since it was bound not be understood in the wider Greek-speaking world, Paul re-cast Palestinian Christology in terms that, Bousset admits, are already beginning to break through in the later Synoptics Luke and Matthew. Thus Luke and Matthew occasionally present Christ in a way that implies his pre-existence, as in Lk. 10.18 and Mt. 11.25-30. In the former passage Jesus says 'I saw Satan fall from heaven like a flash of lightning'. Bousset comments: 'certainly the time is not far off when Jesus will become a spiritual being, heavenly, pre-existent, coming down from above'.[27] Bousset classed Mt. 11.25-30 as a 'migratory saying' that is clearly dependent on Hellenistic Christianity in its affirmation of Jesus as the unique Son to whom God the Father has revealed himself and who brokers this revelation to those God chooses. These developments will be articulated in the Pauline corpus, Bousset argues, and will be further developed, at a later time, in the FG in dependence on Paul.[28]

Paul, a Jew from Tarsus in the Hellenized world, and the Jerusalem community have little to do with each other.[29] His conversion 'by apocalypse' on the road to Damascus set him apart and contributes to his tortuous relationships with the Twelve. His contact with the Greek-speaking Hellenistic community in Antioch, a community in which there were (non-Jewish) Greeks (Acts 11.20-21), was crucial for the development of his Christology. In place of the Son of Man Christology of the Jerusalem and the Palestinian communities, the title Lord, κύριος, comes to the fore. This title, Bousset observes, 'dominates' the Pauline letters and marks a decisive Christological development.[30] That the title is a mark of the Hellenistic community can be established by its common use in Greek religion, a usage to which Paul refers in 1 Cor. 8.5-6.[31] The κύριος was pre-eminently present in the cult. Such an overtly Hellenistic title could not have originated on Jewish Palestinian soil, Bousset argues.[32] As κύριος, Jesus

26. Ibid., p. 39. Cf. *1 Enoch* 45–48, and note James C. Vanderkam, 'Righteous One, Messiah, Chosen One, and Son of Man in *1 Enoch* 37–71', in James H. Charlesworth (ed.), *The Messiah: Developments in Earliest Judaism and Christianity* (Minneapolis: Fortress Press, 1992), pp. 169–191 (esp. pp. 185–191).

27. Bousset, *Kyrios Christos*, p. 48.

28. See also B. W. Bacon, *The Fourth Gospel in Research and Debate* (London/Leipzig: T. Fisher Unwin, 1910), pp. 534–536. 'It was reserved to Ephesus to produce a truly "spiritual" gospel, interpreting the synoptic tradition of Jesus' life and ministry from the standpoint of Paul's doctrine of the redeeming Spirit' (p. 534).

29. Bousset, *Kyrios Christos*, p. 119.

30. Ibid., p. 122.

31. Ibid., p. 147. See also Rudolf Bultmann, *The Theology of the New Testament, Volume One* (New York: Charles Scribner's Sons, 1951), pp. 124–125.

32. Ibid., p. 147. See also Joseph Klausner, *From Jesus to Paul* (London: Allen & Unwin, 1944), p. 484. Bousset (*Kyrios Christos*, p. 123) notes that Jesus is addressed as κύριε only once genuinely in

was ever-present in the cult of the Pauline communities, in word and sacrament. Concomitantly the presence of the Spirit of the Lord was experienced by believers as the power of God that empowered them to fulfil the demand of the law and to restrain the lusts of the flesh.[33] It is for this reason that Paul had little purpose for the historical Jesus save to know the theological significance of his death.[34] His immediate presence in the cult overshadows all aspects of the Palestinian gospel such as we encounter in the Synoptics. The FG will invest the tradition of the historical Jesus with 'myth' and 'dogma', fashioning the story with the exalted Christology that developed uniquely in the Hellenistic community. Paul was a second founder of Christianity, wrote Wrede.[35] The FG built upon his foundation and actualized Pauline theology.[36]

The use of κύριος in the LXX for God, a term that in time was to be applied to the exalted Jesus, required for Paul the development of a Christology of Christ as the Son of God. While the title κύριος places the exalted Jesus close to God, θεὸς, the terms 'Father' and the 'Son of God' hold 'God' and the 'Lord' apart.[37] The FG built on this Christology and on the presence of the Spirit of Christ in his community.[38] The FG inhabits the same Hellenistic milieu as Paul.[39] But, Bousset points out, while there are commonalities there are discontinuities too.

First, while Paul is not at all interested in the historical Jesus, the FG is profoundly so. In the FG, Bousset writes, the earthly life of Jesus takes on 'a new and unprecedented significance'.[40] In the evangelist's presentation of that

the Synoptics, where (not surprisingly) it is used by the Syro-Phoenician woman (Mt. 15.27; Mk 7.28). The discussion in Bousset about the origin of the Aramaic acclamation *Maranatha*, 'our Lord, come', is enlightening. On p. 129 he argues that the formula could not have arisen in the early Palestinian community but in the 'bilingual region of the Hellenistic communities of Antioch, Damascus, and even Tarsus'. This matter will be further discussed in Section IV.

33. Bousset, *Kyrios Christos*, p. 163. Bousset cites Rom. 8.4 and Gal. 5.16, 25 as evidence.

34. The crux is 2 Cor. 5.16 and the meaning of no longer knowing Jesus 'according to the flesh' (κατὰ σάρκα). Klausner, *From Jesus to Paul*, pp. 312–315 remarks that Paul regards the earthly Jesus to be irrelevant because that would 'call attention' to the fact that he did know Jesus in Palestine during his lifetime but as one who had opposed his message while Jesus was still alive. Note also Eva Aleith, *Paulusverständnis in der Alten Kirche* (Berlin: Töpelmann, 1937), p. 18. It is much more likely that κατα; σαςρκα refers to an inadequate estimate of the worth of Jesus.

35. Wrede, *Paul*, p. 168.

36. Ibid., pp. 170–171; Aleith, *Paulusverständnis*, pp. 18–22.

37. Bousset, *Kyrios Christos*, p. 209.

38. Aleith, *Paulusverständnis*, p. 21. Aleith rightly notes the connections between the pneumatology of Paul expressed in Rom. 8.26-27 and the Paraclete in the FG.

39. A number of scholars single out the supposed use by Paul and John of the myth of the descending redeemer as evidence of their indebtedness to Hellenistic culture. See, for example, R. Bultmann, *The Gospel of John: A Commentary* (Oxford; Blackwell, 1971), pp. 9–10; W. G. Kümmel, *The Theology of the New Testament* (Nashville/New York: Abingdon, 1973), p. 273.

40. Bousset, *Kyrios Christos*, p. 199.

life, even the death of Christ is glorification and exaltation.[41] But for Paul, the cross is the climax of his self-giving and humiliation as one who took the form of a slave (δούλου) (Phil. 2.7). For the Synoptics, the cross is the supreme expression of the lowliness and humility of the now-exalted Son of Man. Robert Kysar aptly summarizes the passion story of the FG as the 'story of the king going to his coronation'.[42] This suggests that the FG is reacting against the Synoptic presentation of the story of Jesus, and especially the Synoptic Passion narrative. Similarly, the emphasis in Paul on the abasement of Jesus that is his suffering is to be contrasted with the theology of the glory of the Christ that is everywhere in evidence in the FG. As Wrede and Aleith remark, the Christ of Paul, exalted, present in the church, appears in the FG in his 'fleshly shell'.[43]

Second, Bousset argues that the title κύριος, so important for Paul, is avoided by the FG in chs 1–19 and is only used in the resurrection stories of chs 20–21. For the FG the title κύριος ought not be used of Jesus prior to his resurrection, since his life was that of a servant and slave (δούλου) among friends (φίλους) whom Christ refuses to call δούλους (Jn 15.15). Paul, on the other hand, accepts the designation δούλου of himself and calls his addressees δούλους, and invokes Jesus as Lord unlike the friends of Jesus in the FG prior to his resurrection.

Third, unlike Paul, the Johannine Jesus openly confesses that he is the Son of Man, investing that title with the divine dignity that it possesses in apocalyptic expectation and which can be especially glimpsed in *1 Enoch*. As Bousset explains, the Palestinian concept of the Son of Man as eschatological judge has become in the FG the judge who presides over judgement in the present (5.27), completely separating the title from its Jewish apocalyptic roots such that the FG 'falls into the danger of completely eliminating the primitive Christian eschatology'.[44]

Fourth, while the FG, like Paul, used the title 'Son of God' of Jesus, the evangelist does so in a way that is quite different to Paul. For Paul, as we have already observed, 'Son of God' permitted a demarcation between God as θεὸς and Christ as κύριος. For John, on the other hand, the title 'Son of God' assumes a metaphysical significance. Christ, on earth, is the incarnation of the pre-existent Son, who exists in the 'bosom of the Father' (Jn 1.18). He is the revealer of the Father's secrets. He has been sent into the world to reveal the Father's love. He returns to the Father. On earth as well as in heaven, the Son exercises the works of the Father supremely in exercising judgement and raising the dead to life. For John, the title 'Son' encapsulates all that Paul 'and popular Hellenistic Christianity' inferred in the title κύριος.[45]

41. Ibid., p. 53.
42. Robert Kysar, *John, the Maverick Gospel* (Atlanta: John Knox Press, 1976), p. 37.
43. Aleith, *Paulusverständnis*, p. 18; Wrede, *Paul*, p. 172.
44. Bousset, *Kyrios Christos*, p. 213.
45. Ibid., pp. 213–215.

IV. *Responses to Bousset*

In a number of articles Martin Hengel has argued the case for greater continuity between the earliest Palestinian community and the theology and Christology of Paul. More specifically he has focused attention on the work of the Hellenists, Greek-speaking Jews living in Palestine, but emanating originally from the cities of the Diaspora. Among the Hellenists were believers who further developed what Hengel terms 'the eschatologically motivated trend of the message of Jesus, which was critical of the Torah'.[46]

It was the Hellenists who, in Hengel's words, 'mediated the spread of the message of the Galilean Jews to the cities of the empire'.[47] Antioch was the first substantial city where their mission is first evidenced. It was in Antioch that the gospel was first preached to (non-Jewish) Greeks. But, as Hengel argues, Hellenistic Christianity, with its outward-looking perspective, had its roots nonetheless in Jerusalem. There were continuities between Hellenist and Aramaic-speaking Christian communities and between the message of the Hellenist believers and Jesus on the law and his attitude towards non-Jews.[48] Here can be found the starting point of the Gentile mission promoted by the Hellenists. There is therefore no need to posit what Hengel calls 'pagan influences' on Christological development as Bousset had done. Bousset had argued, for example, that the motif of the sending of the Son, prominent in the FG, had its origins in pre-Christian Gnostic myth. Hengel, by contrast, contends that the motif is more likely to be dependent on Jewish Wisdom speculation. Furthermore, the Hellenistic religious context was not decisive for the enrichment of the earliest Christology, as Bousset believed, since the acclamation *Maranatha*, 'Our Lord, come', is preserved in Aramaic in Paul.[49] It is much more likely that the acclamation originated in the Aramaic-speaking Palestinian community as the means by which it expressed its enthusiastic expectation for the imminent return of its Lord and attributed a fundamental identity between the heavenly Lord and the believers now led by the disciples of the resurrected Jesus. Thus the hymn preserved by Paul in Phil. 2.5-11, with its ascription of the title 'Lord', κύριος, to the risen Christ under the influence of Ps. 110.1, has already been prepared for in the Palestinian community with its attribution

46. Martin Hengel, *Between Jesus and Paul* (Philadelphia: Fortress Press, 1983), p. 25.

47. Hengel, *Between Jesus and Paul*, p. 26. Hengel calls the Hellenist believers the 'bridge': they were the first to 'translate the Jesus tradition into Greek and at the same time prepared the way for Paul's preaching of freedom by its criticism of the ritual law and the cult' (*Between Jesus and Paul*, p. 29).

48. Hengel notes Jesus' 'sovereign attitude' towards the law in Lk. 10.8 and Mk 7.15, for example (*Between Jesus and Paul*, p. 40), and his openness of Jesus towards non-Jews (*Between Jesus and Paul*, p. 63). For the extensive connection between Judaean Christianity and Paul, see also Larry W. Hurtado, *Lord Jesus Christ: Devotion to Jesus in Earliest Christianity* (Grand Rapids/Cambridge: Eerdmans, 2003), pp. 156–176 (esp. pp. 167–176).

49. 1 Cor. 16.22 preserves *Maranatha*. Note also *Did.* 10.6.

of the exalted title *Mar*, Lord, to Christ.[50] This acclamation, and especially its evocation of Christ as the divine Lord, helps to explain the eclipse of the title 'Son of Man'.[51] James D. G. Dunn has rightly noted that the persistence of the Aramaic *Maranatha* is the 'Achilles heel' of Bousset's theory that the use of κύριος used of Jesus originated in bilingual Hellenistic communities.[52]

Paul built on the Gentile mission begun by the Hellenists. His Christology has significant elements in common with them, especially any speculation on their part about Wisdom in defining the role of Christ. His attitude towards the law is shared by the Hellenists. His confident expectation of the imminence of the parousia can also be traced to Palestine, to the earliest Aramaic and Hellenist communities. Here is fertile ground that helps to explain the presence in the FG and in Paul of some of the themes they share.

V. *Pauline distinctives*

Having traced the contribution of several important scholars seeking to account for commonalities between the FG and Paul, I now propose to consider several themes that I believe show evidence of both juncture and disjuncture.

a. *The law in Paul and the FG*

Paul's attitude towards the Jewish law, the Law of Moses, is the subject of much debate. Let me pose the following summary of Paul's position. The law belongs to an era that has passed away. It has ceased to be determinative of Jewish identity. Keeping the law ought not to be required of Gentile believers. It has no normative role in the communities Paul founded. By virtue of its condemnation of the crucified Jesus as one accursed (Gal. 3.13; Deut. 21.23) – the same Jesus who has been raised from the dead and vindicated by God – the law has been overtaken and rendered obsolete in the unfolding of divine redemptive purposes. Its time of relevance as commandment gives way to a new commandment, that of faith in Christ. The law demonstrated the need for a deliverer. Having consigned all to death, it leads us to Christ. The law presided

50. Hengel, *Between Jesus and Paul*, p. 75. See also Hurtado, *Lord Jesus Christ*, pp. 108–118.

51. Hengel explains in *Between Jesus and Paul*, p. 75, n. 91 (p. 187), that the title κύριος does not imply that Jesus is to be placed on the same level as Yahweh, and he is not to be identified with the Father. Rather, Hengel explains, there is an 'assimilation' of the κύριος to God influenced by Ps. 110.1. Hengel argues that this Psalm exercised a crucial significance in the development of Christology. 'When the earliest community in Jerusalem, driven on by the power of the Spirit, was concerned to work out in theological terms the overwhelming experience of the resurrection of Jesus, it must have very soon have come upon this psalm' (*Between Jesus and Paul*, p. 87).

52. See J. D. G. Dunn, *The Theology of Paul the Apostle* (Grand Rapids: Eerdmans, 1998), p. 248, n. 66. Note also the critique of Bousset in Hurtado, *Lord Jesus Christ*, pp. 13–26 (esp. pp. 19–26).

over a 'no exit' situation, to use J. Christiaan Beker's words.[53] The law, with its ready condemnation of transgressors, was powerless to give life. But now, the law, with its writ against us, has been nailed to the cross of Christ (Col. 2.14). The law poses great risk to those who seek to obey it. Those who place themselves under its yoke are required to exercise consistent obedience to all its demands (Gal. 3.10). For transgression under the law there is no escape, no remedy, no relief. Indeed, in Galatians the world's religious options, including Judaism, make for enslavement to the 'elemental spirits' (see Gal. 4.3). The law perpetuates the deep divisions that exist between Jew and Greek (Gal. 3.28; cf. Eph. 2.11-22). Rather than seek the righteousness that comes by faith, Paul contends that the majority of Jews to whom he has preached have sought to establish their own (Rom. 10.3).[54] Consequently, the works of the law, those requirements that made for a distinctly Jewish life-commitment to God, can now be set aside in favour of faith.

There is an essential congruity between the FG's view of the law and that of Paul, especially as it is articulated in Galatians. Both the Paul of the undisputed letters and the FG might be fairly said to represent the idea that faith in Christ has superseded justification by works of the law and that faith constitutes the demand of God. For both Paul and the FG, the significance of the coming of Christ is such that faith in him eclipses all other loyalties, including keeping the law. Christ ushers in God's decisive saving initiative to which the law must give way. That this is an issue for John is shown by the prominence given to the law and the old dispensation under Moses in the prologue: 'The law indeed was given through Moses; grace and truth came through Jesus Christ' (1.17 NRSV). The Mosaic dispensation, an arrangement ordered by a man ('through Moses'), and the dispensation brokered by Christ, 'the only-begotten God' (according to the best manuscripts) who is in the 'bosom of the Father' (1.18), is profoundly contrastive.[55] There is a comparability of perspective here between the FG and the law 'mediated by angels' in Acts 7.53 and, by implication, Heb. 1.4 and Gal. 3.19, where the Law is given by angels through a human mediator, Moses.

The negative outlook on the law in the FG is further underscored in ch. 10. Here the FG depicts Jesus speaking of those who came before him as 'thieves

53. *Paul the Apostle: The Triumph of God in Life and Thought* (Philadelphia: Fortress, 1980), p. 238.

54. Paul's statements in Romans about the law are cast in more positive, even irenic, terms. For Paul, in Romans the law is 'good and holy' (7.12) and 'spiritual' (7.14). Sin, not the law, is the problem. See also Beker, *Paul the Apostle*, pp. 94–108. The reason for this, Beker explains, is that Galatians is a 'combat' letter reflecting a polemical confrontation with Judaizers. Romans, on the other hand, encapsulates Paul's attempt to persuade the Jews to see in God's act in Christ the provision of salvation from the condemnation of the law (p. 104).

55. For a more positive evaluation of the law in the FG, see Keener, *John, Volume One*, p. 421. Moses remains God's Word; and testifies to Jesus (see Jn 1.45; 5.45-47). The contrast between Moses and Christ is between something good and something better (*John, Volume One*, p. 422).

and bandits' (10.8, 12).[56] That he has the teachers of the law and the Pharisees in mind is implied by the narrative of conflict with them in the preceding chapter, culminating in 9.40-41. This critique of the law takes on further sharpness if the Gospel community is experiencing harassment at the hands of the local synagogue to which the community belongs, as J. Louis Martyn has argued.[57] But regardless of the merit of Martyn's argument, it is hard to resist the conclusion that the law, for the evangelist and the Johannine community, can be consigned a temporary and inferior place in the dealings of God with humankind. Indeed, the role of the law hinted at in Jn 1.17 implies that it was both a temporary and a human expedient. The Jews who oppose Jesus appeal to Moses and the law out of unbelief (Jn 9.28) – out of murderous spite in fact – such that it might be said that the law promotes and inspires unbelief and invites catastrophe (5.45). 'Did not Moses give you the law?' Jesus asks, 'Yet none of you keeps the law. Why do you seek to kill me?' (7.19). Finally, Jesus is presented as one who is completely alienated from his Jewish heritage when he speaks about the law as 'their law' (Jn 15.25; cf. Acts 23.29) and 'your law' (Jn 8.17; 10.34).

This invites us to ask whether the FG is dependent on Paul. The FG emanates from a generation after Paul when the church outside of Palestine might be expected to be more Gentile than Jewish in its constituency. Yet the FG reads more polemically engaged with the issue of the ongoing validity of the law than the post-Pauline letters Ephesians, 2 Thessalonians and the Pastoral Epistles for which the law has ceased to be of interest.

While we do not know which communities first read the FG, it is possible that if these were in Asia Minor then the law-free gospel of Paul, also operative in this area, might have provided the germ of the attitude expressed in the FG that the dispensation of the law had been superseded by faith in Christ. However, it is more likely that the attitude of the FG has arisen out of a polemical engagement of the Johannine community with the synagogue. Nevertheless, faith in Christ, believing in him, is a key theme of both Paul and the FG and marks a discontinuity with the perspective of the Synoptic Gospels with their focus on Jesus' preaching of the imminent arrival of the Kingdom of God. As

56. Paul depicts the teachers of the law as accursed and bewitching. See Gal. 1.8-9; 3.1. Note also Aleith, *Paulusverständnis*, pp. 21–22.

57. J. Louis Martyn, *History and Theology in the Fourth Gospel* (Nashville: Abingdon, 1979). However, note the arguments that the Gospels were intended for a much wider audience than one community that are presented in R. Bauckham (ed.), *The Gospels for All Christians: Rethinking the Gospel Audiences* (Grand Rapids/Cambridge: Eerdmans, 1998), esp. pp. 9–48, and noting Bauckham's comment on Martyn's thesis on p. 23.

Bultmann pointed out, Christ has become the subject of the *kerygma*.[58] Paul and John agree that faith in Christ is God's demand.

b. *'The Jews'*

There exists in the undisputed Pauline letters an unshakeable belief on Paul's part that God has destined the message of salvation to the Jews first (Rom. 1.16; 2.9, 10). Their unbelief is a source of grief to Paul, who can point to a small number, himself included, of those who have believed as evidence of the faithfulness of God to bless his ancient people (Rom. 11.1, 5). The great passage that expresses Paul's confidence in the end-time reconciliation of the nation is Romans 9–11.[59] Here, Paul asserts that the Gentiles have believed, not as the sign that God has passed over his people but in order that their inclusion might finally win the Jews to faith by 'jealousy' (Rom. 11.11). It is an incontrovertible fact, he writes, that the branches broken off the olive tree can and will be grafted back in (11.24). This robust confidence in the eschatological reconciliation of unbelieving Jews, of 'Israel' no less (see 11.25-26), found only in Romans admittedly, is absent in the disputed letters. Quite alien to Paul is the thought expressed in the letter to the Ephesians where Christ is celebrated as the one who has broken down the dividing wall of hostility between Jew and Gentile (2.11-22), making one new nation out of two, in the church. There is no place here for the end-time expectation of the in-gathering of Israel.

In Section II of this essay we noted that there exists a thematic parallel worth exploring between Jn 12.37-40 and Rom. 9.30-31. The FG cites Isa. 53.1 at 12.38b to explain the lack of response to the ministry of Jesus (see Jn 12.37-38a) and Isa. 6.10 at Jn 12.40 to account for the blindness and hard-heartedness of Jews to exercise faith in Christ. And yet there are many, even from among the authorities, who did believe in Jesus (Jn 12.42) but did not confess it for fear of excommunication from the synagogue. The former passage from Isaiah is also quoted by Paul in Rom. 10.16. Despite the paucity of evidence that Jews have put their faith in Christ, resolving instead to continue submitting to the Law of Moses, Paul cannot accept that God has rejected his people (11.1). As noted, his argument will reach its climax in the assertion that in the end all Israel will be saved (11.25-26) as an essential aspect of the eschatological triumph of God. This perception is lacking in the FG.

Paul did have his Jewish opponents who made his life difficult (see, for example, 2 Cor. 11.24-26) and whose opposition led directly to his death at the

58. Bultmann, *Theology of the New Testament, Volume One*, p. 3; cf. *Volume Two*, p. 4: In the FG Jesus 'strives not against self-righteousness and untruthfulness but against disbelief towards himself'. Cf. Scott, *Fourth Gospel*, p. 41; Craig R. Koester, *The Word of Life: A Theology of John's Gospel* (Grand Rapids: Eerdmans, 2008), pp. 161–74.

59. See Beker, *Paul the Apostle*, pp. 328–347.

hands of the Romans. He has harsh words for Jews who reject the message, of which the denunciation preserved in 1 Thess. 2.14-16 is the most striking. Prompted by the mistreatment of the Thessalonian Christians by their Jewish neighbours, the passage draws a bitter parallel between that treatment and the abuse of Christians in Judaea at the hands of the Jews who 'killed both the Lord Jesus and the prophets and drove us out'. Wrath (ὀργὴ), we read in v. 16, has overtaken them (the Jews) 'at last' (εἰς τέλος). Given Paul's unmistakeable eschatological expectations expressed elsewhere for the salvation of the people, the argument that 1 Thess. 2.14-16 is a post-Pauline gloss is strong.[60]

Paul's profound eschatological perspective on the ultimate salvation of Israel is not shared by the FG, which dismissively portrays the opponents of Jesus as 'the Jews'. The term has become a cipher for the nation, the ἔθνος, that is implacably opposed to accepting the truth.[61] In the persistent use of that nomenclature all the particularity of the references to the Jews in the Synoptic Gospels is missing.[62] The Synoptic Jesus certainly has his Jewish opponents, but there are some among the Pharisees, for instance, who support and defend him. Those who clamour for his death are simply portrayed as 'the crowd' (ὄχλον) in the Synoptics, but in the FG it is 'the Jews' who demand his crucifixion.[63] Occasionally Pharisees appear in the FG, though not in a positive light.[64] The one exception is Nicodemus, the mysterious member of the Council who came to Jesus by night and whose subsequent attempt to defend Jesus in Jn 7.50-52 is decisively deflected by his fellow Pharisees. The words of Jesus recorded in 16.1-4 indict the synagogue with murder. His remark that the Jews have the devil for their father (8.44) is even more extreme, and all the more puzzling since earlier in the discourse the hearers happen to be Jews who, the reader is

60. To what event is the author referring when he writes that wrath has overtaken them? A number of suggestions could be made, including the famine of the mid-40s CE, the progressive breakdown of law and order in Judaea once Roman rule was re-imposed after the death of Agrippa I in 44 CE, and the expulsion of the Jews from Rome in 49 CE. The suggestion that the passage is an interpolation that refers to the destruction of Jerusalem and the temple in 70 CE is best. No catastrophe could have given rise to the statement in Paul's lifetime. See the cautious discussion in F. F. Bruce, *1 & 2 Thessalonians* (Waco: Word Books, 1982), p. 49.

61. *Contra* Kysar, *Maverick Gospel*, p. 16. He argues that 'the Jews' are local opponents merely and that the term is 'not an ethnic category in the FG'. Note also Lars Kierspel, *The Jews and the World in the Fourth Gospel* (Tübingen: Mohr [Siebeck], 2006). Kierspel argues that 'Jews', when used in a negative sense, denotes the Jewish expression of disbelief that is a part of the disbelief exercised by the 'world' (κόσμου).

62. The 'Jews' appears six times in Mark, and five times in both Matthew and Luke. Outside the passion narratives of the three Synoptics, Mark uses 'Jews' once in 7.3 (in an explanation of the Jewish practice of handwashing before eating), Matthew once in 2.2 (for king of the Jews) and Luke once in 7.3 (of the Jewish elders who come to Jesus to ask him to heal the centurion's slave). By contrast, 'the Jews' appears seventy-two times throughout the FG.

63. Contrast the use of 'the Jews' in Jn 18.38-40 with Mk 15.6-16; Mt. 27.15-23 and Lk. 23.13-23. The links between the Synoptic Gospel tradition and the FG are generally considered strongest in the Passion narrative, but not at this point.

64. See Jn 1.24; 3.1 (Nicodemus); 7.32, 47-48; 11.47, 57.

informed, believe in him (v. 31). This persistent, conflicted polarity of Jesus and the Jews is not encountered in the Synoptics. Even the bitter reproaches of Matthew 23 are directed to particular Jewish groups (scribes and Pharisees) and not to the Jews as an ἔθνος.

c. *Christology*

Bousset and other twentieth-century scholars argue that there are considerable affinities between Paul and the FG with respect to their Christology. What follows is an analysis of aspects of the Christology of Paul and the FG, aspects of which have been anticipated earlier in this chapter.

For John the Christ is the heavenly Son of Man. He exemplifies all that *1 Enoch* had predicated of that figure. Whereas in the Synoptic Gospels the identification of Jesus and the Son of Man is ambiguous and implicit, in the FG Jesus openly confesses that he is the Son of Man functioning with all the authority of the Father, on earth. There is no ambiguity in this self-identification; no mistaking in Jesus the exalted being with whom he identified even in his humiliation and abasement.[65] Strikingly, in contrast to the Synoptic tradition and the FG, Paul nowhere speaks of the 'Son of Man'. Bousset contends that Paul's message was addressed to the Hellenistic world of the wider Mediterranean for which the term 'Son of Man' would have had little resonance. But the argument for the non-appearance of 'Son of Man' in Paul's letters does not account for the frequency with which the FG uses the same term in the same Hellenistic context. At best Bousset can argue that the evangelist 'still has some connections with Palestine and the Palestinian community'.[66] 'Son of Man' was an integral aspect of the Palestinian tradition that the FG transmitted, though in a 'spiritualized' form. The evangelist gave the term content that conferred on the one who used it the character of a being from the realm of the Godhead, and who, as Son of Man, pre-existed his earthly life and would return to the Father after his brief, but profoundly revelatory, sojourn on earth.

The prologue of the FG speaks of Jesus as the Logos. It has often been observed that outside of Jn 1.1-18 the absolute use of the term does not reappear in the Gospel and is nowhere else encountered in the NT.[67] It would be best to regard the prologue as a reflection, originally composed in Johannine circles, added by the redactor at a late stage of the composition history of the Gospel.[68] The significance of the title Logos is out of all proportion to its frequency of

65. Kysar, *Maverick Gospel*, pp. 36–37.

66. See Bousset, *Kyrios Christos*, p. 213. This is a surprising admission on Bousset's part.

67. Jesus is called ὁ λόγος τοῦ θεοῦ in Rev. 19.13. Following G. B. Caird, *The Revelation of St. John the Divine* (London: A&C Black, 1966), p. 244, the allusion is to the living and powerful Word encountered in Wis. 18.15-16.

68. See Brown, *John, Volume One*, p. xxxviii.

appearance. As applied to Jesus, it claims him as the Word by which God spoke order out of chaos (cf. Gen. 1.1-3), the absolutely true revelation of the character and mind of God, the embodiment of the meaning of the creation and the agent of God for the redemption of the world.[69]

The FG's use of the title 'Son of God' can be compared with the use of the title Logos. For the FG the Son of God, Jesus, is the unique Son, full of the Father's glory, who makes the Father truly known. There could be no mistaking Jesus as a son of god in the Hellenistic sense in which there might be any number of such sons. This Son is unique, especially endowed, indissolubly close to the Father (as indicated by Jn 1.18), and one with God such that one can see the beginnings of the development of an ontology that will assuredly lead to the church's Trinitarian doctrine of three Persons in one God. Paul also calls Jesus 'Son of God', but he does not invest it with any of the ontological overtones of the FG.

The title 'Lord' (κύριος), as we have noted, is frequently used in Paul. Its appearance in the FG is limited, the reason having been suggested earlier, in Section III, but it does occur at the climax of the Gospel – namely, the confession of Thomas recorded in Jn 20.28: 'My Lord and my God'. Bousset and others – Bultmann comes most readily to mind – argued that this title explicitly marks the Pauline letters and the FG as products of the Hellenistic world and distinguishes their Christology from that of the Palestinian community. However, we have seen that this argument is deeply compromised by the use of the acclamation *Maranatha*, 'our Lord, come', a phrase known to Paul operating in Hellenistic circles far removed from the Palestinian community. There are greater affinities here among Paul, the FG and the Palestinian community than Bousset perceived.

As we have already noted, compared with the FG, Paul is much more focused on the humiliation of Jesus, pre-eminently in the suffering he endured on the cross. Paul's own sufferings are explicitly linked to those of Jesus in 2 Cor. 4.7-12 (cf. 1 Cor. 4.8-13). By contrast, and perhaps this is intentional, the FG stresses the lifting up of Jesus on the cross as his glorification. The cross and the resurrection are seen as the one event. In Paul, however, while Jesus is vindicated and raised in honour by God by means of the resurrection, the dishonour, humiliation and degradation of the cross is never denied. The

69. See C. H. Dodd, *The Interpretation of the Fourth Gospel* (Cambridge: Cambridge University Press, 1953), pp. 263–285. Dodd argues that the Johannine concept of the Logos owes much to (1) the Hebraic idea of the 'word of God' by which God spoke the created order out of chaos and the prophets spoke God's mind, (2) Jewish speculation about the role of personified Wisdom in the creation of the world, the revelation of God's will in the Torah and its continuing immanence (note the parallels brought together on pp. 274–275) and (3) Philo's speculation about the divine Logos as the 'meaning, plan and purpose of creation' (p. 277).

cross is the event that displays, par excellence, the humiliation of the Son who 'gave himself for me' and died the death of a slave as evidence of the love of God. Abasement surely leads to exaltation (Phil. 2.5-11); but it was real abasement. The resurrection is Jesus' vindication, but it is an event that by no means evacuates the cross of its horror. But for all that, in both the FG and Paul the cross reveals the character of God and proclaims God's love for humankind.[70]

Moreover, while Paul can speak of the equality of Christ and God (Phil. 2.5-11), his speaking of the self-emptying (ἐκένωσεν) of Jesus is nowhere paralleled in the FG. Paul's proposition that on earth the glory of Christ that he possessed in eternity was veiled and even surrendered is foreign to the FG. For the FG, the earthly Jesus retains the glory of God that shines in him (Jn 1.14) and was never eclipsed, even in death (1.5). That there are those who fail to believe and to perceive who Jesus really is – whence he has come and whither he is going – makes their unbelief that much more culpable.

Both Paul and the FG agree that Jesus is the Messiah. The FG makes little of that affirmation, despite the explicit confession of Jesus in ch. 4. For the FG Jesus is more often titled 'Son of Man' or 'Son of God' or just 'Son' – terms that together invest Jesus with heavenly dignity, ontological unity with God and the functions of God. For Paul, on the other hand, Jesus' Messiahship is proclaimed in his ubiquitous linking of 'Jesus' and 'Christ' (Χριστὸς). He invests the title 'Son of God' with meaning derived in the first place from the Hebrew Bible's designation of the 'Son of David' as 'Son of God'. Thus Paul is content to use 'Son of God' to speak of the honour and dignity of Jesus as Messiah. This can be seen in Rom. 1.3-4, where Jesus is not only termed the 'Son of God' descended from David 'according to the flesh' but also 'Son of God in power' by virtue of the resurrection. Jesus' sonship becomes a term to denote the exalted and unique Son of God whose resurrection means his adoption into the heavenly realm where his saving and redeeming work continue through the Spirit. It would be true to say, therefore, that as Son Jesus is the heavenly Messiah, who has been assumed into heaven there to continue his redeeming work until the *parousia*. Thus in 1 Thess. 1.10 this activity will be decisively concluded by the coming of the Son from heaven 'who will deliver us from the wrath to come'. In the FG 'Son of God' can be understood to be synonymous with the appointed King/Messiah of Israel, as in Jn 1.49 (cf. 20.31). But, as noted, 'Son of God' more accurately denotes Jesus in his eternal relationship with the Father. The Father makes the Son known; the Son whom he has always known. This Christology is foreign to Paul.

Does Paul profess a Christology that affirms the pre-existence of Christ? The

70. It is more correct to say that in the FG the beneficiaries of the Father's love are the disciples and the 'other sheep' (Jn 10.16) of which Jesus speaks.

answer must be affirmative. In Phil. 2.5-11, a piece of hymnic tradition taken over by Paul, Christ Jesus' equality with God (τὸ εἶναι ἴσα θεῷ) is understood as something he might have grasped as his right (2.6). But although he was in the 'form of God' (ἐν μορφῇ θεοῦ) he submitted to the life of a slave. His subsequent exaltation as Lord (2.11), an honour bestowed upon him by virtue of the resurrection, implies he did not enjoy the status of Lord beforehand. Elsewhere he writes that when the fullness of time had come 'God sent his Son' (Gal. 4.4).[71] These assertions of the pre-existence of Christ, Dunn argues, are likely to be dependent on Jewish speculation about the role of Wisdom being sent by God, as in Wis. 9.10: 'Send her [Wisdom] forth from the holy heavens, and from the throne of your glory send her, that she may labour at my side, and that I may learn what is pleasing to her.'[72]

As further evidence of Paul's understanding of the pre-existence of Christ, he assigns a role to Christ as Lord in the creation of the world. Paul writes: 'for us there is one God, the Father, from whom [ἐξ οὗ τὰ πάντα] are all things and for whom we exist, and one Lord, Jesus Christ, through whom [δἰ οὗ τα πάντα] are all things and through whom we exist' (1 Cor. 8.6). In the hymnic passage Col. 1.15-20, this Christology is both restated and further developed. Christ is understood to be the image of the invisible God (1.15), a proposition that invites comparison with not only Jn 1.18 but also 2 Cor. 4.4. All things, says the writer in agreement with 1 Cor. 8.6, were created 'through him and for him' (Col. 1.16; cf. Jn 1.3).[73] But the writer now proceeds to assert that Christ is 'before all things and in him all things hold together' (Col. 1.17; cf. Jn 1.10; Heb. 1.3)[74] and in him all the fullness of God was pleased to dwell (Col. 1.19, cf. Eph. 4.13).[75] The pre-existence of Christ is thus affirmed, as is his pre-eminent role in creating and sustaining the world, and holding all things together. Such functions are predicated of Wisdom in Second Temple Judaism.[76]

71. See the discussion in Dunn, *Theology of Paul*, pp. 267–293.

72. Dunn, *Theology of Paul*, pp. 277–278. Dunn notes that the sending of Wisdom provides a precedent for God's sending of the Son, and observes the parallel with the sending parable of Mk 12.1-9. See also J. Louis Martyn, *Galatians* (New York: Doubleday, 1997), pp. 406–408, who notes the affinities between the sending motif in Gal. 4.4 and God sending Moses and the prophets as well as God's sending his angel, spirit and wisdom to the world in Gen. 24.40; Wis. 9.10 and 17. By contrast, note Hurtado, *Lord Jesus Christ*, pp. 122–126 who advises caution when explaining Paul's affirmation of the pre-existence of Christ in terms of his being the embodiment of Wisdom.

73. Barnett, *Literary Influence*, p. 106, assigns this parallel a B ranking, and regards the phrase πάντα δἰ αὐτοῦ (Jn 1.3) as 'an exact verbal parallel' with Col. 1.16.

74. Ibid., p. 107, assigns this parallel a C ranking, but notes that 'the Johannine idea of the immanence of the Logos closely parallels the thought of Col. 1.17'.

75. Ibid., p. 108, assigns a B ranking to the parallel of Jn 1.14, 16 and Col. 1.19 and a C ranking to Jn 1.14, 16 and Eph. 4.13. The term πληρώματος appears in all three passages.

76. See Peter T. O'Brien, *Colossians* (Waco: Word Books, 1982), pp. 32–57, who rightly notes the parallels with the Jewish Wisdom tradition especially articulated in Sirach and Wisdom of Solomon. See, for example, O'Brien's linking of Wis. 1.7 where Wisdom holds all things together (συνίημι τὰ πάντα)

Moreover, there are essential continuities between the Wisdom Christology of Col. 1.15-20 and the Johannine Logos through whom God created the universe, revealed his character and the purpose of creation, and in whom God continues to be present in his creation. Is there a case here for positing Pauline influence on the author of the FG? Even if it cannot be demonstrated beyond doubt that there is direct influence then we are at least encountering parallel trajectories of thought in which the role assigned in Jewish speculation to Wisdom in creating and sustaining the universe and revealing the mind of God is being ascribed to Christ in Colossians and to Christ as the Logos in the FG.[77]

d. *Eschatology*

Readings that align the eschatological concerns of Paul's letters with an apocalyptic worldview abound in New Testament scholarship of the last half-century or so.[78] Early in the twentieth century, there were contributions, such as Albert Schweitzer's *Geschichte der Paulinischen Forschung* (1912) and *Die Mystik des Apostels Paulus* (1930), that brought the apocalyptic thought of Paul to light.[79] But this enterprise was eclipsed by hermeneutical concerns in which scholars sought to communicate the message of Paul in an intelligible fashion as though apocalyptic was peripheral.[80]

and Col. 1.17 where all things are held together in Christ (τὰ πάντα ἐν αὐτῷ συνέστηκεν) on p. 48. *Contra* E. Käsemann, 'A Primitive Christian Baptismal Liturgy', in *Essays on New Testament Themes* (Philadelphia: Fortress, 1982), pp. 149–168, who interprets the Colossians hymn in terms of the Gnostic redeemer myth.

77. On the pre-existence of Christ and the Wisdom tradition that informs this Christology, see Dunn, *Theology of Paul*, pp. 269–281, and Martin Hengel, *The Son of God* (Philadelphia: Fortress, 1976), pp. 66–76.

78. There are significant methodological issues surrounding the use of the terms 'apocalyptic' and 'apocalypse'. Christopher Rowland, whose major survey of early Jewish and Christian apocalypses and related literature, *The Open Heaven* (London: SPCK, 1982), seeks in part to reorient scholarly discussion of apocalyptic in the New Testament to the content of the apocalypses themselves. In the tradition of apocalyptic readings of Paul, scholars have largely assumed that the content of the apocalypses was dominated by eschatological concerns. The adjective 'apocalyptic' is used as though the content of the apocalypses was thoroughly given over to eschatological concerns. Rowland points out, however, that the apocalypses cover a wide variety of themes and ideas. What marks the genre is not a concern for eschatology but a confidence that the secrets of this age and the age to come are available by divine mediation. Eschatology, Rowland argues, is actually a relatively minor theme in the apocalypses. Paul's eschatology is dependent on the prophets, and that none of his concerns is unique to the apocalypses. This is a radical position. Note the response of Martin de Boer, 'Paul and Apocalyptic Eschatology', in John J. Collins (ed.), *The Encyclopedia of Apocalypticism, Volume One: The Origins of Apocalypticism in Judaism and Christianity* (New York/London: Continuum, 2000), pp. 351–354, who protests that Rowland ignores a central fact of the thought of Paul – namely, that the death and resurrection of Christ do constitute the decisive victory of God expected in the apocalypses.

79. Translated respectively as *Paul and his Interpreters* (London: A&C Black, 1912) and *The Mysticism of the Apostle Paul* (London: A&C Black, 1931).

80. See the brief survey by Beker, *Paul the Apostle*, pp. 138–143. He holds neo-orthodox theologians largely responsible for the discounting of apocalyptic as a 'vestige on the periphery of Paul's thought'. They collapsed apocalyptic eschatology into Christology, Beker argues (p. 139).

William Wrede, in his excellent book on Paul, succinctly identified the ground of the apostle's thought as it comes to speech in the Pauline letters to be fully in accord with the eschatologically focused Jewish apocalypses. Paul, he argued, believed that the world is enslaved by 'dark and evil' supernatural powers, the chief of these being the 'flesh', sin, the law and death.[81] Christ did battle with these powers in the flesh. His assumption of humanity brought him into the sphere of their baneful influence. It was these powers that actually crucified him (see 1 Cor. 2.6-8). The death of Christ, Paul contends, amounts to the victory over these enslaving powers (see 2 Cor. 5.14; Rom. 8.3; Gal. 3.13; 4.3; Col. 2.15). He identified the exalted Jesus who had appeared to him with the divine Christ in whom he had always believed. Yet the outward realization of this victory awaits the appearance (*parousia*) of Christ, an event that is imminent.[82] In the meantime the Christian life is marked by 'suspense'. The gift of the Spirit serves as a foretaste of the blessed future life God has in store for his people in a renewed creation. The Jewish apocalypses are eloquent witnesses to the Jewish hope in an exalted Christ, a heavenly Messiah. In his incarnation and in his death and resurrection there is redemption for humankind, which is nothing less than the promised triumph of God over the evil powers that heralds the inauguration of a new order of things. The victory of Christ is the victory of God over the powers that seek to frustrate his will, a victory confidently expected in the apocalypses. They are redolent of two significant concerns for Paul: (1) cosmological dualism – that is, the concept that there are two aeons, two worlds, one present and earthly in the thrall of evil powers (including the angels who mediated the law) and the other future and heavenly – and (2) anthropological pessimism, in the form of the doctrine of the universality of sin and of death as the consequence.[83] The counterpoint of these two concepts is the Christ as the victor over the powers and as the representative of a new humankind.

More recently, J. Christiaan Beker's *Paul the Apostle* is a bold reading of the Pauline corpus, much indebted to the concisely expressed insights of Wrede, that insists that Paul's thought is undeniably indebted to apocalyptic as its 'central climate and focus'.[84] Beker identifies three key apocalyptic ideas. These are: (1) historical dualism, (2) universal cosmic expectation and (3) the imminent end of the world.[85] He argues that apocalyptic was born out of the sense of the discrepancy between the promises of God and the harsh reality

81. Wrede, *Paul*, p. 92. See also p. 95 on Paul on the powers, forces, dominions, heights at 1 Cor. 15.24; Gal. 4.3, 9; Col. 1.16; 2.10, 15; 2.8, 20. On p. 96, the rulers of this world, 1 Cor. 2.6, 8; Rom. 8.38.

82. See 1 Thess. 4.15, 17; 1 Cor. 7.29-31; 15.51; Rom. 13.11-12; Phil. 4.5.

83. See *4 Ezra* 3.20-22; 7.116-126; *2 Bar.* 54.13-16.

84. Beker, *Paul the Apostle*, p. 144.

85. Ibid., p. 138.

of the beleaguered lives of believers who are threatened with martyrdom. Apocalypticists believed that Satan and the forces of death and evil ruled the present world. The age to come, however, would witness the triumph of God, the vindication of the people of God, and the creation of a new heavens and a new earth. The nearness of the *parousia* of Christ is frequently affirmed in the undisputed letters, as we have had cause to note earlier (see Note 82).

Paul, Beker argues, was an apocalypticist before his conversion, one who trusted in the realization of the apocalyptic scenario of the in-breaking of the messianic kingdom, the resurrection of the dead and the defeat of death, and a Pharisaic 'missionary' with an apocalyptic message.[86] Paul's conversion confirmed his apocalyptic worldview. And yet that worldview is also radically disconfirmed because Christ has been raised from the dead and, as a consequence, the new age is already breaking in. Beker stresses the fact that the resurrection of Christ has ushered in the new age and that the cross is the scene of God's triumph over the powers that enslave humankind. The lordship of Christ in the church, Beker writes, 'is the proleptic manifestation of God's imminent eschatological triumph'.[87] He argues that Paul's thought is rightly termed 'apocalyptic', not 'eschatological', because only in apocalyptic literature do we encounter the confidence that God will radically intervene and finally and everlastingly defeat the powers that hold humankind captive and pave the way for the renewing of creation. Moreover, to use the language of resurrection, whether about Christ or believers, is to use apocalyptic language.[88]

In the post-Pauline letters to the Colossians and Ephesians there is a move away from the apocalyptic eschatology we encounter in the undisputed letters. An exalted Christology that stresses the 'cosmic significance of Christ' as the 'principle of cohesion and unity' replaces the earlier emphases on the imminent *parousia* and the triumph of God.[89] Christ reigns in the present. The blessings of the Kingdom of God are being dispensed. The reach of the Kingdom will encompass the reconciliation of humankind as a whole. The delay of the *parousia* is the likely cause of this change of focus, and the best explanation for the eclipse of the imminent expectation of the triumph of God.

Strikingly, the language of resurrection is used in Ephesians to describe the believer's life in the present. In 2.5-6 we read:

86. Ibid., p 144. According to Acts 9.1-2, Paul sought to confront the Jewish believers in Damascus in belligerent fashion.

87. Ibid., p. 102.

88. Beker, *Paul's Apocalyptic Gospel: The Coming Triumph of God* (Philadelphia: Fortress, 1982), p. 46.

89. R. H. Charles, *A Critical History of the Doctrine of the Future Life* (London: A&C Black, 1913), p. 461.

> But God . . . even when we were dead through our trespasses, made us alive together [συν–εζωοποίησεν] with Christ – by grace you have been saved [σεσῳσμένοι cf. 2.8] – and raised us up [συνήγειρεν] with him and seated us with him in the heavenly places in Christ Jesus.

In like manner, the writer of Colossians speaks of believers who, having been buried with Christ in baptism, have now been raised with him (2.12; συνηγέ ρθητε) and made alive (2.13; συνεζωοποίησεν), the exact word used in Eph. 2.5 where it is synonymous with the state of being raised up in 2.6. In the same manner, Col. 2.12-13 proceeds directly to 3.1 where believers are again described as those who have been raised with Christ and where the verb 'raised with' (ἐγείρονται), used at 2.12, reappears:

> So if you have been raised [ἐγείραντος] with Christ, seek the things that are above, where Christ is, seated at the right hand of God. (Col. 3.1)

By contrast, in the undisputed letters of Paul the resurrection of believers from the dead is always a future, even if imminent, reality and hope.

> I want to know Christ and the power of his resurrection and the sharing of his sufferings by becoming like him in his death, if somehow I may attain the resurrection of the dead. Not that I have already obtained this or have already reached the goal; but I press on to make it my own, because Christ Jesus has made me his own. Beloved, I do not consider that I have made it my own; but this one thing I do: forgetting what lies behind and straining forward to what lies ahead, I press on toward the goal for the prize of the heavenly call of God in Christ Jesus. (Phil. 3.10-14; cf. Rom. 6.5)

Paul's use of ζωοποιέω – synonymous with being 'raised' from metaphorical death as a present experience in Ephesians and Colossians – further highlights the contrast.[90] In Rom. 8.11 the future tense (ζῳοποιήσει) is used of God's purpose to give life to mortal bodies in the eschaton through his indwelling Spirit.[91] In 1 Cor. 15.22, it is the future again that is used (ζῳοποιηθήσονται) of God giving eschatological life to the dead at his coming (παρουσίᾳ, v. 23).

The state of being saved, a present experience of believers in Eph. 2.5, 8 that is conveyed by the perfect passive participle of σῴζω is unknown in the undisputed letters. Salvation (σωτηρία) is a future event (for example, Rom. 13.11; 1 Thess. 5.9), which on occasion is spoken of as present (Rom. 11.11; 2 Cor. 6.2) but in contexts that do not negate its overwhelmingly future

90. Note Barnett, *Literary Influence*, p. 118. The literary parallel between Jn 5.21, 25 and Eph. 2.5-6 is assigned a B ranking by Barnett. The thematic parallel warrants a higher ranking.

91. In Rom. 8.23 Paul calls this eschatological hope the 'redemption of our bodies'.

reference. These ambiguities are expressed in Rom 8.24a, where believers, Paul writes, 'were saved in hope' (γὰρ ἐλπίδι ἐσώθημεν) but this hope has clearly not been attained, as 8.24b-25 makes clear. On occasion Paul speaks of believers going through the process of 'being saved' (1 Cor. 1.18; 15.2; 2 Cor. 2.15). By contrast, σῴζω does not appear in Ephesians in solely futuristic contexts and does not occur at all in Colossians. In the Pastoral Epistles salvation is spoken about in both future and present senses.[92]

Salvation and resurrection as possibilities of existence that might be experienced now are encountered in the FG. Bultmann perceived that the FG had largely emancipated itself from the apocalyptic worldview prominent in Paul and de-mythologized that language to speak of the possibilities of present existence such that the familiar apocalyptic categories – end-time judgement, eternal life and resurrection – are seen to be operative in a person's response to Jesus.[93] Although it must not be forgotten that there are also statements in the Gospel that refer to end-time judgement and resurrection as future events, these are overshadowed by its realizing eschatology.[94] Thus those who believe in Jesus will not be judged but have already passed from death to life. Those who refuse to believe are already judged.

> Those who believe in him are not condemned; but those who do not believe are condemned already, because they have not believed in the name of the only Son of God. (Jn 3.18)

> Very truly, I tell you, anyone who hears my word and believes him who sent me has eternal life, and does not come under judgement, but has passed from death to life. (Jn 5.24)

Likewise salvation as eternal life is a present reality by virtue of believing in Christ, a point of view clearly expressed in Jn 3.15, 16, 36; 5.24 and 6.47

92. In addition to Eph. 2.5, 8 (σεσῳσμένοι), note the aorist use of σῴζω in 2 Tim. 1.9 and Tit. 3.5. By contrast, note the use of the future in 1 Tim. 2.15; 1 Tim. 4.16; and 2 Tim. 4.18.

93. See 'The Eschatology of the Gospel of John', in *Faith and Understanding* (Philadelphia: Fortress, 1987), pp. 165–183 (originally published in 1928) and 'The Christology of the New Testament', in *Faith and Understanding*, pp. 281–283 (unpublished paper). Bultmann acknowledged Paul's debt to apocalyptic thinking, but was unable to give an account of the message of the apostle for today unless that thinking was first recognized as mythological and the apostle's language de-mythologized. See further Bultmann's 'New Testament and Mythology', in H. W. Bartsch (ed.), *Kerygma and Myth, Volume One* (New York: Harper & Row, 1961), pp. 1–44.

94. This is well seen in Jn 11.24 and 25-26. In v. 24 Martha's belief in the end-time resurrection is modified by Jesus in vv. 25-26 by his focus on the possibilities of resurrection and eternal life as realities presently available through belief in Christ. Elements of unqualified futuristic eschatology appear in the FG: there will be a future judgement (12.48), eternal life is a future reality (12.25) and there will be a future resurrection (6.39-40) and Christ will come again (14.1-3). See Kysar, *Maverick Gospel*, p. 91. The evangelist, he writes, wished to preserve traditional materials.

(cf. 1 Jn 5.13). In the same vein the FG uses the language of resurrection to speak of coming to faith in the Son of God.

> Indeed, just as the Father raises the dead (ἐγείρει τοὺς νεκροὺς) and gives them life (ζῳοποιεῖ), so also the Son gives life to whomever he wishes. (Jn 5.21)

> Very truly, I tell you, anyone who hears my word and believes him who sent me has eternal life, and does not come under judgement, but has passed from death to life. (Jn 5.24)

By contrast the undisputed Pauline corpus speaks of eternal life as the believers' hope (Rom. 2.7; 5.21; 6.22, 23; Gal. 6.8; cf. 1 Tim. 1.16; Tit. 1.2; 3.7).[95] However, resurrection as a present reality is expressed in Eph. 2.5, 8 and Col. 2.13; 3.1. This is wholly consistent with the dominant point of view of the FG. The delay of the *parousia* is determinative for understanding the FG, Ephesians and Colossians, and has focused attention away from an imminence of the end and the triumph of God to an exalted Christology.[96]

VI. *Conclusion*

The case for the argument that Paul influenced the FG is made more difficult by the fact that both Paul and the FG may owe much to Christian Hellenists who cast the message of the disciples of Jesus into Greek and set about taking that message to the Gentiles of the major eastern Mediterranean cities. Openness to non-Jews and a critical attitude to the ritual and ceremonial law, elements that can be found in the preaching of Jesus, provided the key impetus to the Hellenists. Both of these themes are found in Paul and the FG.

It is also true that Johannine and Pauline Christology are indebted to the earliest Palestinian community. Despite the influential theory of Bousset, Hellenistic, 'pagan' influence is not responsible for the Christological developments we can trace in Paul and John. The survival of the Aramaic acclamation *Maranatha* in Hellenistic Christianity speaks compellingly in favour of continuities with the earliest Aramaic-speaking Palestinian community. But the focus in Col. 1.15-20 on Christ as the image of God, in and through whom all things were made, and who also sustains the universe and through whom the fullness of God has been made to dwell – a Christology that is not found quite in this developed form in the undisputed Pauline letters – is redolent of the Logos Christology of the FG. Hebraic concepts of the role of the word of God

95. The one possible exception is 1 Tim. 6.12: 'Take hold of the eternal life to which you were called.' But here the context supports claiming God's future gift for the present.

96. See Brown, *John, Volume One*, p. lxxxv.

in creation and of the revealing of God's mind through the word that comes to the prophets, and Jewish speculation about Wisdom as the immanence of God and the means by which all things hang together, are essential characteristics of the Logos and Colossian Christology.

For Paul the implication of the appearance of Jesus, the Christ of Jewish expectation, has crucial implications for the ongoing validity of the law, especially in Romans and Galatians. The Christ event is the evidence that God has intervened decisively to fulfil his promises to create a new heaven and a new earth. To that extent theology not Christology is a more prominent concern in Paul. But there is no doubt that Christology is the defining issue for the FG. The Gospel was written that the readers/hearers might come to believe Jesus is the Messiah, the Son of God (20.31).

The presence in the undisputed letters of motifs encountered in the apocalypses, such as resurrection and the imminence of the end, and the fact that Paul is prepared to speak of God's 'revelation' of his Son (Gal. 1.16), as through an 'apocalypse' (Gal. 1.12), requires that we perceive him as one whose apocalyptic worldview has been confirmed in the Christ event. The letters are imbued with that worldview, albeit dramatically and decisively refocused as a result of the resurrection of Christ, but retaining all its futuristic reference. By contrast, the FG prefers to speak of the same apocalyptic motifs – resurrection, eternal life and judgement – as possibilities of present existence. This is nowhere encountered in the undisputed Paulines, but is to be found in Ephesians and Colossians insofar as both speak about resurrection as a present reality (Eph. 2.6, 8; Col. 2.13; 3.1). This commends the argument that between the undisputed letters of Paul and the FG there is a considerable theological disjuncture. Paul's theology takes it rise from apocalyptic Judaism. By contrast the FG, together with Ephesians and Colossians, while employing the same motifs encountered in a number of the eschatological apocalypses, perceive resurrection as a present reality.

The closest thematic parallels between the FG and the Pauline corpus are (1) the realizing eschatology of Ephesians in which the church has become the locus of the reconciliation of Jew and Gentile, (2) the language of resurrection that is used in Ephesians and Colossians to denote the present experience of believers and (3) the developed Wisdom Christology of both Ephesians and Colossians. In the FG there will be no eschatological reconciliation of Israel; indeed, the Jews, by virtue of their present unbelief, can be said to have the devil for their father (Jn 8.44). Any expectation of the imminent *parousia* of Christ is replaced by a realized eschatology that overshadows the traces of the Gospel's futuristic eschatology. The Christ of glory is present already in the community and is dispensing all the benefits of the end-time. The post-Paulines other than Ephesians and Colossians – namely, 2 Thessalonians and the Pastoral Epistles – have engaged with the delay in other ways. The former has interposed an eschatological timetable. In the Pastoral Epistles Christ will certainly return at some time in the future, but in the meantime there is need to ensure that the succession of sound teachers and teaching into the next generation (2 Tim. 2.2).

Ephesians and Colossians were products of Ephesian Paulinists in the generation after Paul, at the very time when and in the very place where the FG was reaching its final form. Although caution prevents us from definitely proposing direct influence, since we cannot know more fully what trajectories and currents of thoughts were making their presence felt in Ephesus at the time, there is good reason for identifying common themes and sensibilities with confidence.

8

PAUL AND JOHN: TWO WITNESSES, ONE GOSPEL

Colin G. Kruse

I. *Introduction*

Within the New Testament there is evidence for three major streams of early Christianity. It is widely recognized that expressions of Christianity in the Jerusalem church differed significantly from its expression in the churches founded by Paul. This is reflected in the differences of opinion concerning what was to be required of Gentiles if they were to be 'saved' and to what extent the Mosaic Law was to be observed by Gentiles who were 'saved'. Some in the Jerusalem church argued that circumcision and the observance of the Law was obligatory (cf. Gal. 2.4-5; Acts 15.5). Others, including James, came to recognize that such demands should not be placed upon Gentiles and supported the ministry of Peter and Paul among Gentiles (cf. Gal. 2.6-10; Acts 15.13-29). Paul strongly opposed attempts to impose circumcision and Law observance upon members of the churches he founded. In Galatians he responds to the trouble caused by Jewish Christians (popularly called 'Judaizers' but to whom Paul refers as 'troublers' [Gal. 1.7: ὁι ταράσσοντες]).[1] Early Christianity in Jerusalem may be characterized as Law-observing whereas this was not the case in the churches founded by Paul.[2]

1. A 'Judaizer' is a Gentile who seeks to live like a Jew. The verb, 'to Judaize' (ἰουδαΐζω) is found only once in the NT (Gal. 2.14: 'But when I saw that they were not acting consistently with the truth of the gospel, I said to Cephas before them all, "If you, though a Jew, live like a Gentile and not like a Jew, how can you compel the Gentiles to live like Jews?"'[ἰουδαΐζειν]).

2. Law observance was held to be very important for Jewish Christians in the Jerusalem church (cf. Acts 21.17-26), though the leaders of this church upheld the right of Gentiles to be accepted into the Christian community without having to take upon themselves the yoke of the Law (cf. Acts 15.13-21). While Paul vigorously defended this freedom on behalf of his Gentile converts, that did not mean he was antinomian. In fact, although he rejected the Law as the regulatory norm for Christian living, he taught that the 'just requirement of the law' would be fulfilled in those who walked according to the Spirit. Further, he found in the Law paradigms for Christian living (see the section entitled 'The Mosaic Law', p. 205).

There is evidence for a third stream of early Christianity, one represented in the NT by the Gospel and letters of John (and some would add Revelation). In these writings there is little evidence of the tensions existing between the Jerusalem and Pauline expressions of Christianity described. The Gospel of John presents an essentially evangelistic message, intended primarily for Greek-speaking Jews, against a background of antagonism towards Jesus from many (but not all) Jewish leaders of the day. The essential issues were not demand for observance of, or freedom from, the Mosaic Law, but rather the claims of Jesus Christ himself: that he had been sent into the world as the incarnate Son of God to testify to the truth about God, to effect salvation and to call out his elect. The letters of John, unlike the Gospel of John, are not evangelistic but were written to deal with serious problems arising within a group of churches (frequently called the Johannine community) as a result of the secession of some of their members who espoused an unorthodox Christology and whose behaviour was sub-Christian. Like the Gospel of John, the letters of John are not concerned with the role of the Mosaic Law either in salvation or Christian obedience.

To provide background for the discussion of Paul and the Gospel of John, it is helpful to note the way the three major blocks of writings in the NT each portray the fundamental message of the gospel. As Ladd pointed out long ago, the ways in which the Synoptic Gospels, the Pauline letters, and the Gospel and letters of John speak of the work of Christ, and thus reflect their understanding of the gospel itself, are all different, but all share a common underlying structure.[3] In the Synoptics the fundamental theme of Christ's preaching is the kingdom of God. Through his life and ministry, death and resurrection and the outpouring of the Spirit upon his church, Christ inaugurated the kingdom of God, and what he inaugurated at his first coming he will consummate at his second coming.

In the Pauline letters the kingdom of God is spoken of, usually in contexts where ethical behaviour is the subject (Rom. 14.17; 1 Cor. 6.9-10), or where the coming of the kingdom and hope for, or warnings about the failure to enter, the kingdom are mentioned (1 Cor. 15.24; Gal. 5.21; Eph. 5.5; 1 Thess. 2.12; 2 Tim. 4.18). However, what takes centre stage in the apostle's understanding of the work of Christ and therefore his gospel is salvation. Christ came, and by his death and resurrection he effected salvation for all who believe so that they may correctly say, *we have been saved* (Rom. 8.24; Eph. 2.5, 8; 2 Tim. 1.9;

Cf. discussion in James D. G. Dunn, *Christianity in the Making: Vol. 2, Beginning from Jerusalem* (Grand Rapids: Eerdmans, 2009), pp. 1171–5.

3. George Eldon Ladd, *The Pattern of New Testament Truth* (Grand Rapids: Eerdmans, 1968), pp. 108–11.

Tit. 3.5). By his ongoing work in believers through the Spirit Christ is presently saving people from the tyranny of sin and Satan, so believers may justly say *we are being saved* (1 Cor. 1.18; 15.2; 2 Cor. 2.15). At his second coming Jesus Christ will bring to completion his saving work for believers (and the creation itself) as they share his glory and inherit eternal life, accordingly they may say, *we will be saved* (Rom. 5.9-10; 1 Cor. 3.15; 5.5; 2 Tim. 4.18). It is noteworthy that often when Paul speaks of the purpose of his ministry he says it is that hearers might be 'saved' (Rom. 11.13-14; 1 Cor. 1.21; 9.22; 10.33; 1 Thess. 2.16).

In the Gospel and letters of John there are few references to the kingdom of God[4] or salvation.[5] The work of Christ is depicted as providing eternal life now for those who believe, life that will be consummated in resurrection on the Last Day. The common factor in these three different expressions of the work of Christ and the gospel message is what Ladd calls 'the pattern of New Testament truth' – that is, that at his first coming Christ inaugurated God's redemptive plan and at his second coming he will consummate it (the well-known 'already-not yet' pattern of New Testament eschatology).

When we compare the Pauline writings with the Gospel of John, then, it will come as no surprise to find there is much in common even though the respective documents date from different periods, address or reflect different concerns, and employ different language and concepts. There appears to be no direct influence of Paul's writings upon the Gospel of John nor does John appear to contain any specific reactions to Paul's gospel or letters. It will also come as no surprise to find that key Christian themes receive attention in the respective documents, albeit handled in different ways. In the case of Paul's writings the themes are usually introduced while addressing pastoral and theological issues that arose in his churches, whereas in the Gospel of John they emerge often in the narrative sections, but also in reported dialogues between Jesus and his adversaries and enquirers, and in teaching given to his disciples. Discussed shortly are a selection of major themes occurring in both the Pauline letters and the Gospel of John with a view to exposing both the similarities and differences that occur between them.

Hereafter, for the sake of brevity and simplicity of expression references in the Pauline letters will often be ascribed to Paul, and those in the John's Gospel

4. The only references are in 3.3, 5, where Jesus tells Nicodemus that he cannot enter the kingdom of God unless he is born from above, born of water and Spirit, and in 18.36, where Jesus tells Pilate that his kingdom is not from this world.

5. The only references are those in which Jesus says he came not to condemn but to save the world (3.17; 12.47), that what he said was spoken so that people might be saved (5.4) and that he himself is the gate for the 'sheep' so that those who enter by him will be saved (10.9).

to John.[6] Also for the sake of brevity references in John's Gospel will be indicated with chapter and verse only – those in Paul's letters will be indicated by the letter concerned and chapter and verse. Unless otherwise indicated all Scripture citations are from the NRSV.

a. *God the Father*

1. Paul's preferred way of referring to God is as God the Father. He speaks of God as the Father of our Lord Jesus Christ (Rom. 15.6; 2 Cor. 1.3; 11.31; Eph. 1.3; Col. 1.3); the Father of believers (Rom. 1.7; 2 Cor. 1.2; Gal. 1.4; Eph. 1.2; Phil. 1.2; 4.20; Col. 1.2; 1 Thess. 1.3; 3.11, 13; 2 Thess. 1.1, 2; 2.16; Phlm. 1.3); simply as God the Father (1 Cor. 1.3; 8.6; 15.24; Gal. 1.3; Eph. 5.20; 6.23; Col. 3.17; 1 Thess. 1.1; 1 Tim. 1.2; 2 Tim. 1.2; Tit. 1.4); as the Father of mercies (2 Cor. 1.3); the Father of glory (Eph. 1.17); and the Father of all (Eph. 4.6). God is the Father of believers in the sense that they are his *adopted* children (Gal. 4.5). As such they have received the 'spirit of adoption' in which they cry 'Abba Father' (Rom. 8.15; Gal. 4.6). This adoption will be consummated in the resurrection of their bodies (Rom. 8.23; Eph. 1.5). Paul says also that to the Israelites 'belong the adoption' (Rom. 9.4), a reference to texts in the OT where the people of Israel are called God's sons (cf. e.g. Isa. 63.8; Jer. 3.19) and the nation of Israel as a whole his son (cf. e.g. Exod. 4.22). Israel's Exodus from Egypt is regarded as the time when God adopted Israel as his son (Hos. 11.1). However, this historic national adoption does not guarantee participation is eschatological adoption, something that is tied to faith in Jesus Christ, as Paul makes clear in Romans 9–11. Paul refers to God as 'the invisible God' (Col. 1.15).
2. John also portrays God as Father. It is overwhelmingly the way he speaks of God. Of the 136 uses of the word 'father' in John's Gospel all but fifteen of them refer to God. Very often God is designated simply as 'the Father'. On one occasion Jesus addresses him as 'Holy Father' (17.11). By far the majority of the occurrences of the designation of God as 'Father' are on the lips of Jesus, either referring to God as his Father in dialogue with the Jews and in instruction given to his disciples, or in direct address to God. Predominately, therefore, God is understood to be the Father of Jesus Christ. God is also understood to be the Father of believers. They become his children *by being born of God* (1.12-13; 20.17), and are the

6. I am well aware of the debates concerning the authenticity of the so-called Deutero-Pauline letters and the authorship of John's Gospel. Because the purpose of this collection of essays is to compare the Christianity represented by individual Gospels and the Pauline writings as they stand, questions of authenticity and authorship are not addressed in this essay.

recipients of his fatherly love (16.27). Jesus says his Jewish opponents do not know the Father (8.19) despite their claim that God is their Father (8.41-42). Instead Jesus says the devil is their father (8.44). John says that God existed in the beginning (1.1, 2), and has never been seen by any human being apart from Jesus (1.18; 6.46). God has life in himself (5.26) and raises the dead (5.21). To know him is eternal life (17.3). He is 'spirit' and seeks those who will worship 'in spirit and truth' (4.23-24).

3. Both Paul and John speak of God as Father, and this is overwhelmingly so in John's Gospel. Both depict God as the Father of believers. For Paul, believers become children of the Father by *adoption*, whereas in John they do so by being *born from above*. Paul says that to the Jews belongs 'the adoption', implying that God is the Father of Israel, but Jesus tells his Jewish opponents that the Devil, not God, is their Father.

b. *Jesus Christ the Son*

1. Paul frequently refers to Jesus Christ as the Son of God (Rom. 1.9; 5.10; 8.3; 1 Cor. 1.9; 2 Cor. 1.19; Gal. 2.20; 4.4, 6; Eph. 4.13). He assumes the Son's pre-existence (Gal. 4.4; Col. 1.15-17) and says that God sent forth his Son to be born as a man (Rom. 1.3-4; 8.3; Phil. 2.6-8), born of a woman, and born under the Law (Gal. 4.4-5). Because he was obedient to the point of death God exalted him, proclaiming him Son of God with power and bestowing upon him the name above all names (Rom. 1.4; Phil. 2.9-11). Paul employs Wisdom categories when he describes Jesus as 'the image of the invisible God', the one through whom and for whom all things were created, the one in whom all things 'hold together' and in whom 'all the fullness of God was pleased to dwell' (Col. 1.15-19). Some have suggested that Paul was not interested in the human Jesus. Bultmann, taking his cue from 2 Cor. 5.16, argued that Paul showed little interest in *κατὰ σάρκα Ξριστόν* (interpreted as 'Christ in the flesh'). Paul's interest was in the kerygmatic Christ, not the historical Jesus.[7] However, this is based on an unacceptable exegesis of 2 Cor. 5.16, which speaks not of his being κατὰ σάρκα Χριστόν but of Paul's previous understanding of Christ being κατὰ σάρκα. All such attempts to drive a wedge between the historical Jesus and the exalted Christ would have been foreign to the apostle. For him the exalted Christ and the Christ of the *kerygma* was none other than the historical Jesus crucified and risen. It is true that Paul had relatively little to say about the historical Jesus, but this does not mean he was ignorant of him. He speaks of Jesus as one who was descended

7. Rudolph Bultmann, *Faith and Understanding I* (ed. Robert W. Funk; trans. Louise Pettibone Smith; London: SCM, 1969), pp. 217, 241, 277.

from Abraham (Gal. 3.16) and David (Rom. 1.3) and lived under the Jewish Law (Gal. 4.4). He was betrayed, and on the night of his betrayal he instituted a memorial meal of bread and wine (1 Cor. 11.23-25). He endured death by crucifixion (1 Cor. 1.23; 2.2, 8; 2 Cor. 13.4; Gal. 3.1; 6.14), a Roman form of execution, although Jewish authorities of the day shared responsibility for his death (1 Thess. 2.15). He was buried, rose the third day and was thereafter seen alive by eyewitnesses (1 Cor. 15.4-8). Paul's letters reflect knowledge of the historical Jesus' character: his meekness and gentleness (2 Cor. 10.1); his selflessness (Rom. 15.3) and humility (Phil. 2.5-7), and also of his teaching (Rom. 12.14, 17, 19, 20-21; 13.9-10).[8] While it may be questioned whether the apostle ever simply equated Jesus Christ with God (the title θεός is generally reserved for God the Father, and Jesus Christ is generally called κύριος), Paul's statements imply the closest possible relationship between God and Christ: Christ is the Wisdom of God (1 Cor. 1.24, 30; Col. 1.15-20); and existed in the form of God (Phil. 2.6-7). God was in Christ (2 Cor. 5.18). Christ as life-giving Spirit, exercised a divine prerogative (1 Cor. 15.45), and OT references to Yahweh are applied by Paul to Christ (cf. Joel 2.32/ Rom. 10.13; Isa. 45.23/Rom. 14.11; Phil. 2.10-11).

2. John makes clear that God the Father has one unique and only Son (3.16, 18). John employs Wisdom categories when describing the Son of God as the Logos who was with God in the beginning. He has no hesitation in equating the Son with God (1.1). He asserts that the Son of God (as the Logos) is the one through whom all things came into being (1.3) and yet was incarnate as the historical Jesus in whom the glory of God was revealed, a glory consisting of grace and truth (1.14, 16) but revealed only to his disciples. He is close to the Father's heart and has made him known (1.18). Upon him God placed his seal of approval (6.27), gave him power over all things (3.35; 13.3; 16.15). God granted him to have life in himself (5.26) and the responsibility for judgement (5.22), both divine prerogatives. The Father loves the Son (3.35; 5.20; 10.17; 15.9; 17.24), glorifies him (8.54; 12.28; 17.5; 13.31-32) and testifies to him (5.37; 8.18). The Father is one with the Son (14.7, 9-11, 20) yet greater than him (14.28). He teaches him (8.28), sends him into the world (3.16, 17, 34; 5.36, 37; 6.57; 8.42; 10.36; 14.24; 20.21), works through him (5.17-19; 10.32) and tells him what to do (10.18; 12.49-50; 18.11). Those whom he has given to the Son (6.37; 10.29; 17.24) he teaches and draws to the Son (6.44-45, 65).
3. Both Paul and John teach the pre-existence of Christ who was the agent of creation. Both employ Wisdom categories in their depiction of him, but

8. Cf. F. F. Bruce, *Paul: Apostle of the Heart Set Free* (Grand Rapids: Eerdmans, 1977), pp. 95–125.

John does so more explicitly when he describing him as the Logos who was with God in the beginning.[9] Like Paul, John asserts that Jesus Christ (as the Logos) is the one through whom all things came into being. Paul, though aware of the historical Jesus, does not focus upon his ministry, focusing instead upon his death and resurrection, whereas John's Gospel, by virtue of being a gospel, has much to say about this. Unlike Paul, John has no hesitation in equating the Jesus with God (1.1).

c. *The Holy Spirit*

1. Paul's letters abound with references to the Holy Spirit. The Spirit raises Jesus from the dead (Rom. 8.11) and vindicates him (1 Tim. 3.16) – through the Spirit Jesus was declared to be the Son of God with power by his resurrection from the dead (Rom. 1.4). The Spirit revealed to Paul the mystery of the gospel (Eph. 3.5) and by the Spirit's power the apostle preached the gospel around the Mediterranean world (Rom. 15.19; 1 Thess. 1.5). In his ministry Paul was entrusted with the 'ink of the Spirit' to write 'letters of Christ' in the hearts of his converts (2 Cor. 3.3). It is the Spirit who gives life, whereas the Law brings death (2 Cor. 3.6). By the Spirit people experience rebirth (Tit. 3.5). God gives the Spirit to believers (1 Thess. 4.8) so that they corporately (1 Cor. 3.16) and individually (1 Cor. 6.19) become the temple of the Holy Spirit. Believers receive the Spirit by faith, not by performing works of the Law (Gal. 3.2-5, 14). All believers are baptized in the Spirit and made to drink of the Spirit (1 Cor. 12.13) through whom they are sanctified and justified (Rom. 15.16; 1 Cor. 6.11; 2 Thess. 2.13). God seals (σφραγίζω) believers with his Spirit (2 Cor. 1.22; Eph. 1.13; 4.30) whom he gives to them as a down payment (ἀρραβών) to guarantee their final salvation (2 Cor. 1.22; 5.5). The Spirit pours (a sense of) God's love into the hearts of believers (Rom. 5.5) and sets them free from the law of sin and death so that the just requirement (δικαίωμα) of the Law may be fulfilled in them (Rom. 8.2, 4). The Spirit creates in the hearts of believers a sense of their filial relationship to God (Rom. 8.15; Gal. 4.6). The Spirit enables them to confess Jesus as Lord (1 Cor. 12.3) and reveals to them the things of God (1 Cor. 2.10-14). The Spirit provides believers with various gifts for ministry (1 Cor. 12.4-11; 14.2) and produces his fruit in their lives (Gal. 5.22-23). Having been made alive by the Spirit, believers are to walk by the Spirit and not gratify the desires of the flesh (Gal. 5.16-18, 25; Rom. 8.12-14) for by so

9. Cf. I. Howard Marshall, *New Testament Theology: Many Witnesses, One Gospel* (Downers Grove: InterVarsity Press, 2004), p. 594; Andreas J. Köstenberger, *A Theology of John's Gospel and Letters* (Biblical Theology of the New Testament; Grand Rapids: Zondervan, 2009), p. 360.

doing they will from the Spirit reap eternal life (Gal. 6.8). Through the Spirit believers have access to God (Eph. 2.18) to whom they pray in the Spirit (Eph. 6.18) and whom they worship in the Spirit (Phil. 3.3). They are to be filled with the Spirit (Eph. 5.18). They are strengthened in their inner beings by the Spirit (Eph. 3.16) and experience joy inspired by the Spirit (1 Thess. 1.6). Believers must not quench the Spirit by despising prophecy (1 Thess. 5.19-20) nor grieve the Spirit by bad behaviour (Eph. 4.30). The Spirit makes known that in the last days some will renounce their faith (1 Tim. 4.1). There appears to be little in Paul's letters about the personhood of the Spirit, the only exceptions being the fact that the Spirit is grieved by bad behaviour and communicates information about the last days.

2. In John's Gospel Jesus is the one upon whom the Spirit descended and remained (1.32). Unlike John the Baptist, who baptized only with water, Jesus baptizes with the Spirit (1.26, 32-33). Jesus speaks the words of God and what he says is trustworthy because God gave him the Spirit 'without measure' (3.34), possibly distinguishing Jesus from the prophets to whom the Spirit was thought to have been 'measured' (cf. Leviticus Rabbah 16.2). Jesus' glorification (death and subsequent exaltation) was the necessary precursor to the bestowal of the Spirit upon his followers (7.39). Only those who are born from above by the mysterious work of the Spirit can see/enter the kingdom of God (3.3, 5). The words of Jesus that are spirit and life (6.63) mediate this birth from above. The Spirit is the living water that wells up to eternal life within those who believe (4.14), flowing from Jesus to them (7.38). Jesus foreshadowed a time when people's worship would be in Spirit and truth (4.23-24). At the Last Supper Jesus promised his disciples another Paraclete following his departure, one to be with them forever (14.16). The Paraclete is identified as 'the Spirit of truth', who will be in the disciples (14.16-17), teach them and remind them of all that Jesus taught (14.26), bear witness to Jesus alongside the witness of the disciples in a hostile world (15.26-27), prove the world guilty in respect of sin, righteousness and judgement (16.7-11) and will also guide the disciples into all truth, declaring things to come (16.12-15).
3. The role of the Spirit is a significant theme in both Paul's letters and in the Gospel of John. In both, the new birth of believers is the work of the Spirit; in both, the Spirit also indwells believers. In both, prayer/worship is engaged in through the Spirit. Paul emphasizes the ministry gifts and the fruit of the Spirit, whereas John stresses the coming of the Paraclete who replaces the physical presence of Jesus with his disciples. The major difference between Paul and John is that the Spirit who is just beginning

to be depicted as a personal being by Paul is presented clearly as a person by John, especially in the farewell discourses.

d. *The Scriptures*

1. Paul's classic statement concerning Scriptures is found in 2 Tim. 3.16-17: 'All scripture is inspired by God and is useful for teaching, for reproof, for correction, and for training in righteousness, so that everyone who belongs to God may be proficient, equipped for every good work.' What Scripture says is God's word (Rom. 1.2; 9.17; Gal. 3.8) and therefore authoritative. While the Scripture (OT) was written long ago it stands written now for our instruction and encouragement (Rom. 15.4). The apostle appeals to Scripture frequently to support his teaching (cf. e.g. Rom. 4.3; 10.11; 11.2; 16.26; 1 Cor. 15.3-4; Gal. 4.30; 1 Tim. 5.18). He introduces Scripture quotations with the expression γέγραπται ('it stands written') thirty-one times.[10]
2. John regards the Scriptures as authoritative – Scripture cannot be annulled (10.35). The Scriptures testify about Jesus (1.45; 2.17; 5.46; 5.39). When John appeals to Scripture it is mostly to show that it was fulfilled in Jesus' life (7.42), ministry (12.14-16; 15.25), betrayal (13.18; 17.12), death (19.24, 28, 36, 37), resurrection (2.19-22; 20.9) and the gift of the Spirit (7.38). Jesus' opponents cite Scripture when taking issue with him (6.31) and Jesus cites Scripture when responding to them (5.39; 6.45; 8.17; 10.34).
3. For both Paul and John Scripture is authoritative – it is God's word written. The difference in their use of Scripture lies in the fact that Paul employs it for the most part to support his teaching while John uses it mainly as a witness to Jesus and shows how it is fulfilled in Jesus' life, ministry, death and exaltation.

e. *The Mosaic Law*

1. Because of the issues Paul confronted in his churches he had a lot to say about the Mosaic Law. The word 'law' (νόμος) is found 121 times in his letters and all but five of these refer to the Mosaic Law.[11] The apostle insists that it is not hearing or possession of the Law that justifies

10. Rom. 1.17; 2.24; 3.4, 10; 4.17; 8.36; 9.13, 33; 10.15; 11.8, 26; 12.19; 14.11; 15.3, 9, 21; 1 Cor. 1.19, 31; 2.9; 3.19; 4.6; 9.9; 10.7; 14.21; 15.45; 2 Cor. 8.15; 9.9; Gal. 3.10, 13; 4.22, 27.

11. The exceptions are Rom. 8.2 where νόμος is used to denote 'the law of the Spirit of life' and 'the law of sin and death' respectively (though some scholars argue that even here νόμος refers to the Law of Moses, cf. discussion in Colin G. Kruse, *Paul, the Law and Justification* [Leicester: Apollos/InterVarsity Press, 1996], pp. 216–17); 1 Cor. 14.21 where νόμος denotes the OT as a whole, in particular Isa. 28.11-12; Gal. 5.23 where it may relate to law generally; and Gal. 6.2 where it is used in the expression, 'the law of Christ'.

(Rom. 2.13), nor is justification achieved by observance of the Law or submission to circumcision, for even those who are circumcised and have the Law break the Law (Rom. 2.23, 25-27; Gal. 2.21) and come under its condemnation (Rom. 3.20; 4.15; Gal. 2.16; 3.10-13). The Law makes sin known (Rom. 3.19; 5.13, 20). The purpose of the giving of the Law was not to nullify the promise of justification by faith made to Abraham (Gal. 3.17); it was added because of transgressions to function as a disciplinarian for the Jewish people until Christ should come (Gal. 3.19, 23-24; 4.1-7). With the coming of Christ the righteousness of God has been revealed apart from the Law (Rom. 3.21; Phil. 3.9), a righteousness to be received by faith (Rom. 3.28). Believers need to be freed from the Law as a regulatory norm in order to produce fruit for God (Rom. 7.1-6; Gal. 2.19; 5.18). It's not that the Law itself is the problem, but the fact that it has been laid under tribute by sin to deepen human bondage (Rom. 7.7-25; 1 Cor. 15.56). Paradoxically, the just requirement of the Law is fulfilled in believers who are free from the Law as they walk by the Spirit (Rom. 8.3-4). Christ is the end of the Law so that there may be righteousness for all who believe (Rom. 10.4; Eph. 2.15). Love is the fulfilment of the Law (Rom. 13.8, 10; Gal. 5.14). While the apostle defends believers' freedom from the Law as a regulatory norm, he nevertheless frequently appeals to the Law as a paradigm for Christian living (1 Cor. 9.8-9) and to illustrate and support his teaching (1 Cor. 14.21, 34).

2. There are fifteen occurrences of the word 'law' (νόμος) in the Gospel of John, all but one denoting the Mosaic Law. John says the Law was given through Moses but grace and truth came by Jesus Christ (1.17; 7.19), implying an antithesis between Christ and the Law. The Law plays a positive role testifying to Jesus (1.45; 5.46). Jesus' opponents, and sometimes the Jewish crowds, cite to the Law in their controversies with Jesus (8.5; 12.34) as Jesus does in his responses to them (7.23; 8.17; 10.34). Jesus' opponents appeal to the Law when bringing charges against Jesus before Pilate (19.7). Jesus cites the Law to illustrate the need for the Son of Man to be 'lifted up' (3.14).
3. The Mosaic Law does not feature as extensively in the Gospel of John as it does in Paul's letters. The way the Law is employed by Paul and John is quite different. Paul introduces references to the Law in his teaching about sin, justification and Christian freedom, and appeals to it in support of his teaching. John shows how the Law testifies to Jesus, and how it featured in Jesus' controversies with his Jewish opponents. John implies that there is an antithesis between the Law that came through Moses and grace and truth that came through Christ, something reminiscent of Paul's Law/faith antithesis in Galatians. John differs from Paul in that the strong insistence

that no one is justified by works of the Law in Paul's letters is missing in John's Gospel, as are the contrast between Law and faith, the faith and works of Law antithesis, and the connection between the Law and sin. There is no hint in John's Gospel that Law observance is a condition for receiving eternal life (only faith in Jesus is required) nor that it functions as a regulatory norm, and in this respect John parallels Paul.

f. *Humanity and its need*

1. Paul depicts the human condition apart from Christ as a parlous one. Sin is a tyrant, an alien power, under whose dominion men and women are held captive. All people outside of Christ are under the power of sin (Rom. 3.9; 6.12; Gal. 3.22). Sin exercises its dominion in death (Rom. 5.21; 6.16-17, 20, 23; 7.5; Eph. 2.1) and commandeers the Law, as an unwilling ally, to further increase its sway over humanity (Rom. 7.5, 8-9, 11, 13-14; 1 Cor. 15.56). Human beings apart from Christ languish under the threefold tyranny of sin, the law and death. However, it is not only the tyranny of sin and death that threatens humanity. Human beings apart from Christ are susceptible to the wrath of God. God's wrath is being revealed from heaven against all ungodliness of human beings (Rom. 1.18) and their impenitence is storing up for themselves wrath on the day of God's wrath (Rom. 2.5, 8; Eph. 5.6; Col. 3.6). Unbelievers are by nature children of wrath (Eph. 2.3).
2. John depicts humanity outside of Christ as slaves to sin (8.34). Unless they are rescued from this tyranny they will die in their sins (8.24). The fundamental sin is failure to believe in Jesus Christ the Son of God (16.8-9). When Jewish people reject the word of Jesus Christ and fail to recognize the significance of his works, they have no excuse for their sin (15.22, 24). Their bondage is apparent in that they hate the light and love the darkness because their deeds are evil (3.19-21). Walking in darkness they do not know where they are going (12.35). Satan, the ruler of this world, has no power over the Lord Jesus Christ (14.30) but can enter the hearts of other human beings and incite them to perform evil deeds (13.2, 27). John teaches that human beings apart from Christ are susceptible to the wrath of God and that it hangs over those who do not believe in the Son (3.36).
3. Both Paul and John depict the human condition as a parlous one: human beings are slaves to sin, and exposed to God's wrath. In Paul the sin that attracts God's wrath consists primarily of evil deeds, whereas in John the fundamental sin is unbelief. Paul stresses that human beings outside of Christ are under bondage to sin, the Law and death, and John says they wander in darkness not knowing where they are going.

g. *The work of Christ*

1. Given humanity's parlous state, it is no surprise that Paul shows that the work of Christ is to rescue people from their fate. In depicting the work of Christ Paul does not focus upon the ministry of the historical Jesus, but jumps straight from his incarnation to his death and resurrection, and explains how these effect salvation. Paul's classic definition of the work of Christ is found in 1 Cor. 15.3-4: 'Christ died for our sins in accordance with the scriptures, and that he was buried, and that he was raised on the third day in accordance with the scriptures.' In Rom. 4.25 Paul says: '[Christ] was handed over to death for our trespasses and was raised for our justification.' The mechanism of salvation is spelled out in more detail in Rom. 3.22b-25a: 'For there is no distinction, since all have sinned and fall short of the glory of God; they are now justified by his grace as a gift, through the redemption that is in Christ Jesus, whom God put forward as a sacrifice of atonement by his blood, effective through faith.' Most striking of all is Paul's statement in 2 Cor. 5.19-21: 'In Christ God was reconciling the world to himself, not counting their trespasses against them. . . . For our sake he made him to be sin who knew no sin, so that in him we might become the righteousness of God.' Paul employs three primary categories to describe the work of Christ. The first and most frequently used is the concept of 'salvation'. The noun 'salvation' (σωτηρία) is used seventeen times and the verb 'to save' (σῴζω) twenty-nine times in this connection. People may be said to have been saved by the work of Christ and through faith in him (Rom. 10.10; Eph. 2.5, 8; Phil. 2.12; 2 Tim. 3.15; 2 Tim. 1.9; Tit. 3.5), to be being saved by Christ and the sanctifying work of the Holy Spirit (1 Cor. 1.18; 15.2; 2 Cor. 2.15), and that they will be saved on the last day (Rom. 5.9-10; 8.24; 13.11; 1 Cor. 3.15; 5.5; 1 Thess. 5.8-9; 2 Tim. 2.10). The second primary category Paul employs to depict the significance of the work of Christ is 'redemption'. The noun 'redemption' (ἀπολύτρωσις) occurs seven times in Paul's letters. Redemption is effected through Jesus Christ (Rom. 3.24; 1 Cor. 1.30) and by his blood (Eph. 1.7). Redemption is identified with the forgiveness of sins (Col. 1.14). The 'adoption' for which believers wait is described as the 'redemption of our bodies' (Rom. 8.23; cf. Eph. 4.30), and the Holy Spirit is given them as a pledge (ἀρραβών) and they are 'sealed' (ἐσφραγίσθητε) by the Spirit for their final redemption. The verb ἐξαγοράζω is used to describe the redemption effected by Christ: He redeems us from the curse of the Law by becoming a curse for us (Gal. 3.13), thus redeeming those who are under the Law (Gal. 4.5). The verb λυτρόω is used once to describe Christ's redeeming work: 'He it is who gave himself for us that he might redeem (λυτρώσηται) us from all

iniquity and purify for himself a people of his own who are zealous for good deeds' (Tit. 2.14). Paul's understanding of redemption is primarily freedom from sin's penalty (forgiveness) and its power in the present time. While redemption is experienced in the present time, it will be fully realized on the last day and will include the 'redemption of our bodies', that is resurrection to immortality. The third of the primary categories is 'atonement'. The word ἱλαστήριον translated in the NRSV as 'sacrifice of atonement' is found only once in Paul's letters (Rom. 3.25). Possible meanings of ἱλαστήριον include: the removal of guilt and the purifying of the sinner (expiation),[12] the appeasing of God's wrath towards sinners (propitiation)[13] and the mercy seat in the tabernacle,[14] and each of these represents one aspect of Christ's atoning sacrifice. In the context of Romans, where Paul says 'the wrath of God is revealed from heaven against all ungodliness and wickedness of those who by their wickedness suppress the truth' (Rom. 1.18), and where he warns those who judge others for their sins while practising the same things themselves that they are storing up wrath against themselves on the day God's wrath (Rom. 2.5), the idea of propitiation cannot be excluded from Paul's use of ἱλαστήριον. To adopt this interpretation would not exclude allusions to the mercy seat, as in the OT it was on the mercy seat that the blood of the sacrifice was sprinkled on the great Day of Atonement (Lev. 16.14-17). It must be stressed that the context makes clear that propitiation must not be thought of in pagan terms to mean overcoming of the wrath of a hostile God, for God himself took the initiative in providing his own Son as the atoning sacrifice for our sins.[15]

2. Apart from the prologue (1.1-18) and epilogue (21.1-25), John's Gospel consists of two major parts described as Jesus' work in the world (1.19–12.50) and Jesus' return to the Father (13.1–20.31). In the former Jesus' work is

12. C. H. Dodd, 'ἹΛΆΣΚΕΣΘΑΙ, Its Cognates, Derivatives, and Synonyms, in the Septuagint', *JTS* 32 (1931), p. 360; T. C. G. Thornton, 'Propitiation or Expiation?: ἱλατήριον and ἱλασμός in Romans 3:25', *ExpT* 80 (1968–69), pp. 54–5; Douglas A. Campbell, *The Rhetoric of Righteousness in Romans 3.21-26* (JSNTSup, 65; Sheffield: JSOT Press, 1992), pp. 188–9.

13. Leon Morris, *The Apostolic Preaching of the Cross* (London: Tyndale, 3rd edn, 1965), p. 206; David Hill, *Greek Words and Hebrew Meanings: Studies in the Semantics of Soteriological Terms* (Cambridge: CUP, 1967), pp. 37–8.

14. Nico S. L. Fryer, 'The Meaning and Translation of *Hilastērion* in Romans 3:25', *EvQ* 59 (1987), pp. 105–11.

15. The ἱλαστήριον cognates in both the LXX and the NT relate for the most part to atonement and forgiveness. In many cases they denote cleansing from or forgiveness of sins, and in a significant number of cases where ἐξιλάσκεσθαι is found appeasing of wrath is clearly intended. Atonement in the OT is best understood comprehensively to include both forgiveness of the sinner and turning away of God's anger. All this suggests that neither the idea of expiation nor propitiation can be ruled out as possible meanings for ἱλαστήριον in Rom. 3.25.

portrayed predominately, though not exclusively, as a teacher sent from God,[16] whereas in the latter preparation of his disciples for, and Jesus' actual return to the Father through death and resurrection, predominates. In the former part, Jesus the teacher reveals the Father through his words and works and invites people to believe in him, so that they may know the Father and experience eternal life. In the latter part the focus is upon Jesus' betrayal, death and subsequent resurrection. By his death on the cross Jesus makes possible cleansing, the forgiveness of sins, for all who receive his word. By his death and resurrection the new age is inaugurated in which his disciples experience the presence of the Paraclete, the Holy Spirit, who continues Jesus' teaching work among his disciples. While the latter part focuses upon the death of Christ, in fact the whole Gospel is structured so as to point the reader to the glorification of Jesus in his death. This is achieved by employment of the theme of Jesus' 'hour'. There are nine references to Jesus' hour dispersed throughout the gospel (2.4; 8.20; 12.23, 27; 13.1; 16.32; 17.1). In the early chapters the refrain 'my hour has not yet come'/'his hour had not yet come' indicates that the event towards which everything is moving has not yet arrived. Then at 12.23 it changes to 'the hour has come'/'I have come to this hour', and this refrain governs the remaining chapters. The trigger for this change is the coming of the Greeks seeking Jesus during his final visit to Jerusalem. This caused Jesus to speak of his impending death in terms of a kernel of wheat that falls to the ground and dies but then produces many seeds (12.24). The 'hour' towards which everything moves in John, then, is the death of Jesus and his subsequent exaltation. In 1.29 the Baptist hails Jesus as the Lamb of God who takes away the sin of the world. Christian readers of John naturally infer that this is an allusion to his sacrificial death by which he atoned for the sins of the world. However, some have argued that John was identifying Jesus as the apocalyptic warrior lamb referred to in Jewish writings (e.g. *1 Enoch* 90.9-12; *T. Jos.* 19.8-9), as does the author of the book of Revelation (Rev. 5.5-10; 17.14), though the latter fused the idea of the powerful lamb/lion of Judah with the sacrificial lamb. By the time the Fourth Gospel was written Jesus had been recognized as the one whose death had atoned for human sins, and John probably hoped his readers might appreciate its double meaning. In 3.14-15, concluding his response to Nicodemus' question about how a person can be born from above, Jesus says: 'Just as Moses lifted up the serpent in the wilderness, so must the Son of Man be lifted up, that whoever believes in him may have eternal life.' The verb, 'to lift up' (ὑψόω) is used five times in the Fourth Gospel

16. Cf. Marshall, *New Testament Theology*, p. 595.

(3.14 [2×]; 8.28; 12.32, 34) and in every case it is used in an allusion to Jesus' crucifixion.[17] As the lifting up of the serpent in the wilderness was God's provision for salvation from physical death for rebellious Israelites, so now the lifting up of the Son of Man (his crucifixion) is God's provision for salvation from eternal death for all who believe. In 13.8, when Peter objected to Jesus' desire to wash his feet, Jesus responded, 'Unless I wash you, you have no share with me.' Such a response makes no sense if all that was involved was foot washing. The meaning of Jesus' response, therefore, must be sought at a deeper level. Jesus' self-humiliation in washing his disciples' feet symbolized his self-humiliation in accepting death upon the cross to bring about their cleansing from sin.

3. Because of the very nature of John's Gospel as a gospel, the work of Christ is presented differently from the way Paul presents it in his letters. Paul's focus is upon the significance of the death and resurrection of Christ. He was made sin for us so that we might become the righteousness of God in him. He died for our sins and was raised for our justification. His death effects salvation, redemption and atonement. John portrays Jesus' work as a teacher sent from God, and does not contain the same sort of explicit teaching about the significance of Jesus' death as that found in Paul's letters, but such teaching is not altogether missing. The structuring of the Gospel around the theme of Jesus' hour points to culmination in his death and exaltation. Jesus is the Lamb of God who takes away the sin of the world, the one 'lifted up' so that those who believe in him might have eternal life, and who in the foot washing symbolized the cleansing from sin made possible by his death on the cross.

h. *Union with Christ*

1. Whether or not union with Christ is the central theme of Pauline theology as some have argued,[18] it is certainly a key element in Paul's writings. He uses the expression 'in Christ' (ἐν Χριστῷ) seventy-three times, frequently describing believers and fellow workers as those who are 'in Christ' where it seems to mean they are Christians (e.g. Rom. 16.3, 7, 9, 10; Phil. 1.1; Col. 1.2), and often in relation to the blessings of the gospel enjoyed by those who are 'in Christ' (e.g. Rom. 3.24; 6.23; 8.1, 39; 1 Cor. 1.2, 4; Gal. 3.14, 26; Eph. 1.3; 2.13; 3.6). Paul employs the expression 'with Christ' (σύν Χριστῷ) to depict believers' participation in Christ's

17. The lifting up of Jesus on the cross denotes, paradoxically, not only his suffering but also the means of his departure from this world and his return to glory.

18. So, e.g. E. P. Sanders, *Paul and Palestinian Judaism: A Comparison of Patterns of Religion* (London: SCM, 1977), p. 502, says that 'the real bite of his [Paul's] theology lies in the participatory categories'. Cf. Albert Schweitzer, *The Mysticism of Paul the Apostle* (ET; London: A&C Black, 1930).

death (Rom. 6.8; Col. 2.20). A particular emphasis of Paul's is that believers have died to sin and been made alive to God 'in Christ' (Rom. 6.3-8, 11; 8.2; 1 Cor. 1.30; Gal. 2.19-20; Eph. 2.4-6). The union of believers with Christ is the basic assumption underlying Paul's use of the image of the body to depict the ministry of members of the church (Rom. 12.4-8; 1 Cor. 12.2-31) and the relationship of the church to Christ (Eph. 1.22-23; 4.4, 12, 16; 5.23, 30; Col. 1.18, 24; 2.19; 3.15).

2. In John's Gospel union with Christ is a key concept in the teaching of Jesus. In heavily metaphorical language, describing those who believe in him, Jesus says: 'Those who eat my flesh and drink my blood abide in me, and I in them' (6.56). This mutual indwelling of Christ and the believer, modelled on the mutual indwelling of the Father and the Son (cf. 17.21-23), is developed in the farewell discourses. So in 14.18-20 Jesus says: 'I will not leave you orphaned; I am coming to you. . . . On that day you will know that I am in my Father, and you in me, and I in you.' In 14.23 he says: 'Those who love me will keep my word, and my Father will love them, and we will come to them and make our home with them.' In 15.2-7 the mutual indwelling of Christ and his followers is depicted with the image of the vine and the branches. Jesus says: 'Abide in me as I abide in you. Just as the branch cannot bear fruit by itself unless it abides in the vine, neither can you unless you abide in me' (15.4). Because of the vine/branches metaphor this has often been interpreted as an organic union between Jesus and his disciples. It is unlikely that the disciples who heard Jesus in the upper room thought of their connection with him in that way. Most likely they thought of it in terms of loyalty and fellowship that would continue as they obeyed his word. Likewise, it is unlikely that the disciples thought of Jesus abiding in them in any organic way. Again, we should think in terms of continuing fellowship, this time of Jesus with his disciples. The means by which Jesus abides in fellowship with his disciples cannot be the same as the means by which the disciples abide in fellowship with him. Jesus does not keep his disciples' commands! While physically present with his disciples Jesus abided in fellowship with them by committing himself to be with them and for them. When he returned to the Father he did not leave them alone (cf. 14.15-18), he came to them again in the person of the Spirit and then his abiding in them took on a deeper meaning. It is the combination of the disciples' abiding in fellowship with Jesus by obeying his word, and Jesus' abiding in his disciples through the coming of the Spirit that produces 'fruit' that satisfies the Father.

3. The theme of union with Christ is important in both Paul and John, though it is employed differently. Paul speaks of believers being united with

Christ in his death and resurrection, using this to stress that Christians can no longer live in sin. It also underlies his use of the image of the body to depict Christ's relationship to the church. John emphasizes the mutual indwelling of Christ and believers, stressing that believers remain in Christ by obedience, and Christ remains in them through the Spirit.

i. *The church and its ministers*

1. Paul provides more information about the nature and ministry of the church than any other NT writer. As noted, union with Christ is the basic assumption underlying his use of the image of the body for the church. It enables him to describe the nature of the church: Christ is the 'head' and believers constitute the other 'members' of the body (Eph. 1.22-23; 4.4, 12, 16; 5.23, 30; Col. 1.18, 24; 2.19; 3.15). It also enables him to describe the various functions of members of the church who make up the body of Christ. Being recipients of gifts for ministry provided by the Spirit they minister to one another and proclaim the gospel in the world (Rom. 12.4-8; 1 Cor. 12.2-31). Pauline churches constituted charismatic communities, each member being a recipient of one or more gifts of the Spirit (χαρίσματα) and exercising them in the congregations. This did not mean there were no 'official' ministers/leaders in these churches. From the earliest days there were paid teachers (Gal. 6.6) as well as those appointed as elders/bishops (Phil. 1.1; 1 Tim. 3.2; 5.17, 19; Tit. 1.5, 7) and deacons (Rom. 16.1; Phil. 1.1; 1 Tim. 3.8, 12). The function of elders/bishops was to teach (1 Tim. 3.2; 5.17; Tit. 1.9) and manage (1 Tim. 5.17) the congregation. Paul's letters contain very little about the function of deacons, the only exception being what he says about the deacon Phoebe: 'she has been a benefactor of many and of myself as well' (Rom. 16.2).
2. There is a lot in the Gospel of John concerning believers' individual relationship with Christ, and of the importance of individual obedience to his commands. It was written so that *individuals* might believe that Jesus is the Christ and receive eternal life. There are numerous examples of *individuals* coming to faith in Christ: Nathanael, Nicodemus (eventually), the Samaritan woman, the royal official, the man born blind and, supremely, Thomas. There is a strong emphasis upon the importance of the *individual's* obedience to Jesus' word. But on first reading there appears to be a lack of emphasis upon the people of God as a communal entity. Kysar notes that the Gospel of John does not include Jesus' Caesarea Philippi statement to Peter about the church. It does not use the word ἐκκλησία nor show any interest in the apostolic foundation of the

church or its institutionalization.[19] Despite these appearances, however, we are not entitled to conclude that interest in the church is completely absent. In fact, a review of relevant texts reveals several implied images of the church: believers constitute the community among whom God's glory dwells (1.14); together believers make up the bride of Christ (3.28-30); they are those given by God to Christ as his own people (6.37, 39; 17.6); they are the flock of God (10.1-6), the dispersed people of God gathered into one (10.16); they constitute the community in which mutual service (even lowly service) is carried out (13.13-17); they are those who will be gathered around Christ in the heavens and see his glory (17.24); they are the community in whom the Spirit dwells (14.15-17; 16.7); the people among whom the Father and the Son make their home (14.23); and they are branches in the vine (15.5). Therefore, despite the emphasis upon the individual's need to believe in Christ, there is sufficient data to show that John has a concept of the church.[20] The Fourth Evangelist appears to 'democratize' church order: no distinctions are made among believers that might become the basis of official leadership. It does not use the word 'apostles' and it uses the word 'disciples' where we might expect 'the Twelve', and by 'disciple' it means simply believers. However, this is not the whole story. The recommissioning of Peter to 'feed my sheep' in 21.15-17 implies a shepherd/teacher role for him in the early church and suggests that this community is structured: some are shepherds, some are sheep.

3. Church and ministry feature much more largely in Paul than John. Paul's fundamental image for the church is the body of Christ, one that enables him to depict the church's relationship to her head, Christ and internal relationships among believers. The church is a 'charismatic community' whose members are endowed with gifts for ministry, and yet still provided with 'official' ministers – teachers, elders and deacons. John on first reading seems to have no interest in the church as a corporate body, or in 'official' ministers. However, the church as a corporate entity is implied by images that are employed such as the bride of Christ, the flock of Christ, etc., and Peter's recommissioning suggests some are 'shepherds', others are 'sheep'.

19. Robert Kysar, *John: the Maverick Gospel* (Louisville, KY: Westminster John Knox, rev. edn, 1993), pp. 112–14, 116–18. Rudolph Bultmann, *Theology of the New Testament*, vol. 2 (London: SCM, 1955), p. 91, notes that in the Gospel of John 'there is no interest in cult or organization', adding 'that does not entitle one to conclude that interest in the Church is completely absent'.

20. Cf. Marshall, *New Testament Theology*, pp. 598–9.

j. *Mission*

1. The concept of mission features large in Paul's letters, but for the most part it is Paul's own mission as apostle that is to the fore. He introduces himself as one called to be an apostle (Rom. 1.1; 1 Cor. 1.1) by the will of God (2 Cor. 1.1; Gal. 1.1; Eph. 1.1; Col. 1.1; 1 Tim. 1.1; 2 Tim. 1.1). An important criterion for being an apostle is having seen the risen Lord Jesus (1 Cor. 9.1; 15.8-9), and the marks of a true apostle include 'signs and wonders and mighty works' (2 Cor. 12.12). As an apostle Paul was 'set apart for the gospel of God' (Rom. 1.1; 2 Tim. 1.11) with the primary task of taking it to the Gentiles (Rom. 11.13; 15.16; 1 Tim. 2.7; 2 Tim. 4.17). He places great stress upon the fact that the gospel message is intended for Gentiles as well as Jews (Rom. 15.8-12; 16.26; Gal. 2.8-9; 3.8, 14; Eph. 2.11-16; 3.6). His converts constituted the 'seal' and 'crown' of his apostleship (1 Cor. 9.2; 2 Cor. 3.1-3; Phil. 4.1; 1 Thess. 2.19). Paul says little of the mission of the church as church. He does not appear to have seen the church as the primary instrument of mission, contrary to popular assertions.[21] He did not regard every member of his churches as a missionary, but he did expect them to support those called and set apart for the task of preaching the gospel. He regarded the church not as a society of missionaries but as a missionary society. The church by its very life and existence is a witness to pagan society (Phil. 2.14-15) and to cosmic powers (Eph. 3.8-10).
2. John emphasizes the importance of mission. First and foremost it focuses upon the mission of Jesus. He was sent by God into the world (4.34; 5.23-24, 30, 36-38; 6.29, 38-39, 44, 57; 7.16, 18, 28-29, 33; 8.16, 18, 26, 29, 42; 9.4; 10.36; 11.42; 12.44, 49; 13.20; 14.24; 15.21; 16.5; 17.3, 8, 18, 21, 23, 25; 20.21) not to condemn it but that it might be saved through him (3.17). He came to enlighten everyone (3.19-21; 12.46), to bear witness to the truth (18.37), to speak the words of God (3.34) and to work the works of God (9.4). He came to take away the sins of the world (1.29) so that those who believe in him might be saved (12.47) and have abundant life (10.10). Though his mission was primarily to Israel, he also came to bring in 'sheep' that do not belong to the 'fold' of Israel (i.e. Gentiles who hear his voice) and so create one flock, with one shepherd (10.16). He came to be glorified (12.23) and to glorify his Father's name in his death (12.27-28). Jesus explicitly aroused awareness in his disciples of the needs of the harvest (4.35) and sent them to labour in it (4.38). Following his exaltation the disciples are to be witnesses to Jesus with the help of the Holy Spirit

21. Cf. Paul Bowers, 'Church and Mission in Paul', *JSNT* 44 (1991), pp. 89–111; Marshall, *New Testament Theology*, p. 600.

(15.26-27). Through their witness the Spirit will prove the world wrong about sin, righteousness and judgement (16.7-11). The crucial text in John's Gospel in relation to the mission of Jesus' disciples is 20.21-22: 'Jesus said to them again, "Peace be with you. As the Father has sent me, so I send you." And with that he breathed on them and said, "Receive the Holy Spirit."' The disciples are sent by Jesus to continue his mission, just as the Father sent Jesus to carry out his mission. The corollary is that the reception accorded the disciples by those who hear them will be regarded as their response to Jesus who sent them and to the Father who sent him. If they hated Jesus they will hate them also; if they kept Jesus' word they will keep their word as well (15.18-21). The Trinitarian nature of mission is apparent in this text: Jesus sends his disciples as the Father sent him, and he breathes on them, telling them to receive the Holy Spirit who will empower them for their mission. Köstenberger comments: 'It can be truly said, not only that John's mission theology is Trinitarian (which in and of itself is a significant statement) but also that his Trinitarian teaching is part of his mission theology – a truly revolutionary insight.'[22]

3. Mission is an important theme in both Paul and John. In Paul's letters the primary focus in this regard is upon the mission of the apostle himself. He was called and set apart for a mission to the Gentiles. He has little to say about the mission of the church, which he seems to have regarded less as a society of missionaries than a missionary society. John highlights the mission of Jesus. He came to bear witness to the truth, to lay down his life that those who believe in him might have eternal life, and that Gentiles as well as Jews might be brought in. Unlike Paul, who seems not to have laid upon members of his churches the obligation for missionary work themselves, in John's Gospel Jesus explicitly arouses awareness in his disciples of the needs of the harvest and sends them to labour in it. As the Father sent him, so Christ sends his disciples.

k. *Israel/The Jews*

1. Reflected in Paul's letters is the fact that the apostle suffered persecution at the hands of his own people. He suffered largely because of his commitment to the Gentile mission and his proclamation of a Law-free gospel. He preached the faith he once tried to destroy (Gal. 1.23); he devalued things that zealous Jews held important, their Jewish pedigree and piety, and even described those things as rubbish (Phil. 3.4-9); he was thought to encourage Jews to neglect the Law and the traditions (cf. Acts 21.18-21);

22. A. Köstenberger, *A Theology of John's Gospel and Letters* (Grand Rapids, MI: Zondervan, 2009), p. 545.

he waived the requirement of circumcision (Gal. 5.11); and was thought to be advocating the abolition of ethical standards (Rom. 3.8; 6.1, 15).[23] Paul responded to this persecution on one occasion with hostility (1 Thess. 2.14-16), but his more characteristic response was concern for those from among whom the persecution emanated. His heart's desire for the Jews was that they might be saved (Rom. 10.1). While his own evangelistic efforts were directed primarily towards the Gentiles, it did not prevent him from engaging in a ministry to Jews as well. He became like a Jew to save Jews (1 Cor. 9.21). The salvation of his fellow countrymen was something for which Paul would be prepared to be accursed and cut off from Christ (Rom. 9.3). He wrestled with the problem of rejection of the gospel by the majority of the Jews, explaining it in two complementary ways. On the one hand he argued there had been no failure of God's word, for there had always been a division within Israel as a result of God's free sovereign choice – not all Israel was (true) Israel (Rom. 9.6-33). On the other hand he laid the blame at the feet of unrepentant Jews themselves. Seeking to establish their own righteousness, they refused to submit to God's righteousness (Rom. 10.3). God had held out his hands all day long to 'a disobedient and contrary people' (Rom. 10.21). But this was not the end of the matter. Paul hoped his ministry to Gentiles would provoke Jews to jealousy, as they saw Gentiles enjoying the blessings first promised to them, and cause them to repent and find salvation (Rom. 11.13-14). Though many of his Jewish kinsfolk were like branches cut off from the 'olive tree' of Israel, God who cut them off could also graft them in again (Rom. 11.16-24). Paul looked forward to the day when 'all Israel' would be saved – that is, when the full number of the elect of Israel will have given their allegiance to Christ and will find salvation (Rom. 11.25-27).[24] Paul insisted that not all Abraham's descendants were Abraham's true children. Abraham's children are those who have faith in Jesus, Gentiles

23. Cf. Colin G. Kruse, 'The Price Paid for a Ministry among the Gentiles: Paul's Persecution at the Hands of the Jews', in *Worship, Theology and Ministry in the Early Church: Essays in Honour of Ralph P. Martin*, eds Michael J. Wilkins and Terence Paige (JSNTSup 87; Sheffield: JSOT Press, 1992), pp. 260–72.

24. This statement of Paul's is susceptible to several interpretations. Stephen Voorwinde, 'Rethinking Israel: An Exposition of Romans 11:25-27', *VoxRef* 68 (2003), pp. 5–12, documents three main approaches to the interpretation of Paul's statement that all Israel will be saved: (1) All Israel as the elect, including believing Jews and Gentiles. In this case 'the Israel of God' includes the elect from among both the Jewish and Gentile communities. (2) All Israel as the elect Jews throughout history. In this case 'the Israel of God' consists of the Jewish elect of all ages that will reach its fullness by the end of the present age. (3) All Israel as the majority of ethnic Jews in the future. In this case there will be at the end of the age, or at least at some point in the future, a large ingathering of Jews as they are converted to Christ, and then the time of the hardening of Israel will have come to an end. Ben L. Merkle, 'Romans 11 and the Future of Ethnic Israel', *JETS* 43 (2000), pp. 709–11, lists the same three positions.

as well as Jews (Gal. 3.8-9, 14, 28-29). In Gal. 6.16 Paul invokes a blessing upon 'the Israel of God' (a *hapax legomena*) by which he may mean either believing Jews and Gentiles or believing Jews who are, with Gentile believers, part of the church of God.

2. Reflected in the Gospel of John is the fact that Jesus suffered persecution at the hands of his Jewish opponents because they thought he was flouting the Law of God, in particular the Sabbath law (5.9-10, 16, 18; 7.23; 9.16), and, more important because he claimed equality with God (5.18). John depicts the Jews as those proud to be Abraham's children (8.33, 39). While acknowledging that they were Abraham's descendants, Jesus denied they were his 'true' children. They did not act as Abraham did – Abraham heeded God's word whereas they were seeking to kill Jesus because he spoke the truth (8.37, 39-40). John portrays Jesus as the king of Israel. The Baptist says his own reason for coming was that Jesus 'might be revealed to Israel' (1.31); Nathanael acclaims Jesus as the 'King of Israel' (1.49); and when Jesus entered Jerusalem in passion week the crowd shouted, 'Blessed is the one who comes in the name of the Lord – the King of Israel!' (12.13). Employing prophetic imagery that depicts Israel as the flock of God and God himself as their shepherd (Isa. 40.11; Jer. 31.10; Ezek. 34.15), Jesus proclaims himself as Israel's true Shepherd (10.11, 14). By so doing he arrogates to himself the place occupied by Yahweh in the OT. He insists that those who are the 'true' sheep of Israel hear his voice (10.4). Beyond all expectation Jesus said that the Good Shepherd would lay down his life for his sheep (10.11, 15, 17-18). In line with another prophetic image that depicts Israel as God's 'vine' (in particular Isaiah 5), Jesus declares himself to be the true 'vine' (15.1). And those who make up the branches of the vine are those who believe in him.
3. Reflected in Paul's letters and in the Gospel of John is the fact that both Paul and Jesus suffered persecution at the hands of their own people. Paul suffered because he proclaimed a Law-free gospel, devalued Jewish pedigree and piety, was thought to encourage Jews to neglect the Law, and undermine ethical standards. Jesus suffered at the hand of his Jewish opponents because they thought he was flouting the Law and claimed equality with God. Both Paul and John depict the majority in Israel as rejecting the gospel. At times Paul felt estranged from many of his own people (cf. 1 Thess. 2.14-16) and the emphasis on the rejection of Christ by many of the Jews in John's Gospel may reflect a sense of alienation in the community in which it was written. Just as Paul spoke of Israel as the 'olive tree' whose unbelieving branches were cut off, so Jesus spoke of Israel as the 'vine' whose unfruitful branches are also cut off (15.6).

II. *Conclusion*

There are a number of other themes that are found in both the letters of Paul and John's Gospel (e.g. divine sovereignty and human responsibility and the ethic of love). In addition, there are in the letters of Paul significant themes that do not appear in John's Gospel (e.g. the flesh/Spirit antithesis, justification by faith and reconciliation), as there are significant themes found in the Gospel of John that do not feature in Paul's letters (e.g. the Logos, the relationship between signs and faith and the cosmic trial). Space does not allow discussion of all these things. However, the various themes discussed in this essay are sufficient to show that, while there is little evidence that John's Gospel is dependent in any way upon Paul's letters, nor that it was written in reaction to them, both Paul and John drew upon the same wellspring of primitive Christian tradition, that in turn is dependent upon God's supreme revelation in Christ. While this is the case, common themes are expressed differently, not least because Paul's writings are letters and John is a gospel, but, perhaps more important because each reflects differently upon the significance of the Christ event and expresses that reflection in his own idiom and thought patterns.

9

THE *GOSPEL OF THOMAS*'S REJECTION OF PAUL'S THEOLOGICAL IDEAS[1]

Christopher W. Skinner

1. *Introduction*

The title of this essay is intentionally provocative and calls for some clarification. First, this study proceeds under the assumption that the *Gospel of Thomas* developed over a lengthy period of time before becoming fixed in the form we currently possess. This means that the final form of *Thomas* contains disparate traditions rather than a unified theological logic.[2] However, when I use '*Thomas*' in the present study I am referring to the final form of the document, as if it were always possible to speak of a coherent 'theology of *Thomas*'.[3] Second, in using the term 'rejection' it is not my intention to suggest that *Thomas* as a whole is consciously 'anti-Pauline' or that the entire text somehow reflects a conflict with Pauline Christianity. I have argued elsewhere that such

1. Several individuals took the time to converse with me and interact with the ideas presented in this essay. In particular, I am thankful for the insights and thoughtful input provided by Michael Gorman, Kelly Iverson, Frank Moloney and Kurt Pfund. Their comments, both written and oral, have improved this essay. Any mistakes or oversights that remain are solely my own responsibility.

2. Over the years scholars have tried to trace *Thomas*'s internal logic with little success. Helmut Koester has commented that there seems to be no logic behind *Thomas*'s ordering of material: 'What is most puzzling about the composition of sayings in this wisdom book is the arrangement and order of the sayings. There is seemingly no rhyme or reason for the odd sequence in which the sayings occur in the *Gospel of Thomas*'. He goes on to say that 'several attempts have been made to find the author's compositional principle, [but] none of them [are] convincing' (*Ancient Christian Gospels: Their History and Development* [Harrisburg, PA: Trinity Press International, 1992], p. 81). One of Koester's former students, Elaine Pagels ('Exegesis of Genesis 1 in the Gospels of Thomas and John', *JBL* 118 [1999], p. 481), encourages readers to adopt 'the hypothesis that the sayings are not randomly arranged, but carefully ordered to lead one through a process of seeing and finding "the interpretation of these sayings" (log. 1). This is not to suggest, however, that the author follows an obvious or syllogistic rationale'. Another Koester pupil, Allen Callahan, attempts to demonstrate the author's 'compositional principle' by examining catchphrases, conceptual links and sequential links within the gospel (see '"No Rhyme or Reason": The Hidden Logia of the *Gospel of Thomas*', *HTR* 90 [1997], pp. 411–26).

3. As a narrative critic, I recognize that *Thomas* became fixed in its final form for a reason and that it possesses an internal unity and coherence, despite problems that might suggest otherwise.

a line of reasoning is often misguided.[4] Rather, I hope to demonstrate that, in several places, traditions contained in *Thomas* show knowledge of Paul's writings and a reworking of 'Pauline language for un-*Pauline* ends'.[5] In the course of its development, *Thomas* incorporated and modified traditions that were decidedly different from the emerging mainstream (viz. proto-orthodox) forms of Pauline and Johannine Christianity. Where parallels to the Johannine and Pauline traditions exist in *Thomas*, they are used quite differently than in their original sources. Finally, I must admit that in examining the relationship between Paul and *Thomas* in light of the aims of this volume, I could think of no better word than 'ideas' to serve as a drip-pan designation for the different Pauline formulations *Thomas* seems to incorporate and modify. *Thomas* is inherently theological but its seemingly random arrangement and lack of narrative structure do not lend themselves as easily to systematic discussions of topics such as Christology, soteriology, eschatology or the use of the OT as do the writings of Paul. With these qualifications in place, it is now possible to proceed to the discussion at hand.

Identifying influences or locating parallels between *Thomas* and the Pauline literature is an undertaking not unlike jumping out of a deep well. Not only does the task seem difficult to complete, but where does one begin? Throughout its history Thomasine scholarship has been dominated by questions of *Thomas*'s relationship to the Synoptics,[6] though a more recent trend has sought to focus on the relationship between *Thomas* and the Fourth Gospel.[7] Apart from the

4. See Christopher W. Skinner, *John and Thomas: Gospels in Conflict? Johannine Characterization and the Thomas Question* (PTMS 115; Eugene: OR, Pickwick, 2009), esp. pp. 227–33.

5. This phrase is borrowed from Simon Gathercole, 'The Influence of Paul on the *Gospel of Thomas* (53.3 and 17)', in J. Frey, E. E. Popkes and J. Schröter (eds), *Das Thomasevangelium: Entstehung – Rezeption – Theologie* (BZNW 157; Berlin: de Gruyter, 2008), p. 84 (emphasis his).

6. For a helpful overview of material related to *Thomas* and the Synoptics see Christopher Tuckett, 'Thomas and the Synoptics', *NovT* 30 (1988), pp. 132–57. See also Stephen J. Patterson, 'The *Gospel of Thomas* and the Synoptic Tradition: A *Forschungsbericht* and Critique', *FFF* 8 (1992), pp. 45–97, and the pertinent sections in Francis T. Fallon and Ron Cameron, 'The *Gospel of Thomas*: A *Forschungsbericht* and Analysis', in W. Haase and H. Temporini (eds), *ANRW* 2.25.6 (New York: de Gruyter), pp. 4213–23, and Nicholas Perrin, 'Recent Trends in Gospel of Thomas Research (1991–2006): Part I, The Historical Jesus and the Synoptic Gospels', *CBR* 5 (2007), pp. 191–8.

7. Over the last decade and a half an influential cadre of American scholars have argued that the Fourth Gospel is a conscious response to theological developments within *Thomas* or to the sayings tradition that stands behind it. See e.g. Gregory J. Riley, *Resurrection Reconsidered: John and Thomas in Controversy* (Minneapolis: Fortress, 1995); Elaine Pagels, 'Exegesis of Genesis 1'; idem, *Beyond Belief: The Secret Gospel of Thomas* (San Francisco: HarperCollins, 2003); April D. DeConick, '"Blessed Are Those Who Have Not Seen" (Jn 20:29): Johannine Dramatization of an Early Christian Discourse', in John D. Turner and Anne McGuire (eds), *The Nag Hammadi Library after Fifty Years: Proceedings of the 1995 Society of Biblical Literature Commemoration* (NHMS 44; Leiden: Brill, 1997), pp. 381–98; idem, 'John Rivals Thomas: From Community Conflict to Gospel Narrative', in Robert T. Fortna and Tom Thatcher (eds), *Jesus in the Johannine Tradition* (Louisville: Westminster John Knox, 2001), pp. 303–12; idem, *Seek to See Him: Ascent and Vision Mysticism in the Gospel of Thomas* (VCSup 33; Leiden: Brill, 1996); idem, *Voices of the Mystics: Early Christian Discourse in the Gospel of John and Thomas and Other Ancient*

occasional footnote or passing reference to potential parallels between the two, *Thomas* scholars have had little to say about the possibilities of a genetic relationship between Paul and *Thomas*, and Pauline scholars have virtually ignored *Thomas* altogether. Aside from a helpful recent essay by Simon Gathercole, little has been written on the topic.[8] Gathercole himself acknowledges that he is 'not aware of a single article or book on the subject'.[9] This fact makes it even more difficult to approach the topic and obviously allows for few conversation partners. Add to this that there is little consensus on the major issues in Thomasine studies and the prospects for exploring a possible relationship between Paul and *Thomas* seem even more tenuous.[10]

I find myself in substantial agreement with Gathercole's conclusion that there are a handful of instances where *Thomas*'s knowledge of Pauline traditions can be detected, but I believe this thesis can be taken a step further. In what follows I plan to investigate instances of Pauline influence on several logia in *Thomas*. I will then consider how the Pauline traditions have been modified, reworked, or completely rejected in the light of *Thomas*'s peculiar theological interests.

II. *Starting points: Problems, limitations and assumptions*

a. *Dating* Thomas *and the Pauline tradition*

Theories abound as to the date of *Thomas*'s composition and there is no consensus in sight. The question of dating *Thomas* is often raised vis-à-vis the canonical Gospels, with some arguing that *Thomas* was composed in the mid- to late second century[11] and others arguing that it emerged as early as the Gospel of Mark (c.70 CE).[12] Few scholars are willing to make the extraordinarily tenuous leap to a

Christian Literature (Sheffield, Sheffield Academic Press, 2001). This idea has been challenged by the recent works of Ismo Dunderberg (*The Beloved Disciple in Conflict: Revisiting the Gospels of John and Thomas* [Oxford: Oxford University Press, 2006]), and Skinner, *John and Thomas*.

8. Gathercole, 'Influence', pp. 72–94.

9. Ibid., p. 72.

10. There is significant division among scholars as to *Thomas*'s date, theological outlook, relation to the canonical gospels, and compositional language. For an overview of these debates and the major players involved in the discussions, see Christopher W. Skinner, *What Are They Saying about the Gospel of Thomas?* (Mahwah, NJ: Paulist, forthcoming).

11. The most notable recent attempt to situate *Thomas* in the second century is that of Nicholas Perrin. Reviving and reworking a theory earlier espoused by Gilles Quispel and later modified by A. F. J. Klijn, Perrin argues that *Thomas* was dependent on Tatian's *Diatessaron*, a Syriac harmony of the four canonical gospels that is generally dated to the 170s CE. For Perrin, this means that *Thomas* is from the late second century; he also argues that it was originally composed in Syriac. For a fuller exposition of Perrin's thesis, see *Thomas and Tatian: The Relationship between the* Gospel of Thomas *and the* Diatessaron (Atlanta: Society of Biblical Literature, 2002); idem, 'Thomas: The Fifth Gospel?', *JETS* 49 (2006), pp. 67–80; idem, *Thomas: The Other Gospel* (Louisville: Westminster John Knox, 2007).

12. See, for instance, the influential work of Stephen J. Patterson, *The Gospel of Thomas and Jesus* (Sonoma: Scholars, 1992).

pre-Pauline *Thomas* tradition, though there is at least one recent scholar to argue along these lines.[13] There is a broad consensus among scholars that, apart from the letter of James,[14] the letters of Paul are the earliest Christian writings we possess, though this consensus in itself proves nothing.[15] Nevertheless, there is firm evidence that the Pauline correspondence began to appear as early as the late 40s CE, while the picture of *Thomas*'s emergence is not quite as clear. There is a high degree of probability that there was a substantive body of Pauline letters in circulation prior to the emergence of the *Thomas* sayings tradition, though we will not take that assumption for granted here.[16] In what follows we will examine each text on its own without assuming an overarching theory of compositional chronology.

b. *Limits of literary comparison*

Because there is only one complete extant copy of *Thomas*, and that preserved in Coptic, it naturally follows that we are severely limited when it comes to looking for strict verbal parallels in the Greek texts of Paul's letters. Nonetheless, the nature of our study is literary and we must necessarily focus on the texts themselves. This means we will seek to identify in Paul and *Thomas* the same or similar words, phrases, ideas and contexts. An investigation of this sort will then assist us in answering questions about which texts preceded and influenced the others.

13. April D. DeConick argues that *Thomas* is the product of a 'rolling corpus'. She locates four layers of tradition. First there is the 'Kernel', which dates to 30–50 CE. The sayings represented here are essentially apocalyptic in nature and reflect the early Thomasine community's expectation that Jesus would return to bring judgement. The second layer of tradition contains accretions reflecting the community's struggle with a changing leadership. These traditions are dated to a period between 50 and 60 CE. The third layer of tradition reveals a change in the community's eschatological expectations, largely based upon the delay of the *parousia*. She dates these to the period 60–100 CE. The fourth layer is dated to around 120 CE. See her discussion of the 'Kernel' in A. D. Deconick, *Recovering the Original Gospel of Thomas: A History of the Gospel and its Growth* (London: T&T Clark, 2005), pp. 64–110.

14. James was likely written in the mid- to late 40s CE and probably predates both 1 Thessalonians and Galatians – the writings usually regarded as Paul's earliest. On issues related to the early dating of James, see Luke Timothy Johnson, *The Epistle of James* (AB 37A; New York: Doubleday, 1995), pp. 118–22. Among recent commentators, Abraham Malherbe (*The Letters to the Thessalonians* [AB 32B; New York: Doubleday, 2000], pp. 71–4) dates 1 Thessalonians to 49 CE. On the dating of Galatians the ongoing debate about the letter's destination impacts the question of dating. Those who favour the so-called 'North Galatians' theory argue for a date around 57–58 CE, while the advocates of the 'South Galatians' theory place the letter between 51 and 54 CE.

15. When describing Paul's writings as 'Christian' texts, I want to be careful to avoid the trap of speaking of Paul as the 'inventor of Christianity' or 'the first Christian'. On this issue I cite my former colleague, Michael J. Gorman, who is quick to remind us that 'Paul was born a Jew, lived a Jew, and died a Jew. It was therefore obviously as a Jew that he experienced the once-crucified Jesus as the resurrected and exalted Lord. Paul did not set out to found a new religion but to call Jews and especially Gentiles to confess Jesus as Messiah. . . . In retrospect, we can of course say that Paul was a 'Christian' – one who confesses and follows Jesus as Christ and Lord. But we must do so without forgetting the inherent Jewishness of this very term ("Christian") and of the great Christian apostle Paul' (*Apostle of the Crucified Lord: A Theological Introduction to Paul and His Letters* [Grand Rapids: Eerdmans, 2004], p. 40).

16. My own view is that *Thomas* developed during the period between 70 and 150 CE, and that those responsible for its composition had some awareness of the Synoptic tradition.

We must also keep in mind that the earliest Christian documents emerged in what was largely an oral culture. In the regions where Christianity developed most rapidly, few people could read and write. Scholars have long recognized that most early Christian storytelling existed in performative, liturgical and homiletic forms before it ever became fixed in a documentary form.[17] This means that the vast majority of the early followers of Jesus were not able to read the story for themselves, but rather relied upon a small group of educated individuals to either read to them or perform for them. An awareness of these factors has implications for our study inasmuch as it is not always possible to establish that a relationship between two or more ancient Christian documents goes back to a written text. A given saying may have circulated widely in oral form, and the decision to incorporate that saying into a written text may have been made without recourse to a written source. This fact must be kept in mind so as to avoid the illegitimate application of a modern 'cut and paste' model to our discussion.

III. *Paul and* Thomas*: Texts and traditions*

Here we will examine several Paul-*Thomas* parallels. Following *Thomas*'s order of sayings we will consider the possible relationship between: (1) *Gos. Thom*. 3 and Rom. 10.5-8, (2) *Gos. Thom*. 17 and 1 Cor. 2.9, (3) *Gos. Thom*. 53 and Rom. 2.25-29 and (4) several texts from *Thomas* and Paul in which the flesh/spirit dichotomy appears. After these parallels have been examined, we will proceed to a discussion of theological formulations in *Thomas* and their relationship to Pauline ideas.

a. Gospel of Thomas *3 and Romans 10.5-8*

Gospel of Thomas *3*	*Romans 10.5-8*
Jesus said, 'If your leaders say to you, "Look, the kingdom is in the sky," then the birds of the sky will precede you. If they say to you, "It is in the sea," then the fish will precede you. Rather, the kingdom is within you and it is outside you. When you know yourselves, then you will be known, and you will understand that you are children of the living Father. But if you do not know yourselves, then you live in poverty, and you are the poverty.'	5 Moses writes concerning the righteousness that comes from the law, that 'the person who does these things will live by them.' 6 But the righteousness that comes from faith says, 'Do not say in your heart, "Who will ascend into heaven?"' (that is, to bring Christ down) 7 'or "Who will descend into the abyss?"' (That is, to bring Christ up from the dead). 8 But what does it say? 'The word is near you, on your lips and in your heart.'

17. For a helpful overview of recent scholarship on orality as it relates to biblical and early Christian studies, see Kelly R. Iverson, 'Orality and the Gospels: A Survey of Recent Research', *CBR* 8 (2009), pp. 71–106.

On the surface there does not seem to be much to commend the view that these two passages share a common heritage. The context associated with each saying is quite different as Paul is focused on justification (δικαιωσύνη) and its relationship to the Torah while *Thomas* is interested in expounding the nature of the kingdom. There are a few verbal similarities, but how far can they be pressed? A potentially illuminating observation is that both Paul and *Thomas* seem to be adapting or borrowing from a tradition influenced by Deut. 30.12-14.[18] Our analysis begins here.[19]

As far back as 1969, Peter Nagel sought to draw a connection between Rom. 10.5-8 and *Gos. Thom.* 3.[20] In an article simply titled 'Considerations on the *Gospel of Thomas*' ('Erwägungen zum Thomas-Evangelium'), Nagel began his discussion of this potential parallel by commenting on Paul's use of Lev. 18.5 and Deut. 30.12-14 in Rom. 10.5-8. He then noted similar terminology and themes in *Gos. Thom.* 3. Nagel identified four changes that Paul made in incorporating these texts into his argument: (1) Paul has replaced the Deuteronomic phrase 'between heaven and *beyond* the sea' with the dichotomy 'in heaven'/'*in* the abyss' (εἰς τὴν ἄβυσσον); (2) in Deuteronomy 30, attempting to obtain the command from heaven or beyond the sea is futile, while for Paul, these questions are refuted in light of the consequences that would result from them; (3) Paul adds the benefit that one is blessed through confession and belief, an element missing from Deuteronomy 30; and (4) Paul wants to connect 'confess' with the mouth and 'believe' with the heart.[21] Following these observations Nagel

18. It has not been uncommon for scholars to recognize a connection among *Gos. Thom.* 3, Romans 10, and material in Deuteronomy 30. For instance, the earliest English translation of the *Gospel of Thomas* (*The Gospel According to Thomas: Coptic Text Established and Translated* [trans. by A. Guillamont, H.-Ch. Puech, G. Quispel, W. Till and Yassah 'Abd Al Masih; Leiden: Brill, 1959], p. 59) contained a note suggesting the relationship of *Gos. Thom.* 3 to Deut. 30.11-14 and Rom. 10.6-8. Cf. also T. F. Glasson, 'The Gospel of Thomas, Saying 3, and Deuteronomy xxx 11-14', *ExpT* 78 (1967), pp. 151–52; and Richard Valantasis, *The Gospel of Thomas* (New Testament Readings; London: Routledge, 1997), pp. 58–59.

19. For purposes of comparison, the MT and LXX versions of Deut. 30.12-14 are provided here:

MT	LXX
12 לא בשמים הוא לאמר מי יעלה־לנו השמימה ויקחה לנו וישענו אתה ונעשנה ויקחם לנו 13 ולא־מעבר לים הוא לאמר מי יעבר־לנו אל־עבר הים וישמענו אתה ונעשנה 14 כי־קרוב אליך הדבר מאד בפיך ובלבבך לעשתו	12 οὐκ ἐν τῷ οὐρανῷ ἄνω ἐστὶν λέγων Τίς ἀναβήσεται ἡμῖν εἰς τὸν οὐρανὸν καὶ λή μψεται αὐτὴν ἡμῖν; καὶ ἀκούσαντες αὐτὴν ποιήσομεν.13 οὐδὲ πέραν τῆς θαλάσσης ἐστὶν λέγων Τίς διαπεράσει ἡμῖν εἰς τὸ πέραν τῆς θαλάσσης καὶ λήμψεται ἡμῖν αὐτήν; καὶ ἀκουστὴν ἡμῖν ποιήσει αὐτήν, καὶ ποιή σομεν. 14 ἔστιν σου ἐγγὺς τὸ ῥῆμα σφόδρα ἐν τῷ Στόματί σου καὶ ἐν τῇ καρδίᾳ σου καὶ ἐν ταῖς χερσίν σου αὐτὸ ποιεῖν.

20. P. Nagel, 'Erwägungen zum Thomas-Evangelium', in F. Altheim and R. Stiehl (eds), *Die Araber in der alten Welt*, vol. V, part 2 (Berlin: Walter de Gruyter, 1969), pp. 368–92.

21. Nagel, 'Erwägungen', pp. 368–9.

examines the similar use of Deuteronomy 30 in *Gos. Thom.* 3 and notes that certain elements peculiar to Paul's use of this OT tradition are also present in the *Thomas* logion.[22] Specifically, and most important, *Thomas* also changes Deuteronomy's '*beyond* the sea' to '*in* the sea' (the Coptic reads ⲥϩⲛ̄ ⲑⲁⲗⲁⲥⲥⲁ though the Greek Oxyrhynchus fragment reads 'of the sea', τῆς θαλά[σσης]). For Nagel, the presence of this change in both *Thomas* and Romans, and its absence in all other extant versions of the saying, means that Paul and *Thomas* are sharing a common tradition. He goes on to conclude that *Gos. Thom.* 3 is an older version of the saying, adding that the Thomasine text must have been in Paul's consciousness when he wrote his letter to the Romans.[23]

Similarly, Simon Gathercole recognizes the use of Deuteronomy 30 by Paul and *Thomas* and asks, '[D]oes *GThom* employ Deut in a reasonably direct way, or is *Deut* 30 mediated to *GThom* through a pre-existing interpretative tradition?'[24] Like Nagel, he observes that all of the pre-Pauline interpretations of Deut. 30.13 (including the LXX, Baruch and Philo) retain 'a contrast between "up in heaven" and "*across* the sea"', while Paul and *Thomas* both 'contrast the heaven above with what is *below*'.[25] The three examples from Deut. 30.13 (LXX), Philo (*De Posteritate Caini* 84-85), and Bar. 3.30 all read πέραν τῆς θαλάσσης, and this is where both Paul and *Thomas* depart. Gathercole writes:

> Paul calls it the 'abyss', and presumes that it is the region where the dead reside: it is the place from which you might at least imagine 'bringing Christ up from the dead'. Thomas calls it the region 'under the earth', where the fish are. These are the same place – not across the sea as in *Deut*, *Baruch* and Philo, but in the *tehom* under the earth, where people sleep with the fishes.[26]

Thus, it seems that both *Thomas* and Paul have changed not only the preposition but also the concept associated with location 'sea'. From this, Gathercole concludes, like Nagel before him, that this is likely an instance of shared tradition, though he argues that the direction of influence goes from Paul to *Thomas* and not the other way around as Nagel suggests.[27]

22. Ibid., p. 371.

23. Ibid., pp. 370–2. Nagel discusses some potential objections to the conclusion that Paul used *Thomas* (see especially p. 372), but defends his thesis against each one. For his part, Nagel is concerned to establish the thesis that the *Thomas* sayings tradition derived from an Aramaic tradition that found its way into Coptic without passing through a Greek intermediary.

24. Gathercole, 'Influence', p. 80.

25. Ibid., p. 81 (emphasis in original).

26. Ibid.

27. I am indebted to Dr Gathercole for pointing me to Nagel's article. During a brief conversation in New Orleans at the annual meeting of the Society of Biblical Literature (November 2009) he mentioned Nagel's essay, noting that he discovered it subsequent to his own research on the topic.

Two questions emerge from the foregoing discussion. First, the observations made by Nagel and Gathercole are compelling but are they enough to demonstrate that this is an instance where Paul and *Thomas* share a common tradition? And, if they are sharing a common tradition, is this enough to demonstrate the dependence of one document on another? To be sure, these conclusions are not as self-evident as one might hope. For his part Nagel seems confident, though Gathercole is less optimistic, giving the probability of his conclusion only a 'good sporting chance'.[28] Second, if there is a borrowing of tradition, who influenced whom? Once we answer the first question, the answer to the second question seems to follow quite naturally.

Even though the final forms of *Gos. Thom.* 3 and Rom. 10.5-8 are quite different, it is difficult to ignore their similar changes to Deuteronomy 30, especially in light of the other existing traditions that do not agree. When that agreement is taken into account, there are at least two points in support of the general conclusion that *Thomas* and Paul share material, and the specific conclusion that *Gos. Thom.* 3 is dependent upon Paul for the tradition.

First, Paul shows a remarkable knowledge of the OT throughout his letters, with the highest concentration of citations appearing in Romans.[29] Paul cites directly from Deuteronomy at least fifteen times in his writings and alludes to Deuteronomic themes throughout.[30] In his important book *Echoes of Scripture in the Letters of Paul*, Richard Hays has argued that Deuteronomy provides Paul with the salvation-historical schema that is appropriated in both Galatians and Romans; this includes God's election of a people, the subsequent rebellion of the people, God's judgement and, finally, God's deliverance of his people.[31] Significantly, Hays opens the book, and his entire discussion of 'the puzzle of Pauline hermeneutics', with a consideration of Rom. 10.6-8.[32] Both Paul's use and reworking of Deuteronomic traditions have been a source of significant discussion within Pauline studies. Likewise, James Scott has argued that Deuteronomy is crucial to Paul's thinking and theological formulations. Scott's analysis of Deuteronomic traditions in Paul's thought convincingly demonstrates that Paul appropriates the tradition in both his

28. Gathercole, 'Influence', p. 83.

29. James Scott ('Paul's Use of Deuteronomic Tradition', *JBL* 112 [1993], pp. 645) notes that 'among the uncontested letters of Paul, not only are the explicit citations [of the OT] confined to the *Hauptbriefe*, but fully half are found in Romans alone. And fully half of the OT quotations in Romans are found in chaps. 9-11'.

30. Dietrich-Alex Koch, *Die Schrift als Zeuge des Evangeliums: Untersuchungen zur Verwendung und zum Verständnis der Schrift bei Paulus* (Tübingen: Mohr-Siebeck, 1986), p. 33.

31. Richard B. Hays, *Echoes of Scripture in the Letters of Paul* (New Haven, CT: Yale University Press, 1989), pp. 163–64.

32. Ibid., p. 1.

early (e.g. 1 Thessalonians 2; Galatians 3) and later correspondences (e.g. Romans 9–11).[33]

Thomas's awareness of the OT is unremarkable by comparison and it is not at all clear that it shows independent knowledge of the Deuteronomic tradition.[34] It is therefore difficult to imagine a scenario in which *Thomas* is responsible for the changes to Deuteronomy 30 that are found in both Rom. 10.5-8 and *Gos. Thom.* 3. Given what we are able to know with some confidence about Paul and his relationship to Torah, it seems unlikely that the tradition originated with *Thomas* and *then* found its way to Paul.

A second and related point can be made by appealing to the principle of Occam's razor. If we conclude that Paul and *Thomas* are sharing a common tradition, we must not only ask who is influencing whom but also which scenario is more likely and which more problematic. Gathercole perceptively notes the problematic nature of positing Pauline dependence upon *Gos. Thom.* 3 when he writes:

> [T]o suppose that *GThom* influences Paul here would mean something like the following: *Deut* 30 made an impression on the author of *GThom* who then thoroughly re-worked Deut 30, changing much of the language and adapting the existing contrast to one which contrasted heaven and the abyss, perhaps for cosmological reasons. Then Paul, coming across a sayings tradition which included something like *GThom* 3 adopted the saying, *but then reintroduced some of the Deuteronomic elements which the sayings-tradition had dropped.* The economy of supposing Pauline influence on *GThom* means that one need not resort to elements being dropped and then later reintroduced.[35]

Constructing the argument in this way solves the greatest number of problems while raising the fewest questions, unlike the corollary, which would create a rather far-fetched and unlikely scenario. In light of these arguments, there is a very strong likelihood that *Thomas* made use of Rom. 10.5-8, though I do want to be careful here to recognize that we cannot know for certain that *Thomas* is relying upon a *written* text of Romans. *Thomas*'s use of this Pauline material may have been mediated through oral tradition, and this too may account for some of the differences we see in *Gos. Thom.* 3. It may, indeed, be the case that the Pauline form of the saying has been altered through oral delivery before reaching its final shape in *Thomas*. Nevertheless, it is safe to conclude that *Gos. Thom.* 3 provides us with our first example of Paul's influence upon

33. Scott, 'Deuteronomic Tradition', p. 647.

34. Several Thomasine logia appear to have been influenced by traditions that were informed or shaped by Deuteronomy. These include logia 23, 32, 53. However, none of these allusions amounts to *Thomas*'s direct or independent knowledge of Deuteronomy.

35. Gathercole, 'Influence', p. 83 (emphasis in original).

Thomas.[36] Although this influence is materially rather insignificant, it is important methodologically for establishing the likelihood of additional Pauline influences on *Thomas* that may be more important.

b. Gospel of Thomas *17 and 1 Corinthians 2.9*

Gospel of Thomas *17*	*1 Corinthians 2.9*
Jesus said, 'I will give you what no eye has seen, what no ear has heard, what no hand has touched, what has not arisen in the human heart.'	But, as it is written, 'What no eye has seen, nor ear heard, nor the human heart conceived, what God has prepared for those who love him.'

The similarities between 1 Cor. 2.9 and *Gos. Thom.* 17 are evident right away though questions about the sharing of tradition prove difficult to answer. To begin with, the proverb appears to draw upon elements of Isa. 52.15, 64.3-4 and/or 65.16, though no part of the saying represents a direct quotation of any OT passage.[37] In addition, this was clearly an important proverb in the early church as different versions appear in 1 Cor. 2.9, *Gos. Thom.* 17, *1 Clem.* 34.8, *2 Clem.* 11.7, *Dial. Sav.* 57, *Acts Thom.* 36, *Acts Pet.* 39, *Protrepticus* 10.94.4 and the Turfan Fragment M 789. Similarities are also present in 1 Jn 1.1, though the context and situation addressed by the Johannine epistles suggest its independence from the tradition shared by these other texts.[38] The widespread appeal of this proverb makes tracing its transmission history a complex task.

If we exclude 1 Jn 1.1, *Thomas* and Paul appear to represent the two earliest extant versions of this proverb.[39] Therefore, the first question to explore is, which version preceded the other? Scholars are split on this question. April DeConick includes *Gos. Thom.* 17 in her list of pre-Pauline *Thomas* sayings, arguing that it reflects the eschatological views of the earliest Thomasine

36. Interestingly, Uwe-Karsten Plisch (*The Gospel of Thomas: Original Text with Commentary* [Stuttgart: Deutsche Bibelgesellschaft, 2008], p. 44) argues that *Gos. Thom.* 3 'has a decisive parallel in Gal 4:7-9, where we also find the motifs of "children of God," "knowledge of God" . . . and "poverty"'.

37. Plisch (*The Gospel of Thomas*, pp. 72–3) comments that the source for this early Christian proverb is Isa. 52.15 and 64.3, while Gathercole ('Influence', pp. 88–9) suggests that the proverb conflates material from Isa. 64.3 and 65.16.

38. The Johannine epistles are addressing an incipient form of docetism that has caused a division in the associated faith community. This split, and the departed group's insistence that Jesus did not 'come in the flesh', together necessitate the author's use of eyewitness claims to have heard, seen and touched Jesus. For this reason, it seems unlikely that 1 John is borrowing from the same proverb used by Paul and *Thomas*.

39. Plisch (*The Gospel of Thomas*, p. 73) suggests that logion 17 'has its most obvious parallel in 1 John 1.1', but this is unlikely given the anti-docetic concerns of the author addressing the Johannine community.

Christians.[40] Patterson, who also regards logion 17 as pre-Pauline, offers the following unqualified assertion about Paul:

> [I]n 1 Corinthians 2 he uses the wisdom style of these opponents to compose his own 'wisdom speech' (2:6-16), only to correct their views with a few well-placed Pauline twists. Interestingly, in the midst of this speech *Paul quotes a saying from the Gospel of Thomas*. . . . The version of the saying quoted here by Paul is not paralleled word-for-word in Thomas, but reflects the sort of differences one would expect to have resulted from oral transmission.[41]

Not all scholars agree with Patterson's bold claim. Thinking along the lines of those who argue that the communities of John and *Thomas* were embroiled in a theological conflict, Plisch suggests that *Thomas* may have altered the saying in response to 1 Jn 1.1,[42] which would mean that the former's version is later than Paul's.[43] Gathercole argues that *Gos. Thom.* 17 has a number of secondary features, all of which indicate that it emerged later than Paul's version.[44]

Among the elements that suggest the *Thomas* logion emerged later than 1 Cor. 2.9 are the former's inclusion of 'hand' alongside eye, ear and heart, and the attribution of this saying to Jesus. First, Paul's version of the proverb refers to the eye not seeing, the ear not hearing and the heart not conceiving. *Thomas*'s version appears to add a reference to what the hand has not touched. This change would provide a fourfold structure and contribute to a greater sense of literary parallelism. Conversely, it would be difficult to explain why Paul would have omitted the phrase.

Second, as with the vast majority of its 114 sayings, *Thomas* attributes this saying to Jesus. It is also difficult to imagine Paul, who at times expends great energy in differentiating between his own words and those of the Lord,[45] altering a received tradition where Jesus was thought to be responsible for the saying. On the other hand, since nearly all of *Thomas*'s sayings begin with 'Jesus said' (ⲡⲉϫⲉ ⲓ̅ⲥ̅) or 'he said' (ⲡⲉϫⲁϥ), it is not a stretch to imagine that *Thomas* transformed a received tradition into a saying of Jesus to fit the content and structure of its other sayings. In addition, most of the later versions of the proverb preserve it as a saying of the Lord, while Paul does not. This is to

40. DeConick does not use the phrase 'pre-Pauline' but the implications of her discussion, as related to the present essay, are clear. See the related discussions in *Recovering*, pp. 97, 113, 118, 129.

41. Stephen J. Patterson, 'Paul and the Jesus Tradition: It is Time for Another Look', *HTR* 84 (1991), pp. 36–37 (emphasis added).

42. Plisch, *The Gospel of Thomas*, p. 73.

43. 1 John is generally dated to the last decade of the first century CE, while scholars believe 1 Corinthians was written around 54 CE, during Paul's third missionary journey.

44. Gathercole, 'Influence', p. 93.

45. See e.g. Paul's teaching on the virtue of marriage, remarriage, virginity and celibacy in 1 Corinthians 7.

say nothing of the fact that attributing the saying to Jesus would invest it with greater authority than it would otherwise wield in the diverse world of early Christianity.

All of this evidence suggests that *Gos. Thom.* 17 is later than 1 Cor. 2.9 but this is not the same as demonstrating its dependence upon Paul. So the question remains: Is there any evidence to suggest that *Thomas* incorporated and modified *Paul's* version of the proverb? In the case of *Gos. Thom.* 3 we argued for Pauline priority, in part, on the basis of Paul's use of Deuteronomic themes and language. We can mount a similar argument here by appealing to Paul's extensive use of Isaiah. Paul cites Isaiah twenty-eight times, more than any other OT book, and his reasons for choosing Isaiah are clear. Hays comments that

> Isaiah offers the clearest expression in the Old Testament of a universalistic, eschatological vision in which the restoration of Israel in Zion is accompanied by an ingathering of Gentiles to worship the Lord; that is why this book is statistically and substantively the most important scriptural source for Paul.[46]

In Isaiah, Paul finds support for his major theological concepts, not the least of which is his understanding of the eschatological inclusion of Jews and Gentiles in God's plan of universal redemption. While several logia in *Thomas* show some familiarity with traditions influenced by Isaiah, little if anything can be said for *Thomas*'s direct or independent knowledge of Isaiah.

As was the case with our consideration of Rom. 10.5-8 and *Gos. Thom.* 3, we must consider which scenario is more likely and which more problematic. Given the similar uses of the proverb by Paul and *Thomas*, it is much easier to account for the changes in *Gos. Thom.* 17 if we assert Pauline priority rather than vice versa. Though the saying consists of original material from Isaiah, it is also possible that this particular form of the proverb originated with Paul, who consistently shows himself to be a sophisticated and creative interpreter of OT traditions.[47] Even if that judgement turns out to be incorrect and the proverb does come to Paul from some pre-existing tradition, he was no doubt drawn

46. Hays, *Echoes*, p. 162.

47. A version of the proverb similar to Paul's appears in Pseudo-Philo's *Liber Antiquitatum Biblicarum* 26.13 ('And then will I take those and many other better than they are from where eye has not seen nor ear has heard and it has not entered into the heart of man, until the like should come to pass in the world'). Gathercole ('Influence', pp. 88–9) argues that the phrase came to Paul as an existing formula from pre-Christian Judaism. However, there is strong evidence that even though *LAB* contains some ancient traditions, the final form did not emerge until the end of the first century or later. Therefore, it is not outside the realm of possibility that Paul is the originator of the proverb and, given his extensive influence, it is conceivable that it found its way into *LAB* and *Thomas*. For more on dating Pseudo-Philo, see D. J. Harrington, 'Pseudo-Philo: A New Translation and Introduction', in James H. Charlesworth (ed.), *The Old Testament Pseudepigrapha* (New York: Doubleday, 1985), vol. 2, p. 299.

to this proverb because of his affinity for the theology of Isaiah. In addition to this, it is clear that both *Thomas* and Paul use the proverb in ways that are similar to one another but different from other existing versions.[48] There is more than enough evidence to conclude that those responsible for the composition of *Thomas* knew and used 1 Cor. 2.9. It is not necessary to suggest that the logion in question was altered through oral tradition because both versions share such strong similarities, but we will remain open to the suggestion that the logion came to *Thomas* orally. Thus, *Gos. Thom.* 17 also shows evidence of having used a Pauline text.

c. Gospel of Thomas *53 and Romans 2.25-29*

Gospel of Thomas *53*	*Romans 2.25-29*
His disciples said to him, 'Is circumcision useful or not?' He said to them, 'If it were useful, their father would produce children already circumcised from their mother. Rather, the true circumcision in spirit has become profitable in every respect.'	[25] Circumcision indeed is of value if you obey the law; but if you break the law, your circumcision has become uncircumcision.[26] So, if those who are uncircumcised keep the requirements of the law, will not their uncircumcision be regarded as circumcision?[27] Then those who are physically uncircumcised but keep the law will condemn you that have the written code and circumcision but break the law.[28] For a person is not a Jew who is one outwardly, nor is true circumcision something external and physical.[29] Rather, a person is a Jew who is one inwardly, and real circumcision is a matter of the heart – it is spiritual and not literal. Such a person receives praise not from others but from God.

With the present parallel, we are on the firmest footing yet in suggesting the presence of a shared tradition between *Thomas* and Paul. Anyone familiar with Paul's letters and his major theological emphases will immediately recognize the Pauline shape of *Gos. Thom.* 53. Given Paul's ongoing dispute with the Judaizing factions, it can reasonably be assumed that questions about the *value* of circumcision arose first in the ministry of Paul rather than the *Sitz im Leben* of the Thomasine community.[49] Issues such as circumcision, dietary laws, and

48. Gathercole comments that it is 'striking that Paul and *Gos. Thom.* use the formula in ways which are similar to each other, but not to their predecessors. . . . As a result, we might reasonably suppose that (given the secondary features evident in *Gos. Thom.*) Paul's interpretation of the formula has influenced Thomas's usage in this respect' ('Influence', p. 92).

49. Paul's experience with the so-called Judaizers is pictured at the Jerusalem Council in Acts 15, and

the relationship of the believer to the Law constitute significant considerations in Paul's letters. By contrast, the Jewish practice of circumcision is not a prominent concern for the Jesus tradition represented by the Synoptics, the Fourth Gospel or *Thomas*, and the 'the peculiar argument rejecting physical circumcision in the second sentence is quite unique and has no parallel in the New Testament or related Early Christian Literature'[50] – all of which suggests the secondary nature of *Gos. Thom.* 53.

Most commentators on *Thomas* draw a connection between Paul's discussion in Romans 2 and the disciples' question in logion 53, even if simply in a footnote. However, few state the obvious connection as clearly as Plisch when he comments that in 'the New Testament, the question of the value of circumcision is mainly *confronted and theologically mastered by Paul*', and that '*Thomas*'s similarity to Paul is quite close, almost verbatim'.[51] Likewise, Antti Marjanen comments that '*Thomas* proves to be part of that tradition in which the "circumcision of the heart" brought about by the Spirit is considered the prerequisite for hearing the word, awakening faith, faithful service of God, and putting off the body of flesh.'[52] He goes on to say that this tradition is represented chiefly by Paul in Rom. 2.25-29 and Phil. 3.3 (though he stops short of arguing that *Thomas* is relying directly upon Paul), and that it is unlikely that *Thomas*'s version represents the earliest stage of the 'circumcision of heart' tradition.[53] These scholars affirm the general impression that *Thomas*'s version appeared later than Paul's.

There are a number of striking similarities between these texts: (1) both passages are concerned with the nature and especially the *benefit* of 'circumcision', (2) each rejects physical circumcision to some degree in favour of a spiritual circumcision (*Thomas* speaks of 'circumcision in spirit' and Paul writes of 'circumcision of the heart'), (3) the question-answer format exists in both texts as Paul addresses an imaginary opponent in Romans 2 and Jesus addresses the direct question of his disciples in *Gos. Thom.* 53 and (4) there may be a faint connection, as Gathercole argues, between the language in Paul's comment about the benefits of circumcision in Rom. 3.2, ('much in every way', πολὺ κατὰ πάντα) and *Thomas*'s affirmation that circumcision is 'profitable in

is addressed directly in Galatians 2. There is also an allusion to Judaizing practices in Phil 3.2. In *Gos. Thom.* 53 is the third in a grouping of three sayings where the disciples question Jesus about beliefs and practices that have greater importance for proto-orthodox expressions of Christianity (viz. resurrection, prophets of Israel, circumcision).

50. Plisch, *The Gospel of Thomas*, p. 136 (emphasis added).

51. Ibid., pp. 135–6 (emphasis added).

52. Antti Marjanen, '*Thomas* and Jewish Religious Practices', in Risto Uro (ed.), *Thomas at the Crossroads: Essays on the Gospel of Thomas* (Studies of the New Testament and Its World; Edinbugh: T&T Clark, 1998), p. 179.

53. Ibid.

every respect (lit. 'has found absolute benefit', ⲁϥϭⲛ̄ ϩⲏⲩ ⲧⲏⲣϥ').[54] The connection between these two texts is strong and the case for Pauline influence is convincing.

As with the previous two parallels, it is difficult to imagine a plausible scenario in which the *Thomas* logion is earlier than Paul's version, and given the multiple similarities between the two, the most logical deduction is that *Gos. Thom.* 53 made use of a Pauline text.

d. *Flesh and spirit in* Thomas *and Paul*

There are a few places in both *Thomas* and Paul where the flesh/spirit (body/soul or external/internal) dichotomy appears. In at least three instances a plausible argument can be made for *Thomas*'s appropriation of Pauline language and imagery in a way that advances the argument that the authors of *Thomas* knew and modified Pauline formulations.

In *Gos. Thom.* 29 there is a reflection on how the 'great wealth' of the spirit has come to dwell in the 'poverty' of the human body. This is similar to Paul's concept of the spirit residing in fragile jars of clay (2 Cor. 4.7), though the link is admittedly weaker than the three parallels examined thus far. The two passages do not share a common vocabulary and evidence of editorial activity is missing. Still, the strong conceptual link exists and it may be that Paul has again influenced *Thomas*. There is not enough evidence to demonstrate that *Thomas* has used Paul (or vice versa), but in light of the conclusions offered earlier, I want to raise the suggestion in much the same way historical Jesus scholars use the 'criterion of coherence'. The criterion of coherence states that what coheres with other established historical material is also likely to be historical. In the same way, material that coheres with established Pauline influences on *Thomas* may constitute evidence of further Pauline influence. We have already seen that the authors of *Thomas* radically reshaped several Pauline texts and, in the case of Rom. 10.5-8, the final form in *Thomas* looks very different from the original Pauline form. Therefore, it is not outside the realm of possibility that this common theme found its way into *Thomas* through Pauline influence.

A second possible body/spirit parallel drawn from material in 2 Corinthians 4 is *Gos. Thom.* 70: 'Jesus said, "If you bring forth what is within you, that which you have will save you. If you do not have that within you, what you do not have within will kill you.' The imagery here may be related to 2 Cor. 4.16-18, where Paul utilizes the distinction between the external (ὁ ἔξω ἡμῶν ἄνθρωπος) and the internal (ὁ ἔσω ἡμῶν) to make his point. There he speaks of wasting away outwardly while being renewed inwardly. The inward/outward

54. Gathercole, 'Influence', p. 78.

distinction is similar here in both Paul and *Thomas* but the texts reach very different conclusions. Plisch sees a potential connection between these texts:

> Especially interesting in our context is 2 Cor 4:16-18, for, on the one hand the opposites there make clear what the inner self signifies, on the other, because it evidences how different the notion in *Gos. Thom.* 70 actually is. According to 2 Cor 4:16-18, the inner being – contrary to the exterior being – the part that shares in transcedence and eternity, is the core of the person.[55]

This parallel may represent another instance of *Thomas* borrowing Pauline language and imagery and using the material in a way different from Paul's original intent.

Finally, in Rom. 7.13-25, Paul writes at length about the war with sin going on inside his body as he longs for spiritual victory. In v. 24 he concludes the section with the woeful statement, 'Wretched (ταλαίπωρος) man that I am! Who will rescue me from the body (ἐκ τοῦ σώματαος) of this death?'[56] In *Gos. Thom.* 87 we read, 'Wretched (ΟΥΤⲀⲖⲀΙⲠⲰⲢΟΝ) is the body (ⲠⲤⲰⲘⲀ) that depends on a body (Ⲛ̄ΟΥⲤⲰⲘⲀ). And wretched (ΟΥΤⲀⲖⲀΙⲠⲰⲢΟⲤ) is the soul that depends on these two.' The shared vocabulary is undeniable and the contexts deal with similar reflections on the internal (soul/spirit) and the external (body). Again, there is not enough evidence here to constitute hard proof, but further investigation may show that *Thomas* was dependent upon Paul in ways we have not yet fully realized.

Space limitations preclude further discussions here, so this question will have to be investigated further in another venue or by another scholar. However, it does seem possible that several Thomasine texts that focus on the interior/exterior polarity drew from and changed Pauline texts. It is hoped that raising questions here about the possible connection between these texts will offer future prospects for further investigation of the Paul-*Thomas* relationship.

IV. *Theological ideas in Paul and* Thomas

Two questions with which this volume is concerned are, (1) 'What is the relationship between Paul and our earliest Christian Gospels', and (2) 'In what way(s), if any, are those Gospels reactions to Paul and his legacy?'

In answer to the first question, I have argued that there are at least three instances where *Thomas* is dependent upon Paul for traditions that are subsequently modified. There also appear to be other, less clearly identifiable instances of Pauline influence on the *Thomas*.

55. Plisch, *Gospel of Thomas*, p. 169.
56. Or possibly, 'This body of death'.

The second question is a little more difficult to answer. If *Thomas* made use of Pauline texts and/or traditions, it follows that substantive changes to the received materials support theological ideas different from those espoused by Paul. Some might be tempted to see a Paul-*Thomas* conflict or even an anti-Pauline polemic emerging from the *Thomas*, and while such a conclusion would certainly be convenient given recent scholarly trends, I do not think the evidence can be pressed that far.[57] However, *Thomas*'s altering of Pauline texts does raise questions that require further exploration.

In the case of *Gos. Thom.* 3 and its use of Rom. 10.5-8, what are we to make of *Thomas*'s nearly complete reworking of both the shape and the context of the Pauline version? In Romans 10, Paul's point is explicitly soteriological. The means of attaining salvation are understood quite differently in Paul and *Thomas*. For Paul, salvation is associated with a cluster of theological realities such as the sacrificial or representative death of Jesus,[58] faith in or the faith of Jesus[59] (depending on one's view on the πίστις χριστοῦ issue),[60] dying and

57. There is no question that both polemic and apologetic are present in most early Christian documents, and this has been recognized by scholars for some time. Both J. Louis Martyn (*History and Theology in the Fourth Gospel* [New York: Harper & Row, 1968]) and Raymond E. Brown (*Community of the Beloved Disciple* [Mahwah, NJ: Paulist, 1978]) pointed this out in their analyses of the Fourth Gospel's *Sitz im Leben*. Each helped to popularize the theory that the Fourth Gospel contains a 'two-level drama', reflecting the Johannine community's internal conflict (possibly with some form of incipient gnosticism) and external conflict (with the synagogue). They argued that the drama is specifically played out in John's polemic against οἱ Ἰουδαῖοι. This approach seemed to morph into a full-blown trend in gospels research in the years that followed. In 1971, Theodore Weeden introduced students of the NT to 'the heresy that necessitated the second gospel' (*Mark: Traditions in Conflict* [Minneapolis: Fortress, 1971]). According to his reading of Mark, the author had a serious theological axe to grind against the historical disciples who held to a flawed and incorrect *theios aner* (divine man) Christology. Thus, for Weeden, the Gospel of Mark contains an 'anti-disciple' polemic that the Markan Jesus continually corrects. This hypothesis led to a whole series of attempts to explain the so-called 'corrective christology' of Mark's Gospel. Today it is commonplace for some Johannine scholars to speak of John's 'anti-baptist' polemic, and there are a handful who argue that John contains an 'anti-Petrine' polemic (cf. Graydon Snyder, 'John 13:16 and the Anti-Petrinism of the Johannine Tradition', *BRev* 16 [1971], pp. 5–15; Arthur Maynard, 'The Role of Peter in the Fourth Gospel', *NTS* 30 [1984], pp. 531–48; and Arthur Droge, 'The Status of Peter in the Fourth Gospel: A Note on John 18:10–11', *JBL* 109 [1990], pp. 307–11), or an 'anti-Thomas' polemic (cf. the works of Gregory Riley, April DeConick and Elaine Pagels listed in Note 7). There has even been a recent attempt to elucidate the 'anti-Pauline' polemic of Matthew's Gospel (cf. David C. Sim, 'Matthew 7.21-23: Further Evidence of its Anti-Pauline Perspective', *NTS* 53 [2007], pp. 325–43). While attempts at persuasion and power are clearly present in early Christian documents, these polemics are simply not as common or as pervasive as these scholars would have us believe.

58. The texts illustrating this idea in Paul's writings are too numerous to cite here. Consider the following: 1 Cor. 15.3; Phil. 2.5-8; Rom. 3.25.

59. Cf. e.g. Rom. 3.22, 26; Gal. 2.16, 20; Phil. 3.9.

60. A seemingly inexhaustible amount of material has been written on this topic over the last three and a half decades and there seems to have been a resurgence of interest in the question in the last five years. Some of the early, important contributions to the discussion were made by Richard B. Hays, James D. G. Dunn and N. T. Wright, though virtually everyone with an interest in Pauline soteriology seems to have weighed in on the topic recently. For an up-to-date bibliography and recent considerations of the

rising with Christ,[61] and the efficacy of the resurrection as a precursor to what will come for all believers.[62] By contrast, *Thomas* states from the outset that eternal life can be attained by properly interpreting Jesus' teachings.[63] Absent from *Thomas* are discussions of Jesus' sacrificial death, participation in Christ, limitations on law observance for Gentiles and the sufficiency of faith as the response to the gospel. Instead, Thomasine soteriological sayings (e.g. 18b, 19c, 37, 111) focus on proper interpretation of the *logia Iesou*.[64] Therefore, it makes sense that when *Thomas* makes use of a Pauline soteriological text like Rom. 10.5-8, the material is altered in a way that will not contradict the former's understanding of soteriology and will help support another Thomasine view – in this case, the internal presence of the 'kingdom'.

In *Gos. Thom.* 17, the material from 1 Cor. 2.9 has not been altered as radically as that in Rom. 10.5-8. Nonetheless, *Thomas* modifies a Pauline instruction concerning wisdom that leads to maturity in Christ, into a rather abstract promise related to inheritance, and likely salvation. In its context, Paul's statement is about the sanctification of the Corinthian believers and how God has already begun a process believers can appropriate. The version of this saying in *Thomas* deals with salvation rather than sanctification. Paul has a developed understanding of progressive growth 'in Christ' while such an emphasis is largely absent from *Thomas*. For *Thomas*, knowledge and wisdom appear to be the path to every spiritual blessing.

Finally, both *Thomas* and Paul reject circumcision as being a source of salvific merit or status, but the former's rejection is more absolute than Paul's. In Rom. 2.25-29, Paul maintains that circumcision has some value since it springs from the religious traditions of the Jews. However, *Gos. Thom.* 53 rejects circumcision completely. The only circumcision that matters is 'circumcision in the spirit', which ultimately provides an absolute benefit. Thus, in typical Thomasine fashion, a great distance is put between *Thomas*'s theological agenda and anything that would have been of value to the Jews, whereas Paul continues to draw upon early Christianity's critical link to Judaism.

All of these observations seem to indicate that the authors of *Thomas* decided

question, see Michael F. Bird and Preston Sprinkle (eds), *The Faith of Jesus Christ: Exegetical, Biblical, and Theological Studies* (Peabody, MA: Hendrickson, 2010).

61. Cf. Romans 6.

62. Cf. e.g. the entire argument of 1 Corinthians 15; Rom. 6.4-6; Phil. 3.9-11; and probably 2 Cor. 5.1-10 (though the concept is never named explicitly).

63. In *Gos. Thom.* 1 we read, 'Whoever finds the interpretation of these sayings will not experience death.' A fair amount has been written on salvation in *Thomas*.

64. Koester (*Ancient Christian Gospels*, p. 115) comments that 'Thomas's hermeneutical procedure is evident. Not Jesus' words themselves but their interpretation gives life, that is, the finding of their hidden truth. This truth is hinted at by different pointers: the finding of Jesus (the Living One), the knowledge of the trees of paradise, the knowledge of one's beginnings.'

to pick and choose elements from Paul (as well as other early Christian traditions) in order to develop and support their theological views. In the end we can simply say that where the authors of *Thomas* used Pauline material they did so in a way that amounted to a rejection of Paul's original point. Even if, in some ways, *Thomas*'s use of Paul is a begrudging nod to the validity of something in Pauline thought, the reworking nevertheless constitutes some degree of rejection. This rejection of Paul's theological ideas appears to be a part of the warp and woof of Thomasine Christianity and its different developing theological perspectives.

V. *Concluding remarks*

In light of the foregoing considerations, it seems clear that at least some elements of *Thomas*'s theology developed later and on a much different trajectory than that of Paul.[65] When the authors of *Thomas* found a given Pauline term, phrase, image or discussion acceptable for use, they also invariably altered the received Pauline tradition to fit a uniquely Thomasine theological perspective. The authors of *Thomas* were familiar with certain Pauline ideas but ultimately rejected them as having any legitimacy for explaining the ongoing significance of identifying with Jesus through confession. Keeping these different presentations of Jesus in mind, I close by enumerating the conclusions of this study:

1. There are several discernible parallels in the writings of Paul and *Thomas*.
2. In each Paul-*Thomas* parallel, it can be demonstrated that the Thomasine version is later than Paul's version.
3. In each Paul-*Thomas* parallel, the Thomasine version shows dependence upon Paul, either directly or as an indirect result of oral transmission.
4. In each Paul-*Thomas* parallel, *Thomas* modifies the Pauline tradition to support a theological idea that is uniquely Thomasine and different from the idea represented by Paul.
5. Thus, the adaptation of Pauline traditions (or the characteristic use of Pauline language for *Thomasine* ends[66]) is evidence of *Thomas*'s rejection of (at least some) of Paul's theological ideas.[67]

65. Though I have not demonstrated it here, it is probably the case that nearly all of *Thomas*'s theological developments are later than Paul's.

66. Here I am modifying the phrase I borrowed earlier from Gathercole. See Note 5.

67. I do not believe that those responsible for *Thomas* had access to all of Paul's letters or ideas. However, a comparison of Paul and *Thomas* would show that the latter rejects a great many of Paul's ideas, even those ideas that were likely not available to its authors.

Appendix: Greek and Coptic texts of the Paul and the Gospel of Thomas texts discussed

#1

Romans 10.5-8 (NA27)	Gospel of Thomas *3* *(POxy 654, 9-21)*	Gospel of Thomas *3*
6 ἡ δὲ ἐκ πίστεως δικαιωσύνη οὕτως λέγει· μὴ εἴπῃς ἐν τῇ καρδίᾳ σου· τίς ἀναβήσεται εἰς τὸν οὐρανόν; τοῦτ᾽ ἔστιν Χριστόν καταγαγεῖν· 7 ἤ· τίς καταβήσεται εἰς τὴν ἄβυσσον; τοῦτ᾽ ἔστιν Χριστὸν ἐκ νεκρῶν ἀναγαγεῖν. 8 ἀλλα τί λέγει; ἐγγυς σου τὸ ῥῆμά ἐστιν ἐν τῷ στόματί σου καὶ ἐν τῇ καρδία σου, τοῦτ᾽ ἔστιν τὸ ῥῆμα τῆς πίστεως ὃ κηρύσσομεν.	(1) λέγει᾽ Ι[η(σοῦ)ς· ἐὰν] οἱ ἕλκοντες ἡμᾶς [εἴπωσιν ὑμῖν· ἰδοὺ] ἡ βασιλεία ἐν οὐραν[ῷ ὑμᾶς φθήσεται] τὰ πετεινὰ τοῦ οὐρ[ανοῦ· (2) ἐὰν δ᾽ εἴπωσιν ὅ]τι ὑπό τὴν γήν ἐστ[ιν, εἰσελεύσονται] οἱ ἰχθύες τῆς θαλά[σσης προφθάσαν]τες ὑμᾶς· (3) καὶ ἡ βασ[ιλεία τοῦ θεοῦ] ἐντὸς ὑμῶν [ἐσ]τι [κἀκτός. (4) ὃς ἂν ἑαυτὸν] γνῷ ταύτην εὑρή[σει, καὶ ὅτε ὑμεῖς] ἑαυτοὺς γνώσεσθα[ι, εἴσεσθε ὅτι υἱοί] ἐστε ὑμεῖς τοῦ πατρὸς τοῦ ζ[ῶντος· (5) εἰ δὲ μὴ] γνώσ<εσ>θε ἑαυτούς, ἐν [τῇ πτωχείᾳ ἐστε] καὶ ὑμεῖς ἐστε ἡ πτω[χεία].	(1) ⲠⲈϪⲈ Ⲓ̅Ⲥ̅ ϪⲈ ⲈⲨϢⲀϪⲞⲞⲤ ⲚⲎⲦⲚ̅ Ⲛ̅ϬⲒ ⲚⲈⲦ’ⲤⲰⲔ ϨⲎⲦ’ ⲦⲎⲨⲦⲚ̅ ϪⲈ ⲈⲒⲤϨⲎⲎⲦⲈ ⲈⲦ’ⲘⲚ̅ⲦⲈⲢⲞ ϨⲚ̅ ⲦⲠⲈ ⲈⲈⲒⲈ Ⲛ̅ϨⲀⲖⲎⲦ’ ⲚⲀⲢ̅ ϢⲞⲢⲠ’ ⲈⲢⲰⲦⲚ̅ Ⲛ̅ⲦⲈ ⲦⲠⲈ (2) ⲈⲨϢⲀⲚϪⲞⲞⲤ ⲚⲎⲦⲚ̅ ϪⲈ ⲤϨⲚ̅ ⲐⲀⲖⲀⲤⲤⲀ ⲈⲈⲒⲈ Ⲛ̅ⲦⲂⲦ’ ⲚⲀⲢ̅ ϢⲞⲢⲠ’ ⲈⲢⲰⲦⲚ̅ (3) ⲀⲖⲖⲀ ⲦⲘⲚ̅ⲦⲈⲢⲞ ⲤⲘ̅ⲠⲈⲦⲚ̅ϨⲞⲨⲚ’ ⲀⲨⲰ ⲤⲘ̅ⲠⲈⲦⲚ̅ⲂⲀⲖ’ (4) ϨⲞⲦⲀⲚ ⲈⲦⲈⲦⲚ̅ϢⲀⲚⲤⲞⲨⲰⲚ ⲦⲎⲨⲦⲚ̅ ⲦⲞⲦⲈ ⲤⲈⲚⲀⲤⲞⲨⲰⲚ ⲦⲎⲚⲈ ⲀⲨⲰ ⲦⲈⲦⲚⲀⲈⲒⲘⲈ ϪⲈ Ⲛ̅ⲦⲰⲦⲚ̅ ⲠⲈ Ⲛ̅ϢⲎⲢⲈ Ⲙ̅ⲠⲈⲒⲰⲦ’ ⲈⲦⲞⲚϨ (5) ⲈϢⲰⲠⲈ ΔⲈ ⲦⲈⲦⲚⲀⲤⲞⲨⲰⲚ ⲦⲎⲨⲦⲚ̅ ⲀⲚ ⲈⲈⲒⲈ ⲦⲈⲦⲚ̅ϢⲞⲞⲠ’ ϨⲚ̅ ⲞⲨⲘⲚ̅ⲦϨⲎⲔⲈ ⲀⲨⲰ Ⲛ̅ⲦⲰⲦⲚ̅ ⲠⲈ ⲦⲘ̅Ⲛ̅Ⲧ̅ϨⲎⲔⲈ

#2

1 Corinthians 2.9 (NA27)	Gospel of Thomas *17*
ἀλλὰ καθὼς γέγραπται· ἃ ὀφθαλμὸς οὐκ εἶδεν καὶ οὖς οὐκ ἤκουσεν καὶ ἐπὶ καρδίαν ἀνθρώπου οὐκ ἀνέβη, ἃ ἡτοίμασεν ὁ θεὸς τοῖς ἀγαπῶσιν αὐτόν.	ⲠⲈϪⲈ Ⲓ̅Ⲥ̅ ϪⲈ ϮⲚⲀϮ ⲚⲎⲦⲚ̅ Ⲙ̅ⲠⲈⲦⲈ Ⲙ̅ⲠⲈ ⲂⲀⲖ ⲚⲀⲨ ⲈⲢⲞϤ’ ⲀⲨⲰ ⲠⲈⲦⲈ Ⲙ̅ⲠⲈ ⲘⲀⲀϪⲈ ⲤⲞⲦⲘⲈϤ’ ⲀⲨⲰ ⲠⲈⲦⲈ Ⲙ̅ⲠⲈ ϬⲒϪ’ ϬⲘ̅ϬⲞⲘϤ’ ⲀⲨⲰ Ⲙ̅ⲠⲈϤ’ⲈⲒ ⲈϨⲢⲀⲒ̈ ϨⲒ ⲪⲎⲦ’ Ⲣ̅ⲢⲰⲘⲈ

#3

Romans 2.25-29 (NA27)	Gospel of Thomas *53*
2:25 Περιτομὴ μὲν γὰρ ὠφελεῖ ἐὰν νόμον πράσσῃς· ἐὰν δὲ παραβάτης νόμου ᾖς ἡ περιτομή σου ἀκροβυστία γέγονεν. 26 ἐὰν οὖν ἡ ἀκροβυστία τὰ δικαιώματα τοῦ νόμου φυλάσσῃ, οὐχ ἡ ἀκροβυστία αὐτοῦ εἰς περιτομὴν λογισθήσεται; 27 καὶ κρινεῖ ἡ ἐκ φύσεως ἀκροβυστία τὸν νόμον τελοῦσα σὲ τὸν διὰ γράμματος καὶ περιτομῆς παραβάτην νόμου. 28 οὐ γὰρ ὁ ἐν τῷ φανερῷ Ἰουδαῖός ἐστιν οὐδὲ ἡ ἐν τῷ φανερῷ ἐν σαρκὶ περιτομή, 29 ἀλλ' ὁ ἐν τῷ κρυπτῷ Ἰουδαῖος, καὶ περιτομὴ καρδίας ἐν πνεύματι οὐ γράμματι, οὗ ὁ ἔπαινος οὐκ ἐξ ἀνθρώπων ἀλλ' ἐκ τοῦ θεοῦ.	(1) ⲡⲉϫⲁⲩ ⲛⲁϥ ⲛ̄ϭⲓ ⲛⲉϥⲙⲁⲑⲏⲧⲏⲥ ϫⲉ ⲡⲥⲃ̄ⲃⲉ ⲣ̄ⲱⲫⲉⲗⲉⲓ ⲏ ⲙ̄ⲙⲟⲛ (2) ⲡⲉϫⲁϥ' ⲛⲁⲩ ϫⲉ ⲛⲉϥⲣ̄ⲱⲫⲉⲗⲉⲓ ⲛⲉⲡⲟⲩⲉⲓⲱⲧ' ⲛⲁϫⲡⲟⲟⲩ ⲉⲃⲟⲗ ϩⲛ̄ ⲧⲟⲩⲙⲁⲁⲩ ⲉⲩⲥⲃ̄ⲃⲏⲩ ⲁⲗⲗⲁ ⲡⲥⲃ̄ⲃⲉ ⲙ̄ⲙⲉ ϩⲙ̄ ⲡⲡ̄ⲛ̄ⲁ̄ ⲁϥϭⲛ̄ ϩⲏⲩ ⲧⲏⲣϥ'

#4

2 Corinthians 4.7 (NA27)	Gospel of Thomas *29 (POxy 1, 22)*	Gospel of Thomas *29*
ἔχομεν δὲ τὸν θησαυρὸν τοῦτον ἐν ὀστρακίνοις σκεύεσιν, ἵνα ἡ ὑπερβολὴ τῆς δυνάμεως ᾖ τοῦ θεοῦ καὶ μὴ ἐξ ἡμῶν.	. . . .ἐνοικ]εῖ [ταύτ]η [ν τ]ὴν πτωχεία(ν).	(1) ⲡⲉϫⲉ ⲓ̄ⲥ̄ ⲉϣϫⲉ ⲛ̄ⲧⲁ ⲧⲥⲁⲣⲝ' ϣⲱⲡⲉ ⲉⲧⲃⲉ ⲡ̄ⲛ̄ⲁ̄ ⲟⲩϣⲡⲏⲣⲉ ⲧⲉ (2) ⲉϣϫⲉ ⲡ̄ⲛ̄ⲁ̄ ⲇⲉ ⲉⲧⲃⲉ ⲡⲥⲱⲙⲁ ⲟⲩϣⲡⲏⲣⲉ ⲛ̄ϣⲡⲏⲣⲉ ⲡⲉ (3) ⲁⲗⲗⲁ ⲁⲛⲟⲕ' ϯⲣ̄ ϣⲡⲏⲣⲉ ⲙ̄ⲡⲁⲉⲓ ϫⲉ ⲡⲱⲥ ⲁⲧⲉⲉⲓⲛⲟϭ ⲙ̄ⲙⲛ̄ⲧⲣ̄ⲙ̄ⲙⲁⲟ ⲁⲥⲟⲩⲱϩ ϩⲛ̄ ⲧⲉⲉⲓⲙⲛ̄ⲧϩⲏⲕⲉ

#5

2 Corinthians 4.16-18 (NA27)	Gospel of Thomas *70*
16 Διὸ οὐκ ἐγκακοῦμεν, ἀλλ' εἰ καὶ ὁ ἔξω ἡμῶν ἄνθρωπος διαφθείρεται, ἀλλ' ὁ ἔσω ἡμῶν ἀνακαινοῦνται ἡμέρα καὶ ἡμέρα. 17 τὸ γὰρ παραυτίκα ἐλαφρὸν τῆς θλίψεως ἡμῶν καθ' ὑπερςολὴν εἰς ὑπερβολὴν αἰώνιον βάρος δόξης κατεργάζεται ἡμῖν, 18 μὴ σκοπύντων ἡμῶν τὰ βλεπόμενα ἀλλὰ τὰ μὴ βλεπόμενα. τὰ γὰρ βλεπόμενα πρόσκαιρα, τὰ δὲ μὴ βλεπόμενα αἰώνια.	(1) ⲡⲉϫⲉ ⲓ̄ⲥ̄ ϩⲟⲧⲁⲛ ⲉⲧⲉⲧⲛ̄ϣⲁϫⲡⲉ ⲡⲏ ϩⲛ̄ ⲧⲏⲩⲧⲛ̄ ⲡⲁ̈ⲓ ⲉⲧⲉⲩⲛ̄ⲧⲏⲧⲛ̄ϥ ϥⲛⲁⲧⲟⲩϫⲉ ⲧⲏⲩⲧⲛ̄ (2) ⲉϣⲱⲡⲉ ⲙⲛ̄ⲧⲏⲧⲛ̄ ⲡⲏ ϩⲛ̄ ⲧ[ⲏ]ⲩⲧⲛ̄ ⲡⲁⲉⲓ ⲉⲧⲉ ⲙⲛ̄ⲧⲏⲧⲛ̄ϥ ϩⲛ̄ ⲧⲏⲛⲉ ϥ[ⲛⲁ]ⲙⲟⲩⲧ' ⲧⲏⲛⲉ

#6

Romans 7.24 (NA27)	Gospel of Thomas *87*
ταλαίπωρος ἐγὼ ἄνθρωπος· τίς με ῥύσεται ἐκ τοῦ σώματος τοῦ θανάτου τούτου;	(1) ⲠⲈⲬⲀϤ Ⲛ̄ϬⲒ ⲒⲤ̅ ϪⲈ ⲞⲨⲦⲀⲖⲀⲒⲠⲰⲢⲞⲚ ⲠⲈ ⲠⲤⲰⲘⲀ ⲈⲦⲀϢⲈ Ⲛ̄ⲞⲨⲤⲰⲘⲀ' (2) ⲀⲨⲰ ⲞⲨⲦⲀⲖⲀⲒⲠⲰⲢⲞⲤ ⲦⲈ Ⲧ'ⲮⲨⲬⲎ ⲈⲦⲀϢⲈ Ⲛ̄ⲚⲀⲈⲒ Ⲙ̄ⲠⲤⲚⲀⲨ

10

Death and the Human Predicament, Salvation as Transformation, and Bodily Practices in 1 Corinthians and the *Gospel of Thomas*

Joshua W. Jipp

I. *Introduction*

An examination of the relationship between Paul's letters and the *Gospel of Thomas* can be approached in at least two ways. One might, as Simon Gathercole has done recently, focus on the linguistic similarities between the two as a means of discerning whether one text has influenced the other.[1] The value of this approach is that it has the potential to establish secure data as to whether one text had knowledge of the other. In this case, however, the results are necessarily limited as one can make a *plausible*, but by no means certain, argument for Pauline influence on *Thomas* in sayings 53 (Rom. 2.25–3.2), 17 (1 Cor. 2.9) and 3 (Rom. 10.7).[2]

Alternatively, one might take a theme or a cluster of concepts that Paul and *Thomas* share and examine it for commonalities, differences and shared religious backgrounds. Gathercole distances himself from this approach claiming that these types of studies 'have tended to focus, if that is the right word,

1. Simon Gathercole, 'The Influence of Paul on the *Gospel of Thomas* (§§53.3 and 17)', in *Das Thomasevangelium: Entstehung – Rezeption – Theologie* (eds Jörg Frey, Enno Edzard Popkes and Jens Schröter; BZNW 157; Berlin: Walter de Gruyter, 2008), pp. 72–93.

2. Saying 53 appears to me be the most plausible candidate for dependence upon Paul but the plethora of other early Christian sayings on circumcision (e.g. Justin, *Dial.* 19.3; *Odes of Solomon* 11.1-3; Col. 2.11-13), some of which are surely no longer extant, that *may have* influenced *Thomas* makes even this claim seriously suspect. With respect to saying 17 and 1 Cor. 2.9, it is again certainly possible that one writing has influenced the other directly. But that *Thomas* may have received this pithy maxim orally, or that it was mediated through another literary source (whether Isa. 64.3; 65.16; *Pseudo-Philo* 26.13; or some source no longer extant) is certainly not beyond the realm of possibility. Further, in order for Gathercole's ('The Influence of Paul on the *Gospel of Thomas* (§§53.3 and 17)', p. 94) emphatic claim that scholarship must now reckon with Pauline influence on *Thomas* to stand, it needs to be demonstrated why and for what purpose *Thomas* would cite small snippets of Pauline text.

on general atmospherics'.[3] It is hard to disagree with this assessment given the general comparisons between Paul and *Thomas* proffered by some fine scholars.

Stevan Davies, for example, impressed with the common ideas of 'image of God' (2 Cor. 4.4) and a 'second Adam from heaven' (1 Cor. 15.45-59), notes that *Thomas* has a 'view of Christian transformation not terribly different from the Pauline view'.[4] For Davies, both Paul and *Thomas* are in agreement that humans can replace the Adamic condition of Genesis 2 with the pristine image of God described in Genesis 1.[5] With respect to ethics and rituals, Davies remarks that both Paul and *Thomas* reject the 'necessity of religious obligations' if one has the Spirit.[6]

Likewise, Stephen Patterson is reminded of Paul when commenting upon the concept of the image of God in *Thomas* and thinks that 'the Pauline tradition' expressed in 1 Corinthians 15 and Col. 3.10-11 'is the world in which those various sayings in *Gos. Thom* that speak of 'the image' . . . are to be understood'.[7] Elaine Pagels suggests that *Thomas* and Paul are indebted to a common exegesis of Genesis, an exegesis that emphasizes transformation, specifically the reclamation of an androgynous unity of the sexes.[8] In an article that argues saying 7 is an allegorical depiction of the resurrection of the dead, Andrew Crislip suggests that *Thomas* evokes a resurrection discourse similar to 1 Corinthians 15.[9] And Risto Uro claims that, like Paul, '*Thomas* can . . . conceptualize future salvation in terms of bodily existence' and that saying 22 is 'a Thomasine version of the Christian resurrection belief'.[10] April DeConick has made an argument for the view that *Thomas* and Paul have been influenced by Jewish mysticism.[11]

3. Gathercole, 'The Influence of Paul on the *Gospel of Thomas* (§§53.3 and 17)', p. 74.

4. Stevan Davies, 'The Christology and Protology of the *Gospel of Thomas*', *JBL* 111 (1992) pp. 663–682, here p. 668.

5. Davies, 'The Christology and Protology of the *Gospel of Thomas*', p. 669.

6. Davies, 'The Christology and Protology of the *Gospel of Thomas*', p. 677.

7. Stephen J. Patterson, 'Jesus Meets Plato: The Theology of the *Gospel of Thomas* and Middle Platonism', in *Das Thomasevangelium: Entstehung – Rezeption – Theologie* (eds Jörg Frey, Enno Edzard Popkes and Jens Schröter; BZNW 157; Berlin: Walter de Gruyter, 2008), pp. 181–205, here p. 193.

8. Elaine H. Pagels, 'Exegesis of Genesis 1 in the Gospels of Thomas and John', *JBL* 118 (1999), pp. 477–496, here p. 479.

9. Andrew Crislip, 'Lion and Human in *Gospel of Thomas* Logion 7', *JBL* 126 (2007) pp. 595–613, here pp. 607–608.

10. Risto Uro, Thomas: *Seeking the Historical Context of the Gospel of Thomas* (London/New York: T&T Clark, 2003), pp. 75–76.

11. e.g. April D. DeConick, *Seek to See Him: Ascent and Vision Mysticism in the Gospel of Thomas* (SVG 33; Leiden: Brill, 1996). Stephen J. Patterson notes that these commonalities include emphases on the image of God, light, glory, the concept of ascent, and soteriological transformation. See his essay 'The *Gospel of Thomas* and Christian Beginnings', in *Thomasine Traditions in Antiquity: The Social and Cultural World of the Gospel of Thomas* (eds Jon Ma. Asgeirsson, April D. DeConick and Risto Uro; NHMS 59; Leiden: Brill, 2006), pp. 1–17, here pp. 10–16.

While Gathercole is right that these, mostly offhanded, scholarly suggestions regarding the similarity between Paul and *Thomas* tend to relate to the most general of similarities, these scholars have highlighted some impressive commonalities that call for a more nuanced comparison. For example, both Paul and *Thomas*: (a) emphasize death as a fundamental human predicament and (b) thereby construct a soteriology that centres upon a transformation that overcomes death – in dialogue with elements of Genesis 1–3, which (c) has direct implications for bodily practices. In this study, I propose to examine the relationship between *Thomas* and Paul, particularly 1 Corinthians, where these themes are articulated the clearest, not as a means for discerning any direct influence (of which I am sceptical), but rather with the hope that the comparison may refine some of our comparisons between Pauline and Thomasine Christianity as well as help us see their own particular contributions to early Christianity.[12]

Engaging in a comparative study of all 114 sayings of *Thomas*'s Jesus with the entire Pauline corpus is beyond the scope of this study, and so in lieu of the fact that scholars most frequently draw comparisons between Paul and *Thomas* at the level of such themes as transformation, 'image' and 'light', and construals of Genesis 1–3, this study will use 1 Corinthians as the Pauline comparison text. Further, the goal of comparison is not the identification of every motif or tradition that Paul and *Thomas* share. Rather, I am interested in discovering *how* Paul and *Thomas* employ similar motifs for their own ends. Additionally, while the compositional unity of *Thomas* is an outstanding question,[13] this essay will treat it as a complete text given that it would have been read as a complete collection of sayings.[14]

II. *Death and the human predicament*

a. Gospel of Thomas

Thomas asks his readers to search out the sayings of 'the living Jesus' so that s/he will 'not taste death' (saying 1). Salvation has as its goal the transcendence of death through interpretation of Jesus' words. One of the most striking

12. I agree with Stephen Patterson ('The *Gospel of Thomas* and Christian Beginnings', p. 16) that 'understanding *Thomas* in itself, as part of the diversity of Early Christianity, will help us to see and understand aspects of other, better known ways of being "Christian" that we had not noticed before'.

13. e.g. DeConick's suggestion of a 'rolling corpus' of orally based sayings collecting over time: *Seek to See Him: Ascent and Vision Mysticism in the Gospel of Thomas* (VCSup, 33; Leiden: Brill, 1996); idem, 'The Original Gospel of Thomas', *VC* 56 (2002), pp. 167–199. For a sage evaluation of DeConick on this point, see Nicholad Perrin, *Thomas, the Other Gospel* (London: SPCK, 2007), pp. 52–69.

14. See Richard Valantasis, *The Gospel of Thomas* (NTR; London/New York; Routledge, 1997) p. 26; also, see Risto Uro, 'The Social World of the *Gospel of Thomas*', in *Thomasine Traditions in Antiquity*, pp. 19–38.

aspects of *Thomas* is its pessimistic portrait of the world and its association of the body and the world with death: 'He who has known the world (ⲡⲕⲟⲥⲙⲟⲥ) has found a corpse (ⲉⲩⲡⲧⲱⲙⲁ); and he who has found a corpse (ⲁⲡⲧⲱⲙⲁ), the world (ⲡⲕⲟⲥⲙⲟⲥ) is not worthy of him' (saying 56).[15] In saying 87 Jesus pronounces a woe upon 'the body which depends upon the body'. That is, the person implicated in the common affairs of the world is dead, while conversely the one who understands that this world is a corpse has transcended death. There is, then, an intense conflict between the empirical world and the new world that Jesus seeks to reveal to the seekers.[16]

Saying 21 makes it clear that the relationship between Jesus' disciples and the world is adversarial as the disciples are compared to those who 'have settled in a field which does not belong to them' and are commanded to be 'watchful over against the world'. Likewise, in saying 80 Jesus says that '[h]e who has known the world has found the body; and he who has found the body, the world is not worthy of him.' The human body is implicated in the corpse-like nature of the world.[17] In saying 29 Jesus claims: 'If the flesh (ⲧⲥⲁⲣⲝ) came into existence because of the spirit, it is a marvel. But if the spirit came into existence because of the body (ⲡⲥⲱⲙⲁ), it is a marvel of marvels. But as for me, I wonder how this great wealth made its home in this poverty.'[18] Flesh and body are associated with 'poverty', and it is wondrous that 'the spirit', that is 'this great wealth', can be united with the body (saying 112).[19]

Humanity's problem is at least twofold. First, something tragic has happened to humanity that has resulted in the division of the original 'image of God' into gendered humanity. Davies and Pagels have demonstrated that *Thomas* shares the Hellenistic-Jewish understanding of creation whereby Genesis 1 refers to God's original creation where God creates a singular androgynous humanity in his own image (Gen. 1.26-27), which precedes the tragic division and separation of humanity into male and female narrated in Genesis 2.[20] *Thomas* reflects

15. I am using Beate Blatz, 'The Coptic Gospel of Thomas', in *New Testament Apocrypha: Volume One: Gospels and Related Writings* (ed. Wilhelm Schneemelcher; Louisville: Westminster John Knox, 2003).

16. See Valantasis, *The Gospel of Thomas*, p. 133.

17. On the near equivalence between 'body' and 'world', see Philip Sellew, 'Death, the Body, and the World in the Gospel of Thomas', in *Studia Patristica XXXI: Papers Presented at the Twelfth International Conference on Patristic Studies held in Oxford 1995* (ed. E. A. Livingstone; Leuven: Peeters, 1997), pp. 530–534.

18. Antti Marjanen ('Is *Thomas* a Gnostic Gospel?', in *Thomas at the Crossroads: Essays on the Gospel of Thomas* [ed. Risto Uro; SNTW; Edinburgh; T&T Clark, 1998]) demonstrates that this aspect of *Thomas* is not uniquely Gnostic and can be found in non-Gnostic texts.

19. Stephen Patterson ('Jesus meets Plato', pp. 189–190) suggests that behind these seemingly dualistic body/spirit sayings may lie an exegetical tradition similar to Philo's interpretation of Gen. 2.7 wherein God breathes the divine spirit into the corporeal and mortal physical body, thus giving rise to a devaluation of the latter.

20. Davies, 'The Christology and Protology of the *Gospel of Thomas*', *JBL* 111 (1992), pp. 663–682; Elaine H. Pagels, 'Exegesis of Genesis 1 in the Gospels of Thomas and John', *JBL* 118 (1999), pp. 477–496.

this notion that the creation of humanity has occurred in two stages: first, singular asexual humanity in the image of God; second, the division into male and female.[21] Humanity's division into gendered persons and its separation from its divine 'image' are for *Thomas* depictions of unenlightened humanity's state of death. Numerous sayings make this clear.[22] Upon seeing some infants being suckled, Jesus tells his disciples that 'these infants being suckled are like those who enter the kingdom' (saying 22). *Thomas*'s Jesus views the infants as innocent asexual beings and temporally closer to their true origin.[23] Jesus makes this clear in his saying on the reunification of the opposites, where entering the kingdom will take place when 'you make the two one . . . and when you make the male and the female into a single one, so that the male is not male and the female is not female' (saying 22).[24] Similarly, in saying 4 Jesus says that a child of seven days is best prepared to tell his disciples 'about the place of life'. Jesus' saying to Peter that he will 'make [Mary] male in order that she too may become a living spirit' should be understood as referring to her return to this primordial human of Gen. 1.26-27 (saying 114).[25] In saying 18 it is the one who 'shall stand at the beginning' who will 'not taste death'. These metaphors of finding the place of life, becoming a living spirit, standing at the beginning, and entering the kingdom refer to humanity's transcendence of death through a return to its original asexual solitary state. Thus, humanity's predicament is that it exists in a state of death so long as it is alienated from its asexual solitary image-bearing existence.

Second, humanity is epistemologically alienated from its true 'image' and its origin from the 'light'. This light is located within humanity, but humans remain unaware of it: 'There is light within a man of light, and he lights the whole world. If he does not shine, there is darkness' (saying 24). But the empirical world blinds humans to this internal light. Jesus claims that when he appeared to them he found them 'all drunk' and 'none among them thirsting' as they are 'blind in their heart for they do not see that they came empty into the

21. See Pagels, 'Exegesis of Genesis 1 in the Gospels of Thomas and John', p. 482.

22. On the myth of a return to androgynous existence, see Dennis Ronald MacDonald, *There is No Male and Female: The Fate of a Dominical Saying in Paul and Gnosticism* (HDR 20; Philadelphia: Fortress Press, 1987); Wayne Meeks, 'The Image of the Androgyne: Some Uses of a Symbol in Earliest Christianity', *HR* 13 (1974), pp. 165–208.

23. There are other sayings in *Thomas* which use infants as symbolizations of those who have returned to their androgynous origins. On this theme, see Howard C. Kee, '"Becoming a Child" in the Gospel of Thomas', *JBL* 82 (1963), pp. 307–314; A. F. J. Klijn, 'The "Single One" in the Gospel of Thomas', *JBL* 81 (1962), pp. 271–278.

24. April D. DeConick, *The Original Gospel of Thomas in Translation: With a Commentary and New English Translation of the Complete Gospel* (LNTS 287; London/New York: T&T Clark, 2006, pp. 116–118), has a list of parallels to this text.

25. See Marvin Meyer, 'Making Mary Male: The Categories of "Male" and "Female" in the Gospel of Thomas', *NTS* 31 (1985), pp. 554–570.

world' (saying 28). *Thomas* characterizes this problem as an epistemological failure. In saying 3 Jesus tells his disciples that if they look for the kingdom in the heaven or in the sea they will be misled, for 'the kingdom is within you and it is outside of you. When you know yourselves, then you will be known, and you will know that you are the sons of the living father'. The one who has knowledge of all 'but fails to know himself misses everything' (saying 67). These sayings contain the sentiment that the empirical world is not the locus for God's saving revelation. Rather, for *Thomas* there is something 'within' humanity that must be known for salvation.

b. *Paul in 1 Corinthians*

One could not ask for a clearer description of the human predicament than what Paul provides in 1 Cor. 15.20-58, for here he not only explicitly refers to Death as the 'last enemy' (15.26) but also he concludes his discussion of the resurrection with a poetic gloat against Death's future defeat (15.54-56). Paul gets at this human predicament through his own messianic rereading of Genesis 1–3.[26] In one simple phrase Paul both sets the blame at the feet of Adam and interprets humanity's resulting predicament in terms of death: 'through a human – Death' (δι' ἀνθρώπου θάνατος, 15.21a). All of humanity participates in Adam and his destiny: 'in Adam all die' (ἐν τῷ Ἀδὰμ πάντες ἀποθνῄσκουσιν, 15.22a). The greatest enemy of humanity is Death: 'the last enemy which is being abolished is Death' (ἔσχατος ἐχθρὸς καταργεῖται ὁ θάνατος, 15.26). Paul's use of the definite article personifies 'Death' and justifies the claim that it is the cosmic enemy of God's people.[27] This reference to Death in 15.26 calls the reader back to Adam as the one through whom death attained its dominion (15.21-22).[28]

Though he is not mentioned, one can see the story of Adam's failure as the subtext behind the description of the Messiah's defeat of Death throughout 15.24-27. As confirmation that Death will be defeated Paul adduces Ps. 8.7, a text which reflects upon God's original intent for Adam and humanity – 'for he has subjected all things under his feet' (15.27a). Psalm 8, like Gen, 1.26-28, is

26. N. T. Wright, *The Resurrection of the Son of God* (Minneapolis: Fortress Press, 2003), p. 334, states: 'The stories of creation and fall, as told in Genesis 1.26–8 and 3.17–19, lie below the surface throughout, and the later parts of the chapter will allude frequently to the same passages.' And David M. Hay, *Glory at the Right Hand: Psalm 110 in Early Christianity* (SBLMS; Scholars Press, 1973), p. 60, suggests that behind 1 Cor. 15.20-58 lies 'congeries of Adamic speculation'.

27. Martinus C. de Boer, *The Defeat of Death: Paul's Apocalyptic Eschatology in 1 Corinthians 15 and Romans 5* (JSNTSup 22; Sheffield: Sheffield Academic Press, 1988), p. 47; J. Christiaan Beker, *Paul the Apostle: The Triumph of God in Life and Thought* (Philadelphia: Fortress Press, 1980), p. 221–234.

28. Richard B. Hays, *First Corinthians* (Louisville: John Knox, 1997), p. 263, argues that 'the manner of Paul's allusion shows that he expects his readers to know the story of Genesis 1 – 3 already. Presumably he had taught it to them during his time in Corinth.'

a description of God's creation of humanity in his own image for the purpose of subduing the earth.[29] Adam, created in God's image, was the agent entrusted with the task of subduing God's creation and ruling righteously over it. Paul assumes a narrative of Adam's failure to fulfil his God-given mandate, a failure that has brought corruption to the earth, the intrusion of inimical powers set against God's creation (15.24) and ultimately Death.[30]

Again, it needs to be emphasized that Paul views humanity's destiny as contained in this figure Adam. We have seen this in 1 Cor. 15.21-22, and it is also mentioned in 15.49 where Paul, speaking of Adam, claims that 'we have worn the image of the earthy one' (ἐφορέσαμεν τὴν εἰκόνα τοῦ χοϊκοῦ). The verb φορέω carries metaphorical connotations of 'wearing' or 'putting on' – often clothing.[31] Thus Adam, as a 'living soul' (Gen. 2.7; 1 Cor. 15.45), and thereby the rest of humanity, is made up of earth and dust and is thereby subject to decay, deterioration and ultimately death. And as Adam died and returned to the dust (Gen. 3.19), so shall the rest of humanity follow his destiny. As Paul says in 15.48b, 'As was the man of earth/dust, so are those who are of the earth/dust' (οἷος ὁ χοϊκός, τοιοῦτοι καὶ οἱ χοϊκοι καὶ οἷος).[32]

It is evident that Paul assumes a particular reading of the Adam narrative in Genesis 1–3 as one of the foundations for his interpretation of the human predicament. God created Adam in his own image, as the corporate representative of humanity, and commissioned him with the task of subduing and obtaining dominion over creation. Adam failed in this task and thereby God's intent for creation was corrupted. Through his failure hostile forces arrayed against humanity entered into creation – the greatest of these being Death. As Adam was composed of the earth and returned to dust, so all who are 'in Adam' (15.22) and have borne 'the image of the earthy one' will die and return to dust. Perhaps most striking about Paul's discussion of humanity and death is his insistence that humanity is entirely embedded within creation. There is no privileging here of some 'more real' or 'more interior' part of the person such as 'the mind' or 'the soul'. While humanity, as created by God out of earth, bears continuity with the rest of creation, Paul also views it as having been set apart from the rest of creation by God and granted a mission to subdue the earth with God's presence (Gen. 1.26-28; Ps. 8.5-7; 1 Cor. 15.25-27).

29. Wright, *The Resurrection of the Son of God*, pp. 334–336.

30. On the figure of Adam as well as the narrative of God and creation in Romans, see Edward Adams, 'Paul's Story of God and Creation: The Story of How God Fulfils His Purposes in Creation', in *Narrative Dynamics in Paul: A Critical Assessment* (ed. Bruce W. Longenecker; Louisville: Westminster John Knox Press, 2002), pp. 19–43.

31. See Gordon D. Fee, *The First Epistle to the Corinthians* (NICNT; Grand Rapids: Eerdmans, 1987), p. 794 n. 34.

32. See Anthony C. Thiselton, *The First Epistle to the Corinthians* (NIGTC; Grand Rapids: Eerdmans, 2000), pp. 1289–1290.

c. *Similarities and differences between* Thomas *and Paul*

Both *Thomas* and Paul use the concept of 'death' as a descriptor for humanity's fundamental human predicament, and therefore the way in which they construct human salvation corresponds to the problem of death. But Paul is much more of a literalist than *Thomas* in this area. Death is humanity's great enemy precisely because it impedes its ability to subdue creation as God's royal representatives. Death further ruptures humanity's relationship to the life-giving God as the body decays and returns to earth and dust. Paul has a strong world and body-affirming theology. The problem is that the body, and creation along with it, grows old and goes out of existence. *Thomas* does not speak of death quite so literally. To talk of bodies and flesh is, for *Thomas*, to talk of corpses and dead stuff. The world and the human body are entangled with death. Further, humanity exists in a state of death now insofar as it is separated from its original 'image'. Humans remain in this state of death so long as they fail to seek and find their original image (Gen. 1.26-27) that was created in the light (Gen. 1.3).

III. *Salvation as transformation*

a. Gospel of Thomas

If *Thomas* views the world and the body as a corpse-like place and humanity as lacking knowledge, divided and removed from its 'image', then how does it construct salvation from this death-like existence? In this section we will see that *Thomas* conceives of human salvation as a protological transformation of the self.[33] This transformation is referred to as a return to 'the light', as a transformation to genderless existence, and as a reunification with one's image.

In saying 18 the disciples ask Jesus: 'Tell us how our end will be.' The 'our' indicates that they are concerned with the question of their own death, hence Jesus' claim that those who heed his answer 'will not taste death'.[34] The disciples' question is similar to the one in Mt. 24.3 where they ask: 'When will these things be and what shall be the sign of the coming and the end of the age?' It is illuminating to note the contrast between Jesus' answers. Whereas in the Synoptics he gives a lengthy discourse concerning future events, in *Thomas* Jesus turns the disciples' attention away from eschatological thinking and redirects it to 'the beginning', which is the place of 'the end'.[35] In other words, knowledge of 'the end' or 'the goal' is attained when one understands

33. I have learned much here from: Davies, 'The Christology and Protology of the *Gospel of Thomas*', pp. 663–682; Pagels, 'Exegesis of Genesis 1 in the Gospels of Thomas and John', pp. 477–496.

34. So Valantasis, *The Gospel of Thomas*, p. 86.

35. Stevan Davies, 'The Christology and the Protology of the *Gospel of Thomas*', pp. 663–682, argues that *Thomas* consistently portrays the kingdom of God protologically and not eschatologically.

and returns to the primordial condition. Jesus' encouragement 'to discover' and 'seek' this place of beginnings indicates, like saying 1, that *Thomas* envisions authentic human existence as a process of transformation through interpretation of Jesus' sayings. That *Thomas* conceives of humanity's transcendence of death as a return to the primordial condition is indicated in saying 19, where Jesus blesses the one who returns to the place of Paradise. The one who attains knowledge of the five trees of Paradise 'will not taste death'.[36] In this saying Jesus pronounces a blessing upon the one 'who was before he came into being'. This blessing indicates that the beginning is actually a return to a time before Genesis 1 and the creation of the material world. Humanity, therefore, has open to it two planes of existence – current existence in the corpse-like world or a temporally prior pre-existent state that is connected to paradise and the transcendence of death.[37]

Sayings 83-85 also envision salvation as a return to one's pre-existent origins:

> 83. Jesus said: The images (ⲚϨⲒⲔⲰⲚ) are revealed to man, and the light (ⲠⲞⲨⲞⲈⲒⲚ) which is in them is hidden in the image of the light of the Father (ⲐⲒⲔⲰⲚ Ⲙ̄ⲠⲞⲨⲞⲈⲒⲚ Ⲙ̄ⲠⲈⲒⲰⲦ). He will reveal himself, and his image is hidden by his light (ⲠⲈϤⲞⲨⲞⲈⲒⲚ). 84. Jesus said: When you see your likeness (ⲈⲠⲈⲦⲚ̄ⲈⲒⲚⲈ), you rejoice. But when you see your images (ⲀⲚⲈⲦⲚ̄ϨⲒⲔⲰⲚ) which came into existence before you, which neither die nor are made manifest, how much will you bear? 85. Adam came into being out of a great power and a great wealth, and he was not worthy of you; for if he had been worthy, [he would] not [have tasted] death.

The sayings are notoriously difficult, but we can draw a few conclusions.[38] First, in conversation with interpretations of Gen. 1.26-28, *Thomas* presents a distinction between humanity's 'likeness' and its 'image'. Whereas the disciples experience the pleasant experience of seeing their own 'likeness', it is the 'images' that have a prior level of existence as they 'came into existence before you'. DeConick notes that this dual level of human existence 'belongs to the early Jewish tradition of one's divine twin, guardian angel, or image from

36. What exactly is indicated by these 'five trees in Paradise' (saying 19) need not detain us here. April DeConick, *The Original Gospel of Thomas in Translation*, pp. 104–105, has made a strong case for viewing this saying as referring to a transformative ascent to Paradise whereby the individual is transformed into its primordial condition through cultivating the five trees of virtue.

37. Richard Valantasis, *The Gospel of Thomas*, p. 89, states it well when he says that this saying constructs 'an alternative world to the cosmic world that has been problematized in other sayings, and constructs a mythological place correlative to the place of pre-existence that never changes and that exists for the disciples' benefit'.

38. A helpful treatment of these sayings is provided by Enno E. Popkes, 'The image character of human existence: *GThom* 83 and *GThom* 84 as core texts of the anthropology of the *Gospel of Thomas*', in *Das Thomasevangelium: Entstehung – Rezeption – Theologie*, pp. 416–434.

which one was separated as the result of Adam's Sin'.[39] And this suggestion makes sense not only of the dual existence of humanity but also of saying 85 where Adam is blamed for tasting death. Jesus' claim that Adam was not worthy of you due to his tasting of death is reminiscent of Jesus' claim in saying 111 that 'he who finds himself, of him the world is not worthy'. Thus, Adam is faulted for his epistemological failure to find his way back to his image.

Humanity's separation from its 'image' is also present in saying 11 where Jesus says: 'When you come to be light, what will you do? On the day when you were one, you became two. But when you have become two, what will you do?' Humanity's primordial origin is 'the light' from which it is now alienated as a result of its division into two entities. Salvation is conceived of as a return to the light. Second, returning to sayings 83-85, the images are not only temporally prior but also they have a higher level of existence as the images do not die, nor are they visible. In fact, the images have an element of the divine within them. This is indicated in the remark that 'the light which is in them is hidden in the image of the light of the Father'. Humans contain within them this light/glory of the Father which is hidden in the light of the Father's image. Humanity's transformation upon encountering 'the image of the light of the father' is likely a description of a vision of the Father's glory in his throne-room – not unlike what one finds in Jewish merkavah mysticism (cf. Exod. 24.10-11; Ezek. 1.26-28; Isaiah 6; *1 Enoch* 14).[40] Given that humanity's image is hidden within the Father's light and that its current existence is only 'likeness-like' suggests that humanity must search for their internal light in order to partake in salvation. Third, the means whereby one reunites with one's light/image existence is through a transformative vision. The sayings emphasize the *revelation* of the images (saying 83) as well as the *seeing* of the images (saying 84). The result of seeing the images is transformative as it results in the reunification of 'the likeness' with 'the image' and the overcoming of death.

Saying 50 also refers to salvation as a transformative vision or return to the primordial light.[41] Jesus tells his disciples: 'If they say to you, whence have you come? Say to them: We have come from the light, the place where the light came into being of itself. It [established itself], and it revealed itself in their image.' Jesus claims that the primordial light of Gen. 1.3 is imbued within the images bestowed upon humanity in Gen. 1.26-27. Humans are the offspring of this light, and their salvation is dependent upon returning to it.

39. DeConick, *Seek to See Him*, p. 164.

40. DeConick, *Seek to See Him*, pp. 100–105, argues that God's hidden glory is only revealed to the visionary mystic. On Jewish ascents to God's throne-room, see Christopher Rowland, *The Open Heaven: A Study of Apocalyptic in Judaism and Early Christianity* (New York: Crossroad, 1982).

41. DeConick, *Seek to See Him*, 43–96, has argued that this saying presumes the context of the interrogation of the soul during a mystical ascent.

As sayings 83-85 and 50 have demonstrated there is a connection between the creation of light and humanity's divine image. Elaine Pagels has shown that *Thomas* interprets Gen. 1.3 as not only the creation of light but also the creation of the primordial man within the light.[42] Saying 77 is of importance here: 'Jesus said, "I am the light that is above them all. I am the all; the all came forth from me, and the all attained to me."' Jesus is identified as the primordial human, and the creation of the cosmos derives from him. As the primordial human Jesus is equated with the creation of light and, therefore, the origin and goal of all existence. Jesus 'is both source and destiny for everything'.[43] Thus, when the disciples ask him about 'the place' where he is so they can 'seek it', Jesus associates his place with the light: 'There is light within a man of light, and he lights the whole world. If he does not shine there is darkness' (saying 24). This divine element is located *within* the disciples, and when they find this internal light they will reflect Jesus as the primordial man of light.

Thomas presents at least two means whereby humans may experience this transformation: the pursuit of visions and self-knowledge. In saying 59 Jesus says, 'Look upon the Living One so long as you live, that you may not die and seek to see him, and be unable to see him.' Again, Jesus redirects their attention away from an eschatological revelation and orients them to seek visions of the Living One now. Given that Jesus is 'the Living One' (sayings 1, 37 and 111), the disciples are encouraged to seek visions of this primordial *Anthropos* (saying 77), who comes from the Light (saying 24), and who is undivided and comes from 'the equal' (saying 61). Likewise, in saying 37 Jesus encourages visionary experiences:

> His disciples said, 'On what day will you be *revealed* to us and when *shall we see you*? (ⲡⲉϫⲉ ⲛⲉϥⲙⲁⲑⲏⲧⲏⲥ ϫⲉ ⲁϣ ⲛ̄ϩⲟⲟⲩ ⲉⲕⲛⲁⲟⲩⲱⲛϩ ⲉⲃⲟⲗ ⲛⲁⲛ ⲁⲩⲱ ⲁϣ ⲛ̄ϩⲟⲟⲩ ⲉⲛⲁⲛⲁⲩ ⲉⲣⲟⲕ)' Jesus said, 'When you disrobe without being ashamed and take up your garments and place them under your feet like children and tread on them, *then [you will see] the Son of the Living One*, and you will not be afraid' (ⲧⲟⲧ[ⲉ ⲧⲉⲧⲛⲁⲛⲁ]ⲩ ⲉⲡϣⲏⲣⲉ ⲙ̄ⲡⲉⲧⲟⲛϩ ⲁⲩⲱ ⲧⲉⲧⲛⲁⲣ̄ ϩⲟⲧⲉ ⲁⲛ).

The vision of the 'Son of the Living One' is not an eschatological hope, but will occur when the disciples strip off their bodily garments and return to the state of purity and childlike existence associated with the original image of God.[44] The statement that they must 'disrobe without shame' alludes to

42. Pagels, 'Exegesis of Genesis 1 in the Gospels of Thomas and John', pp. 479–480; see also DeConick, *Seek to See Him*, pp. 21–24.

43. Valantasis, *The Gospel of Thomas*, p. 156.

44. While J. Z. Smith, 'The Garments of Shame', *HR* 5 (1966), pp. 217–238, argued that this reference to disrobing without shame referred to the ritual of baptism, it makes better sense within *Thomas*'s theology to view this saying as referring to a renunciation of the physical body. For the latter interpretation, see

Adam and Eve in the Garden who were unashamed of their nakedness (Gen. 2.25; 3.7). The visions, then, in sayings 59 and 37 are calls for protological transformation.

In addition to protological transformation through visions, *Thomas*'s Jesus refers to self-knowledge as a means of salvation. We have seen this in sayings 3 and 67 where finding the kingdom and humanity's supreme goal is self-knowledge. Likewise, one must recognize that the world and the body is a corpse and that salvation cannot be found in the physical world (e.g. sayings 56 and 80). Jesus, as the primordial man of light, has undergone this protological transformation, and the disciples are encouraged to seek to see him as a means of recognizing their own origins. When the disciples understand Jesus' words, they will become like him and he like them: 'He who drinks from my mouth will become like me, and I will become like him, and the hidden things will be revealed to him' (saying 108). Throughout *Thomas*, Jesus' words are the means whereby the seeker is transformed into a new person (sayings 5, 38, 91). 'Let him who seeks continue seeking until he finds' (saying 2); 'Seek and you will find' (saying 92); 'He who seeks will find' (saying 94).

We have seen that *Thomas* rejects eschatological, bodily and other-worldly notions of salvation.[45] The kingdom is not in heaven nor is it in the sea; the 'kingdom is within you' (saying 3). When the disciples ask 'when' the kingdom will come, Jesus responds that the kingdom is 'spread out over the earth' but 'men do not see it' (saying 113). Entering the kingdom is associated with a return to childlike pre-Fall existence (sayings 22 and 37).

One final saying that must be factored into our understanding of *Thomas*'s soteriology is saying 51: 'His disciples said to him, "On what day will the rest for the dead come into being, and on what day will the new world come?" He said to them: "What you await has come, but you do not know it."' The disciples are guilty for failing to understand that rest belongs to the living not the dead.[46] As Jesus says in saying 11, 'the dead are not alive and those who are living will not die'. Jesus rejects both premises of the disciples – namely, their future

April DeConick and Jarl Fossum, 'Stripped before God: A New Interpretation of Logion 37 in the Gospel of Thomas', *VC* 45 (1991), pp. 123–150.

45. R. Uro, 'Is *Thomas* an Encratite Gospel?', in *Thomas as the Crossroads: Essays on the Gospel of Thomas* (Edinburgh: T&T Clark, 1988), pp. 153–156, cautions against this claim that *Thomas* rejects all eschatological thinking and claims that there are many sayings which express a future orientation towards salvation. Most of these sayings, however, are either logical futures or envision salvation as a searching-finding process. None of them, insofar as I can tell, envision salvation as a future apocalyptic event.

46. On *Thomas*'s rejection of the apocalyptic resurrection of the dead, see Gregory J. Riley, *Resurrection Reconsidered: Thomas and John in Controversy* (Minneapolis: Fortress Press, 1995).

orientation and their material conception of salvation.[47] Salvation is a present experience for *Thomas*'s seekers.[48]

b. *Paul in 1 Corinthians*

In 1 Corinthians 15 Paul corrected some of the Corinthians who claimed that, while Christ had been raised from the dead, there is no need for a future resurrection of the dead (1 Cor. 15.12, 35).[49] In so doing Paul constructs humanity's salvation from this predicament as a bodily transformation that can be quite simply referred to as 'resurrection from the dead' (15.21). Paul's argument hinges on the readers' granting his premise that the Messiah is their corporate representative.[50] Jesus is then the second Adam, that is God's true human, who bears the image of God (15.49) and thereby reclaims creation through his own resurrection. Again, both Jesus' status as God's true human and the Corinthians' participation in his destiny are indicated in 15.21-22: 'For since through a man came death, also through a man came the resurrection of the dead. For just as in Adam all die, so also in Christ all will be made alive.' The Corinthians participate in, or said differently are united with, the Messiah such that what happens to him will also happen to them. The logical correlate of Paul's belief that Messiah 'was raised on the third day' (15.4) is, then, that 'all those who are in Christ will be given life' (15.22b). According to Paul, then, the transformation of the Corinthians is a two-stage process. Paul says that Christ is 'the firstfruits of those who are sleeping' (15.20), and he indicates that the order goes 'first Christ' and only then 'those who belong to Christ' (15.23).

We see the peculiarity of Paul's eschatological thinking here. The Messiah has already been raised from the dead and exalted to heaven (15.25, 27a). Nevertheless, 'Death' has not yet been abolished (15.26). Some of the Corinthians are dying just as usual (15.20b) and must therefore await their resurrection. That Paul sees this future defeat of Death as the restoration of creation and the accomplishment of the task he originally gave Adam is indicated by his use of Ps. 8.7 – before Death is defeated Christ must subject all of creation to himself (15.27a).[51] When the Messiah finally defeats Death (15.26) and the

47. By 'future orientation' I refer to an eschatological event. Uro, 'Is *Thomas* an Encratite Gospel?', in *Thomas at the Crossroads*, pp. 140–162, here pp. 155–156, is of course correct that many sayings speak of salvation in the future tense given that salvation is conceptualized as a process of seeking and finding.

48. Valantasis, *The Gospel of Thomas*, pp. 129–130.

49. That the situation is a denial of the necessity of a future resurrection from the dead and not a problem of 'realized eschatology' is argued by Dale B. Martin, *The Corinthian Body* (New Haven: Yale University Press, 1995); Wright, *The Resurrection of the Son of God*, pp. 329–331; Hays, *First Corinthians*, p. 269.

50. That 'Messiah' functions as royal title within Paul has been argued by N. T. Wright. For example, see Wright's Χριστός as "Messiah" in Paul: Philemon 6', in *Climax of the Covenant: Christ and the Law in Pauline Theology* (Minneapolis: Fortress, 1991), pp. 41–49.

51. Also, see Wright, *The Resurrection of the Son of God*, p. 335. On the use of the Old Testament in

other anti-human powers (15.24) then God's intent for humanity and creation will have been accomplished and, thus, Paul claims that 'God will be all in all' (15.28b). It is worth emphasizing the obvious point that whereas this process of creation-reclamation has been set in motion through the Messiah's resurrection, Paul's orientation is decidedly towards a future apocalyptic event.[52]

At this point in his argument, Paul's Corinthian interlocutor asks two important questions: 'how are the dead raised?' and 'with what kind of body do they come?' (15.35). And in Paul's ensuing argument, he attempts to answer both of these questions centring upon agency (how can the dead be raised?) and kind (what kind of thing is the resurrection body?). Paul takes the analogy of a seed, which must first die before it can then give birth to a plant (15.36-37). One does not sow an ear of corn into the ground; rather, one sows the seed that will be transformed into the body of the ear of corn (cf. 15.37). Paul is getting at two things here with his analogy. First, as he states explicitly in 15.38, it is God's act as creator which brings forth the fruition of the crop or plant; literally, it is 'God [who] gives to it [the seed] the body just as he desires' (ὁ δὲ θεὸς δίδωσιν αὐτῷ σῶμα καθὼς ἠθέλησεν, 15.38). But second, through this analogy Paul highlights simultaneously the continuity and discontinuity inherent in the transformation of one's identity that takes place in the resurrection. Paul does not conceive of a crude resuscitation of corpses whereby one maintains radical continuity between one's current and resurrection body. Rather, the present physical body/seed must die (discontinuity) before the resurrection body/plant can come into existence (continuity).[53] Paul seeks to stimulate the imaginations of the Corinthians by demonstrating to them that there are different kinds of 'flesh' and different kinds of 'bodies' – humans, animals, birds and fish are all composed of different kinds of 'flesh' (15.39). Likewise, the heavenly bodies such as stars, moons and the sun as well as the earthly materials are composed of different kinds of substances and have their own particular glories or functions (15.40-41).[54] Given that God is the Creator of multiple kinds of bodies and substances, Paul stimulates the Corinthians' imagination into conceiving

our text, see Jan Lambrecht, 'Paul's Christological Use of Scripture in 1 Cor. 15.20-28', *NTS* 28 (1982), pp. 508–511.

52. That 1 Corinthians 15, among other Pauline passages, is infused with apocalyptic motifs and thinking is argued for by J. C. Beker, *Paul the Apostle: The Triumph of God in Life and Thought* (Philadelphia: Fortress, 1980), pp. 135–81; de Boer, *The Defeat of Death*, pp. 93–140.

53. See Thiselton, *The First Epistle to the Corinthians*, pp. 1263–1264; Hays, *First Corinthians*, pp. 270–271.

54. The fact that Paul's analogies are derived entirely from Genesis 1 (humans, plants, birds, fish, heavenly bodies, earthly substances, etc.) should not be overlooked. The exposition of this text in Wright, *The Resurrection of the Son of God*, pp. 329–361, rightly emphasizes how Paul's thinking here is imbued with Genesis 1–3.

of the resurrected body as a transformed substance but one that is in continuity with one's current identity.

Paul draws together the threads of his argument in 15.42a with the sentence: 'So it is also with the resurrection of the dead.' Paul continues again with the seed analogy and draws four points of contrast between current bodily existence and the future resurrected bodily existence. The former is sown in 'corruptibility', 'dishonour' and 'weakness', whereas the latter is raised to 'incorruptibility', 'glory' and 'power' (15.42b-43). It is not quite right to say that the contrast here is between the physical and the spiritual; rather, Paul is contrasting corrupted Adamic-bodily existence with uncorrupted second-Adamic-bodily existence. As the fourth contrast makes clear, Paul's argument pushes human language to its limit. Paul's fourth contrast is between an 'en-souled body' (σῶμα ψυχικὸν) and a 'spiritual body' (σῶμα πνευματικὸν, 15.44). The history of interpretation of this contrast is incredibly messy with many (mis)interpretations that posit a contrast between a physical and a spiritual body.[55] The key to understanding the contrast is Paul's claim in 15.45 where he cites Gen. 2.7: 'the first human Adam became a living soul (εἰς ψυχὴν ζῶσαν), the last Adam became a life-giving Spirit (εἰς πνεῦμα ζῳοποιοῦν)'. Thus, Paul associates σῶμα ψυχικὸν with the first human Adam who was made from the 'dust of the ground' (Gen. 2.7), and in so doing he associates this body with decay, corruption and death (Gen. 3.19). Paul's insistence that the first Adam was corruptible/earthly may be subtle polemic against a Philonic interpretation of Genesis 1–2 that argued the first man of Gen. 1.26-27 was the archetypal man from heaven.[56] At any rate, for Paul it is the second Adam who belongs to an altogether higher level of existence as his body is animated by πνεῦμα. However one might speculate about this last Adam's body, Paul makes it clear that, in some mysterious way, it is animated by and partakes in the very being of God himself. That this is so is indicated by the fact that Christ's σῶμα πνευματικὸν: (a) is associated with God's own animating principle of πνεῦμα, (b) is 'life-giving' (ζῳοποιοῦν) – an attribute true only of God – and (c) is said to have come from 'heaven' (15.47, 49). Christ's new body is not just his, however, but is the pattern and model for all those who belong to him. Just as all humanity partakes in Adam's body and thereby returns to dust (15.47a, 48a), so 'as the heavenly one is [Christ], so too will be those who are heavenly'. That Paul is rereading Genesis 1–3 is indicated once more in his claim: 'as we have worn the image of the earthly one, so we will wear the image of the

55. For corrections of this misinterpretation, see Wright, *The Resurrection of the Son of God*, pp. 347–356.

56. This is suggested by numerous interpreters. See Hays, *First Corinthians*, p. 273; Wright, *The Resurrection of the Son of God*, pp. 352–353.

heavenly one' (τὴν εἰκόνα τοῦ ἐπουρανίου).[57] This restoration of God's image to humanity will occur on the last day when humanity will be transformed and the corruptible will wear the incorruptible (1 Cor. 15.50-55).

It makes sense to conclude this section with Paul's words in 2 Cor. 3.17-18:

> And the Lord is the Spirit, and wherever the Spirit of the Lord is there is freedom. We all, beholding the glory of the Lord (τὴν δόξαν κυρίου) with an unveiled face, are being transformed into the same image (τὴν αὐτὴν εἰκόνα), from glory to glory (ἀπὸ δόξης εἰς δό ξαν) just as from the Lord who is the Spirit.

The sentences are notoriously difficult, but we can draw at least three comparisons with 1 Corinthians 15. First, as the last Adam is a 'life-giving πνεῦμα' (1 Cor. 15.45) for those who belong to him, so here Paul identifies the risen Lord with the πνεῦμα as an agent of transformation into glory. While there is no explicit contrast between Adam and Christ, Paul's emphasis upon the language of 'image' and 'glory' and the quotation of Gen. 1.3 in 2 Cor. 4.6 suggests that his thinking is indebted to Genesis and the hope that humanity will recover and be transformed into the glorious image of God (Gen. 1.26-28). Second, in both passages it is Christ, as the true expression of God's 'image' and 'glory', into which believers are being (or will be) transformed. By gazing upon the glory of the Lord, the Corinthians are in the process of being transformed into 'the same image'. That τὴν αὐτὴν εἰκόνα refers to Christ is suggested by Paul's explicit description of Christ as εἰκὼν τοῦ θεοῦ in 2 Cor. 4.4.[58] Thus, whereas in 1 Corinthians 15 Paul speaks of believers' future bodily transformation, here in 2 Corinthians 3 he refers to the same event as a process already at work in Christ's people.[59] For Paul this transformation is a continuing *visual experience* of seeing the glory of God in the face of Christ.[60] This is indicated by the

57. For example, see Gen. 1.26-17; 2.25; 3.7, 21. On this motif in Genesis and 1 Corinthians 15, see Jung Hoon Kim, *The Significance of Clothing Imagery in the Pauline Corpus* (JSNTSup 268; London/ New York: T&T Clark, 2004), pp. 12–17, 193–209.

58. For more detailed argumentation for this position, see Jan Lambrecht, 'Transformation in 2 Cor. 3,18', in *Studies on 2 Corinthians* (eds R. Bieringer and J. Lambrecht; Leuven: Leuven University Press, 1994), pp. 295–305, here 295–298; M. David Litwa, '2 Corinthians 3:18 and Its Implications for *Theosis*', *JTI* 2 (2008), pp. 117–133.

59. Commenting on the relationship between 1 Corinthians 15 and 2 Cor. 3.17-18, Alan Segal, 'Paul's Thinking about Resurrection in its Jewish Context', *NTS* 44 (1998), pp. 400–419, here p. 413, notes: 'This suggests that for Paul transformation is both a single, definitive event yet also a process that continues until the second coming.'

60. Many scholars have discerned an implicit reference to Paul's Damascus Road experience in 2 Cor 3.17–4.6. See, for example, Seyoon Kim, *Paul and the New Perspective: Second Thoughts on the Origins of Paul's Gospel* (Grand Rapids: Eerdmans, 2002), pp. 165–213. See though Colleen Schantz, *Paul in Ecstasy: The Neurobiology of the Apostle's Life and Thought* (Cambridge: Cambridge University Press, 2009), esp. pp. 123–127, who argues that Paul's references to visionary experiences refer to continuing and ongoing visions.

repeated emphasis on 'seeing' and 'beholding' Christ as 'the image of God' or as 'the glory of God' (cf. 3.18; 4.4; 4.6). Finally, this process of transformation has as its ultimate goal, as with 1 Corinthians 15, the resurrection of the body. Paul's language in 2 Cor. 4.17–5.10 is filled with the belief that while now they are carrying about 'the death of Jesus in their own bodies' (4.10) and while now the 'outer person may be decaying' (4.16) Paul has the hope that 'the one who raised the Lord Jesus will also raise us up with Jesus' (4.15a) and that we will 'be clothed with our heavenly dwelling' (5.2).

c. *Similarities and differences between* Thomas *and Paul*

Both *Thomas* and Paul conceive of salvation as transformation and in so doing employ some similar language and motifs: 'image', 'light', 'glory' and the primordial man. Much of this can be seen to derive from readings of Genesis 1–3. For *Thomas*, however, this transformation is protological whereby the seeker is reunified with his state of existence before the tragic division into gendered existence occurred. In other words, the seeker is reunified with his original androgynous 'image' and discovers his internal 'light' within. This is certainly not a bodily transformation for *Thomas*, but rather a reunion with a part of one's self that is more real and more important than the body. This transformation is accomplished through process seeking self-knowledge, though *Thomas* also advocates visions of the primordial human as a means of gaining self-knowledge. Paul, too, conceives of salvation as transformation, but for him it is a bodily transformation, a transformation which the Jewish Messiah as humanity's prototype and pattern has already experienced. As humans bear the image of the earthly Adam and therefore die, so *they will* bear the image of the man from heaven and thereby receive eschatological life. Paul is emphatic that this transformation is bodily, and he even uses examples from the natural world to make his argument, but it is a new kind of body, a body animated by God's own Spirit. Therefore, while the transformation is a future apocalyptic event, humans experience foretastes of it now as the Spirit transforms and conforms believers into the Messiah. Death will only be overcome when the resurrection of the dead takes place.

IV. *Bodily practices*

a. Gospel of Thomas

The final question to put to *Thomas* is this: Given its view of the world and body as corpse-like and its conception of salvation as protological transformation, what role do bodily practices play in this transformation? One can answer this question by examining two features of *Thomas*: its consistent rejection of Jewish rituals and its promulgation of world-renouncing practices. For *Thomas* the traditional rituals of fasting, prayer, almsgiving and circumcision cannot bring life and are, in fact, part of the corpse-like world.[61] Thus, in saying 14 Jesus says:

> If you fast, you will put a sin to your charge; and if you pray, you will be condemned; and if you give alms, you will do harm to your spirits. And if you go into any land . . . eat what is set before you . . . For what goes into your mouth will not defile you; but what comes out of your mouth, that is what will defile you.

The traditional practices of both Jews and Christians are denounced here as not merely insignificant but as harmful to their identity (cf. saying 6). Traditional pious deeds are at enmity with the process of seeking knowledge of the living Jesus' words. Thus, in saying 53 Jesus claims that circumcision of the body is of no value.[62] Likewise, saying 89 denounces ritual washings, for 'he who made the inside is also he who made the outside'. In saying 104, when some recommend to Jesus that they pray together, Jesus asks, 'What then is the sin that I have done, or in what way have I been overcome?' Those who pray and fast, remarkably, demonstrate their own sinfulness and indicate that they have not understood Jesus' words. Further, Jesus states that 'when the bridegroom comes out from the bridal chamber, then let them fast and pray' (saying 104). The concept of the 'bridal chamber' is complex, but based on saying 75, where it is associated with 'the solitary', we can assume that it is a metaphor for salvation. Thus, Jesus' reference to fasting and prayer being consequent upon the bridegroom *leaving* the bridal chamber, we can be sure that it is a negative depiction of one's abdication of a state of salvation.[63] Rituals, therefore, have no place for *Thomas* in his construction of soteriology or in the ongoing life of those seeking the words of Jesus. While not a ritual, Jesus also recommends the abandonment of the reading of Israel's Scriptures. For when the disciples claim that Israel's prophets spoke of Jesus, he replies to them: 'You have abandoned the living one before your eyes, and spoken about the dead' (saying 52). Insofar as one listens to Israel's Scriptures, the words of 'the living Jesus' (see saying 1) have been abandoned for the dead.[64]

But this rejection of rituals is part of a larger concern that rejects any entanglements with the world. *Thomas* rejects familial ties and loyalties (sayings

61. For a discussion of Jewish rituals in *Thomas*, see Antti Marjanen, '*Thomas* and Jewish Religious Practices', in *Thomas at the Crossroads*, pp. 163–182.

62. On saying 53 and circumcision in early Christianity, see Joshua W. Jipp and Michael J. Thate, 'Dating *Gospel of Thomas*: Logion 53 as a Test Case for Plotting *Thomas* on an early Christian Trajectory', *BBR* 20 (2010): 237–256.

63. On this, see Marjanen, '*Thomas* and Jewish Religious Practices', pp. 171–172; Valantasis, *The Gospel of Thomas*, pp. 184–185.

64. On this saying, see Milton Moreland, 'The Twenty-Four Prophets of Israel are Dead: *Gospel of Thomas* 52 as a Critique of Early Christian Hermeneutics', in *Thomasine Traditions in Antiquity*, pp. 75–91.

55, 99, 101, 105),[65] material wealth and riches (saying 110), the eating of meat (saying 11), a concern with clothing (sayings 36, 78) and may even deny sexual procreative relations (saying 101).[66] *Thomas*'s stance on the world is represented succinctly in saying 42 where Jesus says: 'Become passers-by' (ⲡⲉϫⲉ ⲓ̅ⲥ̅ ϫⲉ ϣⲱⲡⲉ ⲉⲧⲉⲧⲛ̅ⲣ̅ⲡⲁⲣⲁⲅⲉ). In an excellent article Philip H. Sellew has provided a convincing interpretation of this saying.[67] Having noted that *Thomas* views the world as a corpse-like place, he reviews how the buried dead, through ancient funerary epigraphs, attempted to invite ancient travellers into short conversation. *Thomas* plays with this notion of funerary epigraphs, but he subverts it by encouraging his seekers to 'become passers-by' by rejecting any conversations with the dead – that is, entanglements with this world of corpses – and to, instead, 'recognize the world for the corpse it truly as and refuse to be caught up in its ways (*Gos. Thom.* 27; 50; 86)'.[68] The saying is, therefore, a severe pronouncement of rejection of all that is associated with the created world.[69] We have already seen that bodily renunciation is necessary for seeing Jesus (saying 37), and we see a similar sentiment in saying 27 as 'Jesus said: "If you do not fast to the world, you will not find the kingdom; if you do not keep the Sabbath as Sabbath, you will not see the Father."' Note that Jesus' first conditional statement replaces the traditional ritual of fasting with a fasting to the world. Jesus redefines the nature of fasting here, transforming it into disengagement from the world. Likewise, the second statement is not a command for traditional Sabbath observance but rather a call to 'rest' from the

65. On *Thomas*'s rejection of biological family ties, see Stephen Patterson, *The Gospel of Thomas and Jesus* (Sonoma: Polebridge, 1993), pp. 199–202.

66. See, however, Risto Uro, 'Is *Thomas* an Encratite Gospel?', in *Thomas at the Crossroads*, pp. 140–162, who has argued that while *Thomas* does represent strong ascetic inclinations it does not demand renunciation of marriage or sexual relations. Also, see Risto Uro, *Thomas: Seeking the Historical Context of Thomas* (London/T&T Clark: Continuum, 2003), pp. 54–79.

67. Philip H. Sellew, 'Jesus and the Voice from beyond the Grave: *Gospel of Thomas* 42 in the Context of Funerary Epigraphy', in *Thomasine Traditions in Antiquity*, pp. 39–73.

68. Sellew, 'Jesus and the Voice from beyond the Grave', pp. 72–73.

69. There is not enough space to discuss in detail the claims of a few scholars who argue that *Thomas* has a positive view of the world. Risto Uro, *Thomas: Seeking the Historical Context of the Gospel of Thomas* (London/New York: T&T Clark, 2003), pp. 56–58, and Antti Marjanen, 'Is *Thomas* a Gnostic Gospel?', in *Thomas at the Crossroads*, pp. 107–139, esp. pp. 118–126, have suggested that sayings such as 12, 28, 77 and 113 provide evidence that *Thomas* does not view the world as 'unequivocally an evil product or the source of evil'. I fail to see, however, that these sayings support their claim. Jesus' saying that 'heaven and earth came into being' on behalf of James the Just (saying 12) appears to me as entirely ironic (see Valantasis, *The Gospel of Thomas*, p. 73). *Thomas*'s reference to Jesus standing 'in the midst of the world' and appearing to them 'in the flesh' (saying 28) is, indeed, reminiscent of other incarnational claims about Jesus, but it implies nothing regarding the positive nature of human flesh. The point of Jesus' claim that 'the all came forth from me' (saying 77) seems to me to have little, if anything, to do with creation of the cosmos. And saying 113's claim that 'the kingdom of the father is spread out over the earth and men do not see it' is one more saying regarding humanity's unenlightened nature and not a claim that the empirical world reveals the kingdom of the father.

world. In both instances, renunciation of the world is a prerequisite for 'finding the kingdom' and the visionary experience of 'seeing the Father'.

Richard Valantasis has argued that *Thomas* is an ascetical text as it creates an alternative subjectivity for its readers within the dominant majority culture.[70] One of the means whereby it accomplishes this is through the advocacy of alternative practices. As we have seen, *Thomas* envisions a process of seeking the words of Jesus, seeking visions and arriving at self-knowledge in order to attain the goal of singularity, a return to the genderless image of God and a transformative encounter with the primordial light. This identity that *Thomas* fashions can only be harmed and compromised through the dominant religious cultural practices of rituals. Likewise, traditional familial loyalties, economic concerns, food and clothing and other normal aspects of everyday life threaten to compromise the seeker's identity. The world is a corpse-like place and it is not the locus of saving revelation. The world must be disengaged from and rejected as a means of securing one's new identity. Taking the place of rituals and practices that engage the body and the world are performances that centre instead upon seeking knowledge, visions and renouncing the world.

b. *Paul in 1 Corinthians*

We have seen that Paul conceives of salvation as transformation into the pattern established by Christ as the image of God – the Last Adam. The transformation is both a process already underway as well as a future event of bodily resurrection. Our final question for Paul, then, is in what way bodily practices are related to this transformation. While answering this question requires moving beyond 1 Corinthians 15, one should take note of 15.29-34 where Paul argues that belief in resurrection is the necessary premise for certain practices. If there is no resurrection, then why not live by the maxim 'let us eat and drink, for tomorrow we die' (v. 32b)? If there is no resurrection, then why does Paul expose himself to danger 'every hour' (v. 30), and for what purpose did he 'fight with wild beasts in Ephesus' (v. 32a)? And why do the Corinthians (whatever it may mean) practise baptism for the dead if, indeed, the dead are not raised (v. 29)? Whatever the precise meaning of these activities and practices, Paul's point is clear – the resurrection is the foundation for bodily practices. In other words, ontological transformation requires, and is the foundation for, moral transformation. Three texts make this point quite clear.

In 1 Cor. 6.12-20 Paul counters the Corinthian claim that bodily activity, specifically with respect to food and sex with prostitutes, are harmless encounters.

70. Richard Valantasis, 'Is the *Gospel of Thomas* Ascetical?', in idem, *The Making of the Self: Ancient and Modern Asceticism* (Eugene, OR: Cascade Books, 2008), pp. 185–211; idem, *The Gospel of Thomas*, pp. 6–12.

The Corinthian slogan, in fact, reveals a deprecation of the body: 'Foods are for the belly and the belly is for foods. And God will destroy both that [the belly] and those [the foods]' (6.13a).[71] Paul responds to them and counters with a parallel slogan of his own: 'the body is not for immorality but for the Lord, and the Lord is for the body' (6.13b). Paul now must convince the Corinthians that there is indeed a strong relationship between the risen Lord and their own bodies. In v. 14 Paul counters their own deprecation of the body by arguing that just as God resurrected the Lord so he will resurrect the Corinthians. While the Corinthians await their own future resurrection, this power of the resurrected Lord exerts its influence presently over the community now. Further, Paul argues that the Corinthians' own bodies are members or parts of Christ's own body (v. 15). Paul quotes Gen. 2.24 ('for the two shall become one flesh') as warrant for his claim that when the Corinthians unite their bodies with a prostitute they become 'one body' with the prostitute and thereby, unthinkably, they pollute Christ's body by uniting it with a prostitute (6.15-17).[72] In Paul's argument, the 'prostitute' symbolizes the alienated, unredeemed, un-transformed world (cf. 6.9-11) whereas the Corinthian participates in Christ. Thus, for Paul, for the Corinthian to unite together in sexual intercourse is unthinkably heinous as the Corinthian body is both members of Christ's own body (6.15) as well as the temple of the Holy Spirit (6.19).

Some of the Corinthians treated food sacrificed to idols with the same laxity as they treated sex, and thus in 10.14-22 Paul tries to convince them that eating idol-meat in pagan temples is incompatible with their own Christian identity. Eating this idol-meat in temples, Paul argues, is a breach of covenant.[73] This is seen in his warning to them to flee from idolatry (10.14) and his invocation of the warning from the Song of Moses (Deut. 32.21) to watch out lest they make the Lord jealous (10.22a). Paul reasons with them on analogy from their understanding of the Lord's Supper. If the Lord's Supper is 'participation in the blood of Christ' and 'in the body of Christ' then the Corinthians should understand that eating sacred food effects a union with the deity. Paul's argument hinges here on their affirmation of their own experience of the presence of the risen Lord in their community when they eat and drink the Lord's Supper. If this meal establishes κοινωνία between them and the σώματος τοῦ Χριστοῦ, then they have no business eating meals over which other deities preside (cf. 10.21).

While Paul's concern for the corporate and public identity of the Corinthian

71. Most scholars agree that 1 Cor. 6.12-13a contains Corinthian slogans. See Jerome Murphy-O'Connor, 'Corinthian Slogans in 1 Cor. 6:12-20', *CBQ* 40 (1978), pp. 391–396.

72. On Paul's concern with the body's pollution, see Dale B. Martin, *The Corinthian Body* (New Haven: Yale University Press, 1995), pp. 174–179.

73. On the significance of the concept of covenant, both in this text and other Corinthian passages, see William Lane, 'Covenant: The Key to Paul's Conflict with Corinth', *TynB* 33 (1982), pp. 3–30.

community is evident throughout his letter, the backing for this is found in 1 Corinthians 12 where he refers to the community as 'Christ's body' (σωμα̂ Χριστοῦ, 12.27). The presence of the risen Lord through the Holy Spirit within the community is evident throughout Paul's argument (e.g. 12.4-11). Just as a body has many different individual bodily parts, so the Corinthian congregation makes up the parts of Christ's own body. The Corinthian community is the visible and public expression of the Messiah's own body (12.12). It is baptism by the 'one Spirit' that transfers diverse individuals into this singular body (12.13). As individual body parts have their own specific functions and yet are crucial to the body's healthy functioning, so Christ's body is composed of many individuals with different giftings who contribute to the health and unity of Christ's body.

For Paul, the body is crucial to the identity of the Corinthian believer, for it is the means whereby one visibly expresses and demonstrates the presence of the risen Lord through the Spirit. One sees in these texts from 1 Corinthians how Paul's claim in 2 Cor. 3.17-18 that believers are presently being transformed into the image of God by beholding his glory is being worked out practically in how one demonstrates the presence of the Lord within one's own body.

c. *Similarities and differences between* **Thomas** *and Paul*

While it is true that both see certain bodily practices as dangerous and problematic, *Thomas* and Paul diverge from each other the most in their conception of these practices. We have seen that for *Thomas* traditional religious rituals such as prayer, fasting, dietary practices and Sabbath observance are implicated in the corpse-like nature of the world. Loyalty to family, economic dealings and eating meat are entirely rejected. And in their place, *Thomas* advocates the alternative practices of visions and the pursuit of self-knowledge through the interpretation of Jesus' sayings. The empirical world is of no aid in finding salvation, and therefore it must be renounced as Jesus' disciples become 'passers-by'. In constructing a new world and a new subjectivity for the disciples, *Thomas* rejects the empirical world as dangerous and potentially harmful. For Paul, however, given that it is the body that will be transformed when it is given life by God's Spirit, and given that the Spirit is now active and present in the Corinthian community, bodily practices are of supreme significance. The Corinthian community is, in fact, the body of the Messiah. It cannot, therefore, be joined together with something unholy and made one flesh. Neither can one ingest meat sacrificed to idols in pagan temples without becoming partners of the pagan deity. The Spirit of the resurrected Messiah permeates their Corinthian body, and therefore how the Corinthians use their bodies has significant ramifications for Paul.

V. *Conclusions regarding the relationship between Paul and* Thomas

In this final section I draw five provisional conclusions regarding the relationship between Paul and *Thomas* and suggest two remaining questions. It is my hope that this study will stimulate further dialogue and study of the relationship between the two authors.

First, Paul and *Thomas* utilize many of the same motifs and words in their construction of a human salvation. In both one finds an emphasis on death, the image of God, the glory of God, Light, transformation of the self, references to Adam and interpretations of Genesis 1–3. Yet, despite this impressive overlap of motifs, it is rare that they actually interpret or utilize these motifs in the same manner. For example, while *Thomas* speaks of death metaphorically as alienation from one's protological and androgynous beginnings, Paul speaks of it much more crudely and literally as a return to earth and dust. While Paul lays the blame of humanity's and creation's predicament at the feet of Adam, for *Thomas* Adam appears to be an example of one who failed to find his way back to his original image. For *Thomas* every individual must search for their own 'image' to be reunited with it (sayings 83-84), but for Paul it is the Messiah who is 'the image of God' (2 Cor. 4.4) and humans are both now being transformed into that image (3.18) and awaiting their final transformation into that image (1 Cor. 15.49). Thus, second, their portraits of Jesus contain similar motifs but are used for radically different ends. Both, for example, associate Jesus with 'the image of God' and 'the light' (1 Cor. 15.49; 2 Cor. 4.4-6; sayings 24 and 77), use mystical visionary language to describe his role in transformation (2 Cor. 3.17-18; sayings 59 and 77) and describe Jesus as overcoming death (1 Cor. 15.20-28; sayings 18-19). But for *Thomas*, Jesus is the mystagogue who stimulates his followers through his enigmatic sayings as a means of overcoming death. For Paul the words of Jesus are superfluous for human salvation. Rather, Paul sees the destiny of humanity as encapsulated in Jesus as Messiah who overcomes death through his resurrection from the dead. Those who are incorporated into this Messiah are promised that they too will share in his life and receive a 'spiritual body'.

Third, both authors construct their soteriology in conversation with Genesis 1–3, but they read these texts entirely differently. *Thomas* reads Genesis in a way much more comparable to Philo where there is a distinction between the creation of the first primordial human in the image of God (Gen. 1.26-27) and the second account of the creation of humans from the earth (Gen. 2.7). As we have seen, *Thomas* sees this second account as tragic as humanity is alienated from its own image. In fact, insofar as one remains unaware and divided from its original image, humanity exists in a state of death. Paul explicitly rejects this reading of Genesis, however. He directly claims, in fact, that the 'first man' (Gen. 1.26-27) was made of dust and brought corruption and decay to humanity and creation, whereas 'the second man' comes from heaven and restores humanity and creation to its intended glory (1 Cor. 15.23-28, 46-48). Both understand Jesus as originating out of, or in some way connected with, the Light of Gen. 1.3 (saying 77; 2 Cor. 4.4-6). *Thomas* utilizes this as an exhortation to seek to return to the state of Genesis 1, whereas Paul argues that by looking at the light on the face of Jesus believers are being transformed into that eschatological image.

Fourth, directly related to their reading of Genesis, is their disagreements over eschatology. Given *Thomas*'s insistence on returning to Genesis 1 and the state of the primordial human, his soteriology redirects attention away from a future event back to protological beginnings. Conversely, given Paul's insistence on the 'second Adam' as the bearer of the image of God, Paul redirects humanity's focus to a future apocalyptic event whereby death will be defeated and they will be bodily transformed. One cannot, in fact, make sense of Paul's argument in 1 Corinthians 15 without his belief that a future apocalyptic event will erase the power of death over humanity (15.21-28, 50-58). As we have already seen, *Thomas* explicitly rejects this kind of apocalyptic eschatological orientation. He denies a future resurrection from the dead (saying 51; cf. saying 11), reinterprets and rebukes his disciples' eschatological questions (saying 37) and transforms eschatological sayings into protological sayings (sayings 18 and 22). Whereas Paul's thinking about human salvation is infused with Jewish apocalyptic and OT messianic texts (e.g. Pss. 8.5-7; 110.1; Daniel 2 and 7), *Thomas* denies the Jewish Scriptures any role in understanding salvation. *Thomas* also has no place for Paul's insistence on a bodily resurrection from the dead. To talk of resurrection of bodies, one suspects *Thomas* would argue, is to talk about rotting corpses and dead things instead of the living. It in fact follows from *Thomas*'s denigration of the world and the body as a corpse that salvation would not be conceived in such bodily images. This leads to a fifth difference between Paul and *Thomas*; namely, their constructions of the human body. Both agree with each other that certain bodily practices are dangerous: for example, both seem to advocate a critical stance towards the ingestion of certain foods (1 Corinthians 8–10; sayings 11, 60 and 87) as well as certain sexual activities (1 Corinthians 5–6; saying 101). *Thomas*, however, rejects all bodily rituals and worldly activities precisely because they belong to and are implicated within the present worldly structures. The empirical world is simply not the locus of God's saving revelation and it is in fact the adversary of the new world that *Thomas* seeks to create. *Thomas*'s concept of salvation as protological transformation, or reunification with one's original image, leads it to advocate alternative performances – the pursuit of self-knowledge, visions and bodily renunciation. For *Thomas* there is a radical privileging of one's 'image' over one's 'body' (or 'likeness'). While Paul too can be quite critical of certain bodily practices as well as worldly entanglements, the body is for him the visible and public expression of the fact that Christ is, through the Spirit, transforming individuals into the image of God. So much is this the case that Paul even conceives of the Corinthian community as the corporate expression of Christ's own body.

While the final form of *Thomas* seems to me almost certainly later than Paul's first letter to the Corinthians,[74] I find little justification for arguing that it is a *direct reaction* to the Pauline legacy. If Valantasis is right that *Thomas* is an ascetical text that seeks to refashion and transform the self through alternative performances then the identity that it seeks to create can certainly be construed as a reaction against other 'mainstream' influences – including Paul as well as the Synoptic Gospels. Thus, its rejection of Jewish rituals, its dispensing with the Jewish Scriptures, its reorientation from apocalyptic eschatology to protology and its advocacy of alternative practices may be seen as a general reaction to formative (if that is the right word) Christianity as well as the Pauline legacy. We have seen that Paul's thinking is imbued with Israel's Scriptures as well as Jewish apocalyptic scenarios reworked around the advent of the Messiah. While we have not entered into the debate regarding the precise context of *Thomas*'s thought-world (e.g. Gnostic, Hermetic, Middle-Platonic), he explicitly rejects the categories of the Jewish Scriptures and apocalyptic thinking for understanding the identity of Jesus and human salvation. We have seen just how different Paul and *Thomas* are from each other, despite the fact that they employ many similar motifs. But the diverse applications and uses of these common motifs such as light, image of God and readings of Genesis 1–3 are, rather, more plausibly interpreted as demonstrations of the remarkable richness and diversity that comprised the formation of early Christianity than a direct reaction to Paul.[75] If it is the case that *Thomas* is aware of Pauline texts and traditions, it is remarkably disinterested in *direct conversation* with, or polemic against, Paul's legacy, despite its overwhelmingly different constructions of the human predicament, salvation and bodily practices.

74. See, for example, Klyne R. Snodgrass, 'The Gospel of Thomas: A Secondary Gospel', *SecCen* 7 (1989–1990), pp. 19–38; also, see Joshua W. Jipp and Michael J. Thate, 'Dating *Gospel of Thomas*', *BBR* (2010): 237–256.

75. Again, see Patterson, 'The *Gospel of Thomas* and Christian Beginnings', pp. 1–17.

Index of Ancient Sources

Index of Modern Authors

Lightning Source UK Ltd.
Milton Keynes UK
UKOW04f0239280214

227319UK00001B/36/P

9 780567 458124